Social Work as Community Development

A management model for social change

Second Edition

STEPHEN CLARKE
Centre for Applied Social Science
University of Wales Swansea

Ashgate

Aldershot • Burlington USA • Singapore • Sydney

Published by
Ashgate Publishing Limited
Gower House
Croft Road
Aldershot
Hampshire GU11 3HR
England

Ashgate Publishing Company
131 Main Street
Burlington
Vermont 05401
USA

First published in hardback 1996
Second edition published in paperback 2000

Ashgate website: http://www.ashgate.com

British Library Cataloguing in Publication Data
Clarke, Stephen
  Social work as community development : a management model
  for social change. - 2nd ed.
  1. Social service - Great Britain 2. Social planning - Great
  Britain 3. Community development - Great Britain
  I. Title
  361.3'0941

Library of Congress Control Number: 99-75451

ISBN 0 7546 1111 6

Printed and bound by Athenaeum Press, Ltd.,
Gateshead, Tyne & Wear.

Contents

Figures

Preface to the Second Edition & Acknowledgements

I am concerned to provide some more detail to the model which was first described in the First Edition. Testing out the format on students and in the field highlighted the need to provide an additional framework through which the *template* could be applied to the practice situation. The inclusion of a descriptive section on *systems theory* in Chapter 2 helps make up for that shortfall.

It appears that the philosophy which is central to community development is beginning to make a comeback in the developed economies of Europe, and in the U.K. managers and the framers of policy are beginning to seek a mechanism for putting flesh on their public claims for involving the community in schemes as far apart as making public institutions more transparent in their activities to regenerating the heart-lands of the inner city. Professionals in the field can only welcome this turn of events, and hope that it may finally come out of the shadows and become a regular feature of public service agencies, and voluntary effort alike.

There are dangers and traps for the unwary in this potential upturn in fortunes. In a resource-conscious and post-modernist age, quick-fix solutions and window dressing may over-dramatise the potential of community development to solve the pressing problems of the day. It is for this reason, that the contemporary interest in getting 'value for money', and a growing professional interest is the application of evaluations techniques at home which have been a feature of 'overseas' development for years, is very welcome. The application of the *template* approach to the logic framework evaluation process will prove beneficial to those attempting to discover how the social change processes of community development affect people and organisational formations at different levels in the community.

In the production of this volume, I owe a great debt to Terrie McCarthy, who manages to come to the rescue when the production processes are becoming too much. To Ann Meadows, whom I acknowledged in the first edition, I must again express my thanks for the early ideas from which this enterprise arose. Most of all, I again acknowledge the inspiration to the people with whom I have worked on the ground, both in the U.K. and in many other parts of the world. Pillgwenlly, South Wales and Riverlea, South Africa, stand out, particularly as their situations reveal that there might still be a need there for the type of work which we describe here.

The students of the University of Wales Swansea endure it all with good humour, and they continue to provide the impetus for revising, and I hope, improving this approach to social change, people in general, and the professional responsibilities of intervening in the dynamics of community life.

Steve Clarke
Swansea, 2000

Introduction

This volume is an attempt to re-open the discussion concerning the development potential of social work within Britain, a Northern and developed economy. The questions are, can and should social welfare professionals direct their energies and take responsibility for planned social change strategies, especially in the light of the new social policies surrounding Community Care? Along with community nurses, social workers are among the few public officials who are paid to deploy in the community on a full-time basis - in face-to-face contact with ordinary people, in their own homes, with an agenda of social welfare. They are in a unique, and virtually monopolistic position to consider, plan and act on matters which they, themselves, have identified as their vocational priority - the alleviation of social deprivation, and the creation of a less violent and alienated society. It would be ludicrous to suggest that social workers could achieve this all on their own, with the meagre resources at their disposal. However, they are in daily contact with the only untapped force in the social-democratic system - the citizen. Why is it then, that they are not actively seeking ways to forge alliances with the one asset which they have at their disposal? On the contrary, they appear to shy away from them, except as objects of assessment and prescription. In so doing, they are demonstrating just how out of touch they are. British social work is the only institution of its kind in Europe which consigns community to the sidelines. At the same time, they anguish about their own future, and the seemingly insuperable problems with which they contend. Social workers have no natural allies of their own, and they are steadfast in refusing to make any. We hope that this volume will shed a little light on the way in which this position can be reversed.

In Britain, the debate whether or not social work and community development were part of the same profession, was over almost before it had begun. It took place over thirty years ago, but so much has changed in the interim, that it is time that some of the issues were looked at afresh. In the 1970's, both 'sides' retreated in the face of the hostility of the other. Today, few bother to consider whether or not there is even a question worth asking, yet alone differences worth resolving. The social work and community development professions hardly acknowledge the existence of the other. There is virtually no cross-over between the 'Youth and Community Work' training (which is where community development does get some cursory

1

treatment), and the Diploma in Social Work qualifying programme (where it gets virtually none). Even then, the situation is not helped, because restrictive demarcation agreements mean that the respective skills and insights of the two professions are rarely accessible to the other at the work face.

This situation has arisen out of three strands of history and tradition which have conspired to keep the practitioners of each section firmly apart, and, seemingly, deliberately, blind to the advantages that each might offer the other. The primary reason for this hiatus arose when the disparate wings of British social work attempted to form one, unified professional organisation, the British Association of Social Workers (BASW). This movement began in the 1960's. Leading figures in the social work 'wing' gave strong signals that 'community work' had an important part to play in the emerging 'generic', Social Services Departments, which arrived in 1970. Dame Eileen Younghusband, doyenne of the profession, and Sir Frederic Seebohm, who had been charged with the re-structuring of the social services, both gave prominence to the 'development' dimension in their writings on the future of social work (Seebohm, 1968; Younghusband, 1959). Government policies at the beginning of the 1970's indicated that there was a place for community intervention in their vision of the future (Plowden, 1966; Seebohm, 1968; Skeffington, 1969; Youth Service Development Council, 1969), and all seemed set fair. Nevertheless, the fates were against it.

Social Work was still recovering from the attack of Barbara Wooton, who ripped apart the Freudian posturings of the more esoteric elements, and left the activity desperately looking for some new clothes (Wooton, 1959). Stabilising their image, and their practice base, entailed the importation of a considerable amount of theory from the United States, although the choice proved to be selective. Centralisation and case-centred professionalism appeared to be the way. Qualifications replaced 'good intentions'. Hierarchy, supervision and support replaced autonomy, and corporate investment and planning replaced fragmentation. It was certainly the way through which a career structure could be developed (Seebohm, 1968).

The second factor arose out of the growing awareness that Britain's Welfare State had not eliminated poverty, homelessness and social disorganisation (Bailey, 1973; O'Malley, 1970; Townsend et.al., 1965). The persistence of 'class' as a feature of social division was dramatised through the publication of the 'Case Con' commentary on contemporary social work practice, values and priorities. The idea of overt class conflict was not ruled out, and there was a distinct schism regarding the function of social workers in this arena (Leonard, 1975; Wooley, 1970). The 'new' social work profession, which was looking forward to standardised training and unified working conditions for the first time, was divided on the issue of 'professionalism' and 'elitism'. The

2

simplistic Marxist theories of the Left in community work drove a wedge into the constellation of social welfare professionals. When the dust settled over this dispute, it appeared that there was no place for an ideologically-driven faction within 'modern social work practice'.

The third issue arose from another source, and within community development circles themselves. This was the problem of neo-colonialism. At the time, many British community development workers had gained their experience working overseas in British government-aided schemes in the Empire. They were now reluctant to be seen to import a colonial art into the metropole. Because of this, they sought a new name for their professional activity, one that deflected the focus away from its previous associations. This was to prove unfortunate, as it was a time when a high degree of clarity was needed to give experienced and new workers in the field a clear lead to follow. In the main, they were to adopt the title of 'community worker', which could, and did, mean everything and nothing. In their practice, nevertheless, they were more inclined to approach the problems of bad housing, social resistance to deprivation and bureaucratic insensitivity with overt sympathy and developed action strategies for direct engagement. This contrasted greatly with their newly professionalising colleagues in social work, who buried themselves in creating new super structures for their infant service (Calouste Gulbenkian, 1968; Mayo, 1972; Runnicles, 1970; Thomas, 1976).

For the 'community workers', however, this schism had considerable costs. Strategically, community development workers lost a great opportunity when the issue of BASW membership came to a head in 1972 (Cox & Derricourt, 1975). Opting for anti-elitism, they badly misread the way in which the policy and educational tide was running. By not associating with social work as far as official recognition was concerned, they left themselves in the wilderness. It is hoped that the time for reassessment of this situation will come again soon, but nearly thirty years have been lost in the interim. At the present time, there is a ripple of interest again, in a field that has maintained a studied low profile. There have been a number of new books on the subject, and there is also a realisation that recent government policies in social care are going to leave large residual areas of social concern without any provision of state services (Braye & Preston-Shoot, 1995; Mayo, 1994; Popple, 1995).

In the 1970's, whereas professionals were becoming highly charged with the emergent realities of poverty, welfare inequalities and the destruction of community life through planning decisions, they failed to realise that they, themselves, lacked a power base. In particular, they failed to confront the emergent welfare issues from a position which could force local political reactions and remedies. They eschewed *contamination* with domestic issues, focusing their energies on mobilising the entire *working class* instead. This

3

strategy sounded good, but got nowhere. The special knowledge and educational assets of the community development workers, their anthropological insights and their ability to apply it to problem-solving, were ignored.

By failing to clarify the relative weakness of social welfare within the national economic order, many community development workers ignored their own educational assets. One of the most popular books at the time was Marris and Rein's account of the failure of the War on Poverty in the USA. They described the United States' Office of Economic Opportunities initiative to tackle juvenile delinquency through 'Community Organization' methods and direct investment in communities. Established interests just absorbed the impact of these uncoordinated activities, and the problems continued unabated (Marris & Rein, 1967; see also Marris, 1974; Mayo, 1975). In Britain, the majority of workers and projects seemed determined to repeat the history lesson from America. Their failure as strategic analysts was made all the more obvious when the government arbitrarily cancelled their own Community Development Project (CDP) at the soonest possible moment (Loney, 1973).

The twelve CDP projects clashed headlong with their primary paymaster, local government, and they forced central government to back down on this experiment in social reform from below. In so doing, workers failed to take advantage of another example that was happening in North America at the same time. Social work education in the United States was formalising the relationship between 'social casework' and 'community organization'. For them, the connection was obvious; for us, apparently it was not so. Social work practice in America demonstrated that the two could co-exist reasonably happily under one roof, and that there was considerable mutual benefit from this relationship (Brager, 1963, 1973; Cary, 1970; Dunham, 1958; Mizrahi & Rosenthal, 1992; Weil, 1994).

As in America, in the developing economies of Asia and Africa, community development and social work have flourished through active co-operation. This extends into the training regimes, where social work education would be considered deficient without a sizeable community development component. The 'colonial' aspects of 'top-down' initiatives have been subordinated to the overwhelming desire to tackle, head on, the wretched conditions which confront under-resourced peoples. For the empowered communities in corrupt or vulnerable situations, self-help and grass-roots development appeared to be the only way forward. There are no illusions about the uphill task that they face, but the movement to adapt the form and content of community development in these circumstances has changed, evolved and expanded into a critically aware and people-rooted activity (Dasgupta, 1952;

4

Hope & Timmell, 1984: Balleis, 1992: Berridge, 1993). In the UK in the 1970's, there were powerful ideologies at work. Within social work, the drive for professionalism, plus entrenched standing within the state apparatus was one aspect. The other major influence was the need (as state employees) to make a service-providing Welfare State work *for* the people. The idea of people creating their own welfare system flew in the fact of this orthodoxy. The terror of exposure to political incorrectness held sway. The power exercised by the professionals, who monopolised the intervention routes (as administrators, academics, resource controllers, and practitioners), to consign the poor, the homeless and the dispossessed to the 'luxury' of the Welfare State, while they maintained their left-wing posturing. When we study the map of poverty over the decades to 1999, we can see that poverty is rooted in the same geographical areas. Social work has become the servant of poverty and not its destroyer. The map of poverty faithfully plots the intensity of social work activity (Howarth, et.al., 1998). The question, 'Where were you during the 'war'?', is best left unasked. Let those without sin...., etc.

It is necessary, at this point, to provide some definitions so that misunderstandings can be minimised. Community development is a part of the complex of professionally qualified and/or competent people who are engaged in paid, or formalised, social welfare activity. All forms of interventionist activity which deal with aggregates of people, focusing them on the possibilities and practicalities of instituting social change, fall within our definition of community development (Cox, F.M., 1974). We include within this complex all those that consider themselves to be qualified to function as social workers. We specifically include anyone who has attained a qualification in social work. Qualifications in community development were always harder to acquire than those in social work, and the situation has not improved since the earliest studies (Francis et.al., 1984; Popplestone, 1971). We hope to develop the definitions of the professional areas of expertise (in Chapter 1, below), but we see the field as *inclusive* rather that exclusive. Nevertheless, this volume is aimed at all social workers, as much as it is towards specialised community development workers.

The emphasis of this volume is on *development*, and how it is brought about. Social workers, as we have mentioned above, are not the only interested agents of social intervention. Within nursing, there is a growing awareness that there are practices which have been refined elsewhere which could be of assistance to them in their attempting to solve the core issues which they face. Primary health care, and the health education aspects of health are their main concerns in this regard. These professions have long been aware that, unless the objects of their intervention are party to the process at the conceptualisation stage, and if they are not carried along throughout, through consent, participation and, increasingly, into the evaluation stages as well, then the cause is, at best, wasteful, and, at worst, hopeless (World Health Organisation. 1986).

We now include a wide array of community nurses who must demonstrate a competence in community development skills (U.K.C.C., 1998: Clarke, 1998). Modern policies are being based upon the idea that building community can best serve the interests of that community in obtaining the most *relevant* health care facilities, services and support activities (West Wales, 1993). Those responsible for health and nursing policies have not been too shy, nor too proud to adopt practices which have been proved elsewhere. It is evident that 'social work' has had a long start on them when it comes to integrating the methods. Has it failed to appreciate its advantage? The evidence that health care managers and nurses, are reading, absorbing, and writing their own theoretical approaches to the subject, must ring a warning bell for social work (Felvus, 1994; Hancock, 1993; Jones, 1991; Jones & Macdonald, 1993; McMurray, 1993; Macdonald, 1992; Stewart, 1993). In Wales, the Green Paper *'Better Health Better Wales '* outlines a clear strategy for local health development, which links with policies which go up right through the structure of health provision (Secretary of State for Wales, 1998).

Unless the social work profession can focus on the central issue, it may lose out heavily. Social work must review and clarify its objectives. It must consider just what its special contribution to social welfare, and assess how best to bring its considerable expertise and insight into community life to bear on the pressing social issues of today. It must also decide to take the necessary re-organisational steps needed to reincorporate community development within its territory. Unless these decisions are taken, it will lose out to another profession which, like itself, is looking for a route for survival and growth in bad times.

The 'management model' approach

We hope to provide social workers with a model, which will:

♦ allow ready access to the complexities of 'development', and community development in particular;
♦ suggest a framework through which increasingly intricate development processes can be analysed, understood and engaged at every stage.

We have attempted to maintain the connection between the individual, the prime target for social work intervention, at every level of the activity. This is a deliberate attempt to break with the preoccupation which most of the traditional literature has had with group processes. It is not that these are unimportant, but this approach stems more from the actual role that the worker plays within organisational development. In the development process, as the complexity of the structure increases, so the professional is confined more and more to working with key individuals. It is not that the groups, and other formations which make up the vehicles for change, are unimportant. It is the logistical fact that, in complex organisations, the worker cannot be concerned with the day to day contact that might be paid to groups in a traditional 'neighbourhood development' exercise. We are still being fed the 'process' approach, which began in the colonial model of the Biddles, Batten and Murray Ross. This basic structure was taken up with gusto, albeit indirectly, by the structuralist approach of the Community Development Project teams, and the Marxist writers of the late 1970's/early 1980's (Bolger et.al., 1981; Corrigan, 1975; Corrigan & Leonard, 1978). Workers coped with the problem of translating how to intervene with 'the community', 'the class', or 'the trade union', by intensifying one-to-one contact with key individuals. In their theoretical writings, however, they preferred to define activities as class actions, and not as deliberately constructed 'me-led' activities This was one of the issues raised by Fleetwood and Lambert, when they explained the difficulty of launching a world vision with ordinary people, who were beset with oppressive living conditions (Fleetwood & Lambert, 1982). We hope to clarify this issue here.

We have also attempted to use a simplified and staged description of the issues involved, as a progressive and directed support mechanism towards more sustainable forms of community activity. We have begun the process with a skeletal view of the model, described through the application of 'template'. We have then progressed through a number of stages, many of which are familiar to practitioners of community development. The whole dynamic of the scheme rests on the understanding that each step across the 'template' of the model, represents a fresh step in social and operational distance, both between the worker and the target client/client system. In practice, workers will discover that they have simultaneously to maintain many activities, which span a number of the 'stages' which we describe here. This approach represents a progressively widening gap between the community organisation and the worker-as-agent-of-the-employer-agency. As such, the worker is the instrument for delivering some specific social, or related, service to the community, or of achieving a planned outcome of development. The agency may have prescribed goals, and the worker is responsible for managing the contradiction between the goals of the

7

community in self-determination mode, and the objectives of the employer agency. The further away from the starting point that the worker and the client system move across the template/model, the less control the worker, and the agency, will be able to maintain over the process, or its outcome. Progress across the template is a managed process and the model provides the key to this.

Our first task is to relate the social work task to that of community development (Chapter 2). Thereafter, the extension of the social work value approach of support, enablement and empowerment is extended progressively, to its logical extension. This is achieved, in Chapter 6, where the community, through its organisations, decides what form of social welfare service and institutions it wants. The worker is still in touch with this development and, we maintain, can use personal influence (professional skill) to exercise some form of 'control' over the outcomes of this activity. Whether or not workers wish to maintain this position is, of course, up to them. The basic message of this work is that community development is a highly skilled professional activity. As such, it has much to offer on its own terms. This may smack of elitism but it reflects truly the adage, 'Why own a dog and bark oneself?' Some activities are too important to be left to just anybody.

Many aggregates of people in our society live outside the boundaries of conventional 'social' organisation. They socially and economically 'excluded'. These people are in danger of not only being consigned to be aggressed against by a frightened and negatively disposed majority, but they will find that any freedoms which they might enjoy in some form of detached anonymity is eroded steadily away by organised, societal encroachment. Contact with, and the organised resistance of, these groups (the disenfranchised, the marginalised, those without social collateral) are the subject of Chapter 7. We hope that this template model will shed a little light on an approach to this vexing situation, and on the way in which professionals might tackle it. It is in these situations that, despite the lack of formal controls, the disciplines of a management model can be most beneficial. Can power be created for the powerless? This is the question we attempt to answer.

There are instances where the community does not want to develop its own infrastructure, but has a mission to organise against some obstacle, or in order to attain some more political goal. We use a variation of the template which we employed to work amongst the displaced. This is an adaptation of the Alinsky 'community organizing' structure. Here (Chapter 8), the worker is placed in a different form of relationship with the community, being answerable first to them, and not to some distant employer. Can a professional retain 'control' of a situation where the fundamentals of a relationship with the 'client' are dependent on being on the client's payroll?

Finally, we set out some of the ground rules for evaluating the work of community development. We have drawn heavily on the work done in developing economies, where the appraisal, monitoring and evaluation of project work is far advanced. We have found, in practice, that the methods of this crucial aspect adapt very well to application here. This is also true of the many other lessons of success and failure which are well documented in the books and journals on community development. If British social workers wish to understand how issues such as anti-oppressive practice, gender, race, and other sensitive areas might be tackled in their own settings, then they could do worse than consider the lessons of development workers in poor countries, where the risks are higher, the resources minimal and the options fewer. Not all social workers will want to undertake development work, or cope with the many uncertainties that the practice produces. Nevertheless, it is important that they all know what is meant by 'community development', and we hope that this may be a contribution to that process.

1 Social Work and the Development Process

The professional social work task can be seen as seeking to assist a client through the use of direct and indirect intervention strategies. These intervention strategies aim to support, enable and empower the client until at least a state of equilibrium is reached, enabling the client to take stock. Where possible, the first outcome is the establishment of trust and the creation of a helping partnership. From this position, the client can then embark on a fresh approach to personal pressures and difficulties. In some cases, the professional will be able to continue working with the client, developing a different relationship, while the client personally seeks solutions and outcomes to the issues of survival. This further process may be called development. During the first process, and through a programme of development, the professional will use elements of power to aim, steer or control the personal or social changes which occur.

For most professional workers, there are distinct limitations to this scenario. The state, through its legislation, and the shape and direction of Local Authority policies, create power and authority contexts through which the professional must implement a limited range of strategies. These policies and laws become the reference point for the professional. The extent and direction of the application of professional power will be shaped by these constraints.

There are good reasons for this. Firstly, the professional must seek clarity in setting objectives. These will be influenced by the framework of professional knowledge and values which the worker holds, but they will also be constrained by the daily work culture of the agency.

Secondly, there are few employing agencies today who will pay for a product unless they know what they are going to get. They will not be favourably disposed towards objectives which are open-ended, the outcomes of which are ill-defined and which may result in them, or their professional agent, losing financial control over the enterprise. The exercise of direct control over working practices has been one outcome of the 'contract culture' and seems likely to intensify (Depts. of Health, et.al., 1989, p. 42; Audit Commission, 1992b, p. 20).

Thirdly, the professional will also seek personal and career stability which will depend, to some considerable extent, on the maintenance of conformity with the ideology and operational framework of the employing agency. This also includes the expectation that the worker will be loyal to the employing institution itself.

Fourthly, there will also be limits set by each professional's personal perception, skill and motivation to provide certain attainable outcomes to any particular intervention strategy.

Somewhere, in all this, is the client's perspective. This perspective embraces all the personal responses to the predicament at hand. It has a rather less developed concern for the fine-tuning of the politics, administrative processes and power dynamics of the professional world. The client has the 'problem' but professionals lay the claim that their intervention will produce solutions which will be satisfactory to the client. If the above criteria apply, the professional brings conditions to the shape of the 'solution' and sets limitations on the framework through which a solution will be approached. In cases were there is a statutory basis for the intervention of the professional, the statutory framework is itself imbued with the power of being the most 'correct' of all approaches to the issue.

Thus, to what ever extent the social worker may seek to avoid it, the power relationship between the social worker and the client is an unequal one. The social worker's starting point is the authority or the policy through which the intervention strategy is launched and constrained. Objectively, therefore, the social worker is in a privileged and powerful position to enforce, direct and control the whole relationship with a client. The outcome is an agenda which is firmly set before the client's perspective is considered for most questions, save those of detail.

For the community development worker, this form of relationship is problematic. If community development is a part of social work, and if community development workers are employed by agencies which are subject to the pressures of constraint and control which we have described above, then community development workers will find their hands tied in exactly the same way as the general mass of social workers.

The descriptive terminology of the policy documents and theoretical textbooks of community development is set firmly against coerciveness or manipulation. The process of community development is conceived as creating the conditions for social change and supporting the client community through it. The process is supportive until the community can sustain the activity on its own. The self-determination of the agenda and its priorities are clearly identified as the prerogative of the client group.

11

The principles of community development are uncompromising. The community identifies the need to change. The organisation for that purpose and its rooting and sustainability in community culture can only be achieved through the full, voluntary and co-operative efforts of the players. The strengthening of the client population in this process is to be the focus for the intervention of the professional.

Trust between the professional and the client community must be achieved if the supportive, development process is to make progress. As the relationship becomes more inter-dependent and the process more complex, trust will become the bedrock of this central and essential relationship. This trust is established on the basis that the paid worker is not an agent for a prescriptive outcome or a disguised form of colonialism. The dilemma for the professional is whether or not issues such as the 'greatest good for the greatest number', the influence of local, political policies or even the ability to pay the mortgage can be reconciled with the principles of community self-determination, self-help and sustainable development.

Without all the information about the professional's agenda, the client group is not in a position to understand and make a free choice about the direction in which it should go. Without ensuring that the community has this freedom to choose, the professional maintains a paternalistic and elitist position. There is no way in which the client community can challenge the agenda of the professional without threatening the future of its professional support. This is a double bind situation. To challenge it at all threatens the basis of the trust that is the basis of their working partnership. From the client's perspective, the professional has the greatest freedom to act, being in possession of institutional power, personal skills and insight into the affairs of the community.

Even without a hidden agenda for the professional, the forces at work in the arena of change are still far from ideal. If a targeted community has these pressures explained, and it goes about setting its own agenda for development, only certain conditions will allow the community and the professional to work freely together. Only when there is no clash between the client group's change objectives and the policy objectives of the worker's employer, will the professional be truly free to act on the preferred and expressed wishes of the community. To describe it differently would be to misrepresent the situation. It is for these reasons, amongst others, that there have been many criticisms of community development as a vehicle for social change (Corrigan, 1975; Mayo, 1975; Cockburn, 1977). Structural impediments, such as the unequal power relationships in society at large, can only place more barriers in the path of the professional

12

wishing to enable or empower groups or segments of communities. If the direction of possible, or permitted change, is merely that required by the power structure, then how can the role of the worker be justified? For example: A worker is assisting in the creation of a tenants' association on a Council-owned estate. Friction arises over the standards of maintenance. For the worker to be seen to be instrumental in the organisation of a rent strike may alarm elected representatives, cause tension between senior Council officials, and result in direct pressure being applied for the 'initiative' to be terminated.

There are only so many professionally trained people employed to work in the community at the interface between official policies and citizen action. Statutory agencies employing community-based service workers, such as social workers, care managers, primary health care or community nurses, housing officials and youth and community education workers represent a range of these. Others, such as town planners and public health officers have an investment in the opinions, and the levels of active interest of the public in their programmes. The delivery of public services in the community has been the focus of more and more policies over the past decade. There has been increasing control over the amount of public finances available for them, and also regulation over the form in which they are delivered.

The assumption of professional autonomy, or semi-autonomy, is something which may be the subject of increased restriction under the emergent policies of community care. It may be that the distinction between a professional, on the one hand, and a functionary in the chain of delivery of social services, on the other, will be tested at this margin. The ability to act towards goals and outcomes based upon insight, the possession of an organised body of theory and opinion, and the ability to work according to a verifiable practice framework has been the hallmark of the professional (Goode, 1969; Toren, 1969). Decisions have already been taken to devalue the currency of British social work within the European Community through restricting the training period for qualification. This was codified through the Central Council for the Education and Training in Social Work (CCETSW) during a restructuring of training programmes (CCETSW, 1989). The authority and freedom to intervene professionally, on behalf of, or with, those in need, may be already under severe threat.

On the one hand, hopes for the unlimited expansion of services in response to need have been frustrated. On the other, much of the operational flexibility allowed to professionals has been restricted through process monitoring and contractual limits. Maintenance workers in public gardens no longer provide the same social reference point for pensioners or children, as did an earlier generation of 'Park Keepers'. As a larger part of the public service sector is contracted out to the 'independent sector', many local and national voluntary agencies may find that they have less flexibility and scope for seeking or developing activities outside their contracted remit. Specific tasks are contracted for on an hourly basis, making flexibility an unpaid-for luxury.

The contractual agreements of the 'mixed economy of care' (Wistow, et.al., 1994) are gradually ensnaring those elements of the statutory agencies, and the larger voluntary organisations which are designated as *service providers*. These contractual service activities will come to absorb the greater part of their total resources. This will bring about, *de facto*, the 'third force' role of service providers which are tied to a service function, and barred from a wider role of social comment.

This is the suggestion that so enraged many readers of the Centris Report (Knight, 1993). Instead of limiting this to Voluntary Sector suppliers, as Centris recommended, large parts of the local authority network will be cut adrift on the same raft, on a sea of contradictions. They will lack the capability to assert any direct influence on their financial controllers or over the scale of the service which they provide. Yet they will find themselves having to face the frustrations of those in need on a daily basis (see Figure 1 below).

Ultimately, it is government which restricts the resources available to the 'purchasing authority', which, in turn, fix the contract levels. The 'service user', on the other hand, only gets to vote for central government every four to five years, and local welfare lobbies cut little ice at election time.

It is claimed that community care should not be a cheap alternative for institutional care (Davis, 1991), then the 'reform' of public finances points to an increase in the incidence of unmet needs (Audit Commission, 1992b, p.37). The professional desire will be to attempt to meet all needs which are considered necessary after a professional assessment of the case. But the financial restrictions imposed through the funding process may rule out anything save for a pre-defined service which has been specifically contracted. If success in winning a contract to provide care also ties the agency's hands when it comes to highlighting the incidence of unmet needs, a powerful mechanism for seeking social reform will have been lost.

This process may also curtail the freedom to initiate activities in the workplace which are not led by the policies and priorities of the funding body. Innovations in technique, the flexibility to respond to the demands of

14

service users for more control, or the ability to vary inputs to conform to cultural imperatives may all be ruled out. This will create a sterile environment for those who claim a vocational motive for their work.

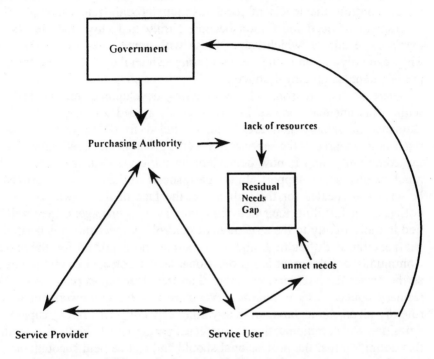

Figure 1: Accountability – the broken link and the residual needs gap

In future, the criteria for sustaining a public service will depend more and more on the funding authority's definition of priority. This will be linked to its ability to pay from fixed resources. Funders may even find that they have too few resources to provide services for those needs which *they*, themselves, define as having the highest priority. The amount may fluctuate from year to year, leaving people without services who once received them. A 'residual needs gap' will be established, which will bring frustration and instability to many in the most vulnerable circumstances (see Figure 1, above).

There has even been talk of curtailing, by statutory means, the scope of 'independent' agencies which hold contracts with the public authorities (Knight, 1993). There is now a potential for a serious gap to emerge between social and health needs and the ability of the professional services to provide for them. As this process unfolds, there is also a gap emerging in the lines of accountability. The purchasers and suppliers of services are supposed to liaise with the service users over the nature and purpose of services which go to make up the 'mixed economy of care', and the contract culture. However, the scale of the operation is fixed by the government, which controls the levels of local taxation through 'rate capping'. The assessment of need must soon become firmly tied to the levels of available resources, which leaves those with unmet need out in the cold. They can only rail on at the local authority, which they will blame for their predicament (see Figure 1 above).

There are two reasons why community development can be justified within this unequal context. Firstly, there is a need for support for those elements of society that are being excluded from the real discussion regarding resources - the service user. This group is the most vulnerable in the community, and is now dependent on the caprices of accountants for much-needed social support. In the past, social workers have not proved to be strong advocates for their clients in the face of their own employers' policies. In fulfilling their new functions as care managers, they will be tied in more tightly to the structures of control. A mechanism is needed to get past these difficulties, and to generate more power for the client. Community development is a professional task which centres on the *citizen* as the target for intervention, rather than the *citizen-as-service-user*. The primary concern of community development is the empowerment of the role of citizen, *per se,* and not in any other capacity. This role is capable of definition and communication to interested parties (see below). It is against this definition that the professional should and can be held accountable. If the client community is made aware of the conflicts of interest that surround community care, they can then assess their own position as citizens more clearly. The role of the professional in this capacity can be thoroughly appraised. If the worker is employed by the 'service purchaser', and is being held accountable by the client community, the transparency of this relationship might constrain an employer from the worst excesses of manipulation or exploitation.

The second aspect concerns the whole question of damage limitation. When the professional is in possession of a clear and uncluttered perspective of the nature and purpose of planned social change, then the costs which have to be borne by the community through the possible loss of control can be minimised. A professional, skilled in the process of focusing community attention on change and in mobilising it for that purpose, must be preferred to another authority figure who is equipped with just technical knowledge about the physical outcome of the policy. Without a focus, and being susceptible to grasping at any straw, people under pressure may react to events in ways which may leave them more vulnerable than before. Development in the community affords people the opportunity to focus rationally on their predicament. An aware citizen is a better citizen and is more likely to conserve resources and target their own activities in more constructive ways than if they are left to the vagaries of chance.

Our task in this volume is to provide a model from which the professional can establish an analytical perspective. The basic theoretical issue here is whether or not there is a consistency in the way community development principles and skills are applied through a changing and increasingly more complex process of intervention? It is our contention, that there is such a consistency and that it is in the interests of practitioners to consider how their practice, principles and skill application can be analysed and then modified in order to provide consistency. For this reason, we have constructed a model which lends itself to this purpose. It takes the form of a 'template' which can be applied over social development situations of varying complexity. It allows for the clarification of certain presumptions about the focus for intervention strategies, and then suggests how the analysis can be made.

In order to begin the analysis, certain definitions are needed.

Definition: community development

> Development is a totality. It is an integrated cultural process comprehending values such as the natural environment, social relations, education, production, consumption and well-being. Development is endogenous, it can only come from within a society, which defines in total sovereignty, its vision and its strategy, and counts first and foremost on its internal strengths and co-operating with societies that share its problems and aspirations. (Dag Hammarskjold Foundation, 1975, cited in Lopes, 1994, p. 37)

The standard definitions of community development consider the process of group formation, need identification, resource development and then action. Results are then reviewed and modifications are made to the original methods employed. It may be necessary also to modify the outcome expectations of the whole strategy. In most definitions, the function and role of the individual is omitted or passed over without sufficient attention (although: see Biddle, 1966, p. 12). The actual role and function of the professional is also skirted over. It is necessary for our purpose that these omissions are rectified.

17

In line with our earlier description of the process of community development, it is presumed that:

♦ community development is a professional function, it is carried out by employed, specially trained personnel who are under some form of contractual obligation (to either their employer, which is external to the community, and/or to the community itself) for the delivery of a service;
♦ community development is geared to develop and consolidate the forces of social change in ways which are quantifiable and qualifiable;
♦ community development's focus on social change will, under most circumstances, centre on the creation of organisations and the mobilisation of power for their members.

There are many definitions of professional activity which, at some time, have been grouped together under the umbrella of 'community work'. These include: community organisation, social animation, social education, social action, community action, social development, service extension, etc. It is possible that any real distinction between these may be more in name only (Biddle, 1966, p. 5). Employers and workers may be inclined to describe this activity more in keeping with their own style or image, rather than with a desire to conform to a professional convention. It is possible to give more precise definitions to some of these terms and it is our purpose to tighten these definitions in this volume.

The term 'community social work' has also been employed over a wide time scale (du Sautoy, 1966, p. 54; Smale, et.al., 1988). It denotes the redeployment of welfare professionals into the community. Their role involves the mobilisation of the community itself for the provision of services. These services are in keeping with the form which the service agency might itself provide, had it not motivated the community so to do.

Words such as decentralisation, participation and consultation nowadays occur frequently in policy documents and plans. They carry with them an expectation of potential empowerment for citizens through an action process. For those seeking to recast social relationships, or to reshape the way in which political or public decision making takes place, these terms imply that both community and public resources must first be mobilised and organised for that purpose. *Development* must take place.

In all these circumstances, the intervention of the professional results in changes in social orientation, the acquisition of skills and the creation of new roles the individuals and groups involved. Individuals and groups can,

18

of course, initiate changes without the intervention of any professional. They may, or may not, seek advice, or obtain expert support or technical input along the way. In these circumstances, it may be possible to plot the impact of the activity, the directions in which it moves, and the nature of social change which results. Historically, it may be important to do so. But in these cases, the group or community is in charge of its own destiny. There is no third party that can be held to account for the success or failure of the enterprise.

There are many circumstances where the community is not equipped to embark on such change strategies unaided. In addition, there is no third party that can maintain a detached objectivity over the nature and progress of the developmental process. 'Objectivity', as we shall see, is itself a relative concept, but community-grown development processes are likely to prove less sustainable, more vulnerable to deflection from their task, or susceptible to take-over or hi-jack by vested interests than the community itself might consider desirable. We set a great deal of store by the concept of professionalism. We have already recognised that the professional is vulnerable to compromise through pressures from employer or personal preference. Nevertheless, the potential for the professional to deliver that essential, detached, and analytical ingredient, coupled with persistence of effort, remains the overwhelming justification for their use in social change strategies. The purpose in analysing the professional task, which is elaborated below, is to provide citizens, workers and employers with a framework through which the professional activity, in these circumstances, can be understood and judged.

We have been considering development as a 'positive' enterprise, with the benefits being measurable in terms of more of something, raised standards of living, greater communication ability, etc. It may have a negative side as well. In many instances today, the effect of development decisions are explicitly designed to produce restructuring of society which will produce negative effects in the immediate, and medium term. The restructuring of the British economy in the pursuit of lower public expenditure, low inflation and fewer 'frictions' on the supply side of the economic equation has had significant effects on the community structure (Mayo, 1994; Schorr, 1992; Toye, 1993). It has caused the dislocation of local communities through prolonged and widespread unemployment and the social consequences of bitter and unsuccessful human resistance to these processes (Fisher, 1993; MacGarry, 1993; Phillips, 1987).

This is also a process well known in those countries with 'developing economies'. The World Bank has placed swingeing restrictions of the nature, scale and direction of public expenditure in order to create economic conditions compatible with 'sustainable growth' and the 'free market'. This is called 'structural adjustment'. Economic restructuring is 'development' of the most traumatic variety for populations which are affected directly, or indirectly. It has incurred the wrath of those who, in parallel with these policies, have been trying to train and deliver community development training. Community development has given way to programmes for survival and social defence because of the arbitrary intrusion of policies which have removed the fundamentals of social and economic existence (Balleis, 1993; Booth, 1994; Clark, 1992; Cornea, 1987; Lopes, 1994; MacGarry, 1993). In countries like Zimbabwe, scarce, skilled human resources are being drafted into the distribution of relief instead of being directed towards the developmental assistance of the community (Hay, 1989).

Above all, community development is about the planning of purposeful change. The recognition of need, and the assembly of concepts, resources and social relations to grapple with its demands, requires reflection and focus that transcends the present, and projects the concerns of the group, or the community, into aspirations for the future. Insofar as 'development' includes the bringing of change to the human condition, we include it within the definition of community development. Community development embraces all the terms which are included below.

Definition: social development

We have been discussing the situation of the citizen as a potential target for intervention by the professional development worker. The citizen has been described as the subject of, and, in many cases, the victim of economic, social, administrative and political pressures. One reason for this is there is no holistic strategy for the satisfaction of the majority of human needs. Where development programmes are designed to encompass the whole social being, as well as the economic and institutional environment of the citizen, then the programme can be said to have a social development orientation. This approach has variously been defined as the 'whole economy' model, or 'to give people some form of control over all aspects of their lives', or simply, to make things 'better' (Friedmann, 1992; Pratt & Boyden, 1985). Midgley puts it thus: Social development ...(is)...'a process of planned social change designed to promote the well-being of the population as a whole in conjunction with a dynamic process of economic development' (Midgley, 1995, p. 25). It is this concept which drives the government of Ireland in its *Programme of Prosperity and Fairness*, where the social economy is placed on a parallel footing with the economic

20

planning process, and community development processes are to be brought to bear on a holistic approach to Ireland's growing social inequalities (Taoisearch of Ireland, 2000).

This is a process that cannot be achieved through the effort of the people alone. The conceptualisation of the issues involved, the concentration of resources, and the deployment of suitable personnel must be the prerogative of the state and its allies. It is the planning for the whole which marks out social development policies from isolated initiatives which might tackle some social issue here, some welfare problem there, and an economic disaster somewhere else.

With this emphasis on planning, and on the centralisation of strategic thinking, there is the expectation that the various sectors of national administration will be drawn in to assist. It is the integration and co-ordination of effort across the full range of social concern. The Oxfam Handbook identifies two major strands of activity to achieve these ends: the removal of the barriers to people's development, and the stimulation of greater self-determination and awareness among people about the possibilities for development (Pratt & Boyden, 1985, p. 140).

Into these processes must go the combined resources of the whole development complex. Chambers envisages the people as the focus of the entire enterprise. The definition of the initiative must begin with their needs and the priorities of the traditional methods of planning without the people must be reversed (Chambers, 1986). Social development programmes are associated with developing economies, where the focusing of national resources is a feature of development policies. This is social planning with a human face. Midgley lists six characteristics:

> it is linked to economic development; it has an inter-disciplinary focus; it involves a sense of process; it is progressive in nature; it is interventionist; it fosters its goals through a strategic approach, it is inclusive, or universalistic in scope; and it promotes social welfare (Midgley, 1995, pp. 25-27).

Strategic thinking must take into account the unevenness of previous inequalities and structural disadvantages in the market or social environment. It is for this reason that gender issues, and those concerning ethnic minorities, are prominent in the thinking of policy planners (Cernea, 1985; Daley, 1994). Various writers describe the problem of distinguishing the most beneficial approach to this issue.

Without empowerment of the group in focus, the effects of a programme can reinforce the status quo, or leave the supposed beneficiaries worse off than before (Anderson, 1992; Moser, 1989; Smithies, 1993). Dixon points to the difficulty in getting across to sponsors the value of social development initiatives which cannot produce tangible proof of their effects. Indicators of measuring process goals must be recognised as valid if programmes are to be credited with their full importance (Dixon, 1995).

Definition: 'community' in development

There is no satisfactory definition of community for our purposes. Previous attempts to do this include references to geographical area, aggregates of people with common cause or groups of people who have been defined externally, by other people's characteristics. These may all become the focus of professional attention for the purposes of development. All are imprecise in that they are doomed to be arbitrary (Cox, 1974). Who is responsible for making such a decision? Should such a decision be made? Does the, so defined, 'community' have the final say itself? For the community involved, and for the professional worker, any decision about defining the nature and extent of any 'community' will actually be a political one. From the citizen's perspective, inclusive definitions may be variously opportune, culturally offensive, or a lever with which to persuade neighbours where their interests lie.

'Community', for the purposes of the professional may, or may not, be a warm, supportive institution, through which its members share cultural ties. It may be a goal for the worker to establish a 'community' for the sake of an operational outcome. In this regard, the writings of Etzioni are pertinent. He calls for a halt to the moral and social decline of society, and the development of social institutions which create new communities. Here there will be mutual support, collective economic co-operation and a sense of moral connection between the participants (Etzioni, 1993, 1995a, 1995b).

Can the re-creation of the community become a justifiable state activity in the face of some perceived social disorganisation? Would the intrusion of a professional worker, with the agenda of seeking a moral consensus, be a legitimate activity? What if the people developed their own agenda for action which did not agree with that of the state? The protectionism implicit in the *communitarianism* movement (see below) is explicitly promoted as a higher moral value (Atkinson, 1994, 1995; Etzioni, 1993). Under such circumstances, the consensus, or consent of an aggregate of people may well be an end in itself for a targeted intervention process. This leaves the worker in the role of a promoter of basic populism, without reference to a wider value system. 'Community' becomes just a functional concept (Biddle, 1965).

By contrast, to local politicians, and others in authority, the arbitrary definition, or non-definition of a community may be seen as a decision best left in their hands. They may like to feel that they are 'in charge' of civic or economic affairs, but do not often recognise the significance of this issue to local people. Personal or collective investment in the community can be high, and its form or purpose may differ widely from the official perspective. The expression of community feeling may not reveal itself until a sudden mix of social forces unleashes it. In Britain, we have been reluctant to formalise the concept. The publication of the Skeffington Report brought some of the issues into focus, but the issue is still being debated (Skeffington, 1968).

The question often arises out of disputed planning applications, where public or private bodies contest the legitimate 'interest' of petitioners to hold up suggested changes to the environment. For the community, 'community' is more than a structural concept. If there should be development workers active in an area such as this, how are the terms of reference established to the satisfaction of all? Could it matter if the employer of such an agent was also the agency for social administration and planning? This issue is the underlying discussion of this study. The ethical basis of professional activity must remain constantly in focus. As so many planning decisions are dictated by commercial interests, the seemingly arbitrariness of decisions often place professional workers in invidious positions.

It is not necessarily in the professional's interests to define a rigid boundary for any voluntary social grouping. Any working definition will be temporary and it will become more or less inevitable that some are excluded or included against their will. The professional worker will seek to define all these who are, or who are not included for working purposes. To the extent that certain categories of potential players are excluded, so the professional must see these people as potential for other intervention initiatives or potential obstacles to the purpose for and in which the professional is engaged. The model, which we describe below, will seek to make this clear. For the professional using this model, the concept of community becomes a point of reference for dynamic interaction and a target for constant monitoring and potential revision. For the sake of workaday practice, the term 'community' can be used as a professional shorthand for the target or object of the professional intervention.

For the community development worker, the concept of community must be fully explored. It is a concept which can, and will be, manipulated by the professional when working towards social objectives. Likewise, it will be manipulated by supporters and opponents of this process. It is in this manipulation of the dynamic forces of community, both functional and structural aspects, that the resourcefulness, and ultimately the success, of the worker will be tested.

Definition: communitarianism

Of late, there has been the emergence of another political rallying cry which, without any reference to the idea of deliberate intervention, or 'development', calls for society to transform itself into a new collective state of responsive and dutiful citizens. The people are asked to transform their social environment into a participatory social system which targets the family, schools, neighbourhood and community values. This is a selective and narrow approach as it calls for solidarity of those who are able, without any mention of those who are might not be structurally free to respond - the poor, the disabled, the victims of discrimination, etc. It makes no concession to the forces of the market and makes no linkage between how cherishing the local school, on the one hand, will overcome structural issues such as poverty, homelessness and unemployment on the other. It also pays scant regard to the ethnic and cultural mix of society, but presumes some sort of social uniformity.

This is an first step appeal to the middle classes to look to the social strengths of their residential and domestic associations. How it is ever going to appeal to loose aggregates of the poor and dispossessed is never addressed. This form of transformed society is promoted by Etzioni (Etzioni, 1993) and other members of the 'communitarian' movement (Sacks, 1995; Hattersley, 1987). There is a call for the re-establishment of 'traditional' values (Sacks, 1995; Atkinson, 1994), and the Leader of the Labour Party, Tony Blair is calling for something very similar (*The Times*, 25th March, 1995).

These appeals seem to be naive, or calculated to create an image of promise. They fail to show how the spirit of public consciousness can actually be induced to work against the forces of the market and consumerist pressures (Scott, 1994; Social Trends, 1994). Long-term unemployment has remained over, or near, three-quarters of a million for over ten years (Employment Gazette, September, 1995, pp. 352-8) and patterns of family income now depend heavily on the income of women, who were cast in another role when the book of traditional values was written. The debate about the nature of the supportive community is, nevertheless, welcome. In an age of positivist approaches to social care

24

and social relations, the skills of the development professional might have to concentrate on establishing contracts as the medium for confirming relationships between neighbours. If all else fails, this may be better than nothing. Communitarianism may be a label with which to dress social agreements. It might also be a vehicle with which professionals with a wider vision might effect access to an area. In other words, it may mean jobs.

Definition: social work & social change

Social change occurs when the social relations of society are forced to adjust to pressure. This pressure can originate outwith a particular social system, or from within. Structural changes, such as natural disasters, economic decline or war can totally distort social patterns, and social institutions have to adjust to these changes. Failure to do so will result in their decline and/or replacement by other mechanisms of social structure. The nature of social change can vary considerably: from orderly, incremental and slow to disorderly, sweeping and rapid. The effects of change can be keenly felt by the individual, where they might manifest themselves as changes in patterns of behaviour or personal values. These, in turn affect the associations with others, which may be dramatically affected. One purpose of social work in these situations is the support of people through the transition to a new equilibrium. Social work is also about initiating the process of social change (*pace* Martin Davies). This can take the form of going beyond the basic support to the enablement of a client. This is to appraise, with the client, how the balance of social forces might be rearranged in order to mitigate the most adverse effects of pressure. Restoring a balance then allows a fresh appraisal to be made of the possibilities for further changes, in a positive direction. In most cases, the lone efforts of the individual cannot make much impact on the situation. Whether this individual, plus the support of the social worker, *can* make an impact, is a moot point. In the 'market' role which is now prescribed for the social worker, there is not much room to manoeuvre. The relationship is tied to the minimal resources which can be mustered in an environment which has already been seen to be unstable.

Purposeful social change concerns the control and directing of power in a social system. In order to discover whether or not social work can be an influence in this process, a thorough reappraisal is required of the forces which are involved. The opportunities must be assessed for mobilising sufficient power to resist or confront those forces, which promote social inertia and negative situations. New forces need to be set up which will

25

allow for change in the direction which is desired by a client. If change is deemed possible, then decisions must be made about the most appropriate form of action. If it is, then social work for social change will have the opportunity to demonstrate its prowess. Social work for social change is *development*. For the client, this process will entail the deliberate modification of the patterns of social life and the acquisition of new skills. For the social worker, it will entail considerable modifications to the relationship which is maintained with the client. As the *enabling* role of the social worker is balanced by the assumption of personal power by the client, the professional role will shift again.

Very often, the initial social work task is to bring stability to a social situation which is deemed, professionally, to be unstable or beyond easy regulation by the client. On the scale of one worker to one individual, the professional is in some control over the process of change as it unfolds. The more that the professional role moves from 'support' to 'empowerment', the less professional control can be maintained over the situation. This will entail the worker taking more risks. The 'empowered' client will be able to make more free choices. Eventually, the professional worker decides that the client is in a stable enough position for the relationship to be severed.

The secret, for social workers, is to maintain the relationship on a one-to-one basis, and to set the horizons of change within manageable limits. This usually means bringing stability to the client *within a given environment*. The client has been empowered *in relation* to the social forces which may prevail at a certain time and place. The social forces which caused the intervention of the social worker still exist, and the vulnerable in society remain susceptible to their pressure. Any weakening or loss of stability by the client, will find these forces reasserting their earlier pressure. The likelihood is that they will again have their earlier effects. This is a potential revolving door situation. If the target for social change is to altogether modify the social circumstances, such that the forces which once assailed the client can no longer have their effects, then a different approach is needed. This will entail the worker increasing the scale of the intervention operation, and taking responsibility for the simultaneous empowerment of a number of clients, with the target for change being the social forces, and not the client's behaviour. This demands a different perspective on the nature of social forces and the exercise of different skills.

The collective activities of groups or whole communities can take control of their own destiny in a much more forceful way than can an individual. For the professional, it is often impossible to exercise any direct control over these collective activities, even if such control was considered necessary. Under some circumstances, merely staying in touch with the process can require special talents and qualities of endurance. If a professional wants to make an impact on such an activity, the method of intervention is problematic. How is acceptance into the activity achieved? What role is to be assumed, and how will it be respected by the other participants? How is any effect of the intervention to be measured? How can the quality of any professional contribution be isolated and assessed? Workers, themselves, are often reluctant to make any claims regarding their own prowess or influence on such collective processes. If they are seen to heavily involved and exerting some form of influence, then their intervention might be seen as paternalistic or manipulative. Over-statement of supposed power and influence can have negative effects on the acceptance of the worker within the group. In development terms, this can weaken the worker's credibility and standing within the community.

There are circumstances where it is considered necessary to employ a professional development worker to intervene in a group or community situation. The agenda is to effect a process of social change. Does such a decision denote that there is a genuine need for a professional input? Does the agenda of the employing agency determine the nature of the relationship between the community and the worker? If the community cannot organise itself to the level required for the desired social changes to occur, how can the engagement of a professional 'change agent' be justified? The decision to engage a development worker presumes that there has been some earlier discussion on this point. Was the community consulted in advance of this move being taken, or has the employer agency taken an arbitrary step on its own? Is there a presumption that certain social change goals will be the outcome of this intervention?

Use of systems theory

Development occurs as changes in the social and economic circumstances begin within a defined area. Community development charts the same ground, but it is the planning and active engagement with that process which marks out the distinctively professional nature of the task. Community development is planned change through the medium of organisational change and growth. For this to be effective, the professional must be in a position to grasp and manipulate some essential features of organisations, their composition and their dynamics. To facilitate this, the adoption of a stripped down version of systems theory is appropriate. We offer below some insight into how the professional can readily assess the potential for change within organisations using this analytical tool.

The essentials of systems theory are:

- management as an essential entity;
- control of organisational boundaries through active managerial functions;
- the management and control of processes which breach/pass through those organisation boundaries; and
- the regulation of functions within the organisation which respond and react to the movement in and out of the system.

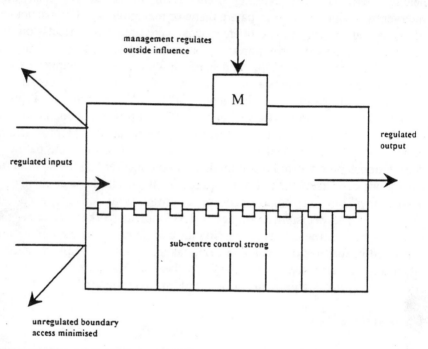

Figure 2: Strong boundary control

Using systems theory shorthand, effective and ineffective management can be demonstrated through the use of diagrams (see above). The management function is represented by the small box at the top of each organisation diagram (M).

A well-managed organisation should be able to control any access to the internal functioning of the organisation through the maintenance of strong boundaries. Strong boundaries are represented by solid lines in the diagram (see Figure 2 above). Uninvited forces seeking access to the organisation, are rebuffed as being inappropriate, by the boundary control mechanisms.

Some forces are allowed negotiated access. In a simple production system, raw materials of an appropriate kind are allowed into the organisation. They are modified internally by the 'production functions', and then allowed out in the desired modified/manufactured form.

The weak organisation will maintain weak boundary control (Figure 3). This weakness is represented by broken lines as boundaries, with a similarly weakened management control system (M), which itself has permeable boundary lines. Forces seeking to access the functions of the organisation, including the management function, can do so with relative ease. This produces unpredictable results, and ultimately the collapse of the organisation.

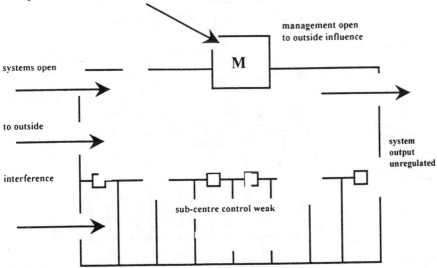

Figure 3: Weak boundary control

Figure 4 amplifies the internal relationships and functions of the organisation. Overall control is vested in the major management box (M), but authority is usually delegated to internal administrative and sub-managerial control levels (sub-centre controls).

These are represented through smaller control/management boxes. Central management sustains control over these management functions and ensures their capacity to function effectively. It also ensures the integration of the delegated task within the overall design and purpose of the organisation. Community development workers should familiarise themselves thoroughly with the nature and purpose of any organisation's boundary and management functions. They should be able to theorise about the organisational requirements for these controls, and also about the nature and purpose of the internal functions of an organisation. Their input, as a consultant to the management of an organisation, will be to strengthen that management's role in relation to its safeguarding the integrity of their organisation, and the success of its desired outcomes. This concerns both the internal functioning of the organisation as well as controlling inputs and outputs. If a new organisation is being built from scratch, then, if possible, an organisational blue print embodying these imperatives should be constructed from the outset.

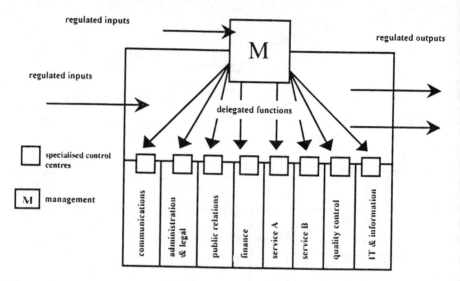

Figure 4: The system, management and delegation (strong boundaries)

Where more complex organisational forms are involved (see Chapter 6 below), this systems analysis has to be just as precise, if not more so. The internal politics of delegation of managerial responsibilities within and between organisations is a much more complicated process. Failure to anticipate these complexities can have considerable negative impact.

In Figure 5, we consider the situation where four autonomous organisations (Orgns. A B C & D) consider two separate transfers of power and responsibility from their respective organisations. The first (in the upper section of the Figure) is to agree between themselves that a new organisation (F) will be created, which will regulate the actions of all of them for certain specific functions. This is the idea of a federal relationship where, for example, the power and responsibility for charitable status, overall policy for expansion/contraction of activities, or public relations might be vested. Each autonomous organisation (A B C D) will be represented on the federal structure (F). This new organisation will make its own policies, and carry out its own activities, through the agreement of the representatives of A B C & D. Once the policies are agreed, they become binding on the constituent members. The dynamics of this form of organisation respond to the relative strengths of each constituent member, and also on the shifting impact which organisation (F) has on its own action environment. Constituent members will have to devise, through their representatives, how much power, and what directions for action, organisation F can pursue.

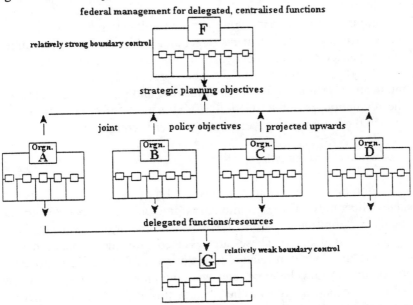

Figure 5: Complex organisations and their sub-parts

In the lower section of Figure 5, a service agency (G) has been created by the same four autonomous organisations. In this case, it has been agreed that this new organisation will be a functional workhorse for the participating members, and it will have little autonomy of its own. An appearance of autonomy may be given to it, but the reality of the power relations is that organisation (G) has to do the bidding of A B C & D. The boundaries of management at (G) are open to incursion by the power bloc above it. In this situation, there can be no question of organisation (G) exercising any power over its controlling organisations. An example of this

31

type of organisation might be where a number of voluntary service organisations decide to create a consortium to bid for a local authority contract to provide care services. The consortium constitutes organisation (G) to become the bidding agency. If it is successful, a delegated management structure is set up which can assume responsibility for managing the contract, and supplying the care service. The 'parent' organisations, A B C & D, can remain reasonably detached from the whole process. On-going relations between organisation (G) with the local authority, or with other interests (such as the carers of those getting the service), will be independent of the functioning of the original organisations.

A community development worker has a consultancy role in this process. Advice on structuring arrangements, legal and public responsibility duties, and, most particularly, on the dynamic process of managing (or being managed by) a number of separate organisations. Patterns of communication, protocols for decision-making and policy implementation, and the regulation of public relations are all aspects of organisational life with which the community development worker is conversant.

The professional and the citizen

At the beginning of this chapter, the description of social work activity was selected deliberately. This definition was gradually expanded to include, eventually, a definition of forms of activity that require the engagement of groups of individuals. These are assisted, by the professional, in transforming their position relative to major social forces. This process is called community development, and we have chosen to include it within the definition of social work, rather than setting it apart, as a distinct and separate activity. Since the earliest literature on the subject, definitions of community development have concentrated on group processes, and, within these, the objective of producing trained and formal leadership. This leadership provides structure for the group and lends stability for what becomes a community of activity. This community then becomes the target for the continued professional intervention. Today, in Britain, within the context of contemporary social work, the concept of social change is one, which is in grave danger of being swept out of the collective consciousness. Workers are continually under pressure to convert their talents into the twin requirements of the management of care, and the protection of the vulnerable. These are both functions of control, and not the forces for change, liberation or transformation. People who fall under the influence of these new professionals cannot expect the world to move for them. They are more likely to be processes, than become a part of a process themselves. These forces are also reactive, whereas development has a pro-active message in its planning mechanism.

Because of a possible conflict between the aspirations of the client and the prescribed function of the professional worker in this setting of social control, we have to seek another mechanism through which the client can work for social change. Community development is one such mechanism, but this is not without its own contradictions, which need to be explored. The skill of the development worker lies in the ability to plan and deliver a strategy of intervention, which will be set to achieve predetermined goals, be they 'tangible' (material) outcomes, or the establishment of sustainable processes. The development worker achieves the goals of the strategy through (amongst other methods) the manipulation of groups. These groups are not 'clients' in the normal sense of the word. These clients are citizens, who are targeted in order to improve their functioning as such. The *client-as-citizen* is the fundamental value of this branch of social work. These citizens will, however, have been identified because of some perceived condition which is described as in some way deficient. Without this condition, they would have no need of the professional input. This confronts both the professional and the citizen client with the unending pressure of contradiction. Who is in actual control of the action process? For example: can the citizen go it alone, or can the professional act behind the scenes as a 'fixer'? Professionals learn rapidly how to survive within these contradictions. They may either deny that they exist, or they may decide that to be employed, and prudent, is worth more than to be idealistic, and unemployed. They may prefer to attempt to fudge the situation as long as they can. In any case, the paradox remains.

A citizen who is faced with a process of change and empowerment, can contemplate new possibilities for social activity. The change also produces a growing awareness of the qualities of the relationship that has developed with the professional. There will be a growing sense of awareness that, even although the basis of 'citizenship' has been established from the start, the relationship is an unequal one. It will also emerge that the professional is perhaps constrained in the degree to which some of the citizen's goals can be given professional support. Areas where there may be policy clashes with the worker's employer, are such examples. If the relationship is to be based upon trust and confidence, the citizen needs to be aware that the resources of the professional are going to be available when the action requires them. The sudden abandonment of the cause by the worker, or the 'counselling out' of setting certain goals altogether, is a situation which needs to be worked through by both parties. The logical extension of the citizen's search for power comes when there is a breakdown of confidence between the governed and the governors. If the citizen considers that all out confrontation with established authority is in order, where does the professional worker stand?

The model which is the subject of this volume, is an attempt to explore the interaction of professionals and non-professional citizens as they grapple with the many situations that emerge during social change. Community development is about understanding social change, and being able to influence it through the application of sophisticated skills, such as planning, intervention and evaluation. There is a need for awareness of the conflicts of interest that will emerge, of choices that have to be made, and of the dilemmas which beset those coping with the shifting raft of values, which emerge from the development of power systems. We hope to address these issues through gradually introducing a change process of increasing complexity.

More recently, and certainly with a high profile at the level of delivery in the field, moneys targeted at development have been accompanied by conditions which emphasise the need for a high level of public participation in the project work. This public participation somehow translates into the understanding that the public actually approved of the activity in which they engage. This might not necessarily be the case. In Britain, the catch-phrase is 'partnership'. Which requires central government grants allocations to be tied to a contribution from local government. This local financial investment must also be accompanied by evidence that local citizens have been involved in the planning process and are active on the ground during the implementation process (Community Development Foundation, 1995).

Where Britain gives aid for projects in developing economies, the level of intervention in stipulating participation is more forceful and direct. Applying the framework of 'social analysis', a prominent government guide for projects defines development as:

> 'the attainment of sustainable improvements in economic growth and quality of life that increase the range of choices open to all, achieved by the people's own efforts in the private sector, or through voluntary activity supported by governments' (Overseas Development Administration, 1995 p. 2).

Broadening 'stakeholder participation' is invoked to ensure that the representivity of opinion is spread wide across the various (legitimate) interests groups in society (Overseas Development Administration, 1995 p. 94).

The combined impact of official administrative support for beneficial social change, plus the strong legacy of democratic and social justice within community development as a profession (see Chapter 2 below), gives rise to certain positive statements about the outputs of community development programmes.

A 'good community development programme' is one where community resources and organisations are involved; more power and influence is gained and the community begins to relate to, and engage in, the wider world. The resultant social change produces a better life quality on a continuing and increasing scale (Barr, et.al., 1996b, p. 9).

We will spend a large part of this volume unpacking these processes and will suggest that many of the changes which 'ought' to be part and parcel of the development process, will not emerge unless they are driven determinedly by the community development professional. We will address the question of verifying actual achievements of development in Chapter 9 (Evaluation) below.

2 Seeking Clarity through a Management Model

The aim of this chapter is to produce a model for the conceptualisation, planning and the analysis of action within the community development process. For the successful application of a model, certain disciplines have to be observed and to do this one has to understand the way in which the model works in application.

High on the agenda is the management of the tension which arises out of the nature of social work practice in an uneven power relationship. It was noted that there was considerable potential for conflict between the principles of community development and the conditions which will usually apply in practice for the professional. The application of professional skills to the relationship between the worker and the client, when they are being controlled by external forces, can be described as manipulation.

The implementation of centrally sanctioned policies using this professional process calls into question the basic presumption of community development. Namely, that it is the people themselves who should set the agenda and decide the action for which they will bear the costs (Armstrong, 1971; Barclay, 1982; Batten, 1957; Biddle, 1968; Calouste Gulbenkian, 1968, 1973; Chekki, 1979; Chanan, 1992; Chanan & Vos, 1990; Cockburn, 1977; Dasgupta, 1968; Macdonald, 1992; McMurray, 1993; Narayan, 1967; Robinson, 1995; Ross, 1955; Rothman, 1979.) The acknowledgement of this tension and its management is one of the purposes of this model (Cockburn, 1977; Corrigan, 1975; Mayo, 1982).

As is explained above, ideal conditions rarely apply to practice, and there is a range of value presumptions behind the different approaches to development (Batten & Batten, 1965; Corrigan, 1975; Specht, 1975, 1976; Alinsky, 1972; O'Malley, 1977; London Edinburgh Weekend Return Group, 1980). Regardless of personal values and position in this debate, the problem for the professional worker is to locate the situation of action and the direction of action in some objective and detached way. From this, the necessary analysis can be made from which to focus, plan decisions, select options and assess a value standpoint. This model will make this process possible, both in a historic and in a planning context.

This model begins with the presumption that there is a basic unit through which the impact of the professional worker is directed or felt. For convenience, in the initial, abstract presentation of the model below, this basic unit is taken as the individual citizen in the community. It is with this unit that the professional has to negotiate a relationship. The selection of the individual, rather than the small group, is deliberate in that it keeps discussion within the boundaries of most social work practice. Secondly, and more importantly, it keeps the individual well within focus. As the dynamics of the model change for different levels of professional intervention, the position of the individual becomes just one in a variety of variables. The focus moves from an individual to an analysis of an aggregate of people, to a group, and on to an organisation. As the scale and the purposes of the intervention change, the position of the individual can become obscured. It is central to our thesis that the individual is essential element in the process of development and must be sustained at the centre of any enterprise that is undertaken.

The second assumption is that, within all social action processes, it is possible for the worker to link the action, or part of the action, to a set of relationships. These relationships are a function of the following:

♦ the degree of independence of the individual citizen (or group or organisation) from close support from the professional;
♦ the freedom of the citizen (or group or organisation) from control by funding or other (commissioning) agency to act towards goals and outcomes;
♦ the nature and strength of structural and institutionalised barriers to citizen action;
♦ the level of awareness and skill of the professional worker.

The first linkage between the above points is to do with functioning ability, autonomy and survival while the second and third are about political awareness and independence. The fourth linkage can have a direct bearing on all three above it. The on-going analysis of these links is an important tool for the work in balancing the relationship with the client.

The third presumption is that there is a point of reference for the (third party) funder of any action programme. Had an employer/commissioning agency remained in control of the process of direct action/service activity themselves, then they would have a set of expectations and boundaries within which they would have anticipated an outcome. If the client is the source of the resources, then there is an added investment in the outcome.

The fourth premise is that the professional will wish to remain in some form of control of the action process until such time as the professional exercises the judgement that it is time for that control to be relinquished. Jacobs rebuts this point, putting the client as the valued arbiter of the choices in directions for development (Jacobs, 1994). But 'the client' can always walk away, and will do so if it is obvious that needs are not being met.

The logic of this model demonstrates that the professional strives to retain control, in some form over the complexities of social change as they follow each other, over the next seven chapters. Loss of 'control' will destroy the ability of the professional to apply best those special skills and values which make community development a professional activity. We realise that this flies in the face of most received wisdom on community development practice and values, but we believe that the reality facing a professional in the field demands that 'social control' be managed as best as it can be. We hope that this 'management model' will provide a framework for this stressful and contradictory process.

The model

The model describes a dynamic and varying relationship between the professional (and the employer agency) and the social action process. This relationship can be described in the abstract through the template below.

The template

FOCUS on the basic-unit- the INDIVIDUAL	INDIVIDUAL as the CONTEXT for ACTION	INDIVIDUAL as the FOCUS for ACTION	INDIVIDUAL as POTENTIAL for ACTION	INDIVIDUAL as a VEHICLE for ACTION	INDIVIDUAL as the MOTOR for ACTION

The template represents a hierarchy of action, starting from the most simple relationship in the left-hand column. The action process is first visualised as a direct intervention, on a one-to-one basis, with an individual citizen. The paradigm of social work intervention comprises support, enablement and empowerment which is adapted by the professional to suit the requirements of social control constraints. This control is dictated by the statutory or policy constraints on the actions of the professional and/or the citizen.

This section seeks to define the boundaries for professional intervention within the most restrictive context. It has the purpose of setting the scene for changes in the professional role as conditions of intervention are modified. In a conventional social work situation, achieving a balance between control and empowerment is of continuing concern. The 'good practice' presumption is that empowerment should always be the goal, and will always (or ultimately) be the outcome of the social work initiative. The procedure of intervention will depend heavily on the professional's original assessment of the citizen's (client's) needs. From this assessment, the professional will make the initial decisions regarding the best way forward.

The degree of freedom or flexibility allowed to the professional is decidedly limited if the specific outcome of the employer's policies is tightly defined. Some services may be offered on an 'all or nothing' basis, e.g. respite care. These conditions apply equally if the boundaries of some relevant statutory framework are precise and binding on the worker. In situations which are defined as 'high risk' in relation to policy or law, then these limitations will exert a high degree of influence on any course of action, e.g. procedures for suspected child abuse.

It could be that the citizen is put under pressure to behave in a certain manner, or to become a certain kind of person to suit the constraints of the policy. These conditions exist when, e.g.: a 'supervised visit' is arranged to a child by its estranged parent. In these circumstances, professional discretion is at its minimum and considerations of duty and responsibility are at their highest.

The desire to implement practice methods which neither oppress nor restrict the freedom of the client may run into conflict with these institutional barriers. Anti-oppressive practice, sensitive to race, gender, age, disability or sexual orientation may require intervention approaches to which those that framed policy paid little or no regard. It is a constant test for the professional, wielding considerable personal and institutional power, that the values which dictate practice methods are continually defended against the generalities of policy (Ohri, et.al., 1982; Dominelli, 1990, 1995). These considerations set up the first elements of risk that confront the professional on a continuum where the introduction of flexibility can be identified with the search for good practice methods. It is this tension which our model seeks to confront.

Where there is tight restraint on the professional and individual caused by restrictive policies, a constricted and controlled relationship results. There is little room for flexibility. Support, enablement and empowerment there may be, but only within a very limited context. Nevertheless, the adoption of certain attitudes and methods of intervention by the professional could cause the reduction of these restraints.

There are situations where the professional determines that there is little risk of conflict between the service requirements of assessed need and the constraints of either policy or law. The amount of scope, and flexibility of a subsequent action programme can then be planned with much less constraint. Under these circumstances, it is likely that the level of professional competence and skill, and/or the prevailing culture of the professional's employing agency, will be the dominant influences on practice. In other words, there are practical and cultural pressures which lead the professional to adopt controlling measures. Support of a 'client' is an on-going part of the professional's rationale but the precise nature of that support will vary considerably.

We now refer again to the template. The six columns refer to a continuum of control over the direction and shape of the action process. The potential for the tightest control exists for work within the left-hand column, where the boundaries around the professional/client relationship are under the least pressure from more general, social forces. A high degree of dependency could easily develop when the professional worker appears to be the only source of support for the client. This applies whether or not official policies or constraints intrude on the relationship. This is typical of social worker/client contact within the confines of the social work agency itself. In practice, this form of relationship is rare, particularly in British statutory social work, where the citizen only rarely attends the Social Services Department. For the present, the community is still the setting of most contact between social workers and their clients. Work in the community forces changes upon the relationship, particularly the degree of professional control which can be exercised.

This shift is represented by the social worker's 'movement' across the template in conceptual terms. Each column in the template represents a different level in a hierarchical relationship between the client and the professional. In re-modelling the relationship, such that the client changes from being a passive object for control and adaptation to meet the needs of welfare objectives, to a situation where the client is in control (the 'motor' for action), the worker has gradually to adjust the nature of engagement. This involves the whole professional relationship with the client. Factors such as specific cultural characteristics (context), locational and intercultural characteristics (focus), and individual capabilities (potential), all determine the pace and success with which a client can be 'adapted' (vehicle) to become (be restored to) an autonomous citizen again (motor).

As the worker adjusts the focus on the client to accommodate more and more of the personal, cultural and environmental characteristics which make up the totality of that client's world, so the constraints of the 'clinical' social work relationship is diluted. The degree of prescription drops, and the capacity of the worker to embrace within the framework of practice the specific requirements of any particular client become less. As the influences of the environment intrude more on the time and space available, the client assumes more and more freedom to act alone. Control over the client's action and responses then becomes a negotiated agreement, with the client in as much real control as the worker. A model for intervention which might have appeared to be appropriate in the seclusion of the office, may prove unworkable in a damp bed-sit basement.

Development for change

The relationship which has been described above has outlined an interdependence which requires a new professional perspective. The social worker seeks to exploit the client's attributes so that a state of (relative) autonomy can replace the dependence or confusion with which the client is presently confronted. To achieve this, the worker must adjust the relationship with the client, adopt fresh professional skills, adopt a different profile and take more risks.

SOCIAL WORK with the INDIVIDUAL	INDIVIDUAL as a CONTEXT for SERVICE	INDIVIDUAL as the FOCUS for SERVICE	INDIVIDUAL as POTENTIAL for SELF-HELP	CLIENT-PLUS as a VEHICLE for SERVICE	CLIENT-PLUS as the MOTOR for SERVICE

As the focus on the template shifts to the right, control over the process of intervention changes. The adoption of practice methods for the greater empowerment of the client, or the absence of restraint by the employing agency will produce a less controlling relationship. As control is progressively relaxed, the professional is forced to restructure the nature of the professional intervention. Control is replaced by support, which, in turn, gives way to an enabling process.

The next stage in the relationship is on to the empowerment of the citizen to implement a process of self-selected activity. Referring to the parameters above, it is assumed that the professional still desires to remain in control of the process. And so, as formal control is progressively relinquished in the process of achieving citizen autonomy for independent activity, so the form of control is also changed to enable the professional to sustain a stake in the outcomes of this action.

Social work as development

In normal circumstances, there are definite limitations to the amount of crude power that the professional can exert (through statutory coercion, for example). Consequently, a degree of planning is necessary to determine, under any particular circumstances, what are the best practice methods. The professional can then begin to work towards a range of outcomes which are compatible with professional or policy guidelines. In the template, we have selected several key stages in the move from control to empowerment. These dictate the form of professional planning and subsequent action. They prescribe variations in skill for their accomplishment and they also require increased or modified forms of monitoring and evaluation if process outcomes are not to fall outside anticipated or prescribed limits. These stages can be described as follows:

Individual as a context for service

Relaxing the control over the relationship between the social worker and the client, by moving the site from which the service is offered, sets off a process of change which can redefine the expectations which each has of the other.

The selection of a geographical location for the site of service delivery, or the targeting of an aggregate of people with similar, specifically defined needs, has an immediate effect on the professional activity. It introduces degrees of flexibility into the approach which must be adopted. Adapting the scale of operation or range of practice methods to suit the general needs of a group (e.g. type of disability) or locality (geographical, or rural/urban) will place pressure on the planning agency. An agency will need to ensure that its workers are expert enough to adopt more flexible approaches to their work, which can handle cultural diversity and difficult working conditions. Often, at this point in practice, strains between actual practice methods and those which need to be adopted in order to minimise oppression, come to the fore. The agency will have to cope with professionals who find that some specific local conditions may require them to conduct their practice with differing priorities and assumptions from those of other workers within the same agency.

From the worker's perspective, freedom to offer a service within the context of the client allows for more professional autonomy and the exercise of discretion in planning and decision-making. On the one hand, the worker has the opportunity to assert personal authority and to decide which of a repertoire of personal skills are most appropriate in this context. On the other, there is more room for failure in addressing the circumstances which may be presented. The mere fact of geographical isolation of a client may necessitate indirect forms of support, instead of routine visiting. Decentralisation in this form is the first step towards recognising that the client is a citizen and has a wider, social reference system which has to be accommodated in the progression of a client towards individual autonomy.

Moving a service away from the administrative centre produces effects that are more far-reaching than mere relocation. Once the service users begin to interact with the agency under influences that can immediately be linked to their own locality, the professional is able to recognise ways in which the services have to be modified. These modifications will be required if the services are to provide for the specific characteristics of local need. The benefits of a more precise tailoring of services to local needs will change the perception of both professional and the client. Good practice would suggest that this is the first step in a communication process towards increasing service relevance. Once this process begins, much more refinement to service structure becomes possible. Planners and workers will become increasingly aware of the complexity of the community fabric around their service delivery systems and how this knowledge can be harnessed. More precise fine-tuning to local needs requires another step across our template.

Individual as the focus for service

In an agency with centralised planning, the nature of the service offered will be reshaped and influenced by the pull of practice expedience and cultural influences of the local community.

It is possible to target intervention much more closely on members of a specific sub-group within any locality. They need to become the object of a deliberate strategy constructed for their own, particular needs. This is the situation which is being implemented progressively through the machinery of the NHS & Community Care Act 1990 (Department of Health, 1990), particularly in the case of block contracts (Department of Health, 1989, p. 27; Audit Commission, 1992a, p. 33).

In the process of fashioning the service more specifically to local needs and group needs, some of the specifics of a service can be modified, replaced or even sacrificed. This shift might demonstrate that the expressed needs of the target (class) type of person are having a direct effect on the design of services. Once need is identified and assessed, planning can be designed to produce certain outcomes. In addition, more specific needs, such as those of people from an ethnic group, a disability group living within a particular location, etc., can be built into the planning framework and a far greater range of sensitivity can be accommodated.

The relationship between the client/citizen and the professional will become broader as the professional begins to operate two systems of analysis simultaneously. One is based on welfare culture and how individual need is assessed by the centralised planners. The other depends on the interaction with the client and on the local culture. There is need for flexibility at the margins between these separate worlds. Centralised planning depends on the creation of 'welfare classes' for the allocation of resources. Personal perceptions of need and socially acceptable solutions to it will influence the acceptance of the professional's intervention. The professional has to become more aware of the interaction between these forces and structure services to be sensitive to them.

This whole process is dependent on high quality intelligence being available into the nature of the complexity of the social context within which the client lives. An accurate 'profile' of the community can locate a client within a particular group or culture. A high degree of professionalism is required to be sensitive to the information and to know how to relate to it in daily practice situations.

It will be noted that the frame of reference for this section is described as for the needs of a *class* of individual in society, rather than for the 'individual' recipient of support found in the first descriptive paragraphs. The resource base for services of this class of need will be planned centrally, policy guidelines for the style and nature of service content will be set centrally, and they will be financed centrally. Priorities of need will also be set at this level and the role and influence of the agency in providing services will be regulated accordingly. The particular characteristics of a local service, for a local group, will be introduced once these broad guidelines are established. This will limit the immediate scope for the workers. It emphasises the point that the individual client/citizen may be the subject of a particular professional intervention but is still an object in a broad planning exercise.

The professional operating in this context will have to demonstrate a high degree of resourcefulness. The maximum amount of flexibility will be required over the allocation of resources, some of which may have already been tied up in block contracts with local service providers. The devising of services which target individual need precisely, and fall within the available resource limits, will become a demanding activity. It is in the targeting of resources to the very sensitive needs of the individual that the potential tensions arise. It may be that some individuals' needs rate below the priority level for the allocation of services. In another situation, a priority rating may change from one financial period to another. When there are insufficient resources, the professional relationship may have to be terminated. In the new scheme of personal needs assessment, a request for care will be given a score. People falling within a priority category of need (a high score) will be provided with services. Those with a lower priority, will not. A person might fall within the priority category during one year, and fall out of it in the next. 'Priority' will be designated according to the pool of resources which are available in each accounting period, thus creating a shifting 'threshold' of priority.

This will create tension and pressure for the worker and considerable frustration for the client. Fallback on the general de-personalised support of public advice services, local charities and family may not be appropriate or sufficient. The possibility of this is identified in the White Paper, *Caring for People* (Department of Health, 1989, cl. 3.1.4.; cl 3.2.12, etc.). Somehow, this deficit of resources must be overcome. What means does the worker possess to enlarge the pool of available resources? Is there a role for the individual citizen in the process of establishing care and/or support systems which meet personal needs?

In exploring a solution to this question, a professional may be led to develop a strategy which provides the necessary resources by alternative means. The motivation for continuing engagement arises out of the professional duty and vocational responsibly to ensure that the requisite amount of support is forthcoming from some source or other. Without enlarging the pool of immediate resources available, there can be no relief for the needs of the client. But attempting to discover or develop them also places fresh responsibilities on the professional. The ensuing progression of the model presumes that there is a role for the client in this process. If this role can be developed, there will be a pay-off for the professional, the client and for the community. It is also supported by the belief that, through personal involvement and taking direct control of the process, the client will become empowered to arrest further deterioration in the situation. By becoming an active player, the client will be drawn into a critical appraisal of the welfare system as a whole.

Some workers may suggest that the introduction of 'alternative' systems cannot ever be justified, others may prefer that this option be introduced at the very beginning of the professional relationship. The generation-old schism between social work and community development in British social work hinges around this issue. It may well be that today's practitioners simply confess that there are no services available for low-priority need cases. The 'case' is then closed or put on 'hold' until circumstances change. One thing is certain. If the worker waits around for a change of government, and then a change in policy, then there is a long wait ahead for the client. In social care, rectitude cannot be abandoned for misplaced righteousness. We are suggesting that there are other solutions to providing resource back-up. Official support is not the only option. But, in this scenario, the professional will have to assume responsibility for the process and outcomes that are not a regular feature of the social work experience.

The failure of most social workers, and social work agencies generally, to come to terms with the structural implications of 'preventative' methods bears out this point. The reluctance to build in the necessary training to fulfil the needs of this role, are evidenced by their omission from the requirements for social work training at qualifying level, despite the criticisms which have been raised along the way (CCETSW, 1989; Leonard, 1975b; Brown et al, 1982).

The whole question of 'individualisation' (Orme, 1993), which has now become a virtual obsessive focus for social work in its new management and/or protection mode, would have to be abandoned once the decision is taken to move beyond this point in the model. If the traditional social work role is further eroded as the introduction of community care progresses (Langan, 1993) then there will be less opportunity for choosing preventative and developmental options. Needs assessment and care management will become the specialised duty of the statutory agencies, and the service providers will be tied to tightly defined and itemised contracts. Under these constraints, it is more likely that there will be a loss of professional consciousness that these options exist at all.

Instead of bowing to these pressures, the worker should be doing another form of assessment. This owes its pedigree to the days when social work prided itself as being a 'generic' profession. It takes the form of working with the client towards establishing a high degree of independence from the service system altogether. It should be based upon the special and personal qualities which the client possesses, together with any immediate support system. It is this system which will become the target for the next stage in the worker's intervention. There will be costs for the client if this process proceeds further, and it has to be established that the decision to move ahead is taken by the client alone, and not under heavy pressure from the professional.

The next stage in the template model represents a time of appraisal, planning and preparation. This process applies equally to the worker, as to the client, as both will need to adjust their outlook and role if the process is to progress further. It is a time for readjustment in the nature of the professional/client relationship.

Individual as potential for self-help

When a shift in methods is contemplated from direct service delivery to the supplement or replacement of services by the community's own efforts, a new working relationship must be developed to undertake an assessment and planning programme.

In order to focus on the structural perspective of this model, explicit developmental methods are now introduced. These change the form of intervention completely as they require the infusion of new kinds of professional skills, for a different type of on-going support. The agenda for changing this relationship is, at the outset, under the control of the professional. Immediately the process of development begins, however, the client-as-citizen perspective changes the balance. The citizen is now free to choose, not between service options, but between co-operation and non-co-operation. The outcome, for the client, is to be enabled and empowered to intervene personally in the process of making care and support available.

This is a phase of assessment of potentials and priorities from the position of self-help. It calls for the development of strategies and the re-working of the professional relationship. The client becomes the focus for an innovative kind of assessment. Personal strengths and weaknesses, the existence of social networks and the needs of culture, personal preferences, etc., are put under scrutiny. This will result in a complete re-appraisal of the client's position, on a different basis from the approach normally adopted by care assessment procedures. The client must be involved fully in this exercise and a special programme of orientation and preparation work must be done at this point. Both the client's perspective and the professional perspective will have to adjust to accommodate the concept of non-professional services, non-statutory support and the self-determination of the client into a free-standing agent of change and development. The professional and the client now become a planning team where each has different skills and resources to offer. It is through this alliance that the client can be enabled to acquire the necessary care and support.

Taking issues such as confidentiality fully into account, the 'team' must consider developing a strategy for transforming the form of service to the

47

client. It is the task of the worker, initially, to identify to the client the range of choice of action which is now before them. The identification and mobilisation of extra resources will take precedence, and will become the foundation of a new working relationship. Once potential resources have been identified and their value assessed, the release of this potential will become the working agenda for the client. Dialogue over goals and understanding the process play a large part in the professional support function at this point. Armed with this information, the worker can assist in extending the client's personal skills. The primary target is the development of the individual's potential to grapple with a new interactive form of care and support, one which is not bounded by the formal constraints and conditions of public service. Rather, the professional task is the preparation of the client as an organiser of care from the resources that are to be found outside the formal systems altogether. This is the primary task of the 'team' during this phase of development.

Network development It is likely that all previous work with this client has been within a small circle of immediate support. In some cases, this may just be the individual client. In other situations, there may be a primary carer, a number of carers or a whole array of active support which might be available. In the assessment of the potential for further development, we are considering the *formalisation* of this system of support; the extension of the client's personal resources into an active, working network. It will be through this network that the practical support of the client will be extended into the community at large.

At this stage, it will be necessary to assess the client as part of such a system - the 'client-plus' network. If no such network exists, the worker may have to consider other approaches to the problem. The recruitment of such a network would then be the immediate priority for the worker before further development work could be undertaken. If need is to be met, then the appropriate amount of resourcing must be mobilised, by whatever means (see Pincus & Minahan, 1973; Goldstein, 1973).

Designing a concept such as 'client-plus', the constraints of confidentiality are being maintained, at least until the potential, purposes and processes of a self-help initiative have been explored. The boundaries of 'client-plus' are limited to the extent to which the professional and the client feel free to expand them as an immediate resource team. In cases where confidentiality, privacy or professional control are the main considerations, the boundaries will only be expanded minimally. Where the boundaries are expanded to embrace a wider network, beyond the family, for example, the skills of the client and professional will need to be developed. The client will have to manage the new dynamics of any interaction and care support which may be forthcoming. The worker will have to support the client through this process until it is rooted in practice.

We are considering a control, planning and action mechanism which comprises the combined resources of the professionals and the 'client-plus' team. This is to be the primary resource team and it will be their efforts and ideas which are to be expanded through making community resources accessible. General, top-up services from the public sector have to be included in any audit of potential help, but they may not be relevant or may get in the way of more personalised development.

The input of the professional is to prepare the client for a series of explorations into the dynamics of community life in the search for mechanisms of support. This can be increased by the inclusion of the professional's knowledge of the resource potential of the community. Community profiling should be a standard mechanism for the assessment of any community's capabilities to support its more vulnerable members (Glampson, et.al., 1975; Hawtin, et. al., 1994). The planning and action 'team' must do a re-assessment of the client's needs and the strengths and weaknesses of the surrounding community as a source of help. Connecting networks will need to be appraised and tested.

The manipulation of the community's resources for the benefit of the client then becomes a strategy for the 'client-plus' team. For this task, the team need to be resourced through special practice exercises, such as how to target individuals or approach organisations and ask for assistance; how to present personal needs publicly in such a way as to protect personal dignity and privacy. This search for support for direct help and assistance may begin with other people in the same need category. The professional will seek to draw people together who have the same needs and to seek to create an alliance between them. The creation of a group approach to this work saves energies and also creates the potential for organised formations of disability groups. They can pool resources and also work for an increased awareness and involvement by the community at large (Adams, 1990).

It must be stressed that the starting point in this process is the preparation of the individual for the activity and the obtaining of consent for the process. Failure to protect the individual's right to privacy is to deny the basic rights of citizenship. It does not mean that the citizen should not be entitled to future support from the formal care system. At this point, this form of support does not exist. The best that can be mobilised are the efforts of the social worker as development worker. The strategic aim of the worker is both to empower the client to participate in formal, or semi-formal mechanisms of self-help, and to develop preventative capacity in the community as a whole. By restructuring the nature of the professional/client relationship, the professional can achieve the following:

♦ the direct involvement of the client in the planning and resource selection of additional, non-statutory services can prepare the client for their control once they are in place. It can also prepare the client for future training and development as a commissioner of care;
♦ the preparation for the introduction of personalised care services can give the client first-hand insight into the development of services. Awareness of this process can raise the client's own awareness of the nature of these needs;
♦ sensitivity to cultural and other needs can become keystones to actual service development;
♦ the client can be made aware that the regulation of services and the appraisal of their performance will be located at the point of delivery rather than through a mechanism of formal monitoring;
♦ the resources of the client will be involved, developed and extended to their maximum possible extent, giving the client the greatest possible sense of involvement and achievement. In this way, the full potential client as a participant can be mobilised;
♦ in the future, some control can be maintained over the direction and extent to which this 'informal' approach extends, or seeks to extend. Professional restraint can be applied to help manage excessive flexibility or 'creativity' which may endanger the initiative.

In times of financial restraint, or where conventional approaches to service are not appropriate, imaginative steps have to be devised. It is also evident that *Community Care* could easily become a contrivance for 'dumping' care onto a captive and under-resourced family or network (Schorr, 1992). These factors place added ethical responsibilities upon the professional. Care is needed where and while it is needed, in a form which will meet the needs of the client. It may be that solutions are sought that provide only illusory alternatives and which create more isolation for the client. Ad hoc solutions may give short-term relief to professional consciences, but they can also create long term vulnerability for the client and future problems for the agency. They do nothing for the client's ability to cope more positively with a bad situation.

This process exposes the professional to the dynamics of sharing, in partnership with the client, the control of service and support. The new mini-team has to discover the reasons why resources are not immediately available and a strategy must be developed to effect their development and/or mobilisation. The degree to which the partnership is an equal one depends on the relationship between three elements:

♦ the degree of control the professional's employers insist upon as a matter of policy (and statutory limitations);
♦ the ability of the professional to manipulate the situation towards a balance which remains compatible with the professional's own desire to retain control; and
♦ the attitude and ability of the client (or client-plus) to assume control.

Part of the professional's skill is to manipulate the employer agency into accepting the allocation of professional time and resources for the task of transferring control across to the client. The employer has to come to understand the value of development and the empowerment of the client as a service goal for the agency. By manipulation, it is meant that the agency has to be offered the opportunity to experience the fruits of such a development. This may require the professional to assume autonomy of action in the first instance and instigate changes as a personal project. In this way, the appropriate prototypes can be developed for demonstration to an agency which is, hitherto, unexposed to these initiatives. Once the prototypes are in place, they can be their own best ambassadors. The clients, themselves, become agents for their own advancement.

Success of this introductory phase will depend heavily on the ability of the worker to create a favourable climate for its acceptance. This may entail the marketing of the idea as a panacea for meeting unmet need, as a cost-saver or as a mechanism through which the agency can avoid criticism for the non-provision of services. The process is no without political risks, either, and these have to be correctly appraised by the worker as a part of the process of empowerment. The freedom to establish this form of working partnership is crucial for the next stage in the process described in the template.

The changed perspective

The process described above is one of changing attitudes and practice methods. These changes are driven by the successive perspectives offered by the template. They represent the movement from the initial, tightly controlling relationship with the client, through processes where the control is steadily lessened. As the model changes through the 'context' and 'focus' perspectives, it dictates that modifications be made to practice methods for

51

the achievement of the agency's agenda. These are, more or less, on the agency's terms and the outcomes required by the agency are kept fully in view. Even in the 'potential' phase, the client's needs are still being appraised in terms of the original needs assessment.

The professional will have to employ a gradually enlarging repertoire of skills in each successive stage of the model. In addition, there will be an extra and varied array of risks which may conflict with professional values and/or prudent employee practice. Certainly, the worker's perception of the client will change, as the need for the relationship to be adjusted impinges on the original ideal of what the nature of the service being offered changes. Awareness of these pressures is essential if the worker is to retain personal and professional control of the situation.

We have already referred to professional autonomy and to some of the limitations which current trends in employment may produce. In situations where a high degree of flexibility is required and where the control element can become less secure due to the 'client-as-citizen' role coming to the fore, the worker must have a clear understanding of what might be involved on the way ahead. Giving prior consideration to both planned developments and unplanned outcomes will give the worker confidence in dealing with them.

The next stage focuses on the development of the client's potential as a service resource. The desired outcome is the development of the client's potential as an active agent in the care/support process itself. The services that might be planned are still those which might otherwise be found on the agenda of the agency. As they are not found there in reality, and because there is now going to be a reduction in the amount of direct control which the worker can exert, outcomes will be far less predictable. This is a natural point of tension within a developmental approach to social work. It is necessary for the worker to be at ease with the problems and dilemmas in the earlier stages before attempting to move further across the template. Failure to do so, might lead to anxiety in the worker and increasing the helplessness of the client in any ensuing service vacuum. The possible exposure of the client to unwarranted pressure, to sudden abandonment due to professional cold feet or to over-extension, cannot be justified unless the costs are at least recognised in advance. It is likely, that the client-as-citizen might never venture along a trail of self-determination unless the support of the professional is built into the plan. Once the crossover is made from 'client-as-potential' to 'client-as-vehicle (see template), the professional and the client are venturing into a different state of mutual dependency. This is one that the professional must anticipate fully before embarking on the next step.

A new focus for service planning and delivery now involves the active ingredient of the community. Professional roles move into a new form of control and partnership. The client system now becomes the focus for a dynamic change process. The aims are to develop, release and sustain the system's full potential to get the client's needs met through exploiting untapped alternative resources beyond the formal care sector. This will be done through developing and supporting the personal resourcefulness in the client system. From the start, an attempt will be made to target resources which can replicate those services which might appear in a care package. This is the outcome of the preparation work done in the previous stage of the model. The crucial difference is that it will be the 'client-as-citizen' who is now easing into the driving seat of this arrangement. The professional's task is to move from being a perceived source of services with the client as a dependant, to a role which is purely developmental.

The professional role is to support the client system in activating this strategy. It entails engaging support from outside the client system through the creation of contacts and networks. These networks will then be strengthened and extended by the work of the client system. The intention is to enlist these networks and contacts into providing care and support for the client. This process is assisted by the worker using indirect methods. This frees the professional from the task of personally developing alternative service systems. It allows for a return to a slightly expanded and modified work regime. The direct care management function has been replaced by one which is run by the client system. It is now monitored and supported by the Care Manager, who has assumed the role of a developer of informal services through indirect means.

This approach generates new importance for those resources on which the client draws naturally as a member of a social environment. In addition to networks such as the family and immediate friends, it focuses on social and recreation activities which might become alternatives to formal support services. These are likely to be resources which are not fully understood by social services or health organisations which have been responsible for the initial, formal assessment of needs. Entry by them into these alternative mechanisms might be difficult to negotiate. For members of the community, they are part of the normal social fabric (Glugoski, et.al., 1994). This is particularly important for clients who are members of minority communities, who may seldom receive what they need in cultural terms from the wider welfare system. These are needs which are harder for an ethnocentric service structure to accommodate (Daley, et.al., 1994).

There are certain considerations which have to be assessed at this point:

- the outlook of the client system and the acceptance of professional support in this process;
- professional's understanding and ability to undertake development-style interventions;
- the resource potential of the local community;
- the release of the professional from the restraints of accountability to the employer for outcomes of this new relationship.

Some of them are clearly explained by Henderson and Thomas in their introductory remarks to social workers on how to utilise community development techniques. They require workers to make an assessment of their own, and the community's capability to deliver the process on an on-going basis (Henderson & Thomas, 1987, p. 10 et. seq). Adams explores them in more depth (Adams, 1990) but without the implication that the relationship will be maintained once the process has become rooted. Smale, on the other hand, is more sanguine and does not suggest a termination of the relationship (Smale et al, 1988). The main section of the Barclay Report, and its Appendix A, advocated for this to be the primary focus of social work (Barclay, 1982). Abrams would caution that the potential of the locality is a variable and over-romanticised phenomenon (Bulmer, 1986).

Of great relevance, is the client systems own assessment of the resources which they perceive as potentially available. We have explored the changed perspectives on the delivery of care, in which the client system, as a care organiser, might replace the professional as the planner and agency for change. The professional role is to advise and assist this system to develop into a planner and commissioner of support within the community. This is a task where the professional helps the client system to discover what skills they need as the process develops.

There will be personal skill development, confidence building and assistance in manipulation information. It is vital that the professional acts in such a way that it is the client system that develops in order to achieve its own goals and that a dependency does not develop for the long-term involvement of the worker. The client system will rapidly develop its own resources for handling this process. This process is the creation and nurturing of social capital, so vital to the sustaining of community vitality at every level.

There is a danger that this is essentially an unrealistic task. The reduced resources of the client, already assessed as being in need (but not too much need) by the authorities, is in danger of being 'dumped' upon by a professional service under pressure to displace its own responsibilities. This is what is happening but, instead of being solely motivated to provide support and care from any source, other than through the official channels, the professional is enlisting development to make the best of a bad situation.

Development, as a vehicle for action, can have limited application unless there is a body of people around who can be moved to offer support. For some individuals and groups in society, this is just not an option. Certain minority groups and others who carry some form of social stigma are going to have difficulty in mustering any support. These are special needs to which the social worker, as developer, must respond and they are dealt with later on. It must be made plain that the development of the community is not a quick or an easy task.

Nevertheless, for those without care from any other source, it may be the only option open. It is in an attempt to counter the trends that bring despair to many that this model is launched (Sachs, 1995; Etzioni, 1993). It is through the next stage in the model that the profile of people in need of support can be raised and the best purpose put to the vehicle of self-help.

Client-plus as a motor for service

The professional has brought the person/client system to the point where services, such as can be provided in the community, are being provided. There are a number of difficulties which will be encountered as this process proceeds. These concern the reliability of the service and also its relevance to the personal, cultural and social environment within which it is being provided.

It will soon be obvious to those in close contact with this system, that there are problems in enlisting the support of others on an on-going and reliable basis. Community members are untrained in the provision of services and they are not professionals, neither are they being paid for it. There are severe weaknesses in volunteer services if they are not developed systematically and with a clear focus on processes and targets. . As it is, they often provide an erratic service, which usually means that the degree of importance and centrality to mainstream activities has to be kept to a minimum. The service providers are not the direct beneficiaries of the process, save that they share the general, social context of the client. They are motivated by idealism or a sense of communal responsibility.

Under these circumstances, the co-ordination of trying to provide a range of support processes with pre-set goals is no easy task. The client system has had no, or little experience of this activity. There are going to be historical expectations that, even in substitute services, certain levels of service might be attained and certain standards should be maintained. There will also be the anxiety of the (sidelined) professional that the new arrangement is not up to scratch. There will be fears that the client will become vulnerable unless adequate coverage and consistency can be maintained. Control of quality is likely to be an uneven feature.

For the worker, there will be the added anxiety that, if the client system does all the organisation of the new service coverage, there is going to be a loss of professional influence over the whole care process. Loss of influence will mean loss of ultimate control of the outcomes. It also means the loss of contact with an erstwhile client of the social services who has been cast aside.

There is a professional responsibility to stay involved. To stay involved brings with it a commitment, if not a duty, to retain some form of influence over the process. This 'control' is part of the preventative function which has to be maintained. In this situation, there is a dependence on the goodwill of systems which are not tried and experienced in the task, and which cannot be held accountable in any realistic way. Intelligence about the welfare of the client is one way to avoid a future scandal for your employer.

The fact that the client has been striving to control the service delivery system, and has been in the position of experiencing the outcomes first-hand, will allow an immediate evaluation to be made. The range and coverage of need, their substance and sensitivity can all be appraised. The purpose of such services, their relevance and their capacity to continue over time will become apparent. The full consciousness of the client, and the client system, will be raised about the predicament of being dependent on this kind of informal support and service.

It is likely that the client system will have been widened in scope as period of self-help and networking develops. There will be others in similar situations to this client and the worker will have made the necessary connections to create a network for mutual support. The opportunity for evaluation will bring about the consolidation of a new consciousness about the nature of welfare services, how they are provided and how they are designed. Sharing this with others will widen this awareness into a system of mutual concern and, potentially, solidarity.

Using the collective view of their situation, the network will develop a critique of the efficacy and purpose of each client's benefit from the system.

It will also acquire a perspective on the overall situation of the whole, residual client group which remains outside the system of official support. They will begin to have definite ideas about what kind of 'service' is most relevant and useful, particularly when it is not being professionally provided.

The worker has a role in this, a third level of intervention. It is a continuation of the indirect method used with the client system, but it is modified in the case of the network to the role of an organisation builder. In the first instance, after effecting the necessary contact between the potential members of the network the worker concentrates on building up communication channels within the extended system and the seeks out ways in which it might extend itself into a semi-formal, or even a formal, organisation to further the interests of the clients and their systems. In that form, they can better mobilise themselves and their support systems for the acquisition of care and any other socio-economic or political purpose which they might decide.

The primary purpose, in this stage in the model, is for the social worker, turned developer, to encourage the formation of a strong network so that the combined effort of the client system group can be employed for their common benefit in a care system. This is the agency priority and it is the process in which the social worker can best provide support and encouragement.

The process will be to assist the client/network to raise confidence and skill in reaching out to mobilise the support, and it should also entail providing support for those newly enlisted through the initial stages of the experience. Systems of control and evaluation will be explored and the client network will be introduced to the benefits of objective analysis for the purpose of improving the impact and effectiveness of the support which is being received. The worker will assist the client to get beyond just 'coping' with the input of outside support. The aim will be to establish the capacity of the client to sustain the service system through the resources which are readily available. This process is not best achieved on the basis of a one-to-one relationship.

The professional now faces another choice of how to intervene further and how to choose direction and remain in control of the process. Not being in the direct employ of the client, the worker is answerable in a number of directions simultaneously. The choices made at this stage in the developmental process can severely affect the freedom of the professional to operate in the community as a free agent. Failure to operate as a free agent will seriously prejudice the capacity of the client-plus system to transcend their present situation.

We must also consider whether, and/or at what point, the role of the professional extends into the realm of prevention through the creation of more competent client systems. Contact with others in the same situation, through the networking mechanisms made available by the professional, will highlight the general situation for people in the locality in similar circumstances.

Discussion

In community care, the targeting of scarce resources solely on those with the greatest need, places additional burdens on those who are not in critical situations. These policies have created an environment which lacks security and stability. Unorthodox methods have to be sought if they are to be dealt with. Client controlled, and community derived, services are a pragmatic solution to this problem which have several overtones for professional values. They not only represent an attempt to substitute the client for the conventional role of the professional. They actively undermine the idea that the civilised society can and should provide for its social and economic casualties. They provide a presence in the community which highlights how expedients of policy affect people who are in need, but not critical need.

This chapter has been concerned with the social work intervention with the individual. We have described a model of good practice methods which can be implemented under circumstances where there were insufficient resources for normal social care support. Using this model, the way in which 'individual' is defined is adapted to take account of the new social and economic facts. From the beginning, it was necessary to extend beyond the constraints of working with one individual client. The client is now perceived to embrace a system comprising the client, plus the immediate support network, such as family, neighbours and friends. From there, the model called for the progressive extension of the target group. The first moves were out into the community immediately around the client and then, through a developmental process, a wider net was cast to construct a service structure out of community-based resources.

Development can also take place in a different direction as an extension, an alternative and/or a complement to the community support system. The collective involvement of fellow would-be service users can be developed. This network can be developed into a self-help, mutual support system, a representative structure for the provision of care and for the promotion of awareness about care needs around their own circumstances.

It is necessary to modify certain social work concepts for the achievement of these goals. The first involves the way in which 'confidentiality' is understood and employed. Service provision for the single client allows for a great deal of privacy for the individual and the immediate support system. Now the client is being offered the opportunity of extending the range of available care by increasing the amount of social support from the community. This will inevitably lead to the community at large becoming more aware of the nature of need in its midst and, the specific needs of this individual in particular. The way in which this is conceived and sold to the client, then how it is planned, contained and possibly exploited is a sensitive part of development work.

The dynamics of this process may lead in a number of directions. Awareness of the care needs can be raised a deliberate strategy during a trawl for support in the community. Alternatively, it can be limited to the gradual leakage of information by those drawn into the support system. Gradually, information will permeate outwards and it is better if the client system attempt to manage this to their advantage. Understanding and acceptance of need is a more desirable outcome than ill-informed labelling.

The boundaries of good practice are extended when the social worker opens up the network to others in the same need category. The agreement of all concerned has to be obtained for bringing this group into contact with each other. After that, developmental support can be added to their efforts to improve their awareness of their own situation within the care system. Self-assessment of care needs and potential for self-help could provide a vehicle for further professional involvement, using indirect methods.

Having bowed to the pressure of unmet needs, the social worker is forced to restructure the form of professional intervention. The role of supporter, enabler and empowerer is sustained as a workable and feasible alternative to being the provider of services. This shift in approach brings with it these additional advantages:

- contact is retained with people who would otherwise be marginalised and their changing needs can be monitored;
- the nature of the relationship with the client changes significantly from that of authority to that of collaborator and partner;
- through the indirect method, the professional can exercise some influence over the direction in which energies are applied;
- concepts such as strategic planning, information analysis and outcome monitoring can be introduced through practical activities as clients control their own service systems;

- the potential of the client system can be expanded through the introduction of training which might be resourced from the employer agency;
- dialogue can be opened about the relationship between public services and self-help, especially around the assessment of need and the designation of priorities.

We are describing a fragile and tentative process which lacks the back-up of the state. There is hardly any justification for the professional to claim that control should still be maintained over any care activities that materialise from this developmental process. What may be unjustifiable in theory may, nevertheless, be prudent practice. We have described methods through which the professional can continue to manipulate the course of events so that control can be maintained. Is it paradoxical that a professional should resort to manipulation in order to ensure that the 'best' form of professional services can continue to be provided?

The rationalisation for this is as follows: Autonomy cannot be retained if the professional is the servant of the client. Without autonomy, objectivity, based upon the value base that informs all practice, cannot be sustained. Once formal care has been refused through the assessment process, the case for continuing professional intervention, using developmental methods, should be negotiated emphasising the importance of the value base which will be employed. This will be the yardstick against which trust can be monitored as the relationship develops.

The kind of authority which goes with community care assessment and management procedures has to give way to another medium of understanding. The professional strives to establish a presence which is free-standing, so that values and expertise justify the authority and control which will be part of the agreement.

One of the deepest tensions between community development workers and their employers hinges around the question of professional autonomy. It manifests itself in the clash between social services conduct protocols which often deny social workers direct access to elected representatives on the Council. Community workers cannot work within these constraints if they are to fulfil their role as enablers and empowerers. It is no less contentious if the worker is the direct employee of the beneficiary client system. This situation occurs regularly when the local population raises moneys for the employment of organisers or other developmental staff for their organisations.

3 Development as Community Development - I

In this, and the following chapter we will consider the application of the model which is presented by the next generation of the template. We will also demonstrate the need for practitioners to consider more seriously the tensions and contradictions which are emerging in the employment of community workers today. The reasons for this are partly historical and partly bound up in the outlook of workers and academics. Most recently, an imbalance has arisen due to the preponderance of concern with 'ends and means' issues, at the expense of the underlying concepts and framework. Values have become confused as the rhetoric changed over the years, and each tack successively bound workers into new orthodoxies, none of which brought much stability to the profession. These have usually been highly selective aspects of political fashion, expediency or opportunism. Our model will assist us to clarify many of these questions.

As with the rest of British social workers, community development workers have mostly been in the employ of others rather than being self-employed and self-regulating. This reflects on the position of social work as an occupation and its relative failure to assume control over its standing in the hierarchy of professional activity. The position of community development within social work received its biggest set-back when the regulations for qualifying training were revised in 1981. Controls were imposed on the community development training programmes which called for the down-grading of specific community development input. The amount of 'generic' content was raised and the approach to 'welfare' issues elevated in priority (CCETSW, 1981). This restructuring applied to the specialist 'community work;' programmes but made no concessions to raise the profile of community development within the on-going 'social work' programmes. A majority of those training programmes, which were forced to withdraw from the CCETSW network in 1982 rather than submit to these controls, consolidated their attachment to the Youth and Community training regime. Under both regimes, the specific 'community development' emphasis was diluted and, after this shake out, only one, specialist community development qualifying programme remained under the jurisdiction of CCETSW. That, too, partly succumbed to the 'genericist' trend within a few years.

The official developments instituted by CCETSW in the early 1980's, reinforced the tendency among employers to consider that any *qualified* social worker, being some sort of genericist, could be adapted for 'community' duties. Specific 'development' qualifications were secondary. This resulted in many workers being given their only training through direct exposure to the work , while those who had undergone formal training in community development, were being left unemployed, at least in social services departments. Where properly constituted development work did take place, its nature and purpose was firmly controlled by the predominant culture of the employer agencies. Workers were often inhibited from gaining greater insight into the aims and goals of community development and acquired little professional flexibility over the choice of targets and outcomes. Even experienced community development specialists often found themselves arranging for the distribution of donated Christmas Appeal toys, and 'pensioners' butter' schemes, as if it was their mainstream activity. This marginalisation led to the fragmentation of their role and function in the agency. These employers have, in the main, been powerful institutions such as local or central government agencies and Voluntary or Non-Governmental Organisations (NGO's).

The funding connection between most independent sector activity and government has also been strong. This ensured that the regulatory force behind community development in Britain has been powerful and fully controlling (Brager, 1969; Farrow, 1993; Lees & Mayo, 1984; Thomas, 1983; Twelvetrees, 1991). Elsewhere in the world, connections between the state, donors and the agency of implementation is as strong as it is in Britain, if not more so (Constantino-David, 1992; Midgley, 1986a, 1986b).

The formal dis-establishment of community development from social work has not really advanced its development as an institution in its own right. However, the rejection of community development by the social work establishment had a knock-on effect in other quarters. A sizeable part of the energy for specialised community work training and accreditation moved out of the formal educational institutions altogether and into the practice arena (Federation, 1990). Those trying to raise the impact of community-strengthening activity without building a superstructure of professional (and, thus, elitist and exclusive) protocols and social distance, began to recruit activists and community leaders.

Formal training, and steps towards accreditation, for this activity began following extensive discussion within the Association of Community Workers (ACW) (Association of Community Workers, 1983; Ohri, 1982;

Stiles & Dean, 1978). The establishment of the Federation of Community Work Training Groups (FCWTG) in the mid-1970's, and consultations nation-wide, led to the process being given a great deal of support at all levels in the profession. Since that date, it has developed considerably but, by design, it has been left to develop in mechanisms outside the recognised educational hierarchy. The journey back to national recognition will not be bridged effectively until, at least, it is linked to the National Vocational Qualifications system. This process has now begun and may now give the education of community development workers a fresh start, albeit at a lower educational level than was enjoyed under the earlier CCETSW attachment. There is still considerable ambivalence towards the problems associated with 'elitism' and 'qualifications' within the networks of community development workers (Federation, 1992).

This mirrors the wishes of many within the profession, especially those who had favoured a complete break with social work from the beginning. Others, still, wished to de-mystify the activity and strip it of its connections with the establishment of academic or public service circles (Wooley, 1970). This anti-elitist tendency, typified by the reluctance to exclude anyone from the ranks of the association (Cox & Derricourt, 1975), has contributed to the bundling together of all in the field with the label of 'community work', a tag which means everything and nothing. In turn, this resulted in the loss of focus and clear standards or the expectation of full professionalism. The profession lost direct control over its own destiny and status. It has also retarded any systematic analysis and consolidation of the theory and nature of community development in this country, any concrete analysis of its effectiveness.

Internal divisions, and the absence of a strong reference point has left the profession with an uncertain view of the way forward. In this, it shares the weaknesses of any unregulated 'movement', being dependent on external reference points to fix its location at any time. It must then succumb to the twin perils of marginalisation and manipulation.

In the 'Youth and Community' arena, youth work activities, club and community centre management requirements predominate in training. Part-time and sessional employment practices contribute to the difficulties workers in this quarter have in making any significant contribution to the discussion about theory. In institutional terms, the opting out by CCETSW from community development training, entrenched the demarcation between local authority Education Departments and Social 'services in their employment requirements for 'youth workers' and 'social workers'. Despite, or, perhaps, in spite, of this confusion, some intellectual energy continues to be deployed, largely through the efforts of the Community

Development Foundation (CDF). CDF had been working, since 1982, with the Calouste Gulbenkian Foundation, to establish a National Centre of Community Development (Mayo, 1994; Standing Conference, 1995).

Success in this field would have consolidated CDF as the main centre for strategic planning within community development in Britain and, because of its strong links with similar institutions in Europe, allowed it to take a more positive lead than it did. For many years, CDF has been instrumental in forging an agreed framework for the activity across the Union. Connections between the work done in Britain and in developing countries has received positive encouragement through the revival of interest in local developments by the Community Development Journal, and its steadily expanding contacts with CDF and other local organisations (Chanan, 1992). There is now a strong official community development presence in Scotland, with their own journal, and a thriving workers' network (Scottish Journal of Community & Development; Scottish Community Development Centre, etc.).

Outside Britain, interest in, and theoretical discussion about, the nature of community development has never abated. In developing countries, the work of the international donor organisations, the United Nations and related relief agencies has continued to spawn a steady stream of books and debate on the subject, its nature and purpose. For some time, focus had concentrated upon macro-economic development issues, and local projects and initiatives were considered in relation to these 'objective' strategic considerations. Only more recently has the discussion returned to the dynamics of the local community and the tensions and costs of imposing national policy constraints, and outcome targets on local communities.

The emergence of human rights issues, particularly the position of women in society, has dramatically redrawn the plans, priorities and methods of approach. There has not yet been any resolution to the conflict between the 'ends and means' debate. This ongoing debate has ensured that a reappraisal of the underlying value system of the whole developmental approach is continuing (Anderson, 1992; Borda, 1992; Braidotti, et.al., 1994; Chinchilla, 1992; Dominelli, 1994; Lovibond, 1990; Moser, 1991; Mosse, 1993; Pityana, 1989; Wilson, 1977, 1990).

Getting women into centre stage has undoubtedly been very stimulating as it has brought in some radical changes in outcomes and outlook. It has highlighted the limitations of simplistic approaches to 'empowerment'. Re-focusing has been good for the whole development approach, but there is always the danger that vested and traditional interests will still take a long time to be accepted (Arce, 1994; Friedmann, 1992; Roche, 1992). This amplifies the problematic contradictions developing at the interface between theory and practice (Oelschlägel, 1991; London Edinburgh, 1979; Wood, 1994).

The challenge of conflicting ideas

These contradictions have been some time in developing. They first emerged in the 1950's, and, although the headline issues may have been modified somewhat, the gaps are still there. In Britain, the problem emerged, and re-emerges, when the predominately reformist practice of most community development work is confronted by a new, purist and radical literature on the subject (Beresford, 1993; Bolger, et.al., 1981; Community Action magazine; Corrigan, 1975; Dominelli, 1995; Fleetwood & Lambert, 1972; Lambert, 1978; Leonard, 1975b; London Edinburgh, 1979; Mayo, 1975; O'Malley, 1977). The radical theorists exhorted workers to choose confrontational tactics while developing strategies for overthrowing anti-democratic systems. This approach draws its inspiration from the Marxist concepts, such as those promoted by Antonio Gramsci, which call for revolution in countries of advanced capitalism (Gramsci, 1971). Failure to adopt these tactics, it is claimed, leaves the professional without ethical substance or any real political relevance (Salmon, 1978).

The radical approach has a number of practical examples from which to draw.   These were the direct action campaigns against poverty, homelessness, public planning policies and housing tenure of the 1960's and 1970's. The most significant example was the government sponsored Community Development Programme (CDP) (Loney, 1983). The CDP was discontinued after only one five-year trial, and it received less than an enthusiastic appraisal from most of its sponsoring local authorities (mainly Labour Party controlled). The well documented projects asserted in an uncompromising way that community development had no place in promoting therapeutic solutions to what were structural problems (Corkey & Craig, 1978), which arose directly out of inequality, political disenfranchisement and poverty. The natural Marxist solution would be to cement an alliance between organised labour at the workplace, and the resources for the reproduction of labour at home and in the community (Cockburn, 1977; Bolger, et.al., 1981; Leonard, 1975b). This line of reasoning had insufficient time to develop under the CDP experiment and it was further weakened through the government abolition of the Greater London Council in 1986, which, with other radical authorities experimented with grant aid and preferential treatment for grass-roots and minority interests (Phillips, 1987). The devolution of many planning and economic development powers to local Development Corporations in 1981 further eroded the democratic accountability of many crisis areas of urban decay and social friction (Lawless, 1989; Robson, 1988). Things have been made worse by the relative decline in the spread and strength of organised labour over the past twenty years. Legislation hostile to Trades Union has had indirect influence on activities outside the immediate workplace and working class solidarity (MacInnes, 1987).

The CDP philosophy has been consigned to the back burner as far as direct action by community development workers is concerned. Nothing of an equivalent scale as been created which might generate enough confidence to confront the prevailing values. Through its contribution to the literature, and the folk law, the CDP still represents the most important influence in the creation of ideas within community development in this country. The fact that this position ran into insurmountable political opposition does not detract from the response that it received at the street level (Benington, 1974; Higgins, et.al., 1983; Loney, 1983). There was great success in organising democratic and popular organisations in virtually every area. The notion of class conflict was probably too extreme for the great British public, but there was sufficient response by ordinary people to rattle vested political interests. This is the main reason why the opportunity which the CDP represented has not been repeated. The structural model for community development which emerged in the literature, broadly represents the analysis gained by the workers from this positive experience.

With the exception of a few local authorities in the North of Britain, most institutional support for community development declined after the closure of the CDP This is caused, partly, by the reliance of local authorities on the central government for special funds to assist in rehabilitating declining city centres. These moneys have been in decline and there has been intense competition for the money (Lawless, 1989; Nevin & Shiner, 1995a, 1995b; Robson, 1988). The absence of the human or social development aspects of all regional aid schemes since the CDP speaks reams. The trend in more recent years has been to offer individualistic responses to local failings of the welfare state through the procedure of the Citizen's Charter. This takes the form of consumerist complaints and token compensation schemes for under-performance (Hogg, 1994). This approach concentrates the resources of the welfare state's services in a reactive and defensive mode. Guarantees are offered of notional standards of quality assurance, rather than make them open to change and user influence.

Forces such as these have undermined and destroyed any freedom workers might have had to stand out against their employers on matters of principle. It has been left to workers in different relationships with the state to try to work out a survival path with the fateful demise of the CDP hanging over them. Tight funding, short-term contracts and clearly defined operational goals became the norm of most workers. However, the redirecting of community development resources allowed for the re-emergence of the mainstream literature, which had been partially submerged by the tide of structuralist perspectives which followed the CDP By the end of the 1970's, therefore, there were actually three strands of literature available to professionals in the field.

The first was conceived of being strictly for export. It was a colonial model, developed by the Colonial Office, Batten and the early North American theorists(Batten, 1957; Biddle & Biddle, 1965; Colonial Office, 1958; Goetschius, 1969; Gulbenkian, 1968; Kuenstler, 1960; Ross, 1955). This was probably the practice model envisaged originally by the Home Office for the CDP, when the programme was launched in 1970. It was the model probably best known to those staff who had seen overseas service in voluntary agencies. Many of them had previously been in the employ of the Voluntary Service Overseas or International Voluntary Service, on projects across the developing countries of the Commonwealth. This model, in turn, developed into a technical approach for the implementation of national and international development strategies in most developing countries. The model comprised the mobilisation of local populations behind the 'extension' policies required in national economic regeneration programmes. It was not until this approach became identified with neo-colonialism that it was seriously challenged (Mayo, 1975). The replacement of a 'neo-colonial' model of community development with one which allows for the pacification of a national population by its rulers can also stand scrutiny through the application of the template model approach (See below page 98).

The second strand of theory grew out of American attempts to cope with the conflicting demands and tensions that spanned the Civil Rights protests, the war in Vietnam and the consolidation of social work as a credible profession (Etzioni, 1969). Social work structure in the United States incorporates 'Community Organization' as a third branch of generic practice in their qualifying process. Community organisation concerns the mobilisation of community resources through the organisation of new social formations, or the co-ordination of existing ones, in social planning exercises. This will usually involve the public authorities, also. The professional role centres on the ability to facilitate communication between complementary interests in a community context. The necessary liaison is effected to enable social issues to be addressed through the collective

67

resources available, and the consolidation of these mechanisms for the future benefit and stabilisation of the community. Community organisation is not about organising rapid or radical social change, unless it is in the interests of the established institutions to do so. (We shall be discussing an associated discipline, Community Organizing, below, Chapter, 8).

Within this context, the 1960's saw the rise of an influential school of thought which embraced consensus, systems theory and structural functionalism (Brager, 1969; Dunham, 1970; Gilbert & Specht, 1974; Pruger & Specht, 1969; Kramer & Specht, 1969; Pincus & Minahan, 1973; Rothman, 1979;). Great emphasis was placed on the place of social research and the application of academically acceptable models of analysis which could provide a sound framework for monitoring and evaluating progress (Cox, et.al., 1979; Rothman, 1974; Warren, 1970).

As disciples of a rationality which sought intellectual, as well as political, respectability, the 'Community Organization' school produced the most enduring models for practice (Rothman, 1979). They distinguished between three levels of professional intervention and activity: locality development, social planning and social action. They were able to accommodate these three under the same umbrella because of an over-riding assumption that, within the great diversity of the United States, there was a profound consensus that the American Dream was somehow attainable. They maintained the faith that the application of professional know-how to seemingly irreconcilable differences could bring about workable solutions (Swedner, 1983). Despite prolonged doubts about the attainment of the 'American Dream' (Kaplan, 1994), the framework for exploring the processes of community development, produced in those more optimistic times, remain strong. Even the radical theorists of the 1970's failed to produce a better tool for the analysis of their product than that produced by the established figure of Jack Rothman.

The advent of the urban stress in the USA of the early 1960's, produced President Johnson's *War on Poverty*. But there were to be irreconcilable differences between the racial assertiveness and demands of Black and Hispanic peoples in the Civil Rights Movement, combined with the revolutionary Left (Carmichael, 1967; Perlman, 1976; Seale, 1970), and the existing political, power structures. The intervention methodology as proposed by the Community Organization school was found to be lacking, and the whole programme failed amid charges of misdirection of public funds and under-funding (Marris & Rein, 1967; Sullivan, 1992). Mass action and direct confrontation with conflict appeared to be achieving rapid progress for those who were oppressed, whereas social work orthodoxy did not have much to offer in the short term. This was a situation in which the fragile consensus rapidly broke down and there was insufficient will for a planned intervention from the centre to arrest it (Sullivan, 1992). There were other strategies for social intervention which claimed legitimacy, such as direct citizen action against targeted problems (Alinsky, 1972; see below, Chapter 8), but these received an uneasy reception in the established circles (Brager, 1969; Specht, 1975). In a market place where ideas perish if they cannot be sustained out on the street, community organisation has had a declining role over the past decade. Some communities despaired of ever obtaining the collective support of the nation for their social and economic predicament, sought to regenerate their own communities from within. They chose the vehicle of the *not-for-profit*, Community Development Corporation, which has endured, and brought some economic prosperity to certain sections of the population (Blaustein, 1972; Peirce, 1987). There is a new optimism in the launch, in 1994, of a new journal which spoke of 'a visible and vital force in American society' for community organization (Weil, 1994).

When the Home Office began to mobilise British government resources for the creation of the CDP, there seemed to have been an almost positive denial of the crucial significance given to ethnic difference in the USA In America, the organisation of ethnic groups, particularly since the turn of this century has tracked the emergence of Community Organization. It created the tensions within the *War on Poverty* which led to the discredit of that form of intervention as a potential unifier of diverse populations (Mizrahi & Rosenthal, 1992).

The British approach was surprising, as it was partly because of the fear of urban unrest in this country that the Urban Programme (and with it the CDP) was launched in 1968. It followed in the wake of the urban and racial tensions of the mid-1960's and heralded the rediscovery of poverty and the chronic state of inner-city housing. In Britain, the community organization approach received scant attention and no alternative approach for tackling the social dimensions of disadvantage emerged in any coherent form. British social work education failed to incorporate it as a formal 'third sector' and there was no place for it in general patterns of social work practice within the 'genericist' teams which followed the Seebohm Report in 1968. As we shall see, the government's own experimental initiative sought another route through which to mobilise the community (Corkey & Craig, 1978).

British social work failed to produce a professional response to the causes and alleviation of poverty and other forms of oppression. For twenty years, since the publication of the Seebohm Report, social services departments developed into huge bureaucracies and attracted a powerful array of statutory duties to sustain their sense of relevance. It is ironic, therefore, that, in 1988, the publication of the Griffiths Report (Griffiths, 1988) should prescribe that the bulk of the social welfare functions of social work be disestablished from the state. This leaves the 'essential social worker' as a prisoner; a functionary within a regulatory system for those in chronic need of protection or control. The profession failed to develop a long-term strategy for itself because it lacked the necessary wherewithal to realise that it needed one (Braye & Preston-Shoot, 1995; Langan, 1993). Now, it is essential that community organisation be re-examined if the full potential of community development principles and methods within British social work are to be understood.

Practitioners of community development are perhaps bemused, if they are affected at all, by this clash of ideas in the literature: the warring factions of the Left, the post-modernists (see below, chapter 7), the consensus school, or 'social engineering through planning' approaches. During times of social change (planned, orchestrated or otherwise), workers are often left confused about what to do with some of the negative after-effects that these processes have on certain individuals and groups. They have sought a method of intervention which lowers the social costs of unforeseen consequences and also allows them to retain the knowledge that it is the people, themselves, who are directing the process rather than the forces of external influence. In their search for a method which might start, rather than end, with the needs of the individual, workers have turned to the Freirean school (Freire, 1972a, 1972b; Hope, et.al., 1984; Popple, 1994).

Feminist writers, also, seek the rediscovery of the whole person through the raising of consciousness and action against repressive institutions (Dominelli, 1990, 1994; Wilson, 1980). This is a more immediate target than the overthrow of the state. A balance for the individual, within the individual's own environment is seen as a priority. It is interesting to note that, in countries where the oppression of colonialism have been cast out, the nation-building ideology of the (often) centralised, national development movements have embraced the consciousness-raising methods in order best to involve the citizens in this task (Balleis, 1994; Berridge, 1993; Hope, et.al., 1984).

Not to be outdone, it seems, by the demands of the radical approach, the reformist (or 'pluralist', see Lees & Mayo, 1984) literature is no less exacting. It, too, calls for purist models of intervention which set up seemingly unattainable targets. These usually centre on the quality of participation, involvement and direct action of citizens in transforming their lives through the development process. In practice, the workers have to approach their tasks within the context of the policy set by the funders or

70

their direct employers. This poses several problems of ethical and practical importance (Brager, 1969; Edwards, 1994; Marsden, 1994a; Oakley, et.al., 1991; Rothman, 1979; Specht, 1976; Thomas, 1976; Twelvetrees, 1982). The professional has to take the decision whether or not to confront the structural limitations to social change.

Many community development projects and programmes call for the greatest feasible levels of participation. Nevertheless, pressure is exerted, explicitly, or implicitly, by the employer or the funder about expected outcomes. This will give the professional 'privileged' insight into the practical consequences of any 'ill-advised' strategy. 'If Jesus had been on the Roman payroll, the history of Christian civilisation would have been different...'(cited in Brager, 1969, p.197). The worker needs defences against this pressure or, at the very least, a framework for understanding how the pressures limit the practice choices that will be sanctioned publicly. Can professional autonomy and/or standards create this sort of protected environment? We think not. Only political protection can produce the 'fire-proofing' that is required. This has its own ethical and practical consequences.

Nevertheless, our model requires that the professional worker maintain a detached perspective on the methods being used, and their effect on the ultimate objectives. It is by using this approach that the stresses and difficulties of the profession can be clarified. On a day to day basis, the worker has to manage a number of conflicting image problems: with those that pay for, and those that use, the professional services. In the final analysis, it is down to the individual worker to calculate what impact the policies and other pressures of a funder, or employer, will make on practice (Smith, 1981). In response to this pressure, the worker must decide how the use of particular practice methods, and their outcomes are best described, justified, or 'sold', to those who might seek to regulate them. The funders will want to see their agreed goals being pursued and that they are not being deceived by their team.

Naturally, the client population will not want to believe that their efforts are being manipulated by external forces, and the suspicions of the 'beneficiaries' of community development are well documented in the literature (Bailey, 1980; Cockburn, 1978; Ellis, 1989; Fleetwood & Lambert, 1982; Mayo, 1975; O'Malley, 1977; Ohri, et.al., 1982; Stiefel & Wolfe, 1994). They will need an explicit reference point so that they can evaluate their relationship with professionals. For the 'objects' of development, who have to make a considerable personal investment, the stakes, are usually very high indeed. They range from providing basic social facilities, to possibly restructuring their entire economic livelihood.

71

The unequal power relationship will, so long as it persists, always give to the professional that extra room to manoeuvre, and the opportunity to manipulate the presentation of choice, and consequences of choice, in the most beneficial light to suit the professional situation.

We now turn to the next dimension of the model and a modification to the template. The description begins with an analysis of the position of the professional in an agency setting. For this example, it is the agency's intention to change, *en masse*, the way of life or material circumstances of an aggregate population. This aggregate may be a 'community' within a geographical or neighbourhood context or it may be an aggregate of people with their 'communality' dependant on some other characteristic. The scale of the operation is dependent on the policy considerations of the agency. The original idea for change has been devised by external forces, and those interests will oversee its implementation and progress. Development, in this case, is conceived of as a controlled process, planned and evaluated to suit those external criteria of success. Certain technical skills will be considered essential for its successful execution and agents with these skills will be engaged for the purpose - community development professionals.

This process is best understood by making a comparison with the powers devolved to planning authorities in Britain, to change the face of the physical environment. In such a developed economy, contact with the recipient community, if any, is on the basis of consultation. The public 'consultation' follows the production of some framework within which the development or change will take place. The process has already involved the active participation and competition of any commercial interests that might become involved in providing some services or physical development. The management and control remains in the hands of the authorities which are undertaking the scheme. These may include central government, local government or semi-governmental developmental agencies (such as a Development Corporation or utility company). It is a pre-supposition of the process that the idea and the general direction of the change is already known. Costs have been analysed and budgets estimated to a fairly high degree of certainty before the proposal is formally made public.

The social and economic impact of a large-scale scheme may have been calculated and, once any consultation process has been exhausted, the implementation will seek to produce the planned outcome. During the implementation stage, there will be rigorous attention paid to those outcomes which form part of the economic or physical targets. With regard to the social outcomes, as many of those which can be realised, will be,

72

within the restrictions of the economic model (Audit Commission, 1989; Department of the Environment, 1988; Robson, 1988).

This approach to planned change sustains the structure of an external authority that retains control of the change process from start to finish. The pressures which fall on the workers, who are responsible for the dynamics and success of this venture, will be discussed. To do this systematically, it is necessary to reintroduce the template which we have already employed above. The template has been modified slightly as there are two separate considerations to be made at this level of intervention. Because the primary target is now the community and not the individual, that section of the template which deals with the targeting of the individual is moved away from the central focus. It remains in the model as an active feature for which the professional remains responsible, but we have moved it across to the right. We will consider the role of the professional in connection with the individual separately, as opposed to the role in the general process of development.

Development as community development

COMMUNITY as the LOCATION for DEVELOPMENT	COMMUNITY as the CONTEXT for DEVELOPMENT	COMMUNITY as the POTENTIAL for SELF-HELP	COMMUNITY as the VEHICLE for DEVELOPMENT	COMMUNITY as the MOTOR for DEVELOPMENT	INDIVIDUAL as the TARGET for DEVELOPMENT

Community as the location for development

If there is to be any expectation of structured social change and/or economic outcomes as part of a development strategy, the infusion of material resources into an area requires planning and management. 'Development' may be the intention to change the physical environment with the building of a new facility, or it may be something less tangible, such as the introduction of an activity programme. Whatever the change, it is desired that it make some impact on the local culture and way of life. There are expectations for its outcome, and staff may, or may not, be deployed to assist in the process. Material development, without active social development, is the norm in most British 'development' schemes.

This approach is the crudest, and most typical, developmental initiative devised by those in authority over public resources. It is common for many public programmes to be introduced with no interaction with the population, other than the posting of the statutory notice which advises of inspection facilities and calls for objections from those with a direct interest in the process. In this kind of development, the adjustment of the local community is not considered until the planning, political and administrative process is virtually completed. The 'location' has been decided. The community will absorb the change and, eventually, it will accommodate it. The 'market' will be left to its own devices. Major schemes, such as the planning of a motor route, are devised with a 'consultative' element but the proposals put forward in 1969, by the Skeffington study, have not been developed. So much hinges on the set-piece, semi-adversarial Public Inquiry procedure that there are few attempts to consider adjustment, accommodation or reconsideration of the original proposals (Skeffington, 1969).

Many physical changes to community life are just left to find their own take-up. Community facilities, such as recreation space, halls and playgrounds, will attract usage of a greater or lesser extent, by one group or another. This may demonstrate the relative success of the planning and any intelligence-gathering exercise which came before. Should there not have been any community participation in the decision-making, then achieving a desired change must be dependent on some degree of good fortune.

Taking a positive role, following externally-planned changes, and steering a community towards social change, will entail more tactical considerations. The application of professional development skills, and the adaptation of technical information for public consumption and understanding will all be part of the approach. Essentially, the main task will be limited to introducing the change and creating an appropriate image, but it will be presented differently. The marketing of any benefits, providing details, technical or otherwise, and fielding complaints will all constitute a public relations function. From the professional's perspective, this represents the simplest form of development intervention. Backed by the resolution of a strong policy and a determined authority, the 'development' worker is the harbinger of good tidings and the manipulator of communications. Much of the 'development' work will be confined to seeking out potential supporters of the change within the community while, at the same time. absorbing and deflection any community resistance. Managing any unavoidable conflict between the power of the planners and the relative powerlessness of the community will have been anticipated. Much will depend on the quality of information and intelligence about the internal workings of the recipient community which has been gathered in advance of the intervention process. Dividing the community's leadership, and bestowing high profile symbols of public approval on those in favour of the planned change, is a tactic well tested in the past. An apparent majority approval for this enterprise is a likely target. If it is thought necessary that some more positive acceptance is to be achieved, then extra developmental skills will be needed to guide that process.

Community as the context for development

The next phase in the model moves the development process into a more interactive mode. When planning and physical development move out beyond the movement of material resources and into the realm of designer facilities for the local community, different techniques are employed. The intention is to prepare a feature of change with this specific community in mind. The community is to be given what it wants, or it will be manipulated to want what it gets. To help them to adjust to any unexplained friction in acceptance, professional assistance will be introduced in the form of community development workers. This is proactive human development in anticipation of planned changes.

The introduction of a physical, or social development programme will be anticipated at the planning stage by the collection of a comprehensive bank of information regarding the location, demographic and cultural shape of the target community. There will be intensive interaction between those responsible for the technical delivery or presentation of the development, and those who are to be the agency's human resource personnel on the ground during the introduction phase. Anthropological insight will be required to assist the planners to design their proposals in such a way that they will gain acceptance by the community (Pottier, 1993). By contrast, in the earlier development example, the emphasis remained on the introduction of a physical change. In this situation, the human dimension of the change process is being targeted. Adjustments will be made in the delivery system to ensure that the change produces the maximum feasible benefit as well as gaining the positive reception from the intended beneficiaries.

In parallel with these behind-the-scenes activities, the community, or some form of representative fraction of the community, will be drawn into a participative process through which the planners can test their ideas and their 'fit' with the community's situation. This is best understood through an appraisal of the amount of influence, which the community may have over the initial idea, and any design of the programme. Involvement with monitoring the project's outcomes and/or the evaluation of any success can also be extended to them as part of a larger design for focusing the community on its own processes (Arnstein, 1969; Burns, 1991; Harding, 1991; Marsden & Oakley, 1991; Marsden, 1994a, 1994b; Oakley, 1984; Oakley, 1991; WHO, 1988). The active involvement of the people in the

75

initial assessment process is now considered essential to justify most intervention initiatives but there is a wide disparity in the objectives of this exercise. There is still a strong determination at this stage in the model, to retain firm control over the process: its scale, purpose, outcomes and practice procedures. Rapid Rural Appraisal (see below, chapter 9) is one method of providing information and, at the same time, providing justification for the shape of planned outcomes. The presentation of 'need' as the rationale for targeting certain outcomes is one method for protecting the interests of experts. The scope of planned change can then be narrowed down and the whole process policed by the planners (Chambers, 1993; WHO, 1988).

Nicholson draws attention to the problem of allowing 'experts' to implement project development which results in the eventual estrangement of the indigenous population (Nicholson, 1994, p. 68). O'Malley, in rejecting the whole approach, draws attention to the ineptitude of the combined (and competitive) forces of the professionals in one of the earlier examples of organised conflict between the planners and community organisations recorded in British community work (O'Malley, 1977,p. 3).

This is the situation which Wooley puts in the classical terms of Class. He claims that the professional takes the initiative away from the local people and subordinates their interests, in this case, to those of the middle class (Wooley, 1970, p. 3). This is precisely the process which is being described as the professional role in this phase of our model. The professional, lacking the authority or the knowledge to share power with the people has to orchestrate a fluid and potentially volatile situation. The problem of social change has been approached from a detached and elitist standpoint: the most efficient and accountable method is to retain control of developments for as long as the employer agency retains an interest. This is accomplished by managing the tensions between the employer/planning agency and the needs of the people through whatever means may be available. The feelings of the people, and the sensitivities of the employer have to be manipulated and contained. Every effort will be made to adapt the plan to the needs of the people, but, by protecting the 'public interest', the original objectives of the plan can be preserved. We shall be addressing the question of power confrontations more centrally in the next chapter. Professionals, working for the state or for NGO's, believe that they have a difficult enough time retaining contact with 'their' development programme once the unpredictable forces of local politics enter the arena (Porter, 1991; Rondinelli, 1993).

In this phase of the model, the first task of the community development workers is to act as a conduit for information and to set up mechanisms for its collection. It can be anticipated that the best designed plans for social development will only approximate the felt needs of the community. The dynamics of change will release new energies, allow fresh agendas to emerge and these may disrupt established leadership and activity patterns. In the sense that the professionals will have taken reasonable steps to ensure that their basic data is correct, they must know that they will need continuing updated material if they are to obtain the maximum impact with their planned change. Their task will be to supply the information and to produce the mechanisms that will be required to make the collection of valid, up-to-date intelligence possible. To do this, they must establish reliable contacts in the community.

Professional penetration of networks and community organisations will become the priority across a wide spectrum of interests, and at every level of scale and importance. If the community does not have effective or sufficient social organisation, then the worker must attempt to establish those organisations which can fit into the needs of the planners. The worker will need to glean high quality information and obtain speedy feedback on initiatives connected to change. Mining the community for insight will give the clearest view of the way in which pressure could and might be applied in order to provide a receptive response to the work of the agency. The worker assumes the role of the elite, who controls through the manipulation of information (Etzioni, 1968). Corporate management in local government, as described by Cockburn, fully accepted that the use of cybernetics is the most painless and effective way of controlling change. Planning with, rather than against, the electorate ensures that the management system is in control of the direction of change at all times. The modern agency has become more consummate in this skill. Its influence over the direction and impact of development, has become more subtle but the boundaries of error have become more clearly defined, especially within the constraints of the 'contract culture' of today's social work (Berkeley, et.al., 1995; Cockburn, 1978; East Dyfed, 1992; Felvus, 1994).

In the idiom of development as practised in the South, the process, which we have described in the above two sections, represent the process of 'extension' of economic or social change. Extension entails transmitting, to the under-developed districts of the nation, the plans for the future development. This also entails imbedding the practices required for this development as devised at the centre, implemented through the channels of the centre, via the ministry of professional experts who are employed from the centre. In the countries of the North, this term is not in use. The language of local politics will not stand for the description of the deliberate manipulation of the electorate to be set out in such bald terminology. Professionals in British community development have to invent their own 'cover' while they work.

Our model of community development divides in two at this point. The first phase is completed if the agency is satisfied with the conditions which are necessary for the agency itself to sustain a service (maintain a facility) within a community with the consent of the local people. 'Development' has taken place and there has been a degree of social adjustment to the process. This situation may need close supervision and on-going manipulation if there is to be a minimum of friction between the planning agency and the people.

The less that the plans of the centre can be modified in order to 'fit' the needs and the cultural expectations of the local people, the greater local awareness will grow of the extent of external influence over their lives. This will set off reactions which will have to be contained. On the other hand, accommodating (appeasing?) local resistance might create rising expectations regarding the scope of future benefits which could be won. The professional will try to avoid being caught in the middle of such a hiatus. The professional will have to make various intervention judgements regarding the degree of personal control which is exercised over the outcomes of development. Managing this rising tide of expectations, and anticipating still further demands from the local people to play a part in determining their own destiny, will tax professional skills and status to the limits.

The professional may be set the task of obtaining the highest degree of 'fit' that is possible in order to head off this pressure. Nevertheless, there will be definite limitations in the degree of flexibility which can be wrung from national or regional policies. In Britain, the pressure has just begun in the defence of the local welfare state against restructuring along the lines of free market principles. Defiance of the government through the refusal of school governors (their own appointees) to reduce further their expenditure, and to sacrifice teachers' posts as a consequence, is a symptom of this trend. In this case, there are no professionals attempting to oil the wheels of change. Also, in community care, local health authorities institute rounds of consultation procedures as they begin to reconcile the conflicting demands of stretching fixed resources (under-used hospital buildings) and health care in the community (Western Mail, 31.3.1995). Human resources are being deployed in some areas in an attempt to reconcile local needs and centralised resource priorities (East Dyfed, 1992; Felvus, 1994). Social services, too, are facing the strain of trying to concentrate their resources on 'those with the greatest needs.' (Department of Health, et.al., 1989, para 1.10; Griffiths, 1988). The people of Gloucestershire and Islington have been to court to challenge the right of their local authority to change their assessment of need (Dobson, 1995). This is a case of expectations of negative 'development' and they want to play a part in the process.

Community as the potential for self-help

The second half of the model arises where the planning agency seeks more ambitious outcomes than just relying on traditional forms of service and delivery systems, even if these can be 'shared' with the local community. There are many categories of people in the community who manifest need. Some of those needs will already be on the agenda of the welfare and health services, others will not, but they will be felt in the community with a greater or lesser degree of public awareness. Some 'needs' will have been removed from the list of those eligible for services under community care priorities (Clarke, 1998).

Providing a state-led service at the level of the community entails balancing the resources which have to be invested in physical plant, such as buildings and equipment, and how much is invested in trained or semi-trained personnel. In a contract culture, this becomes a complicated process of producing a system that is suitably flexible without undermining the business constraints on the providers. However, many of the services which the people require, such as support, respite care, temporary and casual services of a domiciliary nature, do not necessarily require the mobilisation and organisation of a formal agency or a contract. Some may have been provided from a central source in the past and are either no longer available, or are to be down-graded through the restructuring of services through privatisation. Many of them must now be provided through alternative means, informally, through networks and contacts. If the appraisal of service needs and provisions can be approached systematically, and semi-formal, community-led mechanisms developed, there can be spin-offs which act for the long-term improvement and benefit of the whole community.

One of the drawbacks of modern, specialised services is that the workers that deliver them are only in contact with those segments of the community that impinge directly on their professional role. Professionals are often not aware of what other resources are being deployed in, or generated by, the community around their clients. In addition, they are usually pre-occupied with a concept of the kind of contribution that they, as a particular kind of professional, have been trained to consider appropriate. In this context, 'services' are a form of activity which are designed to target specific individuals, making the maximum effective use of professional or technical resources. But the needs assessment process will bring professionals into contact with many for whom there is no allocation of public resources. They might, then, seek alternative approaches in an attempt to get support for these categories of need. To do this, they will have to adopt a new approach and assume fresh roles. The advantages offered through the application of this model are that it immediately involves a constituency wider than the focus of a normal needs assessment. It produces new structures, and it provides genuine control for people who otherwise may be without support at all. We maintain that failure to consider this approach will lead to a growing frustration as the gap between those with services and those without them widens. The earlier that these changes are adopted the better, as community development techniques rely little on traditional roles, image and skills. Practice in their application is needed before the current fluidity in service provision hardens. Pressures are likely to intensify as the constraints of the 'contract culture' and work specifications begin to impinge on more and more service activities.

There is a point of transition where professional judgement is a crucial factor in deciding whether or not to proceed with the development of community-run services. The immediate professional task is to assemble as much intelligence as possible in order to assist in the decision-making. The professional perspective is that of a planner, and the first stage in this process is the assessment of potential of the community. The criteria of assessment will be focused on those forms of activity which can reasonably be accomplished and sustained by the people themselves. The way forward now is closer to action planning but the professional is not in any position to create expectations within the community until this stage is completed. The emphasis is on stabilising the situation, for the professional and for the community, so that assessment and planning can go ahead in a reasoned way.

The tasks fall broadly under three headings:

Assessment The starting point is the needs of the *client* segment in the community. As a starting point, the worker can examine the nature of service being provided or assessed as being required in a particular location/area. The potential of the community to go towards meeting some of the assessed needs can then be appraised, using, initially, the technique of profiling the community's resource base (Glampson, et.al., 1975; Hawtin, et.al. 1994; Henderson & Thomas, 1987; Thomas, 1976). Hawtin describes this approach in the broadest terms, incorporating the straightforward needs assessment which service agencies undertake, the social audit (needs and the resources in place to meet them) to draw up a complete picture of the community as a potential instrument for meeting its own needs.

A community profile might be defined as follows:

> A *comprehensive* description of the *needs* of a population that is defined, or defines itself, as a *community*, and the *resources* that exist within the community, for the purpose of developing an *action plan* or other means of improving the quality of life in the community. (Hawtin, et.al., 1994, p. 5)

This assessment is a large piece of work and may have to be built up over a period of time. It is a task that not only serves the function of mapping the community's resources, but it also is a means to drawing out from the community those human resources that will be the raw material for any future professional activity around the mobilisation of self-help. A vital part of the profile is the recording of the nature, state and level of local community activity. What is organised, for whom, by whom and with what level of competence? The relative strength of the community and its potential for manipulation by the professional can be gauged from the outcome of this study. Does the pattern of activity being undertaken now complement or conflict with any strategy the external agency might like to introduce? Are there any points of obvious weakness that either need support, or, conversely, can be exploited? What level of skill and leadership is being demonstrated? What is the nature of the leadership? Does it have any qualities (charismatic, idiosyncratic, etc.), which will prove sensitive to new agendas being introduced (Clarke, 1970)?

A profile of this kind is not a static artefact. It is the foundation of a dynamic relationship. The information it contains has to be presented and used strategically in the pursuit of the goals of the participants as well as in the interests of the professional, and those service functions which might be developed from them. There is not much evidence to draw upon, but in the United States, there is evidence that professionals can expect more conflict from citizens' organisations if the professionals attempt to maintain a high profile throughout the process (Gilbert & Specht, 1975).

Hawtin's definition contains an additional clause in the section which is quoted above. This reads: 'carried out with the *active involvement* of the *community* itself' (my italics).

The insistence that the community must be fully involved in the gathering and assessment of the information presents certain difficulties for the worker. It could not be accomplished unless a great deal of work is put into the preparation of the community for them to undertake this task. At this stage, the worker is merely involved in an exercise to establish the potential of the community. Does it have sufficient resource potential to meet needs which are being defined by the external agency? Consideration of the active involvement by the community is premature. For information to be reliable, such that it can be used for the purposes of planning services for the vulnerable, it must be tested for certain objective criteria (Glampson, et al., 1975). The involvement of the community might be essential at some stage in the task, but the worker is not going to be in any position to share a preliminary analysis with the community in any meaningful way. This particular phase of the agency's planning phase is strategic, and should be completed and analysed in light of the decisions in principle about future investment which will have to be made. The analysis of this sort of resource by, and for, the use of the community will be the subject of a further section below.

The second aspect of the assessment process is the assessment of the community's own attitudes and priorities for action. There is usually a high degree of informal interaction and other formally organised activities in most communities, however small or economically deprived they may be. The community will demonstrate through its actions just what are its own priorities and ideas. It will also have its own outlook, however fragmented, on the idea that it may be manipulated to displace some of its own activities so that the priorities of the 'state', or some other agency, can be substituted for them. The accusation that substitution and manipulation cannot achieve anything other than the oppression of the subordinate classes is already well made (Cockburn, 1978; Topping & Smith, 1977).

It may well be that many community activities are already completely compatible with the development priorities of the worker. These may not be formally organised or not carried out with any degree of consistency. The worker might seize on these energies for a developmental intervention. Before this can be done, accurate advance information about these activities, and their relevance to the community, would be a definite asset to the worker.

It is very important for the professional to be aware of both dimensions of the question. Assessment of the community's internal capability will suggest what form of inputs will be required, and what form and volume of professional preparation might be necessary once a process of self-help is instituted. How will decisions taken now influence the form of future support and other intervention strategies? On the other hand, it may be that there is no immediate showing of potential for this form of activity. It is at this point that the professional is forced to make certain judgements, and consequently, certain recommendations, to the employing agency about the future strategy for this community, and the form of outside intervention that is most appropriate.

Information and marketing The gathering of technical information, about the nature of need and its alleviation, about the processes of care and networks, has to be acquired by the worker. Knowledge of this kind provides a crucial insight into the purpose of any future planning exercise. This information will broaden the grasp that the worker has over the general shape of service needs, and enable the assessment of the logistics required to provide services of different kinds. The scale of the over-lap between services and the functions that go into their provision can also be calculated. The technicalities: skills, working costs, logistics, etc., of providing and sustaining reliable care services have to be fully understood. The development worker has to become a reasonable 'expert' in most subjects. With a sound basis of understanding of what is involved, priorities for development of local substitutes can then be assigned by the worker, in consultation with the worker's employing agency. The role of the community in all of this is dependant on the nature of relationship which the worker and employer wish to develop with the community. The manipulation of information is a very powerful weapon in the control of political power (Thomas, 1983). Passing on the information in a form which is intelligible to the uninitiated is the next task. It is impossible to translate information into different cultural codes unless a detailed and working knowledge of both the codes and the processes are understood (Marsden, 1994b).

The worker is now in possession of two dimensions of information - the profile of the community and the requirements of services and need. The promotion of community activity, the means to employ this information for the development and benefit of the community, becomes the next task. Priorities for intervention, and strategies for the involvement of the community in meeting them, form the basis of a planning exercise. The human resource potential of the community is a crucial element. It may be that the worker has to consider the recruitment of completely new resources, or the adaptation of proven potential which is currently being deployed on other priorities. The enlistment of the community's goodwill in this endeavour is a priority, one the decision has been taken to proceed.

Of deep significance, is knowledge about the state of the community itself. This may never before have been presented to the community, and it may come as a shock if raw information is dumped upon people who have no means or experience in handling it. Information can empower those already resourced to handle it. For many, however, it serves to reinforce stigma and uncertainties. The management of the process of introducing a community to itself this way is a sensitive and highly skilled task. Once the information about the community becomes available to the community itself, and if it is handled properly by the worker as a part of a prepared strategy of development, there will be a rising tide of interest in the potential that it provides.

The professional manipulation of this flow of information entails selection, presentation and interpretation. The subsequent handling of the people who get it and begin to use it, becomes a skilled operation in itself. Information generates images which have often to be interpreted before they make any sense. Handling this task requires preparedness and maturity. Negative images must not be allowed to contribute further to the oppression of people with whom a positive and ambitious response is to be developed. Minorities can become exposed and undercurrents of community unrest have to be anticipated if the professional is to remain in contact with the process whereby the community 'matures' as it comes to grips with its own problems.

Action programme Having identified those indigenous resources which might be enlisted in the creation of new formations within the community, the worker has to target them as part of a deliberate campaign to draw them together. Many diverse groups of people can be used in this process: those people associated with these needs, which have already given a high priority: civic leaders, service managers and general community organisations. They can all be drawn into a dialogue which the worker will seek to translate into a formal structure over a planned period of time. Unlocking the resources of the community for the benefit of those in need can be achieved once the formal processes of a new organisation take root and begin to exercise their own influence on the participants. Thus, there is a definite agenda for the worker to work through:

♦ assessing the overall resource potential of the community - what are the areas of special need (from the agency's analysis/assessment priorities) that are suitable for transfer to community delivery?
♦ what human resources are immediately available for mobilisation and how might a strategy of orientation be managed to enlist this group for the planning and delivery of services?
♦ what are the short-term and longer-term tasks in terms of enabling, supporting and empowering the identified community personnel in the

build-up of service activities?

This is the subject of the worker's planning process. The ground has been prepared and the worker is in possession of sufficient information to decide whether or not there is sufficient potential to embark immediately on a developmental initiative. There is a great deal of significance to this process. It may, or it may not be possible for those currently authorising this investigation (the agency) to make any alternative resource commitment to the community, other than to support a development programme based on self-help. Failure to advance beyond the planning stage can pose considerable conflicts for the worker who, by now, has developed a detailed understanding of the community and its needs.

The worker may now be in a position to undertake a simple SWOT analysis (Strengths, Weaknesses, Opportunities and Threats), and present a plan for the 'development' of the community. The employing agency is prepared for the contribution it must make in terms of resourcing the worker. It will also be aware that it is in a position of preparing itself for the loss of considerable amount of direct control over the nature and standard of service which may be provided once the community takes over. There are political risks involved in this, and the agency must be aware of what they are and how they might be confronted in the event of something going wrong.

4 Development as Community Development - II

Building the organisation in the community

COMMUNITY	COMMUNITY	COMMUNITY	COMMUNITY	COMMUNITY	INDIVIDUAL
as the	as the	as the	as the	as the	as the
LOCATION	CONTEXT	POTENTIAL	VEHICLE	MOTOR	TARGET
For	for	for	for	for	for
DEVELOPMENT	DEVELOPMENT	SELF-HELP	DEVELOPMENT	DEVELOPMENT	DEVELOPMENT

The detailed planning and preparation of the worker for the next stage in the model is now completed. The worker will now embark on an organisation-building exercise which will achieve two objectives. It will provide a community-based service structure for those in need within the locality, and it will provide a prototype of self-help on which the community can model future activities. We have now moved across the template to the dividing line between worker-led activity and the point, after which, the community itself will provide the motor force for its own growth and enhancement. The first step is the preliminary stage, prior to departure along this path. Developments after this will be shadowed and supported by the worker. The pay-off for the professional, in addition to ensuring that needs which cannot be met from central resources are met locally, is that the role of the professional will ensure that close monitoring and indirect control can be maintained. The level of dependency will be managed by the professional to suit the situation as it emerges. This stage of development allows the worker to manipulate the form in which the intervention is experienced by those participating in the activity in the community.

The development worker is already committed to the task of creating change. Once the initiative takes on an active interventionist phase, expectations will shift on all sides. The outlook of the worker, and the employing agency will be assumed to be positive and reinforcing of any potential which may be identified. The risks should have already been discounted by this stage. If sufficient potential does not seem to exist, then the planning must include a decision-making process. The worker can exercise professional judgement to decide whether or not to deploy

86

resources at the root of the problem, and whether the mobilisation of fresh potential is justified. It may be decided to abandon the initiative altogether. Not all communities will be in a position to supply services on anything like the scale and with the resilience that social care requires. The enlistment of alternative resources such as externally recruited and managed volunteers, might better serve the interests of less well-equipped groups. So much will depend, also, on the outlook of the agency, as well as on the worker. Positive potentials can be identified where there is a will to do so. Much will depend on the detail and the scope of the plan, which will lay out, in advance, the scale and direction of the intervention which has to be accomplished.

Community as the vehicle for development

The professional has assumed, in isolation, that this particular community is a suitable vehicle for a development programme. It is further assumed that after the implementation of the development process, the outcome will be a self-help social action activity (Chekki, 1979). It will now be the worker's task to create mechanisms which will be suitable for this kind if sustained service activity. The sponsoring agency will supply, through the worker, the necessary support and catalytic resources to enable this to happen. For the community to be the vehicle for its own development, the worker must begin by orienting key elements towards that purpose.

There are serious implications in considering this outcome. The agency will be making an investment in a high-risk strategy, the failure of which will have direct effects upon its self-image and its public profile. Failure will have serious effects on internal morale for those members of staff who identify with the agency's public image of service. In the public arena, its reputation of having the responsibility, together with the ability, to meet objective need will be seriously challenged. If the agency is a statutory agency, then there will be political risks as well. From the perspective of traditional professionalism, the agency will be taking another form of risk. It will be investing in a process which necessitates it deliberately divesting itself of control over the service provision.

The difference between this and the 'contract culture' approach is that the outcomes do not just depend on the regulation of financial rewards and penalties. They will depend on the successful mobilisation, organisation and indirect support of independent agents within the community. The time-scale of responsibility is going to remain open-ended. Have the appropriate preparations been made to ensure that the initial intervention is planned and resourced at the appropriate level? Will the intervention be sufficient to enable the community to attain sufficient momentum and expertise for the delivery of a recognisable replacement for the regular service? To what extent are they prepared for conflict of interests and changes in priority?

Does the agency have the necessary will, the policy and reserve resources to replace the community with alternative services if it fails? Abbott describes how the success of such an initiative will depend on the 'openness' of the agency (he uses the government as the model) towards community-led initiatives (Abbott, 1995). If the fruits of development are to be fully harvested, investment must be appropriate for the process, and not pre-determined on an arbitrary basis. Commitments arising out of this form of strategy may increase and be of a more varied and flexible kind than before. This process must be understood, anticipated and not dealt with on a default basis.

For its part, the community will be making a direct investment of human, material and, probably, financial resources. They will discover that their own effort will come to make up the only services to address these particular needs. They will have experienced these needs in the past, to a greater or lesser extent, on an everyday basis, but they will not have considered them from the position of being responsible for care in any formal sense. The people may consider that they have not been fully briefed on the degree of local responsibility that they have to assume. They may not accept that they may have been handed a 'life sentence' of service. It is difficult to prepare people in advance for the unknown and there may be image problems as the community adjusts to seeing its own members in new roles. There will be elements in the community who take fully to the idea, and there will be those that do not. These represent potential political factions which will need to be managed by the community, as well as by the professional worker. All in all, we are looking for a major culture shift, over time, by the whole community.

The worker is in a unique position. Responsibility for the success of the enterprise has to be invested at the point of contact with the community (Barr, 1995). The loss of direct line-management accountability may be difficult to achieve unless all levels of the agency have understanding of what may be accomplished. There are certainly going to be some communication difficulties and some mismatch of expectations along the way. The confidence of the worker to take executive risks will set the limits to the programme. These will entail making working adjustments to the practical issues of the day, provided that they remain within the strategic framework. The degree of professional autonomy (Etzioni, 1964a; Goode, 1969; Toren, 1969), may present some contradictions from

88

a theoretical perspective. But from the point of view of enabling the social change process, the worker must be free to decide on the amount of professional scope and freedom which is required to get the job done (Etzioni, 1964b). All the agency must do is to make a clear statement about the scale and duration of its commitment to this form of activity and remain in close communication with the worker until the new process takes visible shape.

The normal processes of community development now apply. These have been variously described. It is not so much whether or not the method adopted is 'directive' or 'non-directive' (Batten & Batten, 1967; Biddle, 1965; Brokensha, et.al., 1969; Calouste Gulbenkian, 1968; Goetschius, 1969; Henderson & Thomas, 1987; Lotz, 1979; Ross, 1955; Rothman, 1979), so much as whether the goal outcomes are now fixed in the expectations of the worker's employer. The intention of the workers is to create the necessary organisations, which are armed with the relevant expertise and information, to take up, take over or institute the service pattern which the intervening agency has assessed as being of priority.

The salient elements are:

♦ recruitment of essential personnel who will lead the activity;
♦ creation of the organisation-building environment and integration of personnel;
♦ identification of potential and actual resources for the provision of the service;
♦ adoption of work programme and consolidation of organisation;
♦ communication processes, information and networks;
♦ planning the on-going support strategy.

Recruitment People are the raw materials for structural change within the community. This 'workforce' for the new service needs to be identified and persuaded to join in. They need to be convinced that the formation of a new dimension to the community, the provision of a self-help service mechanism, is the only way forward if community needs are to be met. The worker will have already targeted the people with a direct and vested interest in the provision of services. These may be the current users of services, their carers or others with a personal interest in the issue. Many of the early writers on this subject draw attention to the need for careful selection and training for potential activists (Batten, 1957; Batten & Batten, 1965, 1967; Goetschius, 1969; Spergel, 1969; Thomason, 1969). Direct and personal contact will have to be made with all of them. The existence of other self-help and welfare networks will also have been identified. Their membership, and other prominent members of the community will be seen as potential recruitment material. There may be organisations in the area which already have a direct interest in the planned service activity. They will have a membership, some of whom may have a practical need which might be more fully met by this development. There may, also, be those who are already involved in some other form of community activity but who are seeking a new role (or status) within these structures. There will also be identifiable individuals and groupings which are expressing some dissatisfaction with the status quo and who will need little persuasion to volunteer. If the method of direct persuasion fails to produce a satisfactory response, then the worker may have to resort to alternative methods. Marketing and public information activities may have to be tried, but they constitute a less reliable form of recruitment.

Rothman describes research into the rewards and controls which have been employed in this method of selection and support (Rothman, 1979). They are described as *instrumental* (material) or *expressive* (symbolic or personal) benefits. An understanding of the culture and expectations of the local population would give the worker insight about how to package and promote some of these rewards in order to attract interest in the initiative. Diplomacy will have to be exercised if this new activity is not to cause a rift in community relations. The brash intrusion of an upstart worker, offering 'rewards' with insensitive disregard for the local traditions and culture, can create resistance and rejection before the scheme has been initiated.

Nevertheless, if the worker has done the preparatory work, and has produced a profile of need which demonstrates that there is sufficient potential uptake for this activity, then there is likely to be a positive response. There is a need to be met and, therefore, a job to be done. If perseverance, tact and sensitivity are the only price to be paid, then a professional approach will be sufficient. There will be, however, the possibility of some negative responses to change. These may be disorganised and lacking resolve or they may build up into a concerted attempt to spoil the whole activity. Workers must be forearmed for this sort of response. If it shows signs of becoming serious, potential sources of friction will need to be identified and steps taken to neutralise or marginalise them. A strategy of anticipation and early, pre-emptive activity can save the need for wasteful and untidy salvage operations.

Organisation-building The intention is to build a structure that confines its activities to those which are attainable, and those which best meet the needs of the targeted client population. It will be necessary to create a climate that stresses the idea of a 'closed' activity (Gilbert et.al., 1993). This is best suited to the type of organisation which can best guarantee a stable form of service activity. What is needed is a structure which is less susceptible to change, flexibility and deflection from its path. Gilbert, in fact, associates the 'closed' organisational form with the bureaucracies, and describes 'open' organisations as less structured, more flexible in outcomes and high on involvement and the down-grading of the professional input. Nevertheless, it is the intention of this form of development to produce a stable and reliable operation. The beneficiaries of the service cannot suffer the consequences of instability, unreliability or failure of continuity. This is the dilemma which has to be faced by the worker. The spirit of co-ordination may be a better structural goal than a high intensity of 'participation'.

The definition of need and the assessment of service requirements have been carried out from the external world of the employer agency, and not by the community. The development task is now to create the most effective *local* infrastructure for this, and for no other purpose. Consequently, the worker will have to plan the creation of an organisation which can prepare, integrate and deploy the recruits with a degree of competence which will satisfy the basic expectations and needs of the clients. Responsibility for this process must be handled by the leadership of the organisation and not by the worker. However, the resources of the worker and on the employing agency can be involved to maximum effect in providing training and other support for the process. The critical issue for the worker is to create the appropriate atmosphere and forward-looking outlook within the organisation, such that they can consider a sustained service activity with confidence.

The most useful structure for an organisation of this kind will be one with a narrow and clear constitution. It is likely that, in the search for resources to carry out their work, public moneys will become one dimension of the organisation's responsibility. The closer that the operational framework of the organisation can be tied down, the easier control will be of its activities, its image and its leadership. There will be tendency to attempt to build this sort of organisation from the top down.

The integration of the people into the roles that will be required of them is a sensitive and skilled task. Clear expectations can be created in advance. Ross identifies a number of different forms of structure, all of which meet the need of a service organisation (Ross, 1958). Some of these decisions may be decided in advance through the recruitment strategy. If, for example an organisation comprising 'power' figures in the community is desired, then a recruitment strategy targeting that kind of person will be required. If, on the other hand, recruitment attracts only people with little or no experience of public or organisational activity, then a programme to create a new organisation will have to be planned with different training and support features in mind.

Resource mobilisation   The organisation will require a wide range of resources in order to carry out its task: material, financial and human. Each requires special consideration and the development of appropriate skills and managerial approach. For stability, each aspect of the resource base of an organisation needs to be planned and approached strategically over a recognised time period. A culture of resource management needs to be developed within the organisation in order to maximise their use. The worker has a definite role to play in the development of this process. The organisation will need a strategy for the training of personnel, the encouragement of the recruitment of specialists and fund raising. Building up and nurturing contacts and the use of networks in promoting the organisation is essential. Introducing the organisation to the processes of applying for and managing grants from public sources, the cultivation of an image of financial probity and the development of public goodwill are essential aspects of planning and management. The worker must ensure that, as far as the organisation is able, these essential survival mechanisms are taken on board.

The assessment of the resource needs of a service organisation can constitute an invaluable input by professionally competent experts. Once the needs are established, the professional can assemble a resource pool of external contacts and helpful resources. This needs to be planned by the worker from the beginning. It is as important a part of the development strategy as is the recruitment and training of leadership. Bad resource planning can ensure that the organisation begins to decline and lose momentum from a very early stage. There is no intention to exploit the people who take on this responsibility. Full use will be made of their talents and energy, but their ultimate ability to continue to prove vital services for those in need depends on their being fit and willing to continue. The worker's task is to instil competent and aware management systems in order that full autonomy can be attained.

One specific technical area needs to be singled out for special attention. That is the creation of an alternative support network of competent financial advisors to assist the worker to cast off some of the day to day responsibility for the organisation's working. It will also give to the organisation an alternative source of opinion, in a critical area of policy, on the way in which they should proceed with their development. It as been established that the sponsoring agency cannot assume financial responsibility for the provision of the service from central resources. Now it will have to face up to the fact that, as it hands over control for the management of a substitute service, that it will strengthen the power of the organisation. This power will be steadily extended. Having control over the material resourcing of an activity gives virtually absolute power to those that hold it. Once the financial viability for a new organisation has been established, the sponsoring agency, through its worker or otherwise, will have to re-negotiate the relationship afresh. There will, of course, be a delay before the new organisation realises that it has this autonomy. It is the fact of financial survival and development that indicates the success of a community development initiative. It is this fact that demonstrates to the worker just how much of the influence that can be sustained with an organisation in this position depends on the personal qualities of the worker, and not on the status or authority of the outside agency. Professional autonomy is an essential in this situation. The success of this initiative strengthens the hand of the professional in relation to the employing agency. The more success that the worker has in producing sustainable development of service organisation, the greater will become the agency's dependence on the worker. There is likely to be constant tension over accountability issues in this area.

Financial viability and management is only one aspect of the management of resources. Many of a community organisation's resources come from the contributions and goodwill of the surrounding community, and from those who take part in providing its services. Managing this process is one of the key ingredients contributing towards organisational morale. Bad handling of the resource contribution made by the community can seriously damage the image and reputation of the organisation and, consequently, its activities. In addition to building up a base in the community for providing contributions in kind, and regular fund raising activities, the community can be reassured through well packaged demonstrations of efficient and non-wasteful activities. This is part of a public relations exercise which is one of the on-going aspects of organisational survival. It is through opportunities like these that the worker exercises professional support and guidance for the system. Through this relationship, influence is maintained. It is not merely a contrivance, although it is useful as such. The outcome of a successful community organisation is the provision of a stable service for those in need.

The consolidation of the human resources of the organisation is an on-going and important concern, especially for new activities. An important input by the development worker is to spell out to just what the training needs of its members might be. This should encompass the needs of new recruits, and planning the training should begin at the earliest stage. The professional may have personal training skills which can be applied from the outset. But it might be better from the perspective of continuity if the organisation is encouraged to consider either providing its own training for its workforce or to seek it separately from other specialist agencies. It is a valuable professional task to link a new organisation with these appropriate resource agencies, and it is a critical ingredient for the success of a service organisation that as discipline and professional approach to their work can be achieved. Through this, their beneficiaries can learn that they can rely fully on the quality of a service being provided. Training is an essential component of this process.

Work programme and consolidation   An intense amount of work needs to be applied to the leadership of the organisation during this phase. The organisation needs to adopt a planning approach to its work and, as soon as possible, it should be able to test its activities for standards, reliability and continuity. The pace with which it can proceed to assume all these responsibilities rests on the quality and state of preparation of those essential personnel in leadership positions. At this stage of the work, the relationships between the professional and the membership of the organisation need to be re-structured. The professional will apply specialist skills to the top levels of the hierarchy rather than continue any in-depth contact with the rank and file volunteers or members. Initially, adjusting to this new form of relationship may be difficult to handle, for all parties as there may have been a history of closeness which was necessary during the formative period. Many have looked to the professional for personal leadership during this period, and there may be some apparent blurring of responsibilities when initiatives are being planned or implemented This situation often produces some ambiguities which may take some time to resolve.

The worker's priorities are now firmly fixed on creating a permanent structure and are only scarce resources to apply to this process. A professional's image can suffer, especially if attempts are made to keep everybody happy. Workers should anticipate that this change will occur. The leadership will be coming under strain as they take on the responsibility. There is bound to be some tension, but they must believe that they 'own' the organisation. Programming a service can be an exacting task and there will be strains and frictions as 'workforce' and 'management' get used to their roles. At all costs, the worker should avoid appearing to side with the workforce against the management.

The consolidation of leadership is a priority. Its ability to conduct the affairs of the organisation will depend on the speed and resolve with which they take up the challenge, and upon the depth of preparation with which they have been prepared for the task. Plans should include contingency plans for the continuity of the leadership in the event of a possible loss of personalities. The selection and preliminary training of possible successors should be put on the agenda for liaison work from the very start. Community activities are beset with the same problems of staff 'wastage' as the offices of the social services. The problem for the professional trying to ensure that there is some preparation for continuity, is that even mention of the need can be seen as undermining the position of the first incumbents. There is also not a ready pool of potential successors waiting in the wings. If there is, then sensitivity and caution should be exercised.

Communication, information and networks The worker will be concentrating on the adoption by the organisation of the simplest and most effective methods of communication that are possible. Reliable communications with those providing the service, effective communications with sources of resources and/or other players in the field and the establishment of a good public image are all part of the requirements of effective communications (Dixon, 1993). Apart from recognising the centrality of effective communications, the most important tasks are agreeing and setting up the processes. They must be seen to be effective and they must make the work easier and not more difficult. The paths of communication must be set up with the needs of the organisation and its work to the fore. Systems have to be tested, installed, users trained, and the worker can act in a consultative capacity while the needs can be analysed and methods tested. The whole organisation must understand how and why it works best and what sort of investment they all need to make in order to ensure that it remains effective. The leadership has to be convinced that the process is beneficial and that it will work reliably over time.

In assessing the potential for setting up such an organisation, the worker gathered together a comprehensive profile of the area. This information was then integrated with the sponsoring agency's own information regarding the assessed welfare needs for this population. The future relationship of the sponsoring agency and this new service organisation, will depend, to some extent, on: the exchange of ideas and knowledge of the work in the field, the changing needs of the population and the capacity of the organisation to grow and mature in the face of these changed circumstances. The work of the organisation will bring them into daily contact with the reality of life in their patch. Their general links with the whole population, through natural networks and through exposure on the streets will provide them with immediate insight into the patterns of need in the population. Familiarity with the processes of tending to the needs will bring greater abilities to analyse and deliberate on the situation that is around them. The greater the organisation's understanding of these forces, the greater will be their capacity to tailor their own work to meet their requirements.

There are some points of potential conflict here - between the aims of the sponsoring agency and those of the community organisation. The sponsoring agency has the expectation that the organisation will concentrate on meeting the needs which the agency has identified as being of the top priority. This information is supplied to the organisation for that purpose, and there has been considerable investment to this end.

The agency will have formal structures and procedures. These will have definite expectations about the role of, and even the methods to be used by, the new organisation, in tackling the issues in the community. It will probably be accountable to a political constituency for ensuring that these needs are met, one way or another. Those in charge of the process have chosen to follow the community development route as they cannot find the resources for a regular service out of other community resources. Whatever path they are on, they will have expectations that the needs that they have identified will be met, ahead of any other needs that may surface. It has made an investment in the work of the development worker for this outcome.

The organisation, for its part, will get more and more aware of the relevance of their own work to local needs, and the scale of resourcing that is required to meet them effectively. This information can play a big part in determining the direction and purpose of the organisation's development, and it will be discussed below. Of immediate concern is the role of the professional worker in acting as an effective agent for the sponsoring agency and keeping the organisation to its original agenda. The skills required for effective liaison are very sophisticated but they are essential to the worker in maintaining credibility with the employer.

Credibility is also needed with the organisation as the worker's history with the people involved has been one of being available, supportive and, perhaps, even somewhat compliant. Now that the organisation is up and running and the stakes are now more overtly political, the worker has to adjust to the dilemma of having two causes to champion. The worker is contracted to the agency and not to the organisation.

Planning on-going support   The worker now has to negotiate a fresh relationship with the service organisation, based upon the programme of activity which was established in the original intervention. There will have to be recognition that each has something to gain from the relationship and that there is a basis for trust, mutual respect and reliance.

For the worker, the agenda is to retain a foothold in the area, to demonstrate to the employer that there is a responsibility to this organisation and that the pay-off is beneficial to the agency. The closer that the organisation can be persuaded to plan its future in line with the foreseeable needs of the sponsoring agency, the bigger the pay-off for the agency, and for the reputation of the community development process in official circles. Agreement to follow these lines will ensure that those in the community who have already been identified as being in need get the best possible service in the absence of official support. Following these lines of development, the worker will be able to predict for the organisation that there will be continuing support and access to whatever public (or additional) material support might be available. By agreeing to keep to the original agenda, the organisation could bargain more favourable conditions in this regard. This will strengthen the long-term relationship between the two for mutual benefit.

The organisation can benefit from this as it will increase their capacity to plan ahead for the growth of its work. It will also acquire enhanced status in official circles which may increase its standing within its own community, or at least in certain sectors. There will be access to the resource power of the agency in terms of information, up to date insights into techniques and practices and the possibility of formal training within the agency's own programmes. Relationships within the community between the organisation's personnel and those from the agency working the patch will be improved and there will be opportunities for developing co-operation in the future. The organisation's leadership has every chance of being drawn into the planning circles of the agency, and across networks with which the agency is connected. This is more than just status seeking or a sop to political correctness. The community can expect to improve its image, the understanding of its problems by others and, by communicating directly with the suppliers of other services, the allocation of resources to their area. The organisation's representatives can use their influence in many ways, once they have a reputation for well-structured activity for the public good.

There is a question of power, and the way in which the worker retains direct, or indirect, influence over the way in which services and local political formations develop out of them. Being able to influence activities at the grass roots, through local leadership, is the most efficient method. The worker will also be able to use these contacts in other work, with other agencies and organisations and the organisation can be used in the building of networks, within which the worker can exert wider influence.

The agency will know that it has widened the net of service across the locality. They will know that they retain some influence over it, through the activity of their worker, or through the contacts made at network meetings. It can re-deploy resources to areas of greater priority and it can consider the prospects of this organisation as a prototype for similar departures in practice. It will recognise that this new activity is vulnerable and that its failure can bring political repercussions. Nevertheless, without extending its resource commitment, the agency has extended its influence over a wider constituency. Maintaining an arm's length relationship will remove it from the immediate impact of any disaster in the service field and it can always plan for an emergency, and politically conspicuous, relieving operation. It will have lost a degree of direct control, but developments were already beyond its direct external control in the first place.

Community as the motor for development

The professional input to the organisation has been concerned with the development of effective capacity to deliver services within a defined community. The model for this is to produce an efficient and representative organisation which, nevertheless, remains responsive to the needs of the external agency. This is no lightweight expectation but it will have to be managed by the agency or it could be lost to them. The longer that the organisation functions, grows and flourishes, the greater will be its internal cohesion. If it develops along the expected lines, it will soon be realised that the organisation has the sort of effectiveness which might be associated with a small-scale service agency. Good development handling will seek to ensure that the original relationship is adapted to suit the new situation and needs. A spirit of co-operation and collaboration will be the objective for the professional.

As the organisation's service and management systems come to work well, it will generate their own dynamic and the agency will become more confident of its identity. It will gather its own insight into the community which it serves and it will develop a sense of awareness of its function and place in its own society. The organisation may well come to question whether the services which it provides exactly suit the needs of the community. It might then question the nature of its relationship with the eternal agency, and its dependency on the external agenda. This is yet another situation which has to be managed by the worker in an attempt to keep the service function in place.

Corporate effectiveness brings real power and political leverage to any organisation. A community-based organisation, enmeshed in the sensitive networks of social support in its own community, will rapidly develop an image and reputation which it can manipulate to its own advantage at any time that it pleases. The deployment and consumption of community resources, in addition to any that they may receive from the agency or other outside source, will bring home to the leadership of the organisation that they are in a very special relationship with their own community. This is a situation which can be exploited towards a number of different ends. Some of these ends are directly political and will be considered in more detail in the next chapter.

If we confine ourselves to the nature and purpose of the service activities of the organisation, the following possibilities arise:

- the organisation continues to grow and develop along the lines presented in the initial plans;
- the organisation may thrive for some time and then begin to falter;
- the organisation may discover that there are priorities within the community that are more immediate than those presented by the external agency;
- the development of skills by those delivering the services may suggest that the standards and procedures prepared by the agency are wasteful, in-appropriate, or even too low to meet the needs effectively;
- the development of managerial competence by the leadership may lead them to move to tailor their organisational structure more to their own needs. This may bring the functioning ability of the organisation into conflict with the needs of the service structure required by the external agency.

Each of the above presents the worker with a different set of professional tasks and duties. The knowledge that any of them may arise at any point after the organisation has begun to take shape, means that precautions or contingency plans need to be made. It could be stated that each of the above are examples of organisational maturity and that further professional input is redundant. The worker has good grounds for withdrawing from the relationship, and declaring the developmental process to have been accomplished. In all situations, save one, the organisation is now in a position of producing its own strategy for planning and conducting its affairs. We shall argue that this is not a sensible decision in any of these situations.

In the first case, where the organisation adheres to the original operational framework, it might be said that the worker was now superfluous to their needs. The collaboration has been a success. The organisation will now work itself into a new framework which involves the liaison functions of the agency and its service needs. The next phase in the service relationship would evolve, and that would be it. In the case of the organisation faltering, a steady hand on the helm may be all that is needed. The worker can adopt a watching brief. The professional task of servicing the developmental and survival needs of organisations is one of the fundamental skills of the work. These can be called in as required. There are more serious implications involved which dictate other courses of action.

The first two cases represent classic development situations which can be dealt with by employing 'more of the same'. However, once the agency as a whole begins to interact with a new, fledgling service system, the nature of the institutional relationship may be put under pressure. Plans which have been laid during the developmental stage may be open to interpretation or may now not be freely implemented. These plans can often be forestalled due to agency policy, from which the organisation may have been shielded during the formation stage. Agencies will have different policies governing their relations with on-going service organisations, as opposed to 'informal' community groups. The constraints of the 'contract culture' may now set the terms and it cannot proceed in any other way. This may conflict with what the worker sees as necessary regarding the continued deployment of professional resources in the community. Protocols of politics or management may see the worker being withdrawn. Role limitation, demarcation between separate agency functions, and professional jealousy can all be factors in restricting the proper forward view of this process.

These factors make the early anticipation of any of the above scenarios an imperative for the worker. Proactive measures need to be planned as part of a deliberate strategy. Mechanisms for implementing them must be prepared within the framework of the development process and not as a separate, remedial action. If something goes 'wrong', then there must be a strategy for salvaging something of the original design. The professional relationship between the organisation and the worker needs to be adjusted radically if it is to continue. Additional channels of communication need to be established and alternative frameworks created to allow the worker legitimate access to the organisation in the face of contradictory policies from the agency.

Should the organisation not want to continue the relationship, then different strategic considerations need to be evaluated. What investment does the worker, and the agency, have in maintaining active and influential contact with this organisation? Organisations are the source of community power, and voluntarily to cut off a potential lever on that power is not a rational action. If the agency is not aware of this significance, the worker is. The worker activated the 'organisation' model in order to create a power centre in the community, albeit for the benefit of the service needs of the agency. Nevertheless, as it is now a power centre in the community, it can be used as such in the future.

On a more basic level, liaison and planning with community organisations are central to the rationale of professional practice. Contact with this specific community organisation carries particular significance for both parties. The worker has done a good job to help create a viable structure, and the organisation was dependent on this input. The organisation cannot know what its future needs for professional support and consultancy may be. The worker may, or may not, have other *plans* which entail the community as a whole and/or the organisation. These might necessitate the worker manipulating the organisation through the complex of networks within the community, or in the wider society. The relationship with the organisation is a *strategic and political* relationship as well as a product of the development processes. It must not be jettisoned lightly. While it is true that no single personality is indispensable, the worker must recognise that personal influence over community organisations is a factor in the worker's relationship with the employer and the members of the political community of the area. A worker can abdicate this role, but should not do so out of naiveté. The worker, too, has power and only the worker can decide how best it is to be employed.

We have established that the worker can have a large investment in sustaining the relationship with this organisation, even if it is capable of survival and growth under its own steam. This can present the worker with ethical as well as practical difficulties. The conflict of competing pressures will lead to the worker having to carry these contradictions as part of the workload. These pressures were spelled out in ideological terms by the *In and Against the State* group (London Edinburgh, 1979). Here, the range of possible choices was determined by the apparent powerlessness of the worker. An oppressive state apparatus could only be confronted by indirect or by covert means.. In the picture we have described, the centrality of the worker, and the necessity of retaining control of the professional process, substitutes professional autonomy and responsibility as the primary purpose. Whatever the ideological orientation of the worker, the power to operate freely and flexibly will not be achieved without a fundamental commitment to the discipline of the professional task, in all its dimensions.

Operationally, the worker is in an exposed, but privileged position to make decisions and professional judgements. Both the long and the short-term agenda have to be kept under review so that opportunities are not lost. But, as a consequence of the potential strength of the worker within a network of resources and communications, many ethically complex situations present themselves. Should any development plans be based primarily on the priorities and forecasts of the worker? Should the long-term interests of the agency over-ride the needs of 'development'? Perhaps plans should only be devised in conjunction with the perceived needs of the community and in full consultation with the organisation. These are examples of the kind of loyalty conflicts and dilemmas that can arise. The worker is in touch with both agency and organisation on a daily basis but there is an imbalance in the quality of information available. The worker is a party to the strengths and weaknesses of the organisation in a much more immediate way than it is perhaps possible with the agency (particularly a large, complex and, perhaps, a statutory agency). The agency is likely to be out of touch with the specific details of the organisation's situation. By contrast, the worker is not privy to all the pressures and needs of the agency. The agency relies on its worker to keep the relationship intact, subject to whatever changes which might occur, and for whatever cause.

The real power balance between the agency and the organisation may now become apparent. The agency may be led into exerting pressure on the organisation to follow a particular path in order to satisfy a short-term need, or to achieve an outcome determined by new policies emanating from government or head office. The organisation, meanwhile, may, favour different considerations altogether. For example, it may not feel ready or be prepared to operate in a market situation. It is likely that a new organisation will take time to produce its own development strategy. When it does, it will resist outside pressure. It may be in a position to function and deliver much better activities over a longer period, or to different objectives completely. Which way does the worker turn on issues which test loyalty so directly?

If we now consider the situation presented by the remaining three perspectives above: where the organisation is not content to replicate the original service plan but seeks to develop its own approach to working in the community.

The worker is now in a much more sensitive position. Assuming that there was a mutual expectation that the organisation was developed in order to provide for a direct service need in the community, and that it would be guided by the agency on this path, an apparent breach of trust is now looming. The worker's credibility, or even the job, could be on the line. Much would depend on the amount of advanced warning that the worker could obtain and how much influence the worker retained. In the first instance, the worker has to exercise the maximum amount of diplomacy and tact in keeping the agency and the organisation in a working relationship until new roles can be identified and, possibly, new agreements made. The worker will have to demonstrate, to both sides, that there is a valuable professional input that can be made to the organisation while it consolidates itself into a new role. How much influence does the worker have over these circumstances? How much influence should there be?

The agency's original plan is now extremely vulnerable. Despite the large investment which the sponsoring agency has made in getting to this point, the maturity and stability of the organisation have now changed the ground rules. In the drive to create organisations that would be able to apply special, local qualities to the delivery of service, the sponsors have created a potential maverick, over which they have no control. It is in danger of being shut out and of losing a valuable service in the community. It may try to approach this position with the threat of enforcing some form of contractual obligation. This would be impossible to enforce. As the agent of the external agency, the professional could suggest that the agency opened up formal negotiations with its former protégé. The agenda would be a thoroughgoing review of the whole basis of service by and for the community, by their own community organisation. Any other position must surely be untenable, but compromise may not be on the agency's agenda. The organisation can declare that the business of the community is no business of the external agency. In what, up until now, had been an open and free relationship, the organisation has only now come to the position where it can reasonably make rational decisions about its role. The community organisation is capable of voting with its feet and deciding to provide whatever social function it chooses.

The contradictions in deploying professional intervention, with the intention of mobilising scarce community resources for the benefit of an outside system, are apparent. The 'right' of a community to organise itself, for its own welfare benefit, is not in dispute. The flaw in the developmental model is that the goals of the intervention are for the 'benefit' of the external system and its priorities. It is a form of exploitation and colonialism. Had the resources of the centre been placed at the disposal of the community so that they might better organise towards goals of their own choosing, they might have chosen different outcomes or directions. They might, also, have chosen different forms of response. This does not make either solution to social issues essentially better. It just highlights that the professional resources are deployed to set the agenda for action, and then to steer it along a prescribed course. There has been an unequal power relationship from the beginning which has been obscured in the dependency relationship between the worker and the community representatives. In some sense, the potential crisis for the agency if the organisation defects in any way is caused by the very success of the development process. Creating a truly antonymous organisation has empowered it to cut loose from its colonial situation.

A cogent reason for the crisis stems from the agency's inadequate understanding of the development process and the status of its outcomes. This situation can easily arise out of low level priority being given to community development within large, administrative bureaucracies. The idea that it is possible to inject professional skills for a short period and produce docile service organisations is flawed. The community organisation is not just another business, and it has to be handled differently. The idea of permanently resourcing the community so that it can prepare its interactions with the bureaucracy is not considered necessary by officialdom. If it is considered at all, it is perceived as being expensive and time consuming. It also threatens the legitimacy of the local political representatives.

The other cause stems from the unrealistic and idealistic approach of the workers themselves. In social work literature, it is well established that the truly professional relationship is terminated once the contracted goals have been accomplished. It is well established that creating a dependency relationship between the worker and the community is not ethical practice (Henderson & Thomas, 1987; Pincus & Minahan, 1973). It lays the basis for paternalism and colonialism (Cockburn, 1977; Corrigan, 1975; Mayo, 1975). To admit otherwise would be to acknowledge that the forces of social control had been installed in the heart of the community. This must surely undermine the community's ability ever to establish its autonomy. The community must then inevitably become the hapless victim of those in power or authority. It would make them subject to whatever fate that the powerful wished to inflict upon them. Faced with this prospect, received wisdom dictates that the 'contract' of engagement contains a withdrawal, or termination, element. The thrust of motivation is towards establishing autonomy for the client within a structural situation where structural autonomy is not possible.

This 'politically correct' position in effect presents the community with only half of the facts. It implies that they are developing their organisation so that they will assume full autonomy, and that their indigenous resources will be sufficient for them to resist the forces ranged against them. This is a contrived and a dishonest misrepresentation. It arises out of the need of the agency to create a service agency out of indigenous resources. It arises out of the inability of the professional worker to confront the truth of the situation, and to try and establish a realistic relationship on that basis. It begins at the first encounter, based on their inequality of power. It arises, further, from romantic feelings many workers hold about the viability of community organisations. These, in turn, lead to false expectations being created within the agency and in the community. The absence of a set of realistic assumptions leads to frustration and discontent when they are not fulfilled.

To offset this trend, workers need to compensate for the artificiality of the terms which bound their intervention. They may feel prepared to go along with a possible severance of relations, but this is to sell the community short, in the long run. Our thesis is unequivocal. The worker should strive to maintain the relationship with the new organisation for the longest possible time. When the new organisation begins its movement to re-negotiate its relationship with the sponsoring agency, the worker should have a strategy ready for implementation. This should include a prepared initiative for pressurising the organisation to continue to take consultancy from the worker. The strategy will have included a preparatory phase during which the worker will have sought out the channels and devices which will make this leverage possible. It is a time to call in debts, and to approach the organisation's leadership (or its membership at large, if necessary) with the facts about the worker's indispensability. Failure to achieve this level of influence can jeopardise the agency's whole plan for the area and, with it, the workers' credibility. If this approach fails, then an alternative, such as forming a problem-solving group made up of both sides of this hiatus, should be launched - with the worker in the key role of co-ordinator.

General professional considerations

The goal for the professional development worker is oft-times stated (e.g. Batten, 1957; Biddle, 1965; Brager & Specht, 1973; du Sautoy, 1962; Goetschius, 1969; Gulbenkian, 1968, 1973; Ross, 1955; Rothman, 1979;

Schler, 1970; Spergel, 1969; Thomas, 1983; Twelvetrees, 1990). The primary function is to assist a community in the process of self-determination and the achievement of autonomy for its organisations. From the beginning, the negotiation of a withdrawal strategy is usually understood, if not explicitly built into some formal agreement. The professional role is to target the needs and resources within the community and apply to them the skills of development. It is detached role, bearing no act of commitment other than the conviction that the skills of the professional can get the job done. The local culture and political barriers to outside intervention can all be mastered.

There is an actual or implied time boundary contained in the relationship between the worker and the agency. There is usually a detailed plan of how the work can be expected to progress and when certain 'milestones' of development will be reached along the way. These may, later, be discussed with the community, especially leadership figures who take over the directional management of the new organisation. As and when these are achieved, the community's organisation will then begin to assume responsibility for the new service function. Full autonomy will result.

The above conditions for these achievements are theoretical and the reality is more complex. Workers are drafted in and they are expected, by their employers, to start work on the run. For the agency, the operational clock has already begun to run. There are usually clear expectations regarding outcomes and the professional intervention is believed to be an 'add-on', which can be applied without any basic 'feel' for the local culture or any real knowledge of the local community. This is often called 'action planning', which is a term coined to describe a lack of adequate planning. Sadly, this is the form of inadequate preparation imposed on many workers. Often, essential preparatory work, such as gathering a profile of the community, has to be implemented alongside a work programme. As the person on the ground, the worker has to protect the image of the agency form this insensitive approach. Similarly, the organisation must also be protected from the worst effects of this lack of understanding. In this way, the worker's introduction to the community can be seriously distorted.

One of the great failings of community development is the level of collusion which takes place. To get the work in the first place, a certain amount of collusion is necessary. Agreement to unrealistic time-scales and projected outcomes is usually a condition of employment. Workers collude with their employers by agreeing that development, sustainable development, can be packaged, introduced and the product induced on command. Community development becomes a commodity, something that can be turned on and off like a tap. Furthermore, the myth is created that if the professional component can be arbitrarily introduced into an area, it can equally arbitrarily be withdrawn as well. The externally devised plan can be fulfilled in keeping with arbitrary time and budget constraints. The worker will be withdrawn and the community left on its own, changed but somehow completely capable and self-sufficient (Henderson & Thomas, 1987). There is collusion over the amount of preparative work that is needed prior to the intervention. Some work can be done in the detachment of a library or database. But the real information needed for the community to be fully understood can come only from the citizens themselves. There is 'soft' information; networks, traditions, taboos, etc., (Glampson, et.al., 1975) which has to be taken on, as well as 'hard' facts. This takes time and skills. Development needs are must be planned to accommodate these processes, as well as to coincide with the budgeted time period. The worker's judgement should be the arbiter of what the needs are in this respect.

In any specific situation, it may not be discovered that there has been collusion until there is a crisis. Workers, as employees, are in a relatively low position of power when it comes to negotiate the framework for a new initiative. Although workers will become accountable for the outcomes of 'their' project, much will be set up from the start which is beyond their control. The 'participation' of the community will only be elicited once these conditions have been decided and many unrealistic expectations may be planned in before the real work is allowed to begin. If the community were part of the planning process, they might set completely different goals: boundaries of role and influence, targets for social change, boundaries of time and levels of resources.

The situation is made more complex by other factors: Some workers will not want to remain working in a particular area for an extended period. Many more are placed on short-term contracts and will accept the given time-scale of the intervention. There is no national strategy for development, per se, no career structure and no accredited qualification within a discrete professional framework. These factors make it difficult to establish any clear expectations of standards of work or return on investment. Some workers will have reasons other than employment pressures for this standpoint. There is a belief that 'burnout', or, worse, co-option by the community, are inevitable consequences of prolonged exposure to one project.

The investment in a long-term, local development strategy would allow for many of the above dysfunctions to be dealt with. The employment of permanent community development workers would become possible and a framework of assessment could be established to test the viability of their models of intervention, and the true costs of their employment in terms of outcomes. It would create a community setting in which a continual process of action, reaction, pro-action could be instituted as part of the nature of community life. This would limit the scope for fashion changes, expediency and the collusion which is the product of short-termism. Attempts at social engineering would have to gain wider acceptance as awareness of the process became widespread. The community itself would change its perception of the change process and community organisations would become part of a culture of continuity, instead of disconnected beneficiaries of support. At present, sporadic interventions by the planning agencies inhibit the consolidation of community effort and its influence on the shape of service provision. For this reason, they are denied influence over the direction of policy, the level of resources. This limits their capacity and their potential to develop and sustain long-term activities. They become the objects and the victims of change processes and cannot aspire to the stature needed to absorb, or even pre-empt it.

Somewhere in the process of development, the organisation will have developed into a resource-earning agency on its own account. This may have grown out of some contractual arrangement with the sponsoring agency, or it may grow out of the natural developmental needs of expansion. Moneys can originate in fees for services, long-term agreements, and secondment agreements for staff. Sources, such as local government or charitable sources, will also be tapped, for grant aid. Wider sources of development aid, such as national or international grant-making trusts, etc., may also be approached Once this is possible, it is likely that the organisation will have now attained a scale of operation that will allow it to become an employer in its own right. It will begin to rely on its own employees for development initiatives, and new ideas and operational techniques. The professional from the sponsoring agency will have to negotiate relationships with these workers in a number of capacities. Are they now equals in the realm of strategic development planning? What is the status of the relationship between these employees and their own employer? Can the development worker sustain a relationship with all levels, keeping the trust of both and still sustain a role of influence over the leadership, which is vital to the original sponsoring agency?

The resource pool of specialised development workers in most areas is small. There will be a tendency for all those employed to attempt to support each other in general matters and, if linked in purpose across a constituency such as a specific service arena, then they may well seek alliances and shared strategies. Does this link extend to the development worker in this case? The original development worker has to place the relationship with the leadership of the new agency above any new ones that may emerge with the organisation's employees. But with whom will the agency professional be working, and what are the lines of dependency? This is an area fraught with problems and compromises are inevitable.

Individual as the target for development

In these two chapters, we have considered the professional responsibilities of the worker in terms of organisational development. The progressive shift in focus has transformed the nature of the relationship between the agency and the community, and the relationship between the worker and both of these. The agency began its development role by transferring resources to the community. The professional contribution worked to transform this relationship, through a series of recognisable stages, into a new structural alignment. The community's own organisation is now in a position to deliver services to the community. Its capacity is such that it can meet the planning needs of the agency or, should it think differently, it can design its own interventions and develop an independent existence. The community has been transformed from being the *Location* for development by others into being the *Motor* for its own development.

At every stage in this process, the worker has had to readjust the form of intervention, the nature of resource input and the breadth of perception. This has involved the manipulation of structural forces and the establishment of alternative power systems. In establishing objectives in a tactical scenario, the position and personal characteristics of the individuals involved have been depersonalised. Once the groundwork had been done in the community, it might be said that the newly forming organisation became putty in the hands of an experienced operator. Significantly, the channels of communication, the protocols and networks of the sponsoring organisation all have to be put on hold while changes are being developed at community level. They constitute an external framework, which guide policies and which determine resource flows to the community, but they will have to accommodate the changes that are going on at the community level. The process is one of losing direct control, while ensuring that a modified form of control is re-built which does not hamper the outcome: Means to Ends, Inputs for Outputs.

The literature is short on advice regarding the actual process of moving the professional process through the different levels of organisation, beyond the provision of a framework of orientation. For example, Rothman talks about the 'manipulation of small groups', the manipulation of 'mass organisations', etc., while, at the same time, focusing on the people as citizens, consumers or victims (Rothman, 1979). Spergel discusses enabling, providing support and training local leadership (Spergel, 1969) with a section on 'exercising control' and 'Preventing and delimiting riot situations' (p. 147). Much hinges on the creation of a 'positive relationship' with the client. The model put forward by Pincus and Minahan (1973) considers the change agent influencing the client system through a series of contractual relationships, which are, again, predicated to a positive relationship. The 'manipulation' of the client in community development cannot be regulated through the use of statutory powers and so the balance of carrot and stick methods has to be relied upon. Burke suggests that there are a variety of approaches, varying from direct behaviour modification strategies through setting groups goals, through co-optation to offering the influence of power to participants (Burke, 1975).

Without the use of trust, force of personality and a degree of dependency, the worker would rapidly lose the process altogether, or lose control over the outcomes. There is a difficulty, Burke suggests, in making participation the *instrumental goal* of development. This is an issue addressed by Oakley et al., where the value system is founded on an inclusive, 'primacy of the people' principle (Oakley, et.al., 1991). While they present us with an excellent framework, they remain coy on the detail of how the process of *animation* works on the ground. Some commentators subscribe fully to the *instrumental* approach (Etzioni, 1993; Seebohm, 1968), others would see the need for urgent work to be done on this account (Adams, 1990, Baldock, 1974, 1982; Barclay, 1982; Payne, 1986; Smale, et.al., 1988), while another perspective points out the highly exploitative nature of the whole exercise, or have serious doubts (Cockburn, 1978; Corrigan, 1975; Gallagher, 1977). These are the issues that workers will have to continue to carry with them as they work.

One model which does offer considerable advice on the scope of the task to be accomplished, but without spelling out how it is to be achieved, is provided by Daniel Schler (Schler, 1970). Each step in the development of the participative role and the relations between the worker and the structure of participation is laid out in terms of procedural steps, inputs and human interactions. Clearly, it can be seen that the worker has to remain in an active and fully developmental role at each stage. This approach offers a yardstick for the testing of a certain kind of quality. It is one that the employer would understand and compliance with it will produce measurable outcomes. There is a connection between each 'dimension' of the framework and the worker's responsibility is to adapt to the changed circumstances as they arise.

In our basic model, the community was first introduced to the development process through the shift of services or material resources into the area. The community and the individuals were then invited to partake of them. At this point, the professional development worker might have been involved in the primary phase of discovery regarding the nature and culture of the area. It is likely, however, that there would be no development worker near the scene. It is not usual for a development worker to be the early provider of a service to the community. Most specialised social work training available in European social work curricula neglects the development perspective, and we have already described the virtual absence of such training in British qualifying training. This means that the early focus of a service would not seek wider solutions to local issues beyond 'take-up' figures. In related professions, such as nursing, there is evidence that workers discover that there is a need to acquire the necessary development insight and skills, but only after they have assumed responsibility for intervention into a community (Coke, 1991; Felvus, 1994; Jones, 1991; Macdonald, 1992; McMurray, 1993; Smithies, 1991; West Wales Health Commission, 1993; Zutshi, 1991).

Most recently, the governing body for Nursing education, UKCC, has modified the training requirements for post-registration nurses in community settings. These now all contain the requirement in different forms that candidates demonstrate competence in community development or organisational-building techniques (UKCC, 1998).

So far, our new service has not moved to 'develop' the community beyond the physical level. Once there is a desire to adapt the service to be in tune with the actual cultural characteristics of the community, there is a direct need for accurate information about the community. This can only have been developed as a result of systematic contact. Formal research should be launched which looks well beyond the basic 'needs assessment' of a community care exercise. It is at this point that the professional development agent should be introduced. Focused contact with the local population, and the assessment of the community's potential eventually to assume full responsibility for all or part of the service, should begin. The local population (or constituency group) has to be engaged. This is the start of the strategy to draw in participants, to engage in 'consultation' and to establish relationships.

A worker may have all three further stages of the model on the agenda when the first moves are made: assessment of *potential*, the *vehicle* for development, and the *motor* for development. The longer the strategic view that a worker can take, the better will be the assessment process, and the more purpose will emerge to develop relationships over a longer time-scale. In this case, the long-term effects of intervention must be considered. The qualities, which are sought in the community, will be more far-reaching than if merely cultural information is required. Early contacts may prove to be more useful in the long-term, or their potential may not be revealed until the process of development is well advanced. The early promise shown by some local enthusiasts may wither as the scale and the scope of the exercise becomes known. With this amount of local intelligence, the worker has to become a formidable repository of information about the human potential of this community.

There has to be a systematic process of developing relationships, encouraging people to consider, and then assume, responsibility for new types of community involvement and to take on new roles and skills. Some are going to be better than others in the long run. Some will develop political ambitions, both inside and outside the organisation. Others will be repelled by those very same forces, despite their influence on the fortunes of any community-run, service organisation. The worker has to be there, in support, and always mindful of the employer agency's agenda as the unseen influence over the whole process. At the same time, if the community organisation is to be the service, then the people have to be the organisation. The worker has to get them there, to build their viability and to retain the necessary influence to ensure that the community does not divert too far from the agency's needs.

People will come and go, the worker will deploy resources and personal time and emotions in finding, supporting and actioning community plans. There can be no coercion. The worker must strive for credibility as every level, as factions form and fall out within the community and the organisation, as perceptions of the agency change and as the agency's own policies adapt in the face of new, superior pressures. In the final stages of development, towards complete community self-determination within the realm of service provision and as the 'motor' for their own development, the worker must retain influence. This is dependent on the quality of the relationships that have been built up over the whole process, since the first quest for information began.

Some individuals will have been in at the beginning of the process, some will have been veterans on earlier, community initiatives in the same field. Others will have been newly recruited to the process and will be finding their feet in the organisation. They will have mixed feelings and ambitions. Others, still, will be at various other points of familiarisation with the organisation and confidence in their roles. It is an exacting role for the worker to help individuals contain the forces of personal stress, indecisiveness and failure of confidence, all within the dynamic setting of an organisation on the move.

Some will be aware of the organisation's history and aims, others may find that the relationship with the worker appears incongruous within a community structure. This is accentuated in the case where the organisation has established itself as a free agent and is providing an independent appraisal of the community's needs. The worker has to build a form of relationship on this ambiguous ground. The worker is there to support the organisation's stability and quality of service. Dissent about the worker's role has to be dealt with, and the worker's credibility established. Prejudice against the worker cannot be allowed to get in the way of the worker focusing on the welfare of the whole organisation as well as that of its individual members.

The citizen as worker; the citizen as leader; as a member of a team; the citizen as fragile individual, at risk amidst the stresses of the organisation of power; the citizen as ambitious and political - these are some of the characteristics with which the professional has to grapple. Professional contact with, and influence over, the destiny of the organisation remains the goal and it must guide and motivate the relationships with individuals at every level in the process. There will be times when these relationships are placed under considerable tension. Conflicting values, agendas and perceptions of the nature and purpose of the community action will always lurk below the surface. Professionals will attempt to anticipate these shifts and take whatever action may appear to be appropriate. The question of whether or not to manipulate individuals directly, targeting them as personalities rather than as role holders in the organisational context, will become more pointed the more relationships, and the consequent (mutual) dependence, develops. The worker's own fortunes are intimately bound up in the fortunes of the community activity, and there will be ample scope for exercising leverage and influence.

Another problem arises out of the development of close relationships, especially with the leadership of a community organisation. Experience of working closely together, being reliant on each other for personal, as well as work issues, breeds an atmosphere of mutual reliance and expectations of openness. The logic of development insists that the community be in possession of all the facts if they are to be capable of transcending their dependant state and assuming responsibility. But the forces of politics, institutional politics as well as the other kinds, often dictate otherwise. Policies, which concern the agency's priorities and its wider aims and objectives, will sometimes restrain it in committing its full potential support to a particular community organisation at any particular time. All organisations have secrets, and the trade in secrets can compromise the professional worker at times of crisis. It only takes a small indiscretion to uncover a breach of security. The worker will be constrained to observe these conditions, and it will be a professional decision that determines how this delicate matter is woven into the framework of intervention, and the personal relationships that develop.

To what extent will the employing agency's aims and strategies be discussed with the community? The pressure of job security is a two-edged sword in this context. There might be a temptation to share the strategic plans of the agency with the organisation in order to demonstrate trust. But not to share vital information with a vulnerable and dependant organisation also constitutes a violation of the principle of participation. It would be perceived as paternalistic, conspiratorial and manipulative. Leaking confidential information about the agency's intentions might ensure a more robust response from the community at a time when interests diverged. Nevertheless, any hint that the worker was trying to manipulate the employer through the direct action of the community might find the worker rapidly workless! This conflict of interest is most marked where the employer is a statutory agency, with strategies predicated by legal responsibilities and statutory powers. Due to financial constraint, for example, the scope for preventative work under the Children Act 1990 is strictly limited in some local authorities (Smith, 1995). A consequent shortfall in services may over-ride the need to develop a community's service capability at a more natural pace. A negative reaction by the community could create a crisis for the employer agency, and so there will be expectations that the worker will exercise the maximum amount of personal influence to ensure co-operation. Full and frank discussion may be a solution, but the employer will only be satisfied with one outcome. Failure to share this information could come home to haunt the worker later on.

Much of the work which has to be done with the community is not fraught with significance, personal emotion or confidentiality. It is concerned with the creation of a skills pool within the community, vested in the individuals, which can enable the community organisation to carry out its work with confidence. The individuals need to develop the skills of self-management, team membership, information management, decision-making and planning. There will be issues of continuity, replacement and the evolution of leadership. The worker will strive to create within the organisation a system of mutual support and development so that the professional role can be withdrawn to a distance where a detached, monitoring over-view of needs can be established. This work must start immediately the worker is in place and as an embryonic organisation begins to take shape. It is rooted in personal relationships and the quality of the worker's understanding of the local culture. How would the local people prefer to go about change and what are their expectations? Their motivation must be nurtured as they gain interest and skills.

We have shown in these two chapters how the worker manages the evolution of a service into a community-driven activity. The handling of the human factor, its personalities and the complexities of culture within the community are as important as the more strategic considerations of planing organisational form and direction. Once the community is in a position to deliver this process, preferably maintaining a relationship with the worker, then it is possible to extend the role of the community-based organisation still further.

5 Social Planning and Development - I: Simple Organisations

The emergence of a community organisation as a stable and formal mechanism creates the public expectation that it will continue to provide a range of identifiable services on a permanent and institutional basis. The organisation will adapt to this, and it may devote some resources to enhance or protect its image as a service provider. In addition to public perception, its corporate self-image will also become a factor in its outlook towards maintaining service stability. This localised and narrow form of public activity may absorb the organisation's energies completely for some time. Eventually, however, it will learn that it is also capable of making an impact more generally. At first, it will come to realise that its presence is having an effect beyond its service field, on the wider social and welfare structure of the community. Success and continuity will bring public recognition which will be reflected in the amount of influence accorded to the organisation's leadership on matters of more general concern. These changes may not be immediately apparent, but once recognition grows, the effects will begin to be felt throughout the organisation. Will these effects be damaging or beneficial? How does the organisation work this out? Should special provision be made in its structure and style to accommodate it, such as a public relations effort?

Of equal significance, it will discover that its new stature creates development opportunities outside its own community. It discovers that its services are in demand beyond the limits which it originally set for itself, such as geographical area or target population. Once it is providing a stable service within its original remit, it will have to choose whether or not to extend the nature and/or the scope of its services and activities. Some organisations go for growth in their own field, others diversify into new fields as they gain confidence and expertise that is transferable into pastures new. This development has immediate effects on other organisations which are providing services. It also widens the public awareness and the pool of people who become beneficiaries of this extended role. For the organisation, there are questions to be confronted.

116

How will growth be managed? Is the present administrative structure best suited to the changes? Do new opportunities affect the relationship which the organisation has with its community of origin? What internal processes need to be adapted in order to ensure that change does not wreck the whole enterprise?

The politics of maturity

With, or without growth of this kind, the organisation's stable presence in the welfare network will have already made an impact locally, and beyond the original community. By demonstrating its own viability, the organisation has taken the first steps to develop a role which could enable it to influence events and affairs across a broad front, well beyond the confines of home. This role takes on an overtly political character. In the chapter below, we wish to emphasise the duality of role which an organisation fulfils - the service role and the political role. We feel that the latter aspect, which is a natural consequence of development, is often ignored in the textbooks. This is a serious omission as far as the development worker is concerned. Growth in the service sector will require the development and mobilisation of particular kinds of expertise and resources. Likewise, the development of a political role will require new energies, skills and strategic thinking. All service development will carry with it a political dimension. All political decisions will have implications for the development process. Not all organisations will wish to develop this way but there can be great rewards for those that are successful. There are also consequences for not being aware of the significance of this political component of the social welfare world.

There are, potentially, at least three dimensions to this new and complex role:

♦ service work in the community, plus - combining with other local networks to maximise the welfare and/or social impact of community resources (local services and community planning);
♦ service work within and outside the community, plus - liaison and co-operation with other organisations, to assert political influence over the shape of development within the community (general services and social planning) ; and
♦ combining with other organisations, across a broader political front, to influence the allocation of resources at a greater societal or national level (lobbying and socio-economic planning).

117

The organisation may come to be judged by its success in dealing with the demands of the new roles that emerge. It will be a test of its maturity whether or not it accepts each fresh level of responsibility, but only after rational planning and deliberation. Instant success can be a heady but capricious experience. At home, it is of great significance to the dependant, community population that the organisation maintains its original interest in local service. It will be judged there, too. How much significance is accorded to this local activity once the process of growth beyond the community begins, remains to be seen. It is to everybody's benefit that the organisation gains in strength and influence. Confidence, expertise and a broader outlook will all lead to an enhanced service potential, but some of the original qualities may have to change, or become lost altogether. Success of this kind will act as a role model for other, similar organisations. The political significance of a competent player will enhance the reputation of the whole community with the outside world. Such developments may, eventually, add considerably to the resource potential of the wider community and it will bring structural demands on the organisation itself. Failure, meanwhile, can have devastating effects on the resource and service base of the community.

If the organisation responds to all these new challenges, then it will become an agent for change and a participant in policies which affect a far wider constituency than its own. Relationships with the area of origin will be re-shaped as the effects of a wider role exert their influence. They will take on a strategic perspective as well as being part of its organic nature. There may be purely pragmatic reasons for pushing out the boundaries of influence. For example, meeting its local financial needs may rest on its ability to command respect and exert influence in a wider arena. Its own agenda and capabilities will receive formal, and informal, scrutiny as it takes part in liaison and joint activities with other organisations. Contacts made outside of its natural area of interest, may require more investment in time and resources than is anticipated. The calculations needed for survival become increasingly complex as the organisation becomes a part of networks and alliances.

The interests and priorities of the participating organisations within these structures will vary from each other. They will compete amongst themselves and they may seek to compete with other networks and structures beyond their own interest boundaries. The stakes are high, both for the politically aware activists in this larger system, and for the others, who may be left out of vital decision-making processes as a consequence of their non-participation. In many respects, and particularly in an emergent world of the 'contract culture', there is no place for non-participation. In times of change, actual, or contrived innocence will leave the unwary at the mercy of the forces at work within the *politics of welfare*. Decisions have to be made and strategies planned that reflect the conditions of survival in the real world.

There will be competing emphases in this process:

♦ whether to follow a purely political agenda and to achieve political influence for its own sake, using it as a lever for operational goals, or
♦ whether to continue in a developmental direction, consolidating and re-orienting collective activity in accordance with some grander design or strategy, and developing a power base out of operational achievement itself?

Recognising that there is a distinction to be made on these issues, requires skill, as does reading the motives of others taking part. It also requires that the representatives of the organisation fully understand their own priorities, and remain committed to them in all their activities within these wider networks. Participation at this level is intensely political and many organisations may shy away from it once the implications become clear. Members of the community organisation, concerned mainly with their own local agenda, may find that they are confused and repelled by this new, and possibly corrupting influence. In the beginning, they may venture into a wider network, drawn by curiosity or operational reasons born of their own activity. Once they get actively involved, or even if they do not take up an aggressive position, they will, nevertheless, become players in the competitive search for resources, influence and status. Consequently, unless they can establish a presence and command some respect, they may find that their own position is being undermined by competing interests from other quarters. They may even try to share their own expertise and resources and be rebuffed for their pains (Zald, 1975), or they may discover that they are unwittingly exploited. These are some of the unexpected consequences of successful development for an organisation. They are the consequences of the scale of operation, the need to survive and ambition to achieve success. They arise out of the real, or perceived, threat that this presents to other organisations, the personalities within their leadership, and the ties and connections that they have built up.

In this way, development beyond the home base poses dilemmas, risks and conflicts for the organisation, and for the individuals within it. Relationships with its own locality become just one dimension of its mature state. For some time, these may remain unchanged but, as pressures from the outside intrude, they will gradually assume new qualities. Coping with these changes, and distinguishing the varying needs of each, will become another component of the management's responsibility. Dunham describes how this complex process could become an organically coherent progress for a thriving organisation (Dunham, 1958), but reality for a newly emergent organisation is likely to be less ideal. Survival, consolidation and strategic development at each level may take a considerable time and the dedicated pursuit of very ambitious goals. An example of how a strongly held ideal or a compelling social need can give rise to the development of a powerful, international Non-Governmental Organisation is given by the example of the Oxfam, Intermediate Technology or Greenpeace organisations of this world. The continuum of organisational development stretches all this way from the local community to the lobby corridors of the United Nations.

An organisation such as 'Save the Children Fund' (SCF) embraces local, national and international dimensions in its work, each requiring different operational processes and policies within one overall framework. Various writers point out how serious conflicts of interest can develop and how there may be forces which lead to those at the bottom of the hierarchy losing out in the process (Midgley, 1987; Nkukila, 1987; Salole, 1991). For our local organisation, the scale, status and scope of the SCF may be some distance away. Nevertheless, we are taking a positive view of the continuum of development. The essential components in this rise to prominence are vision, determination and a sense of realism. It is possible that the exceptional, local organisation can aspire to, and achieve, many of the accomplishments to which we have referred. It may encounter considerable conflicts of interest as it equips itself to deal with the drive for growth and success. It will require cool and, sometimes, calculated decisions to resolve them. It may have the necessary luck to discover that it has leadership of an exceptional quality, which will steer it through this maze.

The position of the worker

The role of a professional development worker is of crucial importance in this process and can make a unique contribution to its success. Many small organisations are blissfully unaware of the scope of the potential which they possess. Some professionals may seek to preserve this situation, for reasons of their own, or for reasons to do with their relations with their employers. Whatever decisions may be taken in this regard, there can be no excuse for the worker being unaware of the consequences of action, or inaction (Midgley, 1981). Our model requires that we advance through successive dimensions of development, and it is incumbent on the professional to make the necessary personal preparations and to be up to the task. The continuing challenge for the worker is to gain access and influence within the organisation at every stage in the process and to ensure that the professional perspective gets across at each level of decision making. It is essential to the organisation that it obtains competent, expert advice and support throughout the expansion and development of its role in the wider community.

Employer influence   On another plane, and with a different agenda, there is an obligation to extend the intelligence of the worker's employer, the sponsoring agency. Expansion and change of role of the local organisation will affect the plans and expectations of this agency, also. There has been a large investment in ensuring that there will be an on-going service structure in the targeted community. The agency would not like to find that this growth in the local organisation's autonomy acts to prejudice the whole purpose of the development initiative. The agency had hoped to displace the dependency of the community on its own services onto the services of the community organisation. Its on-going contribution to sharing the responsibility is to continue to deploy the development worker for the benefit of the organisation, and to support it through the transition to autonomy. The worker's role at this stage in the development process will be very influential and, as the worker has a deeply rooted relationship in both organisations, both can, and will, choose to exploit it to the full. The skill of the worker will be to ensure that the best professional considerations determine the nature of the role that emerges.

Within the complex of welfare-political organisations, of which the agency is an established player, the emergence of a newcomer is an important event. Potentially, the new organisation can go its own way, using its recent developmental experience as a stepping stone to greater, and different things. The agency has a developmental and a political interest in its progress. Conversely, the agency must monitor any organisation which might come to rival or usurp its own function, challenge its role or show up its methods. More players in the field can be an asset or a threat. There is already a relationship and a great deal of shared information about each other. It is likely there will be expectations on both sides that there should be some sort of alliance between them in the quest for improved services. The worker's employment depends on correctly interpreting this aspect of the changing inter-organisational scene. The organisation's development should be monitored, from as closely as possible, in terms which are relevant to the agency's domestic and strategic needs. The creation of strategic plans by the organisation, which are at variance with the long-term plans of the sponsoring agency, will be perceived as a direct threat. Early intelligence of this development will be required from the worker. The ethical dilemmas are obvious. Within the agency, individuals will also require the worker to keep them informed of the capabilities and potential of individuals within the organisation. These are factors which are significant in the structure of the local political culture which surrounds the co-existence of agencies. The politics of small networks in smaller towns are more sensitive to changes than those found in metropolitan centres.

In addition to the requirement to supply intelligence on the organisation, there will be pressure from the employer agency for the worker to limit or shape the relationship or the extent of the commitment. There is a strong possibility here of a clash between the ethics of professional practice, the personal priorities of the worker and the contractual relationship between the worker and the agency. These pressures have to be weighed by the worker, who must make a personal decision. Does the nature of the relationship with the organisation out-weigh the obligation of the worker to be a dutiful employee? Confidentiality is already under pressure due to the nature of the original purpose of the worker's intervention - to serve the agency's greater needs and to supply a surrogate. The worker now has more irons in the fire and there is more than one strategic interest in the field. The worker has an investment in both, and will have an opinion on what might be the 'best interests' of both, as seen from the grassroots. The worker may consider that a view from the grassroots should carry more influence than it is accorded by the employer:

> The planner may be in the precarious position of having to weigh professional goals and criteria of good social planning against the interests of his would be 'bosses' - existing agencies and supervisors seeking to maintain themselves at all costs; business, civic or political leaders trying to propel their vested interests; citizens' groups espousing 'participation' while eyeing fuller pocketbooks (Meyer Schwartz, 1956, cited in Rothman, 1974, p. 5.)

In the final analysis, the worker will dutifully follow instructions, although there are examples of workers being able to shield their actual activities from their employer for some considerable time. Perhaps these tales are apocryphal. Whatever the outcome of this test of power, the worker should strive to the end to sustain an independent professional perspective on this issue. There may be a fundamental clash of values with the employer, or field level choices and working conditions may simply require changes in institutional thinking or policy. This is a phenomenon highlighted by Midgley, in relation to policies of the state (Midgley, 1987). Where the organisation, or the worker, believes that institutional power is being misdirected by the employer, efforts must be made to clarify the options and define the best choices which are available. Where necessary, a way must be found around a restrictive policy. These dilemmas arise out of the tension generated by the emergence of the organisation as an autonomous body. There are significant questions concerning professional autonomy bound up in this process. A professional may need to have firm guidelines established around a good practice model to defend a hapless community organisation from manipulation (Brager & Specht, 1973).

It may that at this point continued employment by the agency may be impossible for the professional worker. The organisation has now attained a scale of operation and scope of vision which entail ownership of considerable assets: enough to require the employment of development workers of its own. Does our professional, externally employed, now seek employment with the creation that has emerged from the community? What if the organisation employs its own staff who assume a related, but distinctively different role with the organisation than that of our original community developer? A less sophisticated and less politically aware servant might certainly be cheaper, as well as safer!

The basic need for a community development worker is to be 'fire-proofed' against undue pressure, either from within an organisation which is being 'developed', or from without (from financial masters or political scrutineers). Clarke demonstrates how this vulnerability can cause great upsets (Clarke, 1999 - Forthcoming; Porter, et.al., 1991). We shall continue our analysis leaving the professional as an 'external agent' to the organisation, but alternative possibilities and influences on this scenario must be anticipated.

It is the absence of a professional body capable of defending a community development worker when political or employee pressure becomes intense, that highlights the tragedy that befell social work when community development professionals withdrew from BASW in 1972 (see above Chapter 3). Despite the maverick and individualist nature of many community development workers, their political awareness could have provided BASW with much needed collective determination.

Political acumen   The community organisation has become a political entity within its own neighbourhood, area of interest, and beyond. It may, or may not be aware of the implications of this change in profile. It will now have made contacts within networks of influence, both those associated with activities related to its own, but also with individuals with influence on a broader canvas. Personalities within our organisation may revel in the opportunity. They may be sought out, consulted, and included in activities beyond their past experience. The individuals from our organisation are being targeted. Their emergence as part of a formal structure marks them out as potential factors in the strategic thinking of people in other organisations and networks. The local organisation needs to be aware of this process and also it needs to consider what are its own strategic needs, and how it advances them. The individuals from our organisation will also become aware that their personal needs and ambitions, such as political influence, business interests and social status, might well be enhanced if the opportunity is utilised appropriately. All, or some of these pressures will begin to make their mark. It must be realised that these outside personalities and organisations are under the same pressures, to a greater or lesser degree. It is part of the development process for the individuals within any organisation, and the organisation itself, to respond positively, to remain an active player, whatever the direction of that response. To remain passive leaves the initiative in the hands of others.

What is the function and nature of the professional relationship in this process? We have suggested that it is necessary, prudent, politically astute and even personally beneficial for the worker to ensure that the professional relationship is sustained as the organisation grows and develops. In its simplest form, the professional relationship with an organisation, as it enters into a more mature interaction with an organisational network, will be an input of technical expertise. The worker becomes the technical advisor on protocols, how best to contact other organisations formally and informally so as to ensure a dignified and balanced reception. How will diplomatic procedures be handled, what is the currency of trade in the corridors of political negotiation? What does our organisation have to offer and how should it be packaged? Who are the powerful organisations and personages and what are the symbols of status in this community? Many textbooks ignore the politics of this process. They paint a picture of simplistic interactions, where networks of communication somehow appear as if by magic, where there are no trade-offs, no manoeuvring for political and status advantage within the circles of civic circumstance, and no personal ambitions (Dunham, 1958; Henderson

& Thomas, 1987; Leaper, 1968; Morris, 1970, Spergel, 1969; Twelvetrees; 1991).

The professional can, and should, be at the heart of initiatives to create social change, or in inter-group relations, with tactical advice and support. Swedner defines it as ' *a range of activities in which various persons and institutions in the community engage with the object of promoting social changes in the community..... '* (Swedner, 1982a p. 244). The process is one of building legitimacy for the organisation, and this involves an active political dimension (Trepan, 1972). Not all organisations have the capacity or the strategic position to exert the necessary influence. The knowledge and political awareness of the worker is a necessary ingredient in the process of steering the organisation through the ascending levels of complexity which it will encounter as it takes on a power play role in the community at large.

In Party-political matters, especially where the worker is employed directly by the local political structure, the professional cannot claim immunity on the grounds that, suddenly, the activities of the organisation have miraculously crossed the bounds of 'welfare' into the forbidden ground of 'politics'. Politics have been on the agenda since the very beginning.

Local politicians have a direct interest in what happens on 'their' patch. In their personal, or quasi-informal capacities, local politicians may have strong interests in the fortunes of an organisation. Political parties have a responsibility to be aware of, and become responsive to, the formation of social, welfare and/or economic groupings within their constituencies. It is of advantage to these Parties to be in possession of accurate intelligence about the state of local activities. Similarly, in their private lives, professional workers are often members of political parties. They may be put under pressure, whatever their political affiliation, if any, either to put political representatives in touch with key individuals within organisations or to supply intelligence personally.

There may be the desire, by the organisation, in the quest for status, resource-building or support in opposition to central policies which inhibit its work, to align itself with a political party. Politicians may seek to ingratiate themselves with high-status organisations for local political advantage. Personal and professional values may be severely tested under these pressures once these forces discover (rightly) that the professional wields considerable influence over the thinking and decision-making of the organisation.

It is a professional responsibility for the worker to be as up-to-date and knowledgeable about the political attitudes, policies and priorities of all political parties within the constituency. Failure to gather this information will lead a worker to enter strategic discussions with organisations without the necessary insight.

Professional learning The worker, as a n individual player, will want to maintain a position of influence within a dynamic and assertive organisation so that personal and professional interests can be sustained. Some of the worker's personal ambitions may be bound up in the 'success' of an aggressive protégé. This is a time for personal and professional learning, as well as extending the worker's own professional influence. Each level of activity which is attained by the organisation, each stage in the expansion of the participants' horizons, presents a fresh professional challenge to the worker.

The self-development of the community development worker is inextricably bound up in the fortunes of the organisations in which they work. Each successful transition in organisational status, every example of indecisiveness, every disaster, all patterns of choice and each calculation of marginal advantage are all practical lessons for the worker on which professional competence is extended. The worker can only weigh the options on the back of personal and collective experience. The future cannot be predicted beyond certain narrow limits: such is the uncertainty that surrounds the development 'consultant'. The 'benefits' of success or failure are to be best realised by the next client, rather than the current one. Today's client is the beneficiary of yesterday's lessons.

Planning as community development

We have re-cast the template to suit the demands that the organisation will make on the professional relationship. The focal point is now on a more potent mechanism than the small scale and community-sensitive organisation which emerged from the first stage of development. We are now dealing with a more sophisticated entity. It has a potential which greatly exceeds the purpose that may have been in the original plans of the sponsoring agency, and its progress and development will tax the resourcefulness of the professional far more than anything so far.

Those that are party to the process of monitoring its activity, and its position within the networks of the wider system, need to be aware of what is involved. We have described, above, some of the issues which have now to be addressed as major components of the working agenda. For the development worker, the vision is now an agenda with a much sterner task than the community-centric, service model. The relationship between the worker and the organisation will undergo still further changes, there will be more risks involved and many more conflicts of interest.   The new template looks like this:

ORGANISATION with the POTENTIAL for PLANNING	ORGANISATION as the FOCUS for STRATEGIC DEVELOPMENT	ORGANISATION as the COMPONENT of STRATEGY	COMPLEX ORGANISATION as the FOCUS for DEVELOPMENT	COMPLEX ORGANISATION as a STRATEGIC CENTRE	INDIVIDUAL as the TARGET for COLLABORATION

Organisation with the potential for planning

Given the pressures and conditions which we have examined above concerning the politics of social action, the worker's next task is to prepare the organisation for choices about its future.   The quality of the professional relationship will now undergo a profound change, both in terms of the approach to the various tasks which the worker does for the organisation, but also in terms of the form which the relationship takes. The worker will now come to take up a role which must be perceived as being definitely *outside and alongside* the organisation. In earlier forms of the relationship, it may have been easy to blur some of the distinctions, such as: was the worker 'in charge' of the action, working as part of the team, etc.?

From now on, the worker takes on the role of the consultant and the professional approach to 'development' will now be based upon a more visible and equal partnership than before. All vestiges of patronage have to be eliminated. The unity of seeking common goals, and together following an exploratory path to develop service excellence, will be left behind. The relationship must be re-negotiated, and placed upon a more overtly contractual footing.   In the future, the worker will take on the role of 'external advisor'. There must be no grounds for the accusation that the worker is merely loading the guns for action, waiting for the organisation to fire them, thereafter abandoning it to take the consequences on its own. At this stage in the development process, the organisation will become unequivocally clear that it has now to generate and follow its own agenda, and that it must establish fresh relationships with other organisations (including the original sponsoring agency).

The organisation will now be prepared to ask itself the question: is it willing to consider profound change in most aspects of its existence as the way forward?   To answer this, it must be prepared to consider the following: What position would it like to fill in the greater world of welfare and social action? What are its ambitions, and those of its leadership? Does it want to become an influential participant, or even a dominant influence? Does the potential exist, as things stand, for a major transformation from a local service delivery organisation, into a major player within the social action environment? If not, what needs to be done in order to prepare the necessary conditions?

Some of the available choices may flow as a natural progression from earlier success. The worker must strive to present the organisation with a realistic appraisal of its full potential - as a working organisation *per se*, and within the broader context in which it works. What possibilities for change present themselves within the existing framework? Does the organisation have the potential as a power player on a political level? What strategic opportunities present themselves and what change have to be made in order to pursue them? Some of these possibilities can be projected from its current achievements and structure. Others will be developed once the range of choices has been made clear and which of them the organisation selects for consideration. Concrete suggestions for change can follow, but a systematic profile of the organisation is required before any irreversible decisions are made. In the end, it is the organisation which must take the decision, and take up the challenges which follow.

There is nothing new for the worker in all this. It has been on the agenda since the first ideas for a new service organisation began to evolve. The search for suitable people to take a lead in this process began at the same time, not just for starting the simple organisation, but as the future leaders of a far larger entity. This plan has been continuing to evolve ever since that time, each developmental stage being consolidated and projected forwards as it came to fruition. The worker has taken stock of the potential, checked for the appropriate array of structural and personal qualities, and prepared the ground for their adaptation to the needs of the next stage. This is a cumulative process. Each stage is adapted from the successes and weaknesses of the preceding one. It is an intensive and exacting process which requires great awareness, sensitivity and subtly by the worker. Not every organisation will be capable of making the transition. Some will be insistent they can. Others will be reluctant to try. The worker will be making a running appraisal of the potential of the organisation at every stage in its development. This not a publicised activity. There can be no certainty that it will proceed any further than the present.

The foibles of personality or the realities of skill, opportunity and even politics may obscure or obstruct the path. The worker is left with the role of preparing, steering and manipulating the potential as it takes shape. It is an endurance test as well as an opportunist one. The professional advice and influence which may reshape or fix an organisation's role and ambitions must be offered and exercised with great care and with full possession of as much of the relevant information as is possible. Once the decision has been made to move forward, the worker must be in a position to remain in full support of the organisation, at least until it has been able to consolidate its new role.

Although there can be no firm predictions of the environmental conditions which may confront an organisation as it reaches this stage of maturity, the worker must try and equip it with the necessary resources and abilities before it steps out beyond the relative security of its community of origin.. It is for this event that the worker has modified the data and adapted the analysis.' It can now be reassembled for the day when the organisation is preparing to be launched into the more competitive world. This is the form that long-term investment in social development must take. It is one element in the social planning process which is focused entirely on the internal needs of the organisation, and not on the social aspects of change. The worker attempts to establish a firm base of information and clarity of thinking before any further steps are taken along the route to expansion.

Consultancy

The main aim of this form consultancy is to assist the organisation to plan each step in its development, backed with sufficient information for rational decisions, and equipped with the appropriate systems for delivering the changes that are decided. Consultancy is concerned with a qualitatively different form of relationship than the very supportive role which was carried during the early developmental phase. Very often, consultants are 'experts', drafted in to provide a 'quick fix', or and external perspective (Conyers, 1982). The difference is, in this situation, that the worker may well be fully versed in the ways of the local culture, the socio-political system and have insight into the personalities involved. This new form of relationship will take on four distinct components:

♦ preparation for growth and development (includes intensive support for the leadership at the threshold of decision-making for change);
♦ adoption of a 'consultant/client' relationship (technical support during organisational change and consolidation);
♦ provision of strategic advice on relations with other organisations and technical servicing to assist this process;
♦ establishment of new framework for professional in-put appropriate to a mature organisational role.

As the organisation moves for the first time beyond its original local, and reasonably confined boundaries, it may have difficulty in adapting to a new form of relationship with the development worker. The consultancy relationship will have to be introduced at an appropriate point, and in a manner that the organisation can absorb. It has to be accepted on a practical level as well as on an intellectual basis. Various significant decisions have to be made and it is better that the basis of trust that exists between the worker and the organisation is not prematurely disrupted, especially if the outcome of the process is a decision not to proceed any further along the development continuum. For this reason, the process of adjusting the relationship will be delayed until all concerned are convinced that consultancy is the appropriate form for the relationship to take and that the future role of the organisation is prepared for the shift.

Preparation for growth and development The component elements of this stage are:

♦ the preparation of suitable information on which decisions can be taken; and
♦ positioning the organisation for the decision-making process.

The role of the worker is still within the mould of 'enabler', but this stage marks the transition from an almost organic association with most, if not all, its workings, to a more clearly defined, contractual partnership. This phase has to be handled with great skill, and without compromise if the crossover to consultant is to be successful. The form in which these activities and services are carried out and the way in which their outcomes are designed to exclude, rather than be seen as being inclusive of, the worker, will create the pattern for the future. This phase will be used to mark out the new boundaries for the relationship, even if they are not formally spelled out until some later opportunity.

Information The worker has to create a compendium of information which will provide the framework for the next level of professional intervention and arm the organisation for its next steps forward. The worker already possesses much of what is necessary, but the analysis and preparation of an intelligible consultancy report on the organisation must be considered as a discrete task. The focused application of the worker on this report will ensure that the most appropriate and contemporary data is incorporated. It is likely that there will be an immediate need for the organisation to formulate new policies. There may be the need to effect constitutional changes and the agreement of a wider constituency, beyond the intimate circle of the leadership.

This comprises the following:

♦ assessment of the current service capability and its future potential and survival on an autonomous basis;
♦ appraisal of the leadership strengths and human resource needs;
♦ assessment of the mechanisms for processing and digesting information, the abstraction of ideas, capacity for understanding organisational dynamics, and the planning of detailed action programmes;
♦ consideration of the appropriateness of the organisational structure, the competence of management and control functions, and the adequacy of the administrative processes for the current and any future role;
♦ estimation of the material resource needs over a projected development programme, across a range of objectives and growth patterns;
♦ analysis of the relevant network patterns of the welfare and politico-welfare environment and the organisation's place within them;
♦ preparation of opportunity openings for a range of initiatives;
♦ provision of a critique of the public image and public relations needs.

The completion of this process will provide essential intelligence on the strengths, weaknesses, threats and opportunities facing the organisation. Being in possession of significant information is of immense political importance as it provides opportunities for direct, and indirect, influence. No other agent has the strategic opportunity to make this analysis, and to use it. Gaining access to all dimensions of the organisation in order to make the analysis is dependent on the quality of the professional relationship which has been developed up to this stage. Ownership of such privileged information cannot be treated lightly. There is every likelihood that the key personnel in the organisation will not realise the significance of this kind of insight until they discover that their organisation is set to embark on a major step along the road of development. The 'outside' ownership of such information creates vulnerability. It may be that it is only when the organisation's leadership discover the political significance of their prominence in the service sector, that they will also discover that they have unwittingly allowed unfettered access to their organisational secrets to the development worker. This worker is in the paid employ of an agency which is a direct, or potential rival of their own!

The worker will also be known as one who has active membership of many networks, and who has linkages with other players in the politico-welfare sector. Realisation may have dawned some time earlier in the process, and so the worker will have to exercise considerable tact if this stage in the developmental task is to be fulfilled. It is the ultimate test of the trust that has been established whether the organisation continues to allow unrestricted access and discussion of the closest secrets after the development dependency relationship is finally broken and the 'consultancy' phase begins. The organisation will begin to consider how many other organisations offer the worker the same sort of access and how this knowledge may be used in dealings across the entire welfare network. Much will depend on the general demeanour of the worker. Loose tongues lose contacts!

The worker is aware of these factors and yet there is little that can be done in advance to dilute their impact. Things may never be the same again, but they can also be managed sensitively and carefully. The worker is required to sustain the relationship, for personal, professional and employment reasons. It is crucial, at the very least, until the organisation has been able to decide for itself whether or not it possesses the necessary strengths and potential to move ahead beyond its current role. For the organisation to attempt an analysis and planning exercise without the advantage of professional advice and support would be wasteful of the expertise that is there for exploitation. As we shall see below, the stakes for both parties are very high.

Positioning The worker's task is to seek a formal opportunity to share the consultancy analysis with the organisation. It will become a watershed for the professional/client relationship. Careful preparatory work with the organisation's leadership will be needed to prepare them, firstly, for the presentation itself, and, secondly, for the range of changes in their organisation's role which they may have to consider. Each member of the leadership will have a personal investment in its future. The compilation and presentation of such a concentrated digest of information, combined with strategic opportunities may constitute a direct threat to some of them. They may have their own plans, for themselves, and for the future of the organisation. There may be internal political factions which have yet to crystallise. The introduction of a detailed profile may appear to undermine their position or precipitate an internal crisis. Some may be de-skilled by the seeming enormity of the task ahead or they may feel that there is an implied criticism in any shortfalls in coverage that are revealed. Others may be overwhelmed by the complexity of the information which they have received.

As part of the consultancy process, the worker should aim at developing, within the organisation, a mechanism for dealing with the impact of this information. It may be appropriate to suggest, and then to assist in the formation of, a special project group, through which the acceptance and digestion of the contents can be mediated. This group can consider the implications systematically and prepare responses and development choices in more detail. Through this process, the organisation can prepare itself for the decisions that may have to be taken. This mechanism can be used at later critical stages in the organisation's growth and it will reinforce the need for team activities at the top levels of management.

There will already have been an adjustment in the behaviour of the key personnel, once it had been decided to sustain a regular service system within their community of origin. These same people may have different responses to the idea of taking on wider responsibilities. It is likely, that the original decisions to formalise the service entailed the stabilisation of funding and resource planning, such that the organisation became an employer of service, administrative and management staff. Lay membership of the organisation becomes moved more into the wings; management responsibility at the one end, and participation-through-service at the other. Extending the service component still further will make the role of any non-paid personnel dependant upon and subject to the increasing influence of this paid cadre. Not all will want to go down this route and abandon direct control over the service programme. They will recognise that the paths of voluntary service to the community and the rigors of commercial and business practice cross at this point. Should the organisation decide to diversify further across the service front, then there can be no avoiding the structural implications, and the need to place the organisation onto a proper business footing.

The leadership has to be assisted to make the necessary decisions. If it moves ahead for change, then it has to be assisted to prepare itself for the operational changes that will be required of the leadership itself. How will it ensure that it can cope with delegation of control of many of the regular functions to paid staff. The leadership may have made a direct contribution to operational control in the past, and it may be uneasy about moving out of the executive chair and becoming a 'board member', only. How is the 'new' consultancy to be used? This will now replace the 'enabling' developer which had journeyed with them so far, and there will be anxieties about the transition, or even the necessity for any changes to take place. Will any new service staff be seen as surrogate development professionals, and

133

might rivalry emerge between these roles as each works to assume a position for themselves?

Technical advisor In the past, the organisation may have adjusted to the need to accept advice and support from the professional on matters which were linked directly to their own abilities, functioning capacity and orientation towards service to the community. The consultancy task is to change the participant's perceptions of what they are doing, and why.

From the personal and subjectively held feelings of the connection between themselves and the objectives which they sought through the formation of the organisation, the worker has to re-orient them towards the consolidation of this role into a depersonalised and publicly accountable institution. The acceptance of wider responsibilities will have their effects on the original service functions and the relationship with the original client group. Broader horizons, larger scale operations and the rationalisation of resources and policies regarding the stability and scope of the service function will all have their effect. Moving off the home turf will bring a narrower formality to the relationship between the providers and the beneficiaries of services.

If the image of the locally-sprung organisation has not changed before this, it will have to do so now. A business ethos will have to be adopted. 'Contracting for Care' will entail the substitution of a 'not-for-profit' philosophy for the 'voluntary' ethos of the original service idea. This will come to apply to all beneficiaries, and not just those from newly colonised areas or populations. There will now be a premium placed upon the formalisation of decision-making processes, communication systems, resource planning, and even more control over proper practice expectations, organisational image and resource expenditure.

The organisation has now assumed the scale, trappings and outlook of a community-owned business, with business-like methods and values. Boundaries will be drawn around the limits of permitted activities and the values of the organisation will be subject to a greater public scrutiny. There will be the danger of defections and rifts within the organisation. Preparation for these eventualities forms a part of the consultancy.

Organisations as the focus for strategic development

The move to consultancy   The organisation has been prepared and positioned for the changes that it needs to make. Possession of the information and the identification of the decisions which have to be made will highlight the fact that the worker is not *of* the organisation on the same

134

conditions which began their relationship. Making explicit some of the support and resource functions which can now be better offered to an autonomous organisation, and the basis on which they will be offered, is best done just before the organisation begins to fulfil its potential as an empowered entity. To delay it would entail confusion and false expectations, probably from both sides. The move must be accompanied and framed by some form of formal agreement. This is something which usually 'escapes' the attention of the worker at the early stages of a relationship. This is because the worker and the participants in the new organisation may find it difficult to discuss, freely, issues such as trust, ambition and conflicts of role. It is also due to the difficulty in explaining why a 'developer' is required at all. This agreement can describe the rights and duties of both parties - such as the duty to preserve confidentiality, the amount of time and the nature of the processes in which the professional will get involved (e.g. policy development).

This transition will not come easily, despite the seeming logic of the need for it. The quality of the worker's previous relationship is put to the test as the nature and extent of these changes become apparent. There is no possibility that the worker can assist in the implementation of any ensuing policies, save through the circumscribed role of consultant. The responsibility for putting them into operation them is the responsibility of the organisation, alone. Certain 'development' roles will have to be allocated internally. Some will be delegated completely to the hired agents of the organisation, itself. Lay managers will have to take responsibility for 'good housekeeping' - observance of the constitutional framework, public accountability, financial probity, etc. It is likely that the worker would have sustained some form of anxious interest in these matters while the organisation was in the formation stage. The management and the staff will have to be made fully aware that a form of protection for their own positions has been removed.

Strategic objectives   In future, the professional approach towards enablement takes on a different form. Members of the organisation will experience the worker differently and they may feel that they have lost something special in the process. Instead of the close and supportive relationship which may have gone before, the worker is now on a mission to become the technical advisor to the leadership, a facilitator for decision-making processes and a contributor to the pool of expertise. The worker can negotiate a working agenda with the organisation by considering its strategic objectives. These objectives will be found both in the internal mechanisms and processes, as in the organisation's relations with the outside world.

The consultancy task is to demonstrate how the organisation takes the necessary decisions, sets up the appropriate systems for delivering them, monitors progress of all processes and handles crises. Some of the messages may be stern and hard for the organisation to handle. The organisation is now in the big-time, and survival is going to mean dealing with harsh realities in a competitive world. Effective communication systems, the co-ordination of effort and the avoidance of duplication and wastage all require focused attention and concerted action throughout the organisation. The workers task is to advise that these processes are necessary, and then to assist it in establishing them. There is no presumption that a single worker can become skilled in each and every one of these important and technical functions. It is very important, however, that the worker recognises that these aspects of organisational development exist. They will require attention and professional assistance will facilitate the right decisions being taken, and the necessary processes being introduced. Knowledge of where these skills can be obtained, and how best the organisation can avail itself of them, is of considerable benefit to the whole development process. Once the re-structuring is complete, the worker can step back and assist in the evaluation process.

Work objectives The decisions to widen the scope of activity will now have to be placed within a context bounded by specific goals, time constraints, resource needs, and management considerations. What opportunities present themselves? Which expansion moves are to be taken, and in what order? The organisation will probably expand along lines that it can most easily accommodate within its own pool of expertise and experience. Activities similar to its original brief will be undertaken elsewhere and a fresh repertoire will be acquired only gradually. Are there new activities involved and will new skills be required to achieve these goals? The planning of resource needs and creation of the mechanisms for ensuring that they are to hand when needed, is essential. They will be considered in a systematic way and the whole organisation must be satisfied that there is a rational and feasible programme ahead. Human resources will have to be recruited and trained, material resources obtained, and flows and throughputs calculated.

Staffing objectives Preparation of the paid staff for their role as operational managers is another task for the development professional. The interrelated functions of management, administration and service activity must be programmed into the operational culture of the staff. Team functioning, mutual reliance, corporate identity and morale-boosting mechanisms must become built into the structure. Understanding the complexities of managing over a wider scale of operations, planning and logistics, handling public relations and the image of the organisation, quality assurance and control procedures: these are many of the aspects of good practice which extend beyond the basic provision of a service, but without which the whole programme will fail to achieve its objectives.

There will be an interesting shift of emphasis in the culture of lead service organisers and administrators which will become evident as this activity becomes fully operational. As the staff of the organisation assume more and more of the day-to-day responsibilities, the more sophisticated and skilled they become, they will begin to discover that they relate most easily to an alternative reference point outside the organisation. They will begin to associate with, and relate to, other service-providers, in other organisations. These may well become a reference group for the exchange of professional advice and support. The further that this process develops, the more difficult it is going to be for the internal management to retain control over the practice and value priorities of their service organisation. The paid staff will assume the day-to-day responsibilities for the services, they will determine the methods employed for achieving their objectives and they will record and report their achievements. Lay management will become dependant on them for insight and progress reports. As consultant, the worker will need to establish a firm frame of reference in dealing with any conflicts between these factions. One difficulty for our consultant is that this role was once that of 'midwife' and now there are going to be personal as well as professional preferences on the consultancy agenda. Objectivity will be even more difficult to sustain in these circumstances.

Management objectives The quality of management of any enterprise is the key to its survival. The objectives of development are sustainable and incremental progress towards pre-defined goals. Without quality management, control will be lacking, lessons from experience will be lost and clarity of vision will become blurred. In the end, it is all down to management, and the development worker must be equipped to provide the necessary support.

The following areas form the framework for the consultancy input to management:

♦ organisational structure;

- communications; process control;
- financial stability;
- effective decision-making;
- planning, policy review and performance evaluation;
- establishment of sustainable and competent management team;
- accessible administrative systems;
- effective management/staff relationships.

The organisation may have begun its life as a service operation within a small community but its new persona will transform its processes into those of the corporate enterprise. These will require all the checks and balances and all the protocols and formalities which an efficient and successful business would need. From the outset, it will need to demonstrate it vitality by competing with a wide variety of organisations in the 'mixed economy of welfare'. The degree to which the consultant can prepare the organisation for the dynamics of this stern reality, the better. In time, this organisation may wish to transform itself into another form of corporate entity. Management structures should be adequate for any eventuality.

Considering the future   The aim of this phase is the establishment of a fresh and expanded pattern of service activity in the wider community. This will also include attention to the impact that the organisation makes on an socio-economic and political level, but, in the early stages of consolidation, these are not the main priorities to be addressed. The professional has assisted in the setting of the scale and direction of the work, but the responsibility for the implementation of these strategies rests firmly within the organisation. The worker should ensure that there is no ambiguity on this point. Recriminations and soured relationships, born of misunderstandings, must be avoided.

Of immediate concern, is the mobilisation of the organisation's resources, so that they can most effectively respond to the demands of the new role . It may be that the entire internal structure has to be modified, or restructured. This will entail exposing staff and other participants to uncertainty, potential risk and the necessity of adopting fresh methods of relating to the organisation, and to each other. Decisions about how this is to be accomplished will be taken by the responsible management, but the professional consultant will ensure that the best advice is available to them. Resources may be needed to assist management gather contributions from whole organisation.

They will also have to cope with the strains that this process can inflict upon the established patterns of behaviour and the relations between participants. Any breakdown in this process can set back the organisation considerably, often permanently harming relations between personnel and management to the detriment of the whole enterprise. Those that have to deliver the service may justifiably feel that they are in the best position to judge how to effect the changes. This may reflect the best option. Conversely, they may be daunted by the possibility, or internal politics may dictate quite different directions.

Consultancy intervention at this point is very useful to all concerned. Issues can be presented and interactions managed so that views become clarified without irreparable breakdown in trust or relationships. It may be necessary to buy in skills, on a temporary or a permanent basis to assist with the transition. The worker my not possess all of the necessary skills that are required. Consultancy need not depend on the ability to supply all the skilled input from personal resources. A pool of competent and trustworthy experts needs to be sought out over a period of time. Their assistance can been enlisted at times like these, when they are most needed. The value of the consultant's contribution is in the control over the process of bringing expert support to bear on a critical issue.

Once the process of making the case for change has been completed; once the decisions have been taken for diversifying and expanding the role and of widening the collective responsibilities, it is necessary to take stock of the features of the wider environment. A detailed plan must be made of how the expansion strategy is to be implemented. It will be politically astute for new initiative to be accompanied by an image of competence and freshness, for the first impact to be successful and that any potential opposition from outside sources be rendered ineffective. The object is not only to establish that the move out of the old confines was the correct one, but that a positive reputation be established without delay. In this way critics can be silenced and the programme can be implemented within an atmosphere of security and calm.

Organisation as the component of strategy

The consolidation of the new regime has required planning in depth, but it can only be tested in practice. The source, scale and availability of resources will have been determined in advance, but the logistical demands of practice may call for revisions and adjustments. The use of monitoring and feedback data for maximising effectiveness must be integrated into the system. The recruitment and training of personnel for the new activities is stepped up and the lines of communication must be extended. Quality control and accountability systems must be implemented and tested. It will be important that information about the performance and success of any rival in the field be assessed. From the time of arrival and at the first point of intervention in a fresh field, the organisation should be ready to begin planning for the next stage in the development process.

In our model, we have now reached the stage where decisions to proceed can be taken. The action plan can be put in motion and all the planning put to the test. The organisation has successfully made the transition from a localised service activity into a fully-fledged service agency in its own right. It has consolidated itself in a competitive environment, created an image of newness and a reputation of competence. It has negotiated a new relationship with its development worker (still employed by the original sponsoring agency), and it may now begin to exude an air of authority and stability in all that it does. It will discover immediately that its work draws it into new and demanding activities and relationships, about which it may have little fore-knowledge or experience. The role of the consultant, and the scope for further development activity, is far from over.

We shall consider the worker's rationale for wishing to continue the relationship, and we shall explore the role required to gain the most from an on-going investment. Community development expertise, and the special relationship, can be utilised through the following initiatives:

♦ integration and stabilisation of identity;
♦ securing the present role and presence in the welfare complex;
♦ preparation of strategy for development;
♦ mobilisation of linkages.

Integration and stabilisation During times of adjustment to change and the expansion of horizons, the organisation will be unable to do much more than deliver the stable service for which it is contracted. In the short term, keeping the show on the road is sufficient, but, over a longer perspective, the early identification of significant trends and opportunities would be of the greatest value. There are unlikely to be any surplus resources which could be devoted to another detailed analysis of performance, but the development worker is in a good position to provide this service. The worker must strive to convince the leadership that they must not succumb to the strains of the expansion process and become preoccupied with the detail of service provision. They must allow the worker to bring the new structure and activity into focus within the broad context of the welfare economy that confronts them.

Systems The systems, through which communication, control and resource mobilisation are provided, need to be tested for effectiveness and suitability under the new regime. There are bound to be many instances where the old ideas, perceptions of scale and outlooks prevail. These may be partly, or completely, out of touch with the demands of the expanded service. The people in this situation may be experiencing confusion, frustration or disaffection from the whole activity. Fear of failure brings with it fear of humiliation, and this fear must be dispelled. If they are not assisted to stabilise their role and to deliver their skilled contribution with confidence and a rightful sense of belonging to the common enterprise, then the function they serve will be lost or disrupted. Their goodwill will be lost and a possible point of friction created to bedevil the organisation in the future. These systems have to be brought up to date and fully integrated into the structure. The people involved represent an investment which, despite their being out of touch for the time being, is too valuable to be dispensed with, even if replacements were available. The worker is well placed to monitor the functioning of systems, investigate any points of actual, or potential, breakdown in the service, and identify the pressure points. A timely intervention of this sort can suggest remedies early enough to prevent a crisis.

A primary development function is concerned with the management of finances and material resources. Assistance can be offered with the establishment of effective systems for the planning, acquisition, control and deployment of the resources needed for the effective running of the organisation. The worker is able, through a specialised knowledge of the wider service system, to assist those responsible for this function. This includes where to obtain the necessary information regarding the source of appropriate resources, reference guidelines for their control and the availability of training and expert support until an adequate level of competence is achieved. Awareness of the finer characteristics of financial matters is a valued, and politically useful, attribute for any professional, especially when operating at this level in the welfare economy. Anecdotal evidence suggests that, in the U.K. many community development workers are not fully equipped to meet this need. It is alleged that they *read 'The Guardian'*, whereas, in the USA, their counterparts read *the 'Wall Street Journal'*!

Standards Control of standards is an on-going concern to an organisation, particularly one which is undergoing rapid change and expansion. In the realm of social action and welfare, the costs and effects of bad practice are felt by the vulnerable. Detecting how and why this might come about is the

141

first step towards protecting them. The organisation may be placed under pressure to supply services beyond the level which its delivery systems can provide. Resourcing mechanisms may break down, personnel may be drafted into service without adequate training, or misunderstandings can occur where there is the very best of intention. Management, which is the responsible system, may neither be aware of shortfalls or breakdowns, nor be able to cope should standards begin to deteriorate. Professional intervention may be the only opportunity for a remedy before 'custom and practice' take over, and malpractice becomes 'established practice' forever. The institutionalisation of failure on this issue will make victims out of the supposed beneficiaries of the service. Ultimately, this will backfire on the organisation itself. The professional should anticipate the need for this role, and have a good idea about indicators which can be monitored for signs of deteriorating standards. Presenting a framework for this process assists the organisation in establishing its own monitoring and evaluation system.

Today, most welfare service organisations have adopted statements of policy on good practice, for the elimination of discrimination in their employment procedures and for their relations with service beneficiaries and society generally. But procedures for testing the capacity and the will to uphold these ideals can easily be relegated to the background unless they become organically linked to all functioning processes. The development and adoption of a 'house' model for this purpose is especially recommended (Barnardos, 1990), and the services of a professional in steering the organisation towards this outcome can prove to be the decisive factor. It is an activity which the outsider cannot achieve without the close working co-operation of key members of the management and service staff. The building of a code of practice out of the work itself, and its control functions, is an essential element in its subsequent effectiveness. The role of the professional in this, is to assist the participants through sensitive aspects of the process and to help concentrate the activity on the most important questions. Optimum service results, best use of resources and harmonious working relationships are the goals. Conscious practice within readily understood guidelines is the easiest pathway to this result. The worker can seek an active role in helping all concerned to build such a framework out of their working practices. Identifying good practice methods, discovering the results of discriminatory activities and how to combat them, and adopting corporate work methods and attitudes can be done as team activities, thereby gaining the active participation of all in the process. Management, too, must be seen as an active participant in the endeavour.   The professional, alone, has the necessary connections to persuade the leadership that the process should start at the top.

Morale The expansion and diversification of activities bring with them the dilution of contact between the people carrying out different, but essential, functions within the whole. Despite taking on the trappings of a corporate business, this organisation is much more than that. It is the product and the subject of a development process. It embodies the social dimension that originated in its community roots. It has the wider social and political purpose of bringing sustainable change to those who are the victims of previous disadvantage. For these reasons, it must demonstrate its success across a broader range of criteria than just a set of balanced accounts. Consequently, the motivation of all participants must be linked to the same outcome goals with a heightened sense of purpose. Positive identification with the organisation itself and high morale in all its undertakings will further this objective.

In centralised control systems, hierarchies and compartmentalisation create barriers to communication and many of the vital functions become depersonalised and detached. In decentralised systems, inward-looking and small-scale perceptions at the periphery conflict with the need for an over-view of broad strategic factors. Effective communication systems can reduce the problems which these tendencies can bring, but the conscious building of a corporate identity is a strategic goal in its own right. The worker is uniquely placed to devise mechanisms for its achievement.

The collective purpose of the organisation has to be defined and adopted. Staff and management must make this policy common cause at every level, making it public and overtly manifested in all their actions and communications. The paramount value system must be instilled in the working practices and goal planning of all participants. The collective rewards of success must be advertised and success must be reinforced. A framework such as this cannot be left to implement itself. It will have to be worked at and refined until it becomes completely integrated at every level. The values which it comes to embody must reflect the sense of common purpose which the organisation is aiming to achieve. The work and contribution of every person in the enterprise must be seen to be valued and reinforced through the working of this process. Mechanisms for the encouragement and support of everyone can be enhanced through the development of regular contact between those who do not have regular contact or direct operational interactions. The creation of social as well as functional contact can also be fostered. The task is to create a corporate identity out of a social institution, and to retain the best qualities of both.

Role in the welfare complex The reputation which should flow from good practice, and the image which this projects to others, will establish a position for the organisation in and around the complex of activity in the welfare economy. This sector comprises many interests: other service organisations, political and economic interests, and social organisations. The motives for this interest will stem from many sources. Some will have a direct economic link, being donors, suppliers, or purchasers. Users and consumers of the services will be anxious to judge whether or not the conversion of a local service into a corporate enterprise will have direct effects on quality and effectiveness. Others see the organisation as a rival to their own activities, not only on the service front, but also within the networks of social and political connections which sustains the interest for many individuals in a whole range of activities.

Image The management of the organisation will be intent on demonstrating that the standards and reliability of their service are comparable with any other. The promotion of a corporate image must be a priority and. for this, there must be consistency in the messages that those that deliver the services carry with them as they go about their work. Proper credit must be given inside the organisation to those who deliver the whole 'corporate package' when they provide their particular service. This means emphasising the positive aspects of the organisation and its work at all times. Good public relations and marketing are no substitute for excellence in practice, but they do make up part of the packaging which makes outsiders aware of the true value of the work.

No organisation is without its scandals, its secrets, and its disaffected members who spread tales of woe and despair. Performance in the field is the best rebuttal of these insidious forces, but work has to be done to ensure that internal consistency renders futile any attempt to undermine the collective effort.

Managerial integration The functions of management have to be experienced, from inside and outside the organisation, to have an integrated purpose and consistent control function. The management team is a complex and difficult unit to handle effectively. Factionalism and personal ambitions are most acutely felt at this level in the structure. The effectiveness of the whole operation depends on the effective co-ordination of these many and, sometimes, divergent interests. Effectiveness and consistency will be the criteria on which the organisation is judged by rivals, funders and those whose interests lie in making the right connections.

The development worker is in a position to reflect back into the structure, and particularly into the mechanisms of management, the way in which the organisation is experienced in the wider networks. Confronting conflict of interest and formally articulating facts regarding effectiveness, or its opposite, are a function of the trusted outsider. It can be better managed if the process of identifying points of weakness and the need for change come into the organisation from this direction, rather than it being filtered through the veils of gossip and petty intrigue of the wider community. Not all organisations are endowed with their own tame consultant and many consultants are not instilled with the values and goals of social action through development. Many do not know how best to use this endowment, and many consultants do not recognise the need to follow through with the full force of the influence which they wield due to their privileged position. Development workers are in a position to advance the fortunes of the organisation and to advance their own position within it. There is no inconsistency in this, if development is the shared goal. Information is power, and this form of power, with access to bring influence directly to bear, is still more powerful.

Viability The worker's over-riding interest is to create a relevant, viable and reliable service agency. Direct influence is now diluted. Access has to be obtained through a series of contracted servicing inputs and functions, which are seen to be necessary by the 'customer'. Influence has to be exercised sensitively, with great diplomacy and tact. To create stability, the internal systems have to be balanced through a series of checks and balances. The exercise of power by those inside the structure has to be mediated through processes which reduce the effects of dysfunction and enhance communication, consensus and positive outcomes. Where friction over goals, processes or relative personal power disrupt this delicate harmony, the professional has:

♦ to be in a position to recognise that it is happening;
♦ have retained the confidence of all participants to be acceptable as a trouble shooter; and
♦ possess the skills to effect the necessary repairs to the system before it disintegrates.

The larger the organisation grows, the more intricate the tentacles of service extend out into the community, the more vital it is that professional

145

resources are there to assist in avoiding the disruption of the services and, perhaps, even the breakdown of the organisation itself.

Organisational renewal is a very sensitive area for the people within an organisation and for the consultant who has to advise on it and sustain a relationship throughout its progress. There will have been changes in personnel, particularly in leadership, since the organisation began. As the agenda for action broadens and becomes more institutionalised, leadership positions will consolidate. Paid staff will assist in this process out of a necessity for their continued employment, and because they will become adept at 'dealing' with stable management.

The organisation has begun to leave its original roots behind, relegating 'service' to its original constituency. This will become just one 'activity' amid many. What are the responsibilities of the professional worker, the consultant, in this situation? Obviously, any organisation needs new lifeblood drawn in through recruitment. Leadership, too, needs to be renewed periodically (not always a universally popular idea - especially with entrenched leadership), but any attempt to institute change from outside will obviously be resented and distrusted. Indeed, the question needs to be asked: does an 'outsider' professional have any responsibility for the continued vitality and managerial 'health' of the organisation once a certain scale and scope of activity has been attained? It is our contention that the professional relationship extends beyond that of a mercenary/technocrat with developmental skills for hire. There is a residual duty to the original constituency, and to the newly 'developed' leadership of the organisation. It is an ongoing professional duty to ensure that both are successful. The responsibilities of leadership are less of a priority than the continued provision of reliable services and mature representation of the community's will. For this reason, the professional has a duty to ensure that leadership, and the direction in which it steers the organisation, are consistent with the needs of the community. The aim should be to create an organisation which continues to give 'good value for money'. The consultant/professional should not shy away from developing a strategy for ensuring the viability of the organisation. This may entail:

♦ broadening contact within the organisation in search of information and symptoms of decline or ineffectiveness;
♦ seeking out energetic and motivated persons within the organisation who preparation for leadership roles;
♦ providing opportunities for training so that potentials can be enhanced and competitiveness and ambitions harnessed;

♦ ensuring that the organisation takes seriously recruitment of membership from the community, and that it does not begin to rely heavily on paid staff for its ideas and output.

Through the development of a strategy like this, a professional keeps in touch with the internal dynamics of the organisation, while, at the same time, contact with the established leadership is sustained at an appropriate level of intensity.

Strategy for development For the organisation, demonstrating viability is the first step towards establishing a permanent impact on the whole sector. Each step to date has been an adventure in an ever-widening scenario of experimentation and innovation. The emphasis as been on establishing the right to function as a service agency. This is demonstrated by assuming the right, and showing the ability to set policy and outcome goals, independent of outside influence. Viability demonstrates that this right has been established within a competitive environment and the appropriate levels of output at acceptable standards have been achieved. For the first time, our organisation does not have to prove its competence amongst equals, or to superiors. That task is behind it, once and for all. The future needs to be assessed and a fresh strategy planned. This stage is characterised by a series of tactical moves, designed to establish the organisation in a strategic position within the local welfare economy so that it can decide freely which route to follow. The underlying motivation for this is to make a beneficial impact on the whole structure of welfare provision in the locality. This is done through a combination of demonstration and the exercise of power.

Competition When an intruder moves into the domain of other organisations, one outcome is that those under a possible threat of displacement will take stock of the situation. It is likely, that before any direct pressure is applied to respond to the intrusion, an assessment will be made to establish its force, and its possible effects on established activities. These players have to choose whether to follow paths of resistance, co-operation or accommodation. There will be some pressure, experienced by the newcomer, as the others make their assessment and adjust to any changes which will have to be made. An organisation, such as that which our worker has been advising, will not experience much resistance. Standards of competence and well-planned resourcing will demonstrate that there is little that can be done to discredit or deter the intrusion. The effect on our organisation is for it to receive signals about the strength of any opposition and, possibly, information about deficiencies and defects in the existing system as provided by the others until now.

It is in the interests of current professional practice, and those of future development, that intelligence be gathered on the nature and quality of all competing or complementary activities within the service field. Intelligence will inform service delivery systems about the style and extent of other services, what there is to be learned about the service culture and, most importantly, it will inform management about the communication systems between service agencies. Local systems of power and influence can be studied; which agencies, or personalities, dominate the scene. Hard information is needed. It will be discovered that there are myths and false images abounding, amid strands of gossip and misinformation. An organisation with intentions to become more than just a competent player within a circumscribed field, should plan for the acquisition and analysis of intelligence as part of its development process from the very beginning. A permanent investment of some kind is required to ensure that information received is reliable and consistent. The wisdom of the professional can be relied upon to ensure that this advice is proffered at the appropriate stage.

Connections and co-operation Most of the service-delivery agencies will employ similar methods and will share a common culture regarding local perceptions of outcomes, change possibilities and boundaries of operational activity. There is likely to be a great deal of over-lap between activities, wastage of resources and little sharing or active co-operation, beyond that which is unavoidable. There is much to be learned from the way in which things are being done. The priority, for now, is to build up a service reputation which will position the agency at the centre of the established network. It will serve these interests if some practical co-operation and sharing of work and expertise can be engineered. In this way, the most efficient use is made of resources and it is possible to use such opportunities for spreading the message about good practice and values ideas across a wider network. It has the added effect of enhancing the reputation of the new agency and of putting some light pressure on other participating agencies for them to change their ways of working. Co-operation is used as a vehicle for teaching by example. Once the organisation decides that further development is necessary in its role and impact on the welfare economy, all opportunities must be taken to strengthen its image as a dynamic and innovative practitioner.

Alliances Change within the system will be on the agenda, but not immediately. There are many levels of influence and advantage to be explored. Co-operation in field activity is one dimension of the organisation's purpose. Through this wider interest, leaders from our organisation are brought into working relationships with their counterparts from elsewhere. There are shared goals, value systems, complementary fields of activity and/or a common experience of frustration at the shortcomings of the system as it currently exists. The strengthening of the ties between them can become the target for a concerted initiative. Joint initiatives can be instituted, resources pooled and management processes and policy guidelines streamlined to accommodate each other. Combined efforts in the same field will create a more powerful presence than the separate efforts of each on its own. This presence can be used to influence the climate of social action, and to gain prominence for their own agreed priorities.

The organisation will begin to realise the potential that inter-organisational communication and co-operation can bring. To be effective at this level, and to maximise freedom of action, those involved need to develop an over-view of the power structure which surrounds them. This goal can be achieved through obtaining an accurate insight and 'feel' for how the system functions. The competing forces and interests should be analysed. Are any advantages being played out - by whom, and to what extent? The long-term interests of the organisation may be bound up in the survival capability which can be demonstrated through 'success' in this arena. In the immediate period, the organisation may seek merely to continue the co-operation, and the opportunity to participate in mutually acceptable activities. In the long-term, this perspective may change, relationships may deteriorate within the system or objectives of the members may diverge. Consequently, it is of great strategic importance that a position at the centre of the networking process be achieved and consolidated.

It is prudent and politic for all organisations to maintain an intelligent interest in the workings of the formal and informal political systems. A deeper understanding of how the policy framework for the area affects the work of established agencies will facilitate its own plans. Accurate intelligence is obtained only through focused action. What is then done with this information depends on the organisation's strategic objectives? An analysis of the local patronage system, if any, should be attempted and, within the organisation, there should be some agreement about how this can be influenced. Public policy priorities are not only influenced by social need factors, and so the manner in which the organisation handles its diplomacy will have a telling effect on its future within the welfare economy.

149

The worker may advise that the information is used for 'defensive' purposes - stored until public activity shows that some intervention by the organisation is necessary in order to protect an established position. This is in keeping with the model above which sought to consolidate working practices, rather than to confront or disrupt the status quo. There are opportunity costs involved in adopting a defensive stance. Remaining aloof can result in an organisation failing to be aware of changes that occur which could have a significant bearing on its fortunes. Policy decisions could be taken about overall resource levels or shifts in priorities, without the active engagement of the organisation. To be relegated to a state of reaction rather than pro-action in such a crucial process would be problematic for the long-term aspirations of the organisation and its leadership.

Alternatively, intelligence can be used as part of a political offensive, where the objective is to strengthen the organisation's direct influence of the whole system. Here, the objective is to form combinations which have an overtly political purpose and seek to apply direct pressure to alter the operational environment to their advantage. For this approach, the ground has to be carefully prepared. Some, or all, of the organisational linkages which have been made for operational effectiveness may be enlisted in this strategy. For one organisation to attempt to make its own running is to risk exposure and isolation.

Connections should be sought with those who have influence, and relationships are then developed with them. The motive is to gain active participation within the *political* networks which constitute the power connections in the system. Networks exist in many forms. Some will include senior political figures, officials from public agencies and other bodies, business and social personages. Others will be confined to narrow interests, such as service agencies within a particular field. Influence can only be exerted by more indirect means in this context, and so becoming an integral part of these systems is a priority goal for the leadership personalities. Influence will be effected through individual contact, which has to be sustained and understood from the point of view of its strategic importance.

The collective targeting of objectives for political intervention requires systematic planning. Consistency of commitment is required, resource inputs must be agreed and steps must be taken to ensure that participants are able, as well as willing, to play their part. The thing about alliances is that they need not be permanent arrangements, being arranged to suit the political context and being supported at times when it suits the strategic interests of the organisation, and not beyond. They need to be managed carefully while they exist and it is important that the parties have some common understanding and agreed expectations about their nature, purpose, expected duration, and outcomes. Failure to prepare the ground properly could cause the whole fabric to collapse. Mistrust and acrimony between co-existing agencies in a relatively closed social system could seriously affect relationships for a protracted period.

The worker's role in this is a combination of broker and privileged counsellor. It entails acting as a pathfinder to explore the potential of other formations which might be suitable allies. This assessment will include establishing their respective strengths and weaknesses then applying those particular professional insights for the benefit of the organisation. Becoming the advisor to an organisation which is making its entry into a power system in this way, eases the entry of the professional into those same systems. Being accepted as a competent and integrative influence will be made easier if the professional makes some early contribution to the needs or well-running of the whole at the same time. It could be that the worker is already an accepted feature of the network, having made some earlier contribution. This works to the benefit of the newly arrived organisation, as the ground can be prepared for their participation in advance. As the worker extends the facility of dealing with organisations which demonstrate common cause through joining these networks, the opportunity arises to extend the collective influence of those organisation through collective action. The worker will explore the interests, strengths and weaknesses of all the participants. As the situation becomes clearer, it will be possible to suggest opportunities for co-operative action, mutual support systems, joint lobbying for resources, or other political influence.

Effecting contractual relationships, especially in the short-term, for focusing the professional's talents on the attainment of achievable goals widens the scope for professional influence over the general direction of development. Obtaining a balance between competing interests, the pattern of resource outlay and the benefits of outcome is a skilled enterprise. Selling the whole initiative to the participants requires concerted application, detailed knowledge of the facts, insight into the long-term interests of those likely to take part and the production of a model, or route, to be adopted for its realisation. Joint achievements will reinforce the collective interests of all the participants and it will extend the influence of the worker across the whole span of organisations which take part. It is success in this type of activity, where the 'value for money' of the worker is fully tested.

At another level, the worker may be contracted in to undertake intelligence-gathering missions, on behalf of the organisation, but not in its name. Connections, knowledge of the networks and the workings of the system, informal, as well as the formal, and a sense of realism about the form in which information of a political nature should be presented and used is an essential asset.

Mobilising the linkages It is prudent that a newcomer hasten slowly when attempting to bring change to a system. The new agency has joined the network of established organisations and has been entering planned co-operative activities with some of them, to mutual advantage. It is demonstrating its competence in a public manner and it is beginning to influence the structure and direction of the service network to which it belongs. In parallel to this, the worker is gradually working to become the pivotal link in the communication and tactical advice network. Expertise in the preparation of organisations for a role of wider influence has been gained through managing the temporary alliances and co-operative efforts. A detailed personal knowledge of the personalities, at every level, across a broad field, has allowed a thriving pool of contacts to be exploited in most practical situations. Influence within, as well as between, organisations has been extended through the worker's active intervention. Nevertheless, one person's trouble shooter or 'fixer', is another's 'wheeler-dealer'. Quality service to all concerned, openness of approach and clarity of goals will allay most suspicions and enable full co-operation, but a high level of diplomatic must be exercised if it is to be successful.

What is the next step? Our organisation will survey its position within the service network and it will now be in a position to analyse the form of the economy of welfare at this level. It will decide whether or not is satisfied with the way things are running. It will be able to decide whether or not its own position is allowing the maximum satisfaction for its members, the maximum amount of influence for the leadership and, above all, the maximum penetration of the 'good practice model' which it promotes through its service activities. If shortfalls are detected in any of the above, the organisation may seek to change the way in which the system operates, to bring it more into line with what it sees as its own 'advantage'.

It might be questioned how the idea of 'advantage' even appears on the agenda of a service agency? The whole concept is bound up with its image and ambitions. Dissatisfaction with the way that things are going, will lead to action being taken. This might be rationalised thus: It cannot be in the interests of the community at large that organisations with below-standard patterns of activity are allowed to consume the social product without any serious challenge to their methods and accountability. The absence of active competition over the consumption of collective resources leads to the creation of a privileged establishment and rigid systems which work to reinforce the status quo. This, in turn, works to the ultimate disadvantage of those who are supposed to derive their benefit. The organisation, backed by the professional's bank of tactical and strategic expertise, can appraise the whole sector of the social economy in which they have an interest. Gaining 'advantage' in this economy will be both a survival mechanism, and also a necessary step for ensuring that service standards are set at the highest level. More than just technical competence is needed for this strategy to work.

The organisation will cast around to discover the most appropriate way in which to exert power without, necessarily, getting involved in a direct power struggle with the agencies of government. It may also decide that it would be imprudent, publicly, to appear to become a partisan supporter of a single political Party. Politicians can be capricious, and old scores can be settled through victimisation as easily as patronage networks can be set up. Besides the cultivation of politicians is a messy process where the demand for a *quid pro quo* could compromise the organisation and its work. Better for it to become a focus for attention, a centre for excellence and a centre of power in its own right. Let others beat a path to its door, and let politicians look for favour, rather than bestowing it themselves. Nevertheless, politicians should be wooed to ensure that the qualities and status of the organisation are well known in these circles.

Over a considerable period of time, an organisation can build itself into a dominant structure, and a reference point for all others in the field. This comes about through successive phases of expansion, consolidation and diversification. This is highly demanding on leadership, as it affects the internal processes which cater for growth and succession, and many complex planning mechanisms. It is accomplished through long-range strategies, determination and the capacity to change with the times, and the ability to sustain good practice methods. It must correctly read the direction of political and social change, such that it may remain in tune, in fashion and in demand. It would benefit from building its authority across a number of service sectors and networks, and pursuing a policy of active intervention in the corridors of power. The influence which a large and dominant organisation can have is considerable. It may collaborate with policy-makers in setting the bounds of publicly sanctioned activities. It may attract the lion's share of the resources available from public funds or private sources. It may set the standards against which all others are judged.

In times of rapid change, there are a number of factors which militate against this approach:

◆ change may be perceived as being so rapid that it cannot be accommodated without considerable costs, wastage and stress inside the organisation;

◆ the mobilisation of the necessary skills and resources may not be feasible and the internal human resources may be insufficient for the task;

◆ official policy changes, regarding service needs or resource allocation, may be signalled up in advance, showing directions, which may require rapid flexibility and adaptation to the preferred strategy;

◆ there will be many organisations in the field which are not coping with the pressures of change due to rigidity of outlook or inability to compete, and whose eclipse would kill the keen edge of competition;

◆ other organisations, aware of the forces of change and the advantages of scale and stability, wish to protect their interests through any means, and reduce their vulnerability.

In these circumstances, an organisation would be best served if it could 'buy in' the skills and the structures which might make adaptation possible. If the organisation was to absorb, combine with, and/or render marginal any, or all, rivals in the field, it might be able to protect its future. It would need to gather in the necessary resources and expertise to survive the transition in a revamped shape with revitalised energies and policies that could handle the next challenges. The best way forward would be for a complex organisation to be set up by forming a federation with other organisations, or even taking over direct control through mutual agreement. In a process like this, the advice and talents of the professional development worker will continue to be central.

6 Social Planning and Development - II: Complex Organisations

ORGANISATION with the POTENTIAL for PLANNING	ORGANISATION as the FOCUS for STRATEGIC DEVELOPMENT	ORGANISATION as the COMPONENT of STRATEGY	COMPLEX ORGANISATION as the FOCUS for DEVELOPMENT	COMPLEX ORGANISATION as a STRATEGIC CENTRE	INDIVIDUAL as the TARGET for COLLABORATION

The mature organisation which we described in the chapter above, is one where its scale and scope demands respect, both within its own sector and beyond. It is capable of standing on its own and of making its way in a competitive environment. The determining factors for any organisation which develops to this level are bound up in its history, the capability of the central personalities, its own assessment of strategic opportunities, the relative strengths and weaknesses of other players in the field and the wider political context. Whether or not it decides to develop further will be influenced by these factors.

After a certain amount of consolidation of its role, it may undertake a review of its internal qualities and strengths. It may identify that it has developed some or all of the following, or that it has the *potential* for such development:

♦ the capacity to develop and resource a diversity of activities;
♦ the capacity to decentralise its operations into a number of alternative centres of power and discrete structures;
♦ the need for a more complete system of management and control for the whole organisation, including the co-ordination of component functions;
♦ an identifiable and formal corporate identity and unity of purpose.

Possession of this information will allow it to consider whether or not it has reached its full potential. Whatever it decides has to be a feasible proposition in terms of resources, managerial capability and predictions for future viability. Its interests may have to be considered as having two dimensions, internal and external, which may require apparently contradictory policies being pursued simultaneously. The adjustment of purely internal aspects of its form and effectiveness are more easily dealt with. But factors such as freedom of action, influence over public policy and its standing in the community cannot necessarily be dealt with from a narrow power base. Should it decide that it has not yet reached its optimum form, size or influence, it must begin to consider what strategic options are open?

An assessment is needed of any environmental pressures which might have a direct bearing on its current or future activities. For example, there may be real political impediments to further development due to public policies, local political priorities or local cultural perceptions of the organisation's values, practice methods or apparent ambitions. A thorough study and analysis of local patronage and of public policy positions would be invaluable. An assessment might follow of what strategic steps are required to change the balance. For example, a powerful, local politician may have a pet scheme which is likely to be put under pressure if this organisational change is put into effect. How much resistance would be generated? What are the political costs of such a move? The conclusions should indicate whether any planned changes are attainable within the given organisational framework, and whether any predictable and unfavourable consequences can be overcome. Any precautions which can be taken to ease the way forward should be taken. Once these assessments have been made, the decision to change can be taken, and the planning can begin.

Complex organisation as the focus for development

A complex organisation is a structure made up of a number of component parts, each of which, in certain settings and for particular activities may actually be autonomous, with its own structural integrity. In this situation, each part surrenders some autonomy, or diverts some resources, for specified activities within a contracted relationship. Other forms of complex organisation comprise elements which might not be fully independent organisations, being sub-divisions of larger bodies, but which are grouped together for specific, mutually agreed purposes. Each has, or is given, a degree of autonomy or, because of its scale or specialised function, has its own authority and standing and can transact certain affairs on its own account. Each might, with some slight modification or restructuring, become a fully autonomous organisation in its own right. These parts then contract to work collectively, within certain agreed boundaries, as one organisation. The 'old' (British) Commonwealth was an example of this - a number of fully independent countries, tied together, under a nominal leader, for some activities (for example, in their judicial systems). All had started out as colonies, and all had worked to achieve a state of total autonomy, save for the 'voluntary' link (monarchy).

A complex organisation can take on different forms. This is dependent on the authority which its control function has over its own activities, and over the component parts of which it is made. For example, a 'corporation', comprising many divisions but governed by one board of management, will be able to maintain stronger 'line management' systems. Here, authority can be exercised in a hierarchical manner, if this is required. Conversely, a looser, federal structure, with control of the component parts being retained in their own systems, will result in more consultative and guided forms of management. Authority for action has to be negotiated, either directly by the parties themselves, or through a mediating or delegated structure, such as the Secretariat of the European Union (Lehman, 1980).

The coherence of policy and the form of control within a complex organisation depend on the level at which direct control is exercised. If centralisation is maintained at the highest levels of authority within an organisation, and attention is paid to the efficiency of communication systems, then consistency of decision-making may be easier to sustain. The more these functions are decentralised the less consistency will result. How autonomous are sub-levels or component parts allowed to be within the organisation? Delegation of power for self-management, particularly over the selection and pursuit of objectives can place great demands on 'central management' as it strives to keep in touch and sustain its grasp over corporate policies.

The salient characteristic of an organisation has been described as its tendency towards autonomy and defence of its own resources (Benson, 1980). Therefore, within a complex organisation there is likely to be a degree of tension surrounding the exercise of control. Individual power, traditional freedom to act alone, a history of having to give too much and receive too little in return, etc. - all these could cause resistance. The more negotiation that is required to establish authority for action, the more the question of control will be under review and adjustment. Any non-routine activity will bring some changes, which, in turn, will call into question the relationship between the component elements, and their principals in the greater, complex organisation. This will add to the tension amongst the players.

The establishment of a complex organisation can be achieved through a number of different approaches. There are three broad categories:

♦ through internal expansion and diversification;
♦ by colonising, or take-over, of existing organisation(s);
♦ negotiating a federal approach.

Each of the above can be undertaken separately, or elements of each might be woven into a composite strategy.

Internal expansion

The decision whether or not to push out the physical boundaries of operational activity will be based upon the best available intelligence. Areas of need will be identified beyond the boundaries of the current service activities. The absence of comparable or alternative service structures to meet these needs may be one reason for an expansionist drive. Equally, the organisation may regard that its competitors are providing an inferior service, or it may just want them out of the way. There may be greater opportunities for incentives and rewards, either financial or in status, if the organisation expands. Alternatively, there may be a desire to ensure that the field is dominated and controlled by one (i.e., its own) value system. There is no way of disguising the intent of an expansionist organisation once the process begins. The effects of this process will also be felt inside the organisation, as expansion in the internal structure creates its own pressures.

A larger, more centralised structure brings with it a stronger institutionalised approach to managerial and administrative processes. To achieve this, there has to be the will to change the personality of the organisation. Any previous intimacy may be lost as it develops a more impersonal and corporate approach. Management has to be capable of conceptualising the changes and adopting a stronger strategic perspective than before. It must become acceptable to state the organisational objectives in broader terms and to describe the goals more as quantifiable targets. Concepts such as planning, logistics, functional integration and systems development have to be introduced into the organisational culture as the governing logic of policy. Outputs will tend to be standardised, and there will be less dependence on personal approaches and individual qualities. New mechanisms for sustaining morale and motivation have to be developed, based more on the concept of *outcomes* than on personal characteristics (Handy, 1990). Once the impetus begins, the change

158

process becomes continuous, and it extends its influence throughout the structure.

Complex structures require more detailed monitoring if they are to be kept on course. Large-scale activities create a wider impact and it is important that their vitality be sustained and that they do not lose momentum. Drucker describes how not-for-profit organisations become prone to inward looking and how they can become complaisant. They are convinced that they are doing the 'right thing'. 'Are you organised for yesterday rather than today?', he asks (Drucker, 1990 p. 88). For this reason, an on-going strategic review should be maintained. It is not enough to compare goals with outcomes, The field will be changing and the organisation has to remain in touch. New developments in methods of operation, fresh perspectives on values, a broadening vision, or new policies which widen the scope for advances will be weighed for relevance, importance and feasibility of introduction. Once screened and found to be acceptable, the most expedient tactic for adoption will be planned and executed.

A mature organisation is not only able to think strategically, it also develops the capacity to plan and act accordingly. The linear extension of its services requires an element of strategic thinking, but this process, itself, is bound to throw up new possibilities for diversification. By leaving the original narrow field, and widening the sphere of intervention it can capitalise on the benefits of its own internal, functional systems (such as: experienced management, financial control, training, transport facilities, central administration, etc.), and the economies of scale. Goodwill and influence in one sector can be employed to advantage to gain access to others. For example, the absence of alternative suppliers of essential services may be spurring the organisation to diversify into its own service section. Having the power and confidence to act is, on its own, a factor of considerable importance.

Diversification will bring new challenges. Expertise will have to be extended and the relative importance of new initiatives must be balanced against the standing of the traditional activities. Many of the changes that are suggested may not be feasible within the constraints of the present organisational structure. Sheer scale or diversity of outputs may overload the original control function. One approach is to completely re-structure the entire organisation. This may help to stabilise the varied operations through providing more relevant communication, command and resourcing mechanisms. It may also help to bring clarity to problems as they emerge.

This is the first step in moving the 'simple' and direct structure into the form of a complex organisation. Drucker states that, 'the structure has to be organised for business performance...', although, 'Good organisational structure does not by itself produce good performance. But a poor organisation structure makes good performance impossible.' He continues, 'To improve organisational structure will always improve performance.' (Drucker, 1975, p. 274). Hill & Jones discuss the relative strategic merits of structural form: whether to develop a 'flat' scale of management hierarchy in the interests of local operational control, whether to separate out the 'project' (diversity of work/output) activities from the control and developmental functions. They consider whether geographical control is better suited to this organisation than functional control, and how best to ensure that the corporate aims of management are directed towards achieving the best integration of the collective assets (Hill & Jones, 1992, see also Child, 1984). Although this service activity did not start out to take on the trappings of corporate management and structure, the realities of development have forced these changes upon it.

Restructuring, expansion and diversification are very costly in terms of managerial resources. Control, expertise and communications become stretched as the scale of operations widens. Once, it was just a matter of taking on more activities of a similar kind. Existing systems could be diverted or re-focused temporarily, until the new operations were running effectively, and could be integrated into the enlarged web. Where there are completely new forms of control, communication and activity, pressures arise which are more difficult to foresee. Expertise either has to be quickly developed within the organisation, or it has to be brought (or bought) in from outside. In either case, this development brings with it a shift of forces within the structure.

New activities herald new fashions. New fashions unsettle the old ways, and personal feelings, as well as operational systems, are disrupted. A new activity can be over-protected or over-powered and inhibited with undue caution. Opportunities can be stifled and lost through paralysis or ineptitude. Conversely, newness can bring freedom from informed criticism. Initiative and creativity are difficult to monitor and control as they demand trust and low regulation to be effective. Relaxation of control brings relative autonomy and power for those involved. The central control function, as well as some relationships, will be put under strain.

Expansion is a strategy of social planning. Zweig and Morris (Zweig & Morris, 1975) tell us that once the problem has been identified, this should be the guiding influence for the organisation until the solution has been decided, tested and confirmed. The organisation should put a disproportionate amount of its resources into this project and it should have prepared the remaining parts to manage on their own until the new venture has been successfully achieved. In an organisation which has decided to diversify, there are new perils in store. It may be that the new venture is successful, in which case, the allocation of resources may begin to re-orient some part, perhaps some large part, of the organisation in that direction. Conversely, the new developments may not immediately show the promise that was anticipated. This may bring friction into the running of the organisation as component parts strive to win back for themselves that focus of resourcing and status which they were forced to surrender in the name of change. Failure, too, will have adverse effects. Any ensuing confusion can demoralise management, as well as the workers active in the new field.

Recriminations, lost resources, public humiliation, or a retreat back into the old mould will all bring their own form of disruption. There are not many plans that can be made to counter the stresses of change, especially where this scale and magnitude of change is a new experience. Management is an essential control function of the change process, and planning is the insurance against avoidable calamities. At the core of this process is the proviso that the plans contain the flexibility to cater for the unexpected and can accommodate various routes to a satisfactory outcome.

Decision-making systems have to be prepared and ready to respond to the unexpected (Dixon, 1993). Flows of information to the point of decision making and from there to the point of operations need to be tried and tested. People in organisations need to feel that they are responsible for the quality of information which they need to gather, and also for its transmission upwards within the organisation, to where it can do most good (Drucker, 1990). This is especially true during a time of change and potential crisis for management.

Often the structural requirements to carry through the changes are simply not there, or they are perceived as not being there, even in potential. It may be feared that traditional systems will break under the first pressure for adaptation, or there may be defections or passive resistance to change. Overall resistance may be heavier than might be thought possible (Machiavelli, 1975). Uncertainties about loyalty, or other factors, might contribute to the tendency for expansion and diversification to be managed from a centralised position. It stems from fear of the unknown, the desire to be 'in charge' and the notion that the greatest amount of flexibility can be achieved through a single line of command. Where there are doubts about the effectiveness of communication systems, the skill of some segments of the organisation, or the degree of acceptance of the overall scope of the new policy, holding the reins at the centre may appear to be an attractive proposition.

Effective management is one of the greatest assets which an organisation possesses. Any process which can put it at risk is threatening the entire basis of its operations and continuity. Child outlines how bad managerial preparation can result in the whole system becoming over-stretched and demoralised (Child, 1984). This point is also emphasised by Urwick, who places the responsibility firmly at the door of management for any failing in preparation and planning (Urwick L. 1947, *The Elements of Administration*, pp. 5 - 6, cited in Mullins, 1989).

The actual move to effect change, therefore, is best accomplished decisively and quickly. But this should be done only after extensive planning, and the development of a sophisticated strategy and the necessary managerial competence to handle it. In our organisation, the experience of this dimension is likely to be lacking. This means that the role of the professional is going to be a crucial element in the success, or otherwise, of the outcome. The professional must try and ensure that the leadership, at least, understands the value and nature of the planned changes (Resnick & Patti, 1980). This may result in intensifying the feelings of dependence on the professional, and a heightening of investment in the organisational leadership by the professional. The expanding organisation must consider the following:

Service environment

♦ analysis of the forces in favour and against change;
♦ analysis of the sector within which change and expansion will take place;
♦ identification of complementary activities and organisations for targeting.

Organisation

♦ identification of the areas of vulnerability, gaps in provision or expertise;
♦ development of strategy for approach;
♦ creation of the new control and organisational structure.

Action & consolidation
♦ implement strategy;
♦ rationalisation of activities;

♦ re-build public image.

At each stage in this process, the abilities of the worker will be put to the test. A highly political situation will begin to emerge. The investment of all parties will all be reshaped:

♦ personal investment - including principles, history, vision and status;
♦ institutional - collective identity, protocols and procedures, priorities and authority;
♦ public - influence, connections and reference points.

The orchestration of the whole will be the responsibility of the central leadership of the organisation, but it is likely to be untried in such activities. Many of the tensions will have to be managed by the worker until internal experience develops. The consultancy relationship will have to be restructured and the limits of responsibility clearly drawn.

The worker will be providing two types of support during this transition from the mature, one-dimensional organisation to the complex and corporate dimension which it seeks. The most important part of this service is the support of the leadership through the strains of managing change in a fast-growing structure. This will be referred to in detail below, in the concluding section of this chapter, but the role of personal advisor will come entangled in the more detached role of professional advisor to the structure as a whole. The worker, through the strong personal ties that have developed with the leadership and other members of the organisation, will have personal preferences and, perhaps, a personal political investment in the shape and direction of change in which the organisation is involved.

The second function performed by the consultant is the input of certain information and advice for the strategic development of the work. This will translate into key support being given for certain development options. This advice, given by a valued and respected advisor becomes a powerful factor in the political networks within the organisation. This dimension of the relationship will be consciously recognised by different interests within the change process. Their interpretation will colour their reception for the consultancy advice, and the role and apparent influence applied by the worker may be scrutinised closely. A degree of political sophistication is required of the worker to recognise these forces at work and to counter them (or manipulate them?). This process cannot be ignored, and it has to be dealt with. Living with the facts of political differences and factions within an organisation, even for the professional 'outsider', is one of the contradictions that have to be managed by the professional. The worker may *prefer* a particular option, the *facts* may point in another direction, and the preferences of the organisation's leadership may be set on a third possibility. Presenting an 'objective' choice will be coloured by all of these factors.

Service environment Intelligence, analysis and evaluation of the service environment has been possible on a much more detailed level since the organisation became a player of influence within the network. It is prudent for any organisation to stay in touch with developments in its own, and related fields so that it: a) knows from where the changes are coming, and what trends they may reveal about the future; b) understands the nature and purpose of change within the context of the economy of welfare; c) is able to assess the effects of change on its own activities and d) can assess the need in favour or against responding to change.

This activity will absorb energy and resources, but if it is not carried out effectively, far greater wastage may result and the whole basis of the organisation may be undermined. When the signs appear that change is a strong possibility, some organisations just ignore them, waiting for the signals to come from others that there is something significant about to happen. Passivity in these matters is a symptom of deficient management, inappropriate advice and potential redundancy of purpose.

The fundamental quality of the professional-as-consultant is the ability to maintain a compendium of up-to-date intelligence on all matters relevant to an organisation active in the field. The worker will have encouraged the organisation to maintain its own community profile, but this may now be out of date in the light of planned diversification and geographical expansion. Testing the in-house profile for currency, relevance and for its capacity to remain up-to-date in the future, is a first step to assist with the under-pinning of an effective intelligence system. Once the organisation assumes the status of a major element in a wider service sphere, it must be expected that it will maintain its own systems. This is a means of protecting its activities with information, which is especially gathered for its own use, rather than general information of uncertain origin, which may have been interpreted earlier for other uses. We have already emphasised the need for the professional to assist the organisation to think and plan strategically. This quality is the hallmark of the professional consultant. Every aspect of the work done with and/or for an agency must be considered from a 'strategic' dimension, as well as the considerations of the immediate situation. The professional responsibility must extend beyond the level of problem solving, although the organisation may not always be receptive to the long-range implications of the advice it receives.

A professional framework of preparedness also applies to the question of local and national policies, and their relevance to the service activities, which are being planned. Valuable assistance can be given to a group, which wishes to gain direct access to the decision-making strata of the centres of statutory or administrative power. In addition, the consultant has to be up to date with changes in policy and has to be in a position to predict, with some degree of accuracy, what risks an organisation may be assuming if they embark on change. In order to be able to anticipate changes, and to gauge the political climate regarding shades of political emphasis and priorities, the pace of the implementation schedules, and/or the preferences of responsible leaders and officials, the professional has to develop a network of 'insider' advisors. The ability to 'network' the political system can be extremely controversial when the political affiliation of the worker, the stance of the organisation in the face of established policies, or any other instance where doctrinal, ideological or value conflicts are likely to arise. The worker has to judge how best to obtain the most relevant information for the client system being worked.

There are degrees of closeness about professional relationships. The worker could consider whether or not a particular relationship within an active political network is too close to avoid compromising the professional status through which it was forged in the first place. The barrier of professional detachment could be breached, even, or even especially, when there is no ideological conflict to consider. Pressure is just as likely to be applied from within the professional/political network for 'favours', 'leaks' of confidential information regarding private plans, etc., as it is from the citizen side of the equation. Such is the ambiguity of the professional's situation within the political networks, that there is a risk of being compromised by NOT being affiliated to one grouping or another, as well as there might be by establishing a close relationship. There may be factions within the organisation which owe primary allegiance to external political groupings, rather than to the service agency. They may translate the 'bias' of the professional purely in externally relevant political terms, and report this as such to those outside political organisations. This factor is more common in complex organisations, where linkages between people with common goals does not necessarily depend on them having common values. The worker has to manage this situation, perhaps relying on creating a dependable or professional image to those who hold real power in the external system.

Another controversial aspect of the consultancy relationship addresses the question of confidentiality of privileged information. The professional is in contact with many organisations, some of which may be in direct competition with the one now striving to change and grow. The professional may have offered, or is still offering, consultancy support to such organisations during their own expansion/diversification process. The consultant has to maintain the best advice to offer the client, and to provide detailed insight into the strengths and frailties of the 'opposition'. This marks out the really useful consultant from a run of the mill service. In circumstances where the consultant is offering support to organisations across a wide geographical area, the degree of local, specialised knowledge is not presumed to be extensive. On the other hand, the integrity of the local worker, working the home patch, is put under great pressure. The outside world does not go away once the work is completed. A worker may have to live for a long time with the consequences of how sensitive information is handled while under pressure.

Organisation Working on the internal needs of the organisation can carry as many dangers for the worker as trespassing abroad in the political networks. Society's political systems are among the most robust, whereas the ties that bind small organisations together can be very fragile. The consultancy can have a powerful impact on the organisation's ability to cut through history and established approaches to the work. This process may have the opposite effect, however, if it serves only to tear apart the social fabric of the system.

The model we have been following assumes that the worker has been in touch with this particular organisation since its very earliest days, before it was able to offer even the most simple service. An intimate knowledge of the strengths and weaknesses of every aspect of the structure and its personalities has been accumulated over this period. Attempts have been made to influence the quality and direction of the system at every stage in the development process. But now, as the time arrives for the organisation to move beyond its original constraints of a narrowly defined purpose, a penetrating analysis has to be made for any structural weaknesses. These now have to be dealt with, or the new mission will fail.

A worker, who does not share the history of an organisation in the way we have described, will have to consider how to gather, handle and present the detailed information required so that the next phase of development can be initiated on a firm structural base. It is of the nature of the power that a worker possesses that an intimate knowledge of the culture and foibles of the organisation will assist the consultant to give an 'appropriate' range of recommendations. The correct decisions have now to be made regarding restructuring and diversification. Any purely detached and dispassionate analysis of the current structure, and any strictly 'objective' suggestions regarding feasible alternatives, will fail to address the vital issue of this organisation as an organic whole. The nature and personality of all the participants have been stamped upon it, and any change will be rooted in the specific internal culture of the organisation. The worker must be sensitive to this factor when advice is offered. The sentiments that are involved may deeply affect the disposition of the personalities to carry their energies forward into a new era. It is not just a question of tact, although diplomacy may well be employed intensively throughout the process. One special quality that marks out the community organisation from one which is strictly commercial, is the ethos of commonality. A lower priority is accorded to financial and quantitative outcomes, and, notwithstanding the contract culture, there is still an emphasis on citizen involvement and the sharing of value systems which transcend much of the aggravation that the commercial market atmosphere might generate. Consequently, the worker who produces a purely 'consultation' document, with swingeing recommendations for change, and then departs, leaves the organisation's leadership holding a time-bomb which they may not be able to handle. All the strain of breaking the news of impending change, of handling the politics of insecurity, corralling the effects of previously pent-up frustrations which may be released, and manipulating the personalities into a more appropriate structural form may all be too much. Unless there is support and planning, these pressures could cause the collapse of the whole leadership system.

The key to this phase, is the term 'strategic'. Everything about the complex organisation has to be re-oriented towards this approach. The leadership becomes 'management'; the operational framework becomes guided by a strategic plan; and the organisational structure becomes a corporate mechanism which is designed to integrate the needs of these. The planning of the time-scale and the sequence of development becomes a more critical element in structural considerations. Time will begin to shape the integration process, and it will, necessarily, dictate the choice of options and the mobilisation of resources. It will become an arbiter in the evaluation of success and it will become increasingly a factor costed in advance for certain specialised inputs and services. The more that the 'contract culture' impinges on the work ethos, the more time will become a consideration in the allocation of work. It will also act as a restraint and a source of pressure for change to take place, at different points across the organisation, in order to enable the whole to focus on the essential tasks which it has to undertake. Time, long-term planning and costed processes all contrast with the quality embodied in the 'not-for-profit', or 'voluntary', character of most locally developed organisations. The contradictions will have to be confronted and the 'compassion' to which Drucker refers has to be weighed against the need for measurable and accountable outcomes (Drucker, 1990).

Weaknesses have to be assessed and strengths identified. These will include personalities, systems of service delivery and other functional necessities, such as communication, decision-making or image building. Integration will entail some 'wastage' as well expansion. The human resources of the organisation must be appraised for their capacity to: a) cope with the challenge of operating within a large, and more impersonal organisation and an extended, and more objective, control mechanism; b) perform skilled activities which are new both to them and to the organisation, itself; and c) being prepared to be trained, or retrained for strategic, rather than the more personal vocational deployment to which they may have been used. The worker must be able to recommend to the management structure how to integrate training into their service plans, and how to manage the dynamics that this may produce within the operational systems. At the top of the organisation, training for the management cadre, itself, may have to be introduced in preparation for the increased responsibilities which they will have to assume.

The leadership of the organisation will be aware of the points at which pressure should be applied, but they may seek to rely on the intrusion of the 'outsider' for the legitimisation of the actions which have been made necessary. For this reason, there may be pressure for the professional to withdraw early from the scene, leaving behind the report with its problematic recommendations. In this way, certain parties (including the consultant) may choose to escape from the embarrassment of witnessing conflict, pain, and difficult procedure being taken to steer the way through the change. This is convenient for the sensitivities of the worker, but it is not good professional practice for this situation. The possibilities must be spelled out in advance and the expectations of all parties must be explored in anticipation of avoiding, rather than creating, chaos.

The most difficult task will begin with the design and building of any new control structure. The strengths and personalities of the current leadership will play a large part in the choice. Blau & Scott draw attention to the influence of the group's norms and values in determining the most appropriate structure (Blau & Scott, 1963). At this stage in the organisation's development, the values of the past will act as a restraint on the organisation of the future. A yet-to-be-explored activity level must have a new organisational structure built for it. It will be necessary to integrate some components which may have no culture of their own (new development), or established ways of doing things (take-overs and amalgamation), and there may be a tendency to allow the old ways to dictate the way forward by default. It is not just a matter of devising the most appropriate structure, but managing its implementation that will tax the resources of the existing leadership.

The professional contribution will comprise focusing the leadership on the options presented by these three perspectives. This will help to integrate the thinking and will facilitate working through the options in a systematic way, all the time exploring and probing to discover the extent that alternative proposals and routes are fully understood, even if they are not adopted. The worker has to guard against fatigue on the part of the leadership group. New members may have to be specially recruited specifically for this expansion process. The professional may well be needed for this process and in assisting with induction and training for these new members. They will be bombarded by fresh and difficult, often abstract, material. The quality of the professional service will ultimately be assessed upon the leadership being able, in the end, to make an informed and rational choice. They must feel that here is a method through which they can adopt the strategy, and that the implementation process can be achieved within their existing resources. Where a radical new organisational structure is to be adopted, there will be a need for exercises to be devised and training for the leadership so that they can be prepared for the transition.

Action & consolidation   Once the process starts to run, the leadership are going to become completely tied up in the minutiae of the ever-changing scenario which confronts them. These include: new activities, fresh lines of communication, the difficulties experienced by new levels of delegated authority, misinterpretations of intent, and the induced helplessness of some elements. All these will require emergency action, intervention, prophylactic and palliative remedies and a firm and encouraging support system while the new processes work their way into the organisational structure.

The professional will be employed in a monitoring role, assisting the leadership with moral support but also analysing information. Fresh forms of intervention will be considered, scanning the system for significant signs of weakness, devising alternative models and tactical approaches to aspects of the work, while seeking to sustain the structure and integrity of the overall strategy. The professional must strongly resist any tendency for this consultancy function to be sucked into the managerial process itself. It must remain detached and, without appearing to undermine the confidence of those struggling with the effects of change. It should retain a nonpartisan but critical over-view of the process. In this way, the worker can be of the most long-term help to the management, and ultimately, the beneficiaries, of the organisation.

The organisation, itself, will have few spare resources with which to monitor its progress through what will be a difficult phase. The worker, as consultant, can perform an invaluable service and, at the same time, provide a historical account of the change process which might otherwise be lost. The worker will closely observe the implementation process with the objectives of the strategy to the fore. Difficulties with implementation, signs that the direction of change may be diverted through internal or external pressures which had not been foreseen, opportunities for the improvement of systems and an appraisal of the performance of some of the key personalities involved will be the target for this study. The timely warning of problems which might arise, one step in advance of the present action, and a reasoned contribution to the central executive management mechanism will be an invaluable asset to the organisation, present and future. The decisions regarding remedial action, changes in the strategic approach, adjustment of tactics or the deployment of personnel will all be the responsibility of the organisation's own management. But for decisions to be made by those with only a limited perspective on the broader issues involved would prove to be wasteful in the long run. By deploying the services of a consultant in this way, the organisation is acquiring an early warning service about potential weaknesses and it can take early preventative steps to counter them as soon as the stress lessens.

It is likely that the first plans to restructure the organisation and the design of the control function for the expanded programme will only prove partly successful. Plans have to be proved through exposure to the constraints of the real world, and these are going to be no exception. The whole structure may be wrongly conceived, resource deployment and weighting may be inadequate, whole services may fail to reach their targets and the planning model itself may prove to be deficient under the pressures of rapid change. The worker's analysis of the change process will have anticipated some of the points which may require special attention. The worker can make the space for this focus to be made and then provide assistance to the responsible management group. Helping them to take these points on board, at a time when they are under pressure to be satisfied with what is going well and not seek out troubles, will contribute to their maturing as competent managers of their complex organisation. The ability to detach themselves from the pressures of the immediate stimulation, and to consider rationalisation and abstracted problems will also help them to come to terms with the human issues involved when they have to deal with bad performance, wasted efforts, deflected interests and bruised morale amongst their middle managers and front-line workers.

There is no doubt that some hard decisions may have to be made. The professional can assist the management in deciding which are the most crucial, which have to be made by direct intervention and which can be delayed, diverted or alternative solutions found which can contrive to hold an existing service, or other system, together. We refer back to the Drucker quote, above, regarding the need to consider the structure of the organisation. In another place, Drucker continues with the theme: 'Strategy converts a non-profit institution's mission and objectives into performance....An effective non-profit institution also needs strategies to improve all the time and to innovate. The two overlap.... these strategies begin with research, research and more research..... Strategy also demands that ..(it).. organises itself to abandon what no longer works...(and)... that it exploits opportunity, the right moment...' (Drucker, 1990, pp. 75-77).

We have identified that there may be casualties in this process. The power of the organisation will now command more attention and loyalty than the individuals on which it is built. There is a purpose in it all, but the full fruits of this may not be shared by all those who entered into the change process. Rationalisation will entail eliminating over-lap, duplication, less effective activities and, possibly, those activities which cannot usefully fit into the new structure. The latter choice may result in viable and popular activities being abandoned altogether. Strong management will be needed to carry this through. There will also be a knock-on effect of this. Individuals; workers as well as beneficiaries of the services; bystanders and others with political interests in this new growth of power, will react to the changes, either through direct resistance, or through negative propaganda in the community at large. In some cases, this may result in a full-blooded campaign against the organisation for what it is doing. Part of the original strategy may have centred upon this aspect of public relations and the effects of change. It is more likely that it will introduce a negative element at a time when the whole organisation is looking forward with optimism and a certain amount of trepidation at the changes ahead. As such, this will be very counter-productive. Most of those on the inside may have overlooked the possibility of a backlash, or put it into storage, hoping that it may not be needed. The worker will have anticipated this need and made the critical assessment of the change process with this item on the agenda. An opportunity should be sought to broach the subject, so that the organisation can devise a post-change strategy with its public image set as a high priority.

It may be too late to rebuild some of the bridges that may have suffered, but the creation of a positive image must be seen as an active component of policy, even before the changes have been achieved. This is not just about reconciliation. It is an active and positive intervention by the organisation, highly selective and purposeful, which seeks to redress a perceived imbalance. Successful public relations are a highly specialised form of communication, usually aimed at selected targets. The organisation will not have many resources to spare for this form of activity, and so the professional will have to assist in identifying the priorities for action. The best use of scarce resources will be made if the targeting is precise and accurate, but it may be that there are not sufficient resources for the elimination of all the negative consequences of the change. A 'fix' for one critical group may be all that can be hoped for. In this case it must be concentrated and aim to be decisive on the selected target.

Not all image-building arises out of negative situations. At the end of a period of reconstruction and change, it will be generally beneficial if the organisation considers embarking on a publicity drive as soon as it can. It might be imprudent to put out the messages prior to the changes being accomplished. This would give advance warning and concrete information to those who need precise information of this kind in order to attempt to sabotage the strategy. This is one kind of 'organisational secret' which the complex organisation will learn to protect as it gets more involved in the politics of power play and large-scale operations. The professional may not, personally, be an expert manipulator of the media, or be able to select accurately the most cost-effective target for an image-building exercise. But the specialised knowledge of community affairs and culture which the professional brings as part of the consultancy package will enable the organisation to weigh up advice which may be elicited from other, more expert sources.

Colonisation or take over

Realisation of the need to change may strike a number of organisations in the same or related sectors at the same time. New conditions, such as the introduction of the 'contract culture', may leave organisations with an air of uncertainty about their role. On the other hand, they may have a feeling of confusion over apparent contradictions between the new order and their old value base, and concern with their state of operational preparedness to continue to function effectively under a new regime. There are many organisations which may have served a locality or a small-scale needs group and which have never considered the question of 'viability', the 'economy of welfare', or any other corporate or market-oriented system of analysis. These may be vulnerable to take-over by other, more go-ahead organisations.

An organisation seeking to expand, rather than to go through the internal re-structuring necessary, as described above, may seek to accomplish the same result, but to do so through the take-over of one, or more, existing organisations. The approach to this process is more methodical and calculating than the simple expansion model. A set of conditions is required prior to the process being initiated, and the whole operation falls well within a 'conspiracy' theory of social change. This is a contrived move from the beginning and as little is left to chance as possible. Social planning is at the heart of this exercise, as the outcome realises the reformation of social resources into a more tightly controlled and coherent form. Only those organisations which cannot resist the forces for change, will succumb to the sort of inducements which will be proffered and, it might be said, that the introduction of 'efficiency' models into the economy of welfare is long overdue anyway. It is the role that is played by the professional developer that may cause some controversy.

One organisation seeks to expand through the direct take-over of another organisation. It will have its own view of the direction in which it wishes to move, and it will be in touch with many other organisations. This will give it first hand knowledge about what they do, their relative effectiveness and the personalities who make up their leadership. What it needs now is a professional assessment of its own potential as a take-over organisation and a strategy for its accomplishment. It seeks the services of a development consultant and requests advice on how to proceed. The consultant considers the following:

♦ what intelligence is already available regarding the size, strength and viability of other organisations, and what gaps exist in this intelligence that need attention?

♦ given that full intelligence is available, what is known about the internal workings of these organisations and are there any special characteristics which might render some of them more or less suitable for inclusion in a more detailed analysis?

♦ does the worker, or special contacts of the worker, have any privileged insights into the internal workings of these organisations which may be of utility to this study? (This includes leadership qualities as well as operational considerations).

♦ what special political considerations surround the workings of these organisations that might facilitate or retard a take-over approach?

173

♦ what is the potential of the management of the take-over organisation for sustaining a detailed strategy which will result in the absorption of the other(s)?

The result of this investigation will produce an analysis which can be reviewed alongside the organisation's own intelligence. This analysis will have to be made with great tact, within the confines of the strictest confidentiality and with diplomacy and sensitivity. There may be potential 'leakages' from within the planning group, and the worker does not wish to be exposed to accusations which may be compromising. This exercise might be described as 'an evaluation of the mutual benefits arising from an asset rationalisation programme', or it could equally be seen as plotting the elimination of one organisation by another through absorption. The target just happens to be one with which the consultant may already have an established history of trust. In the light of these considerations, the consultant will report on the following:

♦ an array of organisations in the field or within the geographical target area already defined;
♦ a narrowed-down target group of organisations, their resource base and specialised service functions;
♦ a review of the asset value of each of these in terms of their workforce and practice performance, captive market for services, material assets (if any), managerial performance, value base (constitutional, as well as practising), relevance to the established political (and Political) environment;
♦ a description of any salient features regarding the particular vulnerability of any organisation: its track record of service, the relevance of its services, the qualities of its leadership and appropriateness of the control system, and any other factor against which its viability can be judged.

Working with the management of the take over organisation, the worker will prepare a strategic plan. This will be based on the relative advantages which the take-over organisation sees in the options before it. It must consider its own internal potential to translate a successful approach for merger into a successful complex organisation. Depending on the selection of targets, the planning organisation may have to consider a number of internal options, which may include restructuring or 'down-sizing' some of its own operations. The take-over organisation may devote some thought to devising a 'sales package' for itself prior to an approach being made to the target. In this, the advantages, strengths and projected plans might be set out. It will serve to explain to a wider audience what lies behind the bid, and for the need to expand its operations this way. It may also demonstrate to the target's leadership that there is a future for them, and for the work in which they are currently engaged. This might be a political as well as a working tool to assist in the process. The move to absorb another organisation will need to be explained to the wider public, as well as the membership of both organisations. A 'positive' description can serve as a good public relations weapon, if it is needed. The client population can also be reassured through a properly prepared and well-presented explanation in which their own needs are safeguarded.

The next component of the strategy is a detailed blueprint for an approach to the organisation which is identified as being suitable for take-over. This plan might consider any of a series of options regarding the best tactics. They range from: the mounting of a direct 'market challenge' to the other, through an aggressive incursion into the 'turf' of the target, with the intention of exposing its vulnerability and forcing it to panic or seek an accommodation; to preparing an 'offer document', a rational analysis of the mutual advantages which might be realised if the two were to merge. Even the softer approach might be interpreted as a veiled threat if there is an obvious power differential between the two. From the position of the professional consultant, the smoother the process, the better it will be. A smooth take-over would probably mask any role which the consultant played in the exercise. It would also demonstrate that the most beneficial path had been followed.

The leadership of the target organisation needs to be paid special attention. Some of them may have standing within the wider community and their connections might be used to rally opposition to the move beyond the confines of the organisation itself. They may want to resist change at any price, or they may be divided on the issue. Quality intelligence is a great asset in the latter situation. Patti describes these characteristics in terms of 'conservers' and 'climbers', and offers some useful insights for the consultant on how to exploit their strengths and vulnerabilities. Some people are open to flattery, others stand on principle. The human factor is so important, and a project like this must not be seen as a mere exercise in logic, or even a power play (Patti, 1980). It must be remembered that this not a financial take-over bid in the market sense. Voluntary organisations are free from any shareholder constraints, and they may have loyal and devoted supporters/members who may well resist any changes - even those which might prove beneficial to the service users of the target organisation.

Once the decision has been made to launch a take-over, the active organisation must pursue its goal with determination. It has to be done through a direct approach and the consultant will be required to attend any meetings to give detailed advice on constitutional and tactical matters. This is a serious exercise and failure could have far-reaching repercussions across the whole welfare sector, as well as for the parties involved. The take-over organisation might suffer some negative reaction, whatever the outcome of the exercise. If it fails, particularly if it has used its power forcefully, then there are likely to be recriminations and some negative publicity. Even after success, other organisations may have misgivings about the realignment of power within their sector. A general loss of goodwill and trust between organisations may result as there may be speculation that there may be further manoeuvres of this nature. This could undermine the image and confidence across the whole service/welfare community.

Once the bid has been negotiated and accepted, the immediate tasks are to effect the merger and the absorption of the target organisation. The new control function may entail the retention of some, or all, of the original structure and leadership. These will have to be integrated, and everyone within both organisations must be quickly informed about what the new set-up will mean to them, how it will work and who is in control of what. Immediate steps must be taken to ensure that there is no interruption of any of the service activities. Some functions and activities will have to be rationalised and the maximum value realised from the take-over. The role of the consultant in this process is to assist the leadership follow the blueprint and to offer them support and counsel in the early days of decision-making. The members and/or employees/voluntary workers of both organisations will experience some considerable trauma at these events. The consultants role in this aspect of a merger is to advise the leadership of : a) the necessity for the fostering of good internal relations and, b) drawing up a strategy for winning over the *hearts and minds* of all concerned to the new consolidated cause. The end result of this process must be the creation of a new organisation, with one clear image and identity. The take-over task is not completed until this is achieved.

Negotiating a federation

There will be some goals which an organisation wishes to pursue which it finds impossible through merely expanding its own repertoire by direct action. It may wish to expand or diversify and also to maintain some form of direct control over all the main aspects of the regime that results. A straightforward partnership with another organisation is one solution, within a contracted agreement for joint commitments to specified activities. This will achieve the proposed expansion/diversification, with control firmly vested in a new management structure that has been agreed. It is development in a simple form, it is cost-effective and it draws on the established expertise of the participants to mutual advantage. There might be nothing for the development worker to do in these circumstances, but there is a role in bringing the partners together in the first place, and monitoring their joint activity in order for them to obtain the most benefit from the exercise. There will be a need for advice on how individual organisational secrets can be best protected during close working relationships with another (and potential competitor). Mediation may also be required in the event of friction. Evaluation of the activity (see Chapter 9, below) and assessing the progress towards their mutual and separate objectives can also be provided.

But this form of activity does little to enhance the scale of each of the participants. It makes an impression on the service structure of the area, inasmuch as a joint service is created, but the larger power system has been largely unaffected. Also, unless it is specified in the contract, there is little other rationalisation of activities and each is free to go their separate ways in everything else that they do, without any accountability to the other. Of course, there will be benefits in broadening the horizons and testing fresh methods, while sharing the costs with others. Another useful lesson is experiencing the sharing of power, planning, and operational control. This may create a climate through which closer co-operation can be developed.

There are many objectives which lie outside the resource potential of any single organisation and which cannot be realised through joint activities. The mobilisation of the full resource potential of each and the focusing of it on agreed objectives is a process likely to realise social change of a more significant dimension. A power play, aimed at a take-over by any one of them, may be rendered impossible, or imprudent, due to factors in the organisational environment. These include the relative political prominence of potential targets, covenanted funding agreements which might limit the scope of permitted activity, or just mutual agreements between the organisations not to encroach into the territory of the other. Nevertheless, circumstances or opportunities, such as policy changes or a threat from other sources, may dictate that change and expansion be undertaken. A practical solution is to consider the realignment of the structures of existing organisations, so that all the benefits of past experience and current activity can be harnessed without any of the dysfunctions of conflict. The result of a friendly merger may have been discussed but not proved to be feasible and so a third, federal possibility is considered.

Where two, or more, organisations, between which there is little differentiation in either power or scale of operation, agree to pool their resources and create a superior level of control with authority over the participant elements concerning *certain agreed activities*, then a federal structure can be developed. The objective is to create a new organisation which contains within it the structures of its component organisations, virtually unmodified; but with a range of new functions which are accountable to a centralised executive. Original control functions, activities and organisational culture are retained, but there is a new level of supra-organisational control created to oversee the whole and to take specific responsibility for negotiated and contracted activities and functions. All the participants agree to give up a little amount of their freedom to operate (for example, to operate alone in the new area of co-operation) in the name of join activity, managed by this new superior mechanism. The long-term intention of such an arrangement will be that a culture for the whole federated structure will emerge and permeate all the component elements. In addition, various 'federal' structures will emerge, which are responsible for the delivery of services to the whole federation. These may be duplicated in each component, or each lower level structure may agree to have this done for it on a centralised basis.

The purpose behind such an organisational move is to harness the combined weight of the components, to bind each into a framework which will allow this weight to be used as a lever in influencing local public affairs, to create fresh structures for the development of new initiatives - both internal and external, and to allow for the rationalisation of certain activities within the whole to take advantage of economies of scale, etc. The influence exercised by the new structures has to be negotiated and agreed. Each federation will have its own safeguards, and limitations will be set regarding the power of the superstructure relative to its 'subordinate' elements. It is likely that this will be codified in a formal agreement between the parties and a composite constitution will embody the shared aspirations and values of the members.

The professional task in this form of enterprise moves from:

♦ being the broker in the early stages;
♦ setting up the expert system which will enable the parties to begin working constructively together until they can formalise their agreement, and then;
♦ acting as advisor and/or trouble-shooter to the whole on the conduct of its business.

178

The worker will be contracted to all the parties taking part. This immediately restricts the public role which can be carried, but it is likely that there will be demands for a great deal of private consultation which will put pressure on the worker to defend confidences and privileged information.

A worker is likely to be approached by one organisation and the proposition to form some sort of merger will be discussed. During the early stages of the process, the role of the consultant may be very similar to that adopted in the 'take-over' option, which was outlined above. In the event of a federal structure emerging as the likely way forward, the worker will then seek to effect a formal meeting where a simplified proposal can be discussed. If one of the parties is set completely against this form of activity, then the worker may have to seek out alternative potential partners, or assist the original one to defend its image as it beats a retreat. Once communication has been established, the professional role is to assist all the parties to produce a model which can serve as a basis for negotiation. This task may be delegated to the worker, on a consultancy basis, and this is the preferred option. Alternatively, the parties may agree to set up a task group, which the worker will service. It is more difficult to obtain agreement from a round-table discussion than if one party is given the task. For a first draft, the consultant visiting all the parties, eliciting their views, options, preferences and proposals is a more effective way in which to centralise the relevant information. The costs of participation (extended timescale, premature discussion of differences, isolation of minority interests, etc.) may be the price that has to be paid for increased trust.

The worker's most valuable contribution, apart from keeping the communication processes open during the discussions, is the drafting of a model for the control function of the new organisation and also drawing up a draft constitution. The definition of the legal powers of the superstructure is a pivotal function in the progress towards agreement. All parties are going to have to take risks, the advantages to each participant will have to be explored and reasonable predictions made about the losses and dangers which may be incurred. Receiving this information from an independent source may go some way to bring the negotiators together in a positive frame of mind. If there can be agreement on the constitutional framework, then the hard work can begin.

Federation is an evolutionary process, as well as a constitutional edifice. The changes that follow the formal agreement have to be worked out through trial and error by those on whom the daily responsibility rests for running the collective activities. All the participants must be warned that, as the focus shifts towards the emergence of the new creation, so the on-going activities are likely to feel, and be, neglected until things settle down. Those responsible for these activities are going to feel that they are being restrained in what they are allowed to do in the future, due to the imposition of the new constitution. The forces that determine the folklore of organisations must not be allowed to spin their webs without some form of intervention. There can be no escape from the likelihood that there will be 'resisters' to the changes. Some people will lose out and others will perceive that they have lost out. Others, called 'climbers', conversely, will seek to dominate the new processes in furthering their own interests, to the exclusion of all else (Patti, 1980). This will be experienced negatively by any who are not completely in favour of the changes. Placation may not always be possible. But the centralised management/control function should ensure that there are resources diverted to cater with this potential friction. It will serve the new structure well if there is a clear programme for the continuation of the existing activities, within the new structure, and that mechanisms can be activated to highlight the attainment of these objectives as soon as the new structure emerges.

The professional function is to retain a grip on the strategic issues which underlie the federal process. Forces which assist in the focusing of resources, the distribution of power, the enhancement of communications and facilitate the establishment of agreed structures must be kept under constant review. In particular, the behaviour of the human players must be monitored. It is not unlikely that several of them will have their own, private agenda, and they might seek to put it into effect to the detriment of the whole process. The worker is in a delicate position. Loyalties may be presumed which have never existed, or pressure may be exerted to trap the worker into collusive practices. The earlier that a worker can detect that there may be a hidden agenda, the sooner tactics can be developed to deal with them. The worker's 'best interests' may prove difficult to divine.

The interests of the participants may change during the time-scale of negotiations. Anxieties will arise and, as more information is shared and the real nature of all the participants is revealed, there will be moments of doubt and confusion. If the early motives for starting the process are valid, then it is likely that they will still be valid once the process is concluded. The worker is going to be in a more detached position, and will be keeping outside events under scrutiny throughout. As advisor to the whole, it would be legitimate for the worker to caution against carrying through with the exercise if circumstances suggest it.

Once the process is completed and the constitutional structure has demonstrated the effectiveness in the operational world, the worker must once again re-negotiate a relationship with the organisation. Development skills now fall into the 'maintenance' mode.

Comment In this process of developing a more complex organisation out of simple structures, the role of the professional has been forced back into an increasingly detached relationship, the more complex the structure that has been planned. One of the main reasons for this is the potential for the professional role being compromised in the event of a conflict of interest emerging. In the case of the simple expansion process, there is little to hide. The organisation may, however, wish to conceal its activities from potential rivals and it may wish to shield its members from some of the stresses associated with planning, reviewing options and executing trial activities. The planning process for this is likely to be conducted in a closed environment, with the worker playing a close support role.

In the take-over situation, because of the secrecy surrounding the operation in the early phases, the worker has been given the relative freedom of being protected. As the strategy emerges and the hand is played by the take-over organisation, the worker is able to step out of the centre position and to adopt a liaison role if required. This apparent duplicity is not necessarily due to the worker wishing to abandon the process and appear always to remain on the side of the angels. The worker is never more than an advisor, even if the role of co-conspirator might be a more truthful description. It is, and must be, the take-over organisation which initiates the take-over process and takes full responsibility for the outcome. A high profile and public role for the worker in this process will be remembered, especially if there are any real casualties or 'victims' in the end. The professional role is to give the 'best advice', and in these circumstances, the best advice is about the absorption of another organisation. There is no way where many of the conflicts which emerge can be avoided. The worker has to develop the mechanisms to manage them.

One feature of the professional relationship with an expanding organisation is the complexity of the formal relationships which emerge with individuals. Extremely close contact with a small number of people during planning operations is relatively easy to manage. Relationships with others, outside the planning circle, become part of another culture, predicated to technical advice or historical ties with their service function. As the control function (management) of the expanded organisation emerges, the professional will have to forge relationships and trust with a growing number of people, many of whom may have been the target of the original planning exercise. There may have been well-founded fears and suspicions aroused during this process and they will have to be allayed if the worker is to be able to offer a productive and beneficial service to the new structure. It is in the workers, and the organisation's, interests for this to be accomplished rapidly and in a business-like manner. The future leadership of the new structure will emerge from this expanded pool and the intimate knowledge of the workings of the new structure is best known by the worker. Each has something vital to share with the other, especially in the long run. The worker and the organisation's members have a compatible strategic interest in the future.

Complex organisation as a strategic centre

The consolidation of the control systems and re-focused service activities will take up much of the energy of the restructured organisation. There will be a certain amount of self-congratulation if the exercise is accomplished without undue trauma. Those in control of specific functions or activities will experience the satisfaction of the expanded scale and enhanced influence in much that they do. Once the exercise has bedded down, the organisation will be able to assess whether or not the present scale and scope of the operation satisfies their ambitions. Having weathered a process of planning and strategic development of this kind will contribute greatly to the level of expertise and confidence of all the participants. Any perceived need to make further changes in the shape or balance of the structure or activity pattern can now be approached through internal assessment processes.

There may be a tendency to dispense completely with the services of the 'independent' consultant. The benefits of scale which the new operation produces will release new capacities. The integrated system of internal functions will be able to adapt and re-orient its efforts towards new tasks. The planning of fresh expansions and take-overs can now be assessed internally, without any risk of compromise through the involvement of 'outsiders', such as the consultant. The organisation may retain, or re-train, personnel of its own for the planning and execution of 'development' initiatives. It may be that consultancy services are still required for certain activities: e.g.: where alternative or specialised input is required, or where sensitivity may dictate a need for some anonymity, or detachment from the organisation's own management. Generally, however, the professional can expect to have to negotiate yet another qualitatively different relationship with an organisation of this maturity and power.

There is one area of influence and expertise where the professional development expert can exercise considerable leverage. In strategic terms, this has been on the worker's agenda since the very earliest days of the development exercise, when the organisation was just a puny, local service activity. The time is now ripe for the realisation of some of the worker's own strategic goals. This comprises the exercise of political influence over a wider scale, using the weight of several multi-dimensional organisations, working in tandem and under the guidance (and influence?) of the worker. The worker has always been concerned to provide the 'best advice' and to prepare each organisation for the next stage in its development with certain value and operational targets in view. These have been assessed from the perspective of the organisation; its scope, skills, areas of influence, etc. In fact, they have also all been screened through the perceptions of the worker, and this has been a specialised and over-arching perspective across the entire welfare/service economy.

Once a network of 'complex organisations' can be established, each of which maintains a special developmental relationship with the worker, then it is conceivable that this common factor might emerge in a clearer light, and with more explicitly identifiable goals than have ever been expressed before. Can the worker exert influence over the combined power of a whole bloc of organisations? Can their influence be focused and brought to bear upon certain strategic goals for their mutual benefit?. It is likely that the worker has established, over the years of association with each of them separately, that certain value structures and approaches to practice are more appropriate. Additionally, all will have shared in a similar study and analysis of the form and priorities of the established order in the world around them, in the economy of welfare. They will be aware of how these forces affect them, and how political impediments hamper the work that they hope to accomplish. The worker will have a personal strategic perspective on the situation, and so will each organisation, if the preparation work has been done correctly. The next task of the professional is to explore with the constellation of powerful, complex welfare/service organisations how they might conduct their affairs so that they can reduce or eliminate these impediments. A collective approach would concentrate power and influence and allow for a broad agenda to be managed without necessarily over-extending the resource capacity of any individual member of the enterprise.

The task in this phase in the development agenda is as follows:

◆ assessment of potential for collective power-sharing;
◆ creating the collective;
◆ reserving the centre-ground;

♦ sustaining the consultancy.

Assessment of potential   The worker has established an intimate
knowledge of the working methods, strengths and weaknesses and
ambitions of each organisation throughout the developmental process.
Demonstrating that the organisation has a wider role to perform, indeed, a
public responsibility to fulfil should not prove to be difficult to achieve. By
this stage, the organisation will be satisfied that, through its strategic
successes in protecting its position in the field of practice, the scale of its
operations and the levels of competence which it can demonstrate, it
deserves to be rewarded for its efforts. This might be in terms of public
recognition and the opportunity to exercise its talents through having an
influence on policy-making.

Each organisation within the circle of influence of the worker may have
a similar feeling about its own role. However, there are factors which may
militate against these impulses ever being released. There is likely to be
the desire to protect 'turf' or reputation, to be uneasy over entrusting
organisational secrets and ambitions to outsiders, or feelings that things are
best managed through personal intervention.

Not all organisations may prove to be possible allies. Nevertheless,
despite the problems which may emerge, the collective targeting and
mobilisation for strategic change within the economy of welfare can be
shown to be an expedient, as well as an efficient way forward.
Organisations with equal power, discrete, or non-competing practice
activities, and with leadership which believes that there is an optimum scale
of operation and/or complexity of organisation for their practice
requirements will make excellent partners in joint activities. This is
especially true where these are based upon diplomatic initiatives such as we
are describing here. Machiavelli warns against entering into co-operations
with organisations with greater power than one's own. Short-term gains
give way to long-term tensions and possible conflict if all ambitions are not
satisfied. The worker is concerned to protect, as far as is possible, the
interests of all organisations if the consultancy agenda is not specifically
about take-over or merger. Creating alliances within which unequal power
relations may become apparent may result in some elements gaining more
advantage than others (Machiavelli, 1975). Assessing the potential of a
'pool 'of possible co-operators is an essential first task. Where necessary,
the organisations who wish to group together for the purposes of exerting
direct political influence may benefit from having the threats to their
independence explained to them in detail. It is possible to effect

agreements in advance to safeguard the interests of the weaker components of such a structure.

At face value, each organisation needs to know what assets all the others may bring into an association of this kind. The worker is in a good position to supply a suitably tactful and discrete description of many for public consumption. Direct inquiry approaches can usually provide much of what might be required, if this information is not to hand. A more candid appraisal of each may also be possible. It is important that someone (i.e.: the consultant) be in a position to anticipate strengths (power) and weaknesses (lack of resolve) of most of the major players in an exercise of this nature. Whether or not this dimension of the enquiry is shared with any other party is a matter for personal consideration.

The second factor, which has to be public knowledge, is the priorities for action which each organisation has identified. A working list of common interests can easily be put together and circulated. The worker is in the role of facilitator at this stage. Information is gathered, analysed, put into consumable (palatable) form and circulated. Contacts are made and points needing interpretation clarified ahead of any formal interaction. Individually, each possible co-operator must be convinced that it would be futile to attempt an individual effort. As soon as a composite picture is assembled, the next phase can begin. The worker will also be in possession of information about more 'priorities', other than those which the individual organisations may wish to go out into the public domain. Insider knowledge of this sort can be become a manipulative tool between the worker and an organisation. It is necessary to attempt to clarify how live issues such as this might influence future behaviour and tactics. They can never be completely cleared out of the way, but the worker's agenda and commitment needs to be made explicit so that future misunderstandings between the worker and the organisation's leadership can be avoided. Once any serious negotiations begin with other parties, covert agendas can only corrupt the process.

A third factor concerns the quality of leadership of the organisations which have been targeted. There are going to be imbalances in the perceptions and preparedness of the leading personalities across the sector. Some will have developed a vision of their future as influencing the shape of the whole economy of welfare, others will certainly not have such wide ambitions. Each will have a list of personal and organisational priorities, and each will have a personal idea of the benefits of widening the scope of activity. There will be different perceptions of possible personal and organisational risks that may be incurred, especially if there is to be a strategic move on the centre of policy making. Many may share feelings of

185

competitiveness or suspicion about the others in the potential alliance.

The worker will have to identify as many as possible of these factors in advance. An organisational structure will have to be devised which is compatible with the present needs of the participants, and suitable for the needs of future interaction with the structures of authority which are in focus. The degree to which any authority of each participating organisation can be delegated to a central structure has to be negotiated and a firm agreement reached well in advance of an approach being made to the 'other side'. This agreement needs to address what issues might be involved and how decisions might be taken. Agreement will have to be reached regarding the personalities who will be chosen to form an executive, operational, planning and representative core for the whole. Mechanisms for feedback and consultation must also be established. Even if there is no agreement on a formal structure for this function, the role of a liaison process and the impact it may be allowed to make on the behaviour of the participating organisations must become a focus for active consideration. The worker has to shepherd them all along this path. Failure to address the implications of such a development will lead to disarray and confusion.

Creating the collective   The task of the professional is to act as the broker and advisor to this process. In addition, there are special responsibilities regarding the role and approach used by the leaders of any structure that emerges. Do the individually identified priorities combine sufficiently to allow for a collective agenda to be constructed? If not, what might? Mutual and individual advantage have to be brought together. If an agenda can be established, threads of contact between the organisations need to be connected and some form of dialogue started. These strands will be strengthened through taking positive steps to bring all the participants together. The worker must create a working environment in which mutual trust can be established and where the worker's own competence can also enjoy complete credibility.

The professional task is to establish a working framework for the new form of association. This is achieved through:

♦ adopting an agreed direction for development;
♦ the adoption of a servicing mechanism through which appropriate preparation, the input of information, analysis and advice, the facilitation of communication for whatever purposes and the routine administrative duties are fulfilled;
♦ the preparation of individuals for representative activity;

- enabling individual organisations to delegate some responsibilities 'upwards' into the common arena; and
- eliciting the necessary material resources from the participants to allow the new structure to function.

Many of these functions will be carried out by, or facilitated through the services of, the worker. In the longer term, it will be necessary to assist the new formation to decide whether or not their association will take on any permanence. In this case, the constitutional position of the whole, and of the constituent parts, must be clarified, codified, and then the emergent structure must be administered through its own resources.

In preparing individual leaders for their role in this activity, the worker is going to be under pressure to sustain a balanced assessment of the interests of those participants who may not, themselves, seek a prominent position for their own representatives. Some individuals are going to push themselves forward, or they may have heavy responsibilities thrust upon them This will distort their relationships with all the participating organisations. There may be a tendency for the effects of prominence and the pressures that arise out of constantly being at the hub of policy-making to lead these representatives to by-pass the feed-back and consultative mechanisms which will have been set up to allow this structure to emerge. To some extent, similar consequences may be experienced by the person's own organisation. Individuals can become entrenched in positions of power at all levels and considerable effort may be put into protecting this situation by those concerned. Charisma, political skill and high energies in the leadership may condemn everyone else to spectator roles. This will, ultimately, lead to the weakening of the underlying structure, or change the whole nature of the organisation. This will take it further away still from the ethos of the community from whence it sprang.

There is an urgent need to prepare individuals for the role of statecraft; the exercise of collective power, representative and collective responsibility and the capacity to project a stable and positive image while functioning in public. In the end, it will be the trust that these few representatives can establish with those that sent them that will determine whether or not the collective approach can continue. Particular difficulties arise when power has to be delegated for the purposes of negotiation and collective agreements. The worker needs to prepare individuals for the pressures that will arise and also to explore with them the consequences of abandoning representational responsibilities. The worker's relationship with other members of the organisation will also come under scrutiny. Is the consultant's duty only to those at the top? What advice is given to the

187

plotter of a palace coup? What are the limits of confidentiality and trust? The worker must prepare for these situations. By stepping away from a potential conflict, the worker may not be behaving in a strictly neutral manner. Are there grounds for bowing to the superior moral force of 'values' over contract? Many workers may believe so, but the fine print should be consulted early in the process. The worker may find it more difficult, but reconciling the differences may prove more beneficial to the welfare constituency than aiding (or avoiding) the ambitions of a privileged few (Grosser, 1965).

Reserving the centre-ground There are two sides to this equation. The community organisations, in alliance together, and those with, or over which, they seek influence. Each will have its own agenda and vested interests. Each will have established protocols and constitutional ties which bind it to established ways of working.

For the community organisations, the target is the political system, and the way in which it takes decisions and allocates its resources to the wider community (notably, the organisations in question). At the same time, this is a *reformist model*. It does not aim to overthrow the established order. The banner under which this position is announced may imply that a serious challenge is being made on the structure ,but the reality is more modest. The main aim is to apply pressure on the system, through demonstrating that power and influence in the community at large is capable of mobilisation (Brager & Specht, 1973). It is a first step in a strategy for these 'alternative' centres of power to play a role at the centre of the field of policy.

In many respects, the hierarchy of the complex organisation replicates the structures against which it now sets itself. Power has been centralised, work responsibilities have been delegated downward, while executive power and the setting of policy are the prerogative of those at the top. This development is aimed at *intrusion and inclusion* into the active political world of the economy of welfare. This comprises the allocation of public resources, the formation of 'markets' and sectors of activity through policy design, and having a direct influence on planning which will calm the long-term stresses and uncertainties of their theatre of activity. Change is aimed at extending the bounds of influence, and at not replacing them. It is anti-competitive. In many respects, it aims at the creation of a club-like environment for those who enjoy the fruits of mutual confidence. There must be room for some more at the top of the pyramid of the establishment. By broadening the top of the hierarchy, the community's perspective may receive more attention when the planning is done. It is the role of the professional to tend to the needs of this central focus of activity. The position has already been secured on the community side. How a complementary influence is developed beyond that is the subject of a separate strategy.

The worker maintains relationships with people on both sides of the power equation. Officials, powerful people across the political, commercial and administrative spectrum are cultivated as sources of information. They are included in expert learning activities and are fed favours. Opportunities are sought to include them in 'contact' activities with community interests, and the worker acts as the gatekeeper in this exercise. The process of winning and maintaining the respect of this element, while at the same time retaining the freedom to act freely as the consultant to the community organisations, requires the adoption of considerable strategic dedication and a fluid approach. The worker has to introduce to all these contacts the concepts and benefits of community participation, and models through which they can be achieved. The adoption of a 'professional' detachment may serve to provide a rationale for bridge-building, and in being formally accepted as such. The reality is, that games on the playing field of power politics cannot sustain myths of neutrality for very long. The worker will have to work very hard to maintain access and credibility in official circles once they have calculated the intensity of, and the purpose behind, the professional's relationship with the community. Nevertheless, on a purely exchange basis, the worker has much to offer. It is likely that the worker has contacts with, and can offer interpretations of, community activity of which officialdom has little or no knowledge. As the community consortium gains in confidence, competence and ambition, the seriousness of its intentions will become apparent. Political conflicts, between the community and the instruments of policy making, are very untidy matters. The astute politician and planner will choose to avoid open conflict if at all possible; particularly if there is a real threat to their authority in the making. Only commercial interests can afford to remain aloof (see Chapter 8, below) in this form of approach. The worker will capitalise on this knowledge and offer the 'professional relationship' as a partial solution to both sets of needs.

The key bridge-building exercise is between the community organisation and the *official* channels of communication of the establishment. Informal offerings may be made: consultations, information exchanges, social activities, and other forms of therapy (Burns, 1991). Without a seat at the table of real influence, the community organisation is wasting their efforts. Some may be bought off in the short-term. The worker's task is to have prepared them for these kind of developments, and to remain insistent that the representatives chosen for contact and negotiation remain true to their delegated task. Much of this can be planned and rehearsed in advance as part of the consultancy package. To neglect this aspect and to try to retrieve a situation once it has become established is a hopeless task.

The extension of the consultancy role may not be open to the mechanisms of the establishment. It may not wish at any stage to share its secrets with any third party. It may have no legal power to do so, but it may be prepared to allow a form of consultancy to evolve whereby the worker acts as the key player in orchestrating the workings of the bridge between the two interests: consulting participants and shaping the agenda, setting up meetings, preparing for the administrative needs of all participants, record-keeping, etc. The role of the consultant in the function of the secretariat, even without real executive power, can yield great influence if exercised properly. The worker must continue to demonstrate that this role is useful to both sides. This capacity can only come from continuing to offer a real service, but it places the worker in a serious contradictory position, as each may seek to press the new structure into service for its own advantage. Being a servant in the middle is an unenviable position.

If this role can be carried off, it represents the pivotal power position in the network. Much of the communications which pass between the parties, and between the network and other systems, comes under the influence of the secretariat function. The worker is able to access information and be privy to the planning and thinking of all sides. Properly managed, the situation should yield up early insight to the policies of tomorrow, and the role of brokerage for a strategic activity such as this can be used to open other doors, outside the network, but at perhaps higher or wider levels of influence. Certainly, the contacts which can be made can be manipulated to the advantage of the worker, and any personal/professional agenda which is being implemented.

The organisational alliance will come up against the realities of power and the fact that it will have to exercise real power if its own if it wants to have any meaningful influence on the way in which decisions are made. Combining the interests of the component organisations behind the thrust of the collective strategy will take persistent application and skill by the consortium's leadership. Demonstrating to the target power centre (such as the local authority) that they mean business and can stand by any threats or positions they adopt can only be substantiated through action, or convincing pretence of action.

If both sides agree that contact and joint activities are beneficial, then a working structure can be agreed. The form for this should have been central to the discussions from the beginning. Whether or not any agreed form carries a formal constitutional structure, remains a central point for negotiation. The more formal recognition that is accorded to this kind of development, the greater has been the shift in real power towards the community alliance. The shape and limits of any future contracts that may be planned between a 'purchaser' and these potential 'providers' can be influenced through such a mechanism.

Once such a network is created and consolidated into a formal feature and a mechanism is established for: the sharing of information; the planning of services; the allocation of resources; the recognition of mutual interests - the worker can set about tackling questions concerning strategic issues. These can best be met across a broad planning front. They are: values within the system, the 'quality' of the various functions being met, practice methods and standards, and the targeting of priorities for further development. Structural social issues: poverty, social conflict, racial and other forms of discrimination, environmental pollution and central policies which perpetuate disadvantage, can be worked into the working agenda of the network. The pressure from the community base of the pyramid can be filtered through the organisations and can be brought to bear when the values and operational framework for jointly-planned services are constructed.

Keeping the channels of communication open within the community organisations for this purpose is one of the worker's long-term strategic considerations. This mechanism must be keep active throughout this developmental process - from the membership of the organisation to its leadership, from the leadership to the planning forum, from the planning decision into the policy resolution, and into the service structure. Those involved in the daily processes of liaison and negotiation may lose sight of some of these considerations. Timely reminders from the constituency might be welcomed.

Individual as the target for collaboration

The worker will have forged many relationships with the community during the long process of developing their social planning capability. Because of the way in which organisations develop and the way in which power tends to centralise in this reformist model, the higher up, or more centralised an individual moves in an executive capacity, the greater pressure and demands there are going to be. An individual who once began as an activist in a small, community-based service organisation is now performing as a public figure, aspiring to play a full part in deciding on the allocation of public resources and being considered to be a repository of community power. The worker will have had to adapt each relationship as the roles and personalities changes in the face of new challenges.

Skill development and personal growth   The organisation's leadership has had to bridge huge changes in culture. The demands of planning, of conceptualising change in terms of strategic and time-differentiated goals, of objectifying outcomes and the use of technical language, of risking resources other than one's own, of choosing between priorities and allocating scarce resources - all these have to be recognised and learned. Questions of diplomacy (analysing the actions of others for motives, and acting, personally, in concert with collectively agreed political/outcome goals in view, keeping organisational secrets) have to be practised and developed until they can be handled with ease. Taking command of one organisation is one thing, assuming responsibility for the fortunes of a collective requires courage and dedication. The worker is going to be intimately involved in selecting, training and sustaining people as they endure the pressures that these processes create.

Those with leadership responsibilities have to master the art of recognising and being receptive to information from all available sources. Developing the capacity for handling large amounts of information, assessing its value, sifting it for the needs of analysis and marshalling it for the purposes of decision-making are essential skills. The worker will spend a great deal of time and resources in assisting leaders to develop this capacity and to formulate methods of acting upon it in line with the collective (and the person's source organisation's) best interests. The recognition that political processes are as much opportunistic as they are planned and formalised, and that there is a continual need for risk-taking if there is to be growth and change has to be supported by confidence born of a thorough knowledge of the system. These insights are part of the professional's repertoire and have been developed in the leaders over the whole period of organisational change. The worker is aware that if these elements are not formally embedded in the capabilities of the leaders, then the organisation will become vulnerable to manipulation.

Thus, the responsibility of the worker in developing the awareness and competence of the organisation's leadership is bound up in forcing upon them an analysis of structural issues and the relations of power and change in an established system. This may entail dealing with taboo subjects and the exploration of harsh choices, many of which will not meet the essential needs of the organisation in the immediate term. Support through the

192

pressures of taking responsibility is all that the worker can offer as compensation.

The worker's credibility with any party will depend on the quality of the service or the relationship which can be sustained, especially under quickly changing circumstances. The uncertainty of change may rapidly test the dependability of a worker's support capacity. There are going to be failures and unmet expectations, but a worker with a strong relationships is better placed to cope with set-backs and crises when they arise.

Personal dependency and relationships As the complexity of the organisational structure increases, and as the worker is forced to concentrate more and more on the leading personalities, and on setting up operational systems, and all the other channels of communication, a very strong mutual dependency will develop between the worker and certain members of the leadership contingent. Both the worker and those whom are targeted will discover that they change and develop as a consequence of the growth and change in the organisation. The worker sustains a perspective on the people involved that constantly contains a component concerning the future, and their future learning needs. This picture will not be formulated accurately unless the worker can gain the trust and personal commitment of those involved. So the worker will have deliberately set about creating as close and as open a relationship as is possible. This strategy is not without considerable risks. Both sides to the arrangement become vulnerable to manipulation and disillusion. The worker may come to depend on the ties of personal friendship such that the community leader is effectively being morally blackmailed to fulfil work activities. The worker's vulnerability to the vagaries of community sustainability and continuity could lead to the reverse process being activated - where the worker is manipulated on the promise of community activity which is vital for the worker's strategy/timetable, etc.

On a more personal level, a close relationship may reveal personal weaknesses on either side which may lead one or the other losing the basic trust that is necessary for the professional side of the relationship. Too close scrutiny of the professional strategy may also reveal the private agenda of the worker. This process will, in itself, uncover the underlying paternalistic goals of the professional. The worker may be prone to confuse the community representatives' roles and goals, with their positions as ordinary citizens namely: with the right to be less than perfect, with the right to walk away or the right to seek alternative guidance in their struggles to cope with the stress and pressures of personal and institutional change.

The employer agency (and the wider strategies of development)   In the background to all this development sits the worker's employer. This agency will have different demands to make, different information needs and clearer expectations about roles and goals. In terms of sustainable development, the quality leadership which emerges from these organisations is going to be of great concern to the worker's employer. As an agency which employs 'development agents', its own reputation is going to be assessed by the impact these new leaders make. Whether or not the established system takes to the demands for change and inclusion by the outside organisations, they are going to make their own assessment of the significance and quality of the people involved.

One of these may be that the worker has to realise the fruits of their extensive investment in the system by delivering up-to-date intelligence on community/grass-roots feeling and activity. If the worker has concentrated exclusively on the development of the organisations' leadership, then any residual relationship with those at the work face is likely to become diluted and sterile. The worker is likely to lose touch with the swell of grass-roots opinion, particularly with regard to the effectiveness of the services, the leadership of the organisations and the social priorities of the community. The worker will make decisions regarding the priority to give to this form of contact. The prize is in the grasp of the leadership, but the legitimacy lies with the people, both as activists in each organisation and as consumers of its services. In the end, it is all about time, personal preferences and pay-off. Nevertheless, a worker's appraisal of 'good practice' will still depend on the level of support, enablement and empowerment which is experienced by the people.

7 Social Action for Change - I: The Outsiders

In 1977, Gilbert and Specht identified one of the essential factors which distinguishes social work from the 'true' professions. It was, they contended, that social work held no commitment to *welfare* as a whole, despite its obvious commitment to *services* (Gilbert & Specht, 1977 p. 219). By failing to commit itself fully as an instrument of change, social work remained one-dimensional. By defaulting on the challenge presented by the material and social circumstances of the people which it claimed to serve, social work was merely a palliative. Social workers stand accused, as a profession, of avoiding a confrontation with the forces which lie behind the causes of their clients' distress. Except for a minority, social workers have done what they have been told to do, rather than seeking to increase the relative power of their clients. This leaves the client, individualised and isolated by the framework through which social work operates, unable to benefit form the supposed purpose of the social work intervention. The good practice guidelines of 'support, enablement and empowerment' can achieve little for the individualised and powerless victim of structural social and economic forces. Pinker's minority submission to the Barclay Report emphasises the *correctness* of opting out of this conflict. He chooses to segregate social work from a community-change perspective, limiting the action to the 'mandatory and permissive undertakings' (Pinker, 1982; see also, Payne, 1986). Hettne sums up this position when he cites the policy guidelines of the World Bank on this subject. The Bank promotes itself as the champion of 'participation' but not as the champion of 'empowerment'. The reason for this, is that 'empowerment' stands for structural change, whereas 'participation' involves only involvement in the processes of the status quo (World Bank, 1992, *Participatory development and the World Bank*, edited by B. Bhatnager & A.K. Williams, quoted in Hettne, 1995). Recent discussions regarding the nature and purpose of Community Care have reinforced this tendency (Orme & Glastonbury, 1993). Even within community development circles, failure to concentrate on the key issues or confront these contradictions, leads to confusion and lack of effective direction (Kelly, 1991; Mayo, 1979; Standing Conference, 1995). Mayo argues for radical and political goals, whereas Kelly is more concerned with a Gandhian, process concern for the process of engagement. The Standing Conference on Community Development is exploring how a 'representational' position can be maintained, within a position which is hostile to 'partnership' with the state (Kelly & Sewell, 1988, Mayo, 1994, Standing Conference, 1995).

For the profession as a whole, the history of the past three decades has been a painful one in this regard. The challenges posed successively by the Community Development Project (1970's) and, to a lesser extent, by the National Institute for Social Work *Community Social Work* initiative (in the 1980's) appear to have gone unheeded (Benington, 1976; Corina, 1987; Darville & Sprake, 1990; Loney, 1983; Seebohm, 1968; Smale, et.al., 1988; Smale & Bennett, 1989; Specht, 1976; Topping & Smith, 1977). The rift between the Association of Community Workers and the British Association of Social Workers in the early 1970's has continued to have its effects on the formal relations between the two activities (Cox & Derricourt, 1975; Popplestone, 1971). Whereas Younghusband considered the community perspective as a core element of social work intervention (Wilson, 1976; Younghusband, 1962, 1978), thirty years on, the hiatus is firmly cemented in the new regulations determining the scope and standards for qualification as a social worker (CCETSW, 1989). Currently, a community dimension to the work gets the barest of mention. This reflects the steady decline in the Central Council's interest in the subject (CCETSW, 1974;1979; 1981) and there is no hint of a structural approach to the task of intervention. In the face of this official exclusion, only a determined defensive action by a tiny minority of social work training establishments offer their students a balanced development component in their qualifying programmes. The main point here is not whether a definitive solution could have been produced at any specific point across the years, but that meaningful dialogue, and thus any creative, in-house competition, appears now to have been eliminated?

Shortly after the publication of the second Gulbenkian Report, in 1973 (Calouste Gulbenkian, 1973), clear examples of the effects of large scale social engineering were beginning to emerge from the Community Development Project and other grass-roots projects (Benington, 1974; Community Action, 1973; Crummy, 1992; Loney, 1983; Mayo, 1972; Topping & Smith, 1977; Whitfield, 1972). Concepts of class and the realities of deprivation were very much the order of things at that time. This information did not find its way into the models of community work until the 1990's, by which time, their utility as rallying cries for social workers had passed. The thought that community development techniques could be used by a malign state apparatus to pry into, and seek to control the destiny of community life was not considered (Cockburn, 1977; Corrigan, 1975; Leonard, 1975a).

This issue would not be of any consequence if social work was able to isolate itself from the changes going on around it in society at large. But, since the Seebohm Report (1968), which gave early encouragement to the place of community work within social work, the structure of society has been transformed, and the manner in which it is analysed and understood has changed beyond recognition. A structural perspective on the causes of personal disadvantage of the clients of social work, and how to target these pressures as they continue to exert their influence, has never been more urgently needed. In the face of the evidence, mere pleading for more resources and a closer observance of the rules will not suffice (Orme & Glastonbury, 1993).

In Britain today, the nature of employment and job tenure, home-ownership and family structure is virtually unrecognisable compared to thirty years previously. There are now 13.5 million households in their own home, up 35% since 1980 (Local Government I.U., 1995). Unemployment rose from just over 1% in 1955 to stabilise above 8% for the 1990's. Trade union membership has fallen dramatically to just 7.5 million and non-union employment has risen to 17.7 million (Bassett, 1995). The pattern of urban living was transformed steadily since World War II (Ginsburg, 1979; Willmott & Young, 1960; Young, 1957), and the cultural and ethnic make-up of the population has diversified through successive waves of inward migration (Mason, 1995; Jones & Macdonald, 1993; Rex, 1967). Poverty and homelessness have continued to rise. Despite the evidence of causal connections between poverty, the unequal society and the breakdown of the social fabric, social work is now preoccupied with issues of assessment and protection, rather than confront the structural issues which consign its 'clients' into financial and social poverty, and powerlessness (Barclay, 1995; Hills, 1995).

As it has nothing itself to say about society, it is preoccupied with ever more individualisation as it focuses on statutory provision and with providing priority care in the community to those with the 'greatest need' (Dept of Health, 1989; Griffiths, 1988). This does not include the homeless or the destitute (Croft & Beresford, 1989; Popay & Dhooge, 1989). Their plight is largely in the hands of the emergency housing services and/or the voluntary sector. This situation has persisted since the 1950's, when poverty, homelessness and the relative failure of the Welfare State to solve these questions first leaked out into public consciousness (Glastonbury, 1971; Greve, et.al., 1971; O'Malley, 1977; Radford, 1970; Townsend &

Abel-Smith, 1965). The issue of class, direct action and social change was eloquently argued by the activists' magazine, Community Action, between 1972 and 1990. Against a backdrop of vast redevelopment schemes, and the deliberate construction of insensitive and unresponsive systems by the State, time alone, it seemed, was to be the healer of this traumatic social dislocation. Outside the New Towns, few resources were allocated to assist in any social reconstruction. This was to be a process which was to have prolonged effects, and which carried over into the next major 'structural adjustment' of the Wilson-Callaghan-Thatcher era (Else, 1980; Harloe & Horrocks, 1974; Lees & Mayo, 1984). This all added to the justice of the 'Community Action' cause. Here was the ideal opportunity for those who made up the institution of social work to assert their relatively powerful and privileged influence on the side of 'their' clients. After all, it was they who were in daily contact with the victims of this situation; who literally clambered through the decay of working class communities, and who witnessed the accelerating problems of unemployment and poverty. Social work stands accused of being biased towards the values of the middle class (Corrigan & Leonard, 1978; Bolger, et.al., 1981; Hugman, 1991; Jones, 1983; O'Malley, 1970; Wooley, 1970). There is little evidence that it ever accepted the plaintive plea of Runnicles (1970), that it ally itself with direct action and assist the poor to strengthen their role in the democratic structure of the nation. Rather, it took the hint from Popplestone, who, very early on, described the vulnerability of the community work ideology within the social welfare complex (Popplestone, 1971). This might have been an opportunity for pre-empting the accusation of Gilbert and Specht of 1977, cited above. It proved to be beyond their ability. Instead, systems theory emerged as a non-controversial alternative, but this did not make a lasting impact outside the 'therapeutic' wing of social work (Pincus & Minahan, 1973; Smale, et.al., 1988). Increased detachment from *caring for* the client, and a preoccupation with creating '*care*' in its place, may make any journey back very difficult from an institutional standpoint.

Community development practitioners have not got much to boast about either. Losing touch with social work during the 1970's has not driven them to discover a new haven in which to prosper (Waddington, 1979; Thomas, 1995). They have not resolved their own differences, nor have they commanded a place of respect, either around the table of the policy makers or the powerful, or amongst the ranks of the poor. Over many years of evolution, the debate within community development remained rooted in the same questions: what constitutes 'change', what is considered to be the most appropriate method for achieving it, and by whom? Much of the literature on community development remained lost in the blind alley of indecisiveness. It was long on rhetoric, but short on practicalities. The polarisation of the theorists between 'class' and 'reformist' schools has still not been adequately supplanted (Barr, 1976; Barr, 1991; Bolger, et.al., 1981; Corrigan, 1975; Corkey & Craig, 1978; Gulbenkian, 1968; Leonard, 1975b; Loney, 1983, Thomas, 1983). More recently, the 'class' faction has been increasingly ignored, despite, as we shall see, that the debate has been both enriched and confused by the insistent pressures of militant and forceful players who have finally been able to get their voices heard.

The confusion which persisted over the years (Thomas, 1983; Thomas, 1995; Waddington, 1994), is echoed by the consultancy investigation of the International Social Policy Research Unit study of Leeds (Batson & Smith, 1995). Workers, it is claimed, lack direction and certainty about their work and appear to have no particular power base of their own. They lack clarity of goals, allow themselves to be refused permission, or are reluctant to subscribe to values that strive towards concrete objectives for social change. The principles behind their own concepts of good practice might include 'empowerment and change', but process goals appear to dominate the scope of their interventions. They appear to be unprepared for any personal responsibility in deciding on ideological issues, and are either unaware or unconcerned with the effect that this position has on any intervention model (Sayer, 1986). Put altogether, it is not surprising that the overall impact is not winning more support. These issues are raised by Armstrong when he states that community development has not demonstrated its role in community care and, consequently, that its potential has not been realised (Armstrong & Henderson, 1992b). Williams continues in this theme in relating empowerment to the care needs of the community, when she states, '..collective organisation/representation is vital. It is here that questions or patterns of inequality and exclusion can be tackled.' (Williams, 1995 p. 5). More forceful assertion is needed if this message is to get across.

In practice, despite the powerful and continuing call from feminists and black people, to name but two groups, for more radical action and consistency of principle, little has changed. Much of community development is still hiding within the bland, consensus approach of the early theorists - who deliberately avoided identifying and defining the limits of their targets for change. Most of them, generally, agreed with Murray Ross when he rooted his theoretical map of 'Community Organization' (Ross, 1955) in the values of religion and social work. He saw the basic conflict as between ideas, on the one hand, and the unresolved conflict between the community and individual liberty on the other. As far as Ross was concerned the 'community' resolved its arguments around the parish pump. Organising and integrating the debate was the duty of the worker, even when class differences emerge (Thomason, 1969). Ross did not recognise that responding to oppression and the denial of liberty came within the scope of his model. No distinction was made between the collective will of the 'community' and the organs of government. In the early days, Dunham, alone, seems to have anticipated that there was a source of potential conflict over the definition of what was 'socially desirable' (Dunham, 1958).

The history of employment conditions for British community development workers is marked by the low degree of tolerance for actions which create social conflict, or those which place politicians and senior officials on the defensive (Barr, 1991; Batson & Smith, 1995; Glen, 1993; Higgins, et.al., 1983; Loney, 1983; Thomas, 1995; Tracey, 1982). In this sense, workers are accused of perpetuating a form of neo-colonialism. Writers such as the Bryants (Bryant & Bryant, 1982) are exceptions, and their approach to practice combines the European concern with political ideology with the apolitical Alinsky model from the United States. Only in emergencies, does the State appear to tolerate this sort of activity for any length of time (Griffiths, 1974; Wiener, 1980). The theme that strategically placed professionals could be subversive agents, running as part of the system, itself, while acting as catalysis and resource personnel to the community was never developed openly after its initial foray into the literature (London/Edinburgh, 1979).

Movement for change

The structure of this book has set out to offer the practitioner a theoretical basis for intervention. It has sought to provide an insight into the necessary steps and ingredients of thorough development practice within the context of relative social stability, despite the turmoil which faces the victims of social and structural dislocation. The models which have been described up to, and until this point, offer an insight into the framework and dynamics of organisational development, and they were linked firmly within the structural scope of conventional social work practice. They will work, but control over the process by the worker has been deliberately safeguarded. This makes the framework both comprehensible and acceptable to the bulk of practitioners (and, also, to their employers). However, something more is needed if change is to be perceived to be attainable and its effects and benefits experienced by those that expose themselves to the effort and risks of the process - the people on the ground. These are twice-times victims: of structural disadvantage and of professional intervention. Professionals will continue to take arbitrary decisions, and to conceal their actual power when conflicts of interest arise, or when risks appear to be too great for comfort. But the hollowness of the classical 'consensus' approach, or its crude Marxist successor must be put into perspective. There is still a lot of it about, and, it appears, that the poorest and more vulnerable areas, particularly in Africa, are more susceptible to it than others (Barr, 1991; Burkey, 1993; Long & Villareal, 1994; Porter, et.al., 1991; Rondinelli, 1993). Some are grappling with the dilemmas of coping with the crisis of survival (Edwards, 1994; Constantino-David, 1992), and others with the pressures of manipulative and authoritarian regimes (Porter, et.al., 1991; Fainstein & Fainstein, 1993; Mouzelis, 1994; Ntebe, 1994; Rathgeber, 1995). There are stark differences between cultures which have to be taken into account (compare, for example, the essays in Escobar & Alvarez (eds), 1992; Schuurman, 1993b); or Stiefel & Wolfe, 1994, with those in Gibbon (ed), 1993, or Burkey, 1993), and it is obvious that the gulf between the aspirations of theory and the realities of practice will remain. In some low-risk settings, though, so strong is the old ideology of consensus that serial attempts are being made to avoid the problem of risk-taking altogether (Waste, 1986).

The impact of post-modernism It is obvious that the theories and initiatives of the early generations of worker have made only limited impact. This is particularly evident in the failure of the electorate to demand that their taxes be spent on the skills and processes of community development. Community development is still inflicted from the outside, on 'suitable cases for treatment', so to speak (Cruikshank, 1994). But now the gauntlet has been thrown down by critics who will no longer allow their protests at the limitations of the classical approach to go unrecognised. Their criticisms have been in the literature from early days, but they have had to compete with the oligarchy of rival orthodoxies which dominated the presses. Development theories are now becoming absorbed with the debate over which philosophical star to hitch their wagon (Escobar & Alvarez, (eds), 1992; Fisher, & Kling, (eds), 1993; Marchand, & Parpart, (eds), 1995; McLaren & Lankshear (eds), 1994; Schuurman, 1993b; Stiefel & Wolfe, 1994).

The fragmentation and re-appraisal of the theories of the 'Modernity' School, under the cloak of 'post-modernism', is now very advanced (Parpart, 1995; Wilson, 1990). Callinicos presents the thesis that the proliferation of 'schools', or natural groupings, do not go far enough to break completely with the past, despite the desperation that has arisen at the loss of faith in the old order. Is this the fear of abandoning the dream of utopia and emancipation for the oppressed (Callinicos, 1990)?   Post-modernism can, at least, be considered as a valuable tool for investigating 'these new components of the spectacle' (Wilson, 1990). To borrow from Lovibond: '...... (development) ......aspires to be something more than a reformist movement ..... there is a need to know, and post-modernist theory fails to explain how we can achieve a thorough-going revision of the range of social scripts ..... available to men and women...'.(Lovibond, 1990, p. 172). Schuurman analyses the evidence and considers the rise of dissident voices. He considers that feminists, Gramscian Marxists, the interpreters of Castells, up to and including the *Rainbow Coalition*, are really the manifestation of the crisis that is facing 'modernity' in the era where the fruits of its own emancipating forces are being faced. Modernity is not dead, it is merely hiding in *The New Modernity Project*, where emancipation can be realised through a political economy based upon *'Citizenship and Participation'* (Schuurman, 1993a).

In many respects, this discussion is vital to the reformation, and the reclamation, of community development. The voices from the sidelines: Black people and cultural minorities, women, the poor and marginalised, the suppressed movements of the urban proletariat of Latin America, all need the space to review their history. They are now all free to do so, and, in theory, consider the most beneficial path forward. Post-Modernism has exposed the constraints of reductionism (Townsend, 1993) and the (philosophical and verbal) challenge to patriarchy continues unabated, but its material rewards in the field of community development are slow in coming. It is the extreme diversity of the post-modernist assault, and its lack of real success through direct action, which is of immediate concern to us. We must learn from history. The internecine strife and fragmentation of the 'Left' during the Spanish Civil War greatly undermined whatever cohesive resistance might have been possible to Fascism. This contributed significantly to its eclipse and elimination. In community development, the forces of *emancipation* must not be allowed to be swept aside on a similar tide of dissonance, merely because they are not convenient.

Community development can draw on many discourses but, like most of the classical pioneers of the process, it is concerned with the adjustment of power relations within society in the immediate, or short term. It is, therefore, systems-based, seeking compromise, pragmatic action and riposte to counter-action along the way. Community development is not anti-intellectual, but neither is it aspiring towards a purist position. Community development strives for clarity, but it has to rely on opportunism and compromise as much as it does on moral rectitude or contractual probity. Organisation is the springboard for power and organisation is anathema to many of the theorists of the post-modernist approach. And so we must conclude that community development belongs to the modernity school, but it is not concerned with science in the old sense. It seeks its knowledge of the world from the post-modernists, to whom it remains forever in debt. It seeks to re-unify the fragments, such that they may survive to continue the struggle, and to discover some clarity and stability along the way: a *New Modernity Project,* to be sure.

If community development theory is to escape from the sidelines, the time has now come for practitioners to grapple with the intellectual task. They have to break with the inadequacies of the 'old' ideologies, and enter the dialogue. By asserting their presence, they will be able to present a powerful lever in their efforts to regain professional autonomy. The pre-occupation with 'method and process' will no longer do. It is not just that there is a bandwagon out there waiting to be ridden. There is a strong tide running which demands evidence of commitment. It will not be fobbed off with more of the same. This tide has an intellectual dimension, which has been neglected far too long. Without picking up the challenge in its entirety, community development will be brushed aside as irrelevant.

There is a powerful motive for this need to be aware of, and conversant with, the substance at the heart of the 'new social movements', which are both the vehicle and the inspiration for the new wave of ideas and analyses. These 'movements', in all their guises, which have sprung from the rebellion against the strictures of   ideologies and regimes, both past and present, must not merely be seen as the source of intellectual inspiration. They must be seen as the targets for community development intervention. This may present difficulties. Those seeking space, freedom from past perceptions and outmoded controls, will not take happily to what has, hitherto, been described as: colonising, elitist and interventionist;   as patriarchal, diversionary and untrustworthy;   as class-biased and oppressive. Many, particularly women, disability groups, Black people and other minorities, may seek separation and detachment from the vestiges of the bad old days. These were days in which their contribution was derided, their presence queried and marginalised by racism and paternalism, and their whole analytical approach devalued, suppressed or ignored altogether. The presence which the 'new social movements' manifest through their social, economic and theoretical impact represents a distrust for the trappings of the past. In the longer term, and along the road of testing the political viability of their cause, many of them will acknowledge their debt to some of these structures of the *ancien regime.* In their present state, they are, by definition, unstable and lacking in form. Those seeking to resist any manifestation of formality by ensuring the free flow of ideas, but casting their (intellectual) fortunes upon the vagaries of fortune, fashion and the availability of a publisher, are vulnerable to having their message pillaged by opportunists who will claim the authors of the ideas as legitimising their own activities. Getting nowhere may be an aesthetic convenience, but real people are being oppressed and being denied life chances while we await the millennium. This may be already happening, as the 'new social movements' continue to manifest themselves in their shibboleth fashion. To avoid being the passive hostages to fortune, these thinkers will have to seek out the processes and trappings of instrumental power if they ever want to demonstrate that the 'movements' are to become an intellectually coherent and tangible force in society. Community development has much to offer now, while the ground rules are being discovered, and later, when the real quest for power and influence begins.

From the perspective of the community development worker, presentation approaches must be learned to create the image of a credible change agent for every level in this process. A firm grip must be taken over the consideration and description of the most appropriate role. This concerns the definition of values, and what this implies for establishing boundaries for action and practice methods. Principally, practitioners must seek to overcome the difficulties which they have demonstrated in the past. These are: handling risk, political exposure and passive dependence on the patronage of the major employer institutions (such as major Voluntary Organisations and Social Services) (Britton, 1983; Dixon, 1990; Grace & Romeril, 1994; Jordan & Parton, 1983; Wade, 1963). It is not that these agencies should not be sought out as employers. Rather that they, too, be offered a model for application which will produce more thought-provoking, challenging outcomes. Simplistic and 'quick-fix' solutions have served the profession badly in the past. Palliatives are neither cost-effective nor good for credibility. The fault lies, not only in the avoidance of argument with the employers about the nature and purpose of 'outcomes', but in the failure of adopting a consistent strategic and theoretical approach.

Community development has to make itself appealing and acceptable to a wider constituency, but on a revitalised basis. It has been blighted, in the past, by over-extravagant exhortations in the literature, without an analytical model which could translate into practice. Instead, the safe option was to deliver a bland form of uncritical consensus. Reasoned analysis, strategic perspectives and a carefully developed personal (and private) agenda would provide the underpinning for a more dynamic and credible profession. Promotion and careful presentation must be introduced into the professional repertoire.

The worker must consider how a tactical shift of intervention procedure might influence the behaviour of any already captive customer/constituent group. This could result in direct pressure being applied to a potential funder or employer by those currently in a dependant or consumer relationship. They must be persuaded to 'rock the boat' of consensus on their own account. This would change the existing climate and create new perceptions and expectations on all sides. Any previous state of unresolved differences, stratagems or negotiations can now give way to more clearly defined proposals for moving forward. Not 'more of the same', but a fresh strategy, complete with rationale and targets. For this tactic to be successful, credibility must already be achieved with the 'consumers', the constituent population. From the beginning, this must take the form of defining, for the 'fragments', the difference between the 'mob' and an effective organisational process for acquiring power and change (Alinsky, 1972).

Where no consensus is possible As in the earlier chapters above, the workers must approach a target population on the basis of searching out the individuals for engagement. The task is then seeking to find common cause, openings for contributing 'support, enablement and empowerment' in the achievement of social change or other goals. In the example of those groups seeking tangible changes in the socio-political structures in their society, in line with their own strongly held beliefs and aspirations, there is already a clear fissure between these aspirations and those of the target, or object of a change strategy.

The identification of the potential client group may not pose a difficulty for the worker. Nevertheless, there may be difficulties in establishing meaningful contact. In some cases, this target population constitutes a self-defined, or self-definable, constituency of its own. Most ethnic populations contain within their midst many such groupings. There are cultural associations, religious organisations, youth formations, social welfare support systems, etc. Across the whole community, the members of women's groups, the disability constituencies of agencies, categories of assessed 'social need', and the aggregate of any such persons within workable 'catchment' areas or geographical locations might form the nucleus of a similar development strategy. There is no attempt here to gloss over the interventionist measures which are at the fore of a workers tactical approach to such a group of people. The fact that a group is identifiable is enough. That fact, alone, represents the identification of the first hurdle for a development strategy.

However, there are targets, and there are *targets*. There is sometimes a determination in people to establish a separate identity, or to avoid contact with the institutions of the wider society on any terms. This can manifest itself in different ways. Any grouping or aggregate of people which own common sentiments or characteristics, which are more or less freely acquired or held, and which, in themselves, do not constitute an effective block to self-mobilisation, can be tracked down and engaged. Such aggregates are carers of the disabled, for example, who seek privacy for themselves and their family, rather than a public profile for their situation.

But there are loose aggregates of people who do not share these identity characteristics in the same way. The people to whom we refer are those who have fallen out of the conventional patterns of social interaction, for reasons of poverty, despair or confusion, coupled with suffering the active rejection of the larger formations of society (Burghardt & Fabricant, 1987; Devine, & Wright 1993; Donnison, 1991; Field, 1989; Murray, 1994; Scott, 1994). The homeless, the detached and confused casualties and sufferers of stigmatising and debilitating illness, and others, who are non-conforming in this way, make up this constituency. Because of the fragmentation of the means of mutual support for these people, and their dependence on charity or the rudimentary tactics for barest survival, all under conditions of extreme deprivation, this is a target population usually ignored in community development (Brager, 1963; Cannan, 1975; Grosser, 1965). The 'underclass' constitutes bad connections for community development: bad politics, bad publicity and bad odds for successful outcomes (Burghardt & Fabricant, 1987).

From the perspective of the development worker, what characteristics do these different groupings have in common? They are 'separate' to some degree or another. They will not welcome intrusion from outside, especially on any terms which suggest that the established interests of society have an interest in manipulating their relations with the greater community. They have their own codes of behaviour, they have accommodated their contact with the greater community on terms which allow for many real, or imagined frictions to be reduced. From the standpoint of their 'marginal' or 'minority' status, they are owners of cultures which are discrete and self-serving, rather than actively exchanging with the wider complex. They will usually be part of an exclusive system of networks which are private, although some members of these groupings will share extensive contacts *inside* the wider social system. They have no reason to 'share' who they are or what they want to

206

be with any outsider. They are likely to have an analysis of their relationship with the greater community, which defines the benefits and costs of maintaining this status, even if it is not in their power to change it in any way.

We have reconstituted the model which we have presented in earlier chapters, which describes development of community organisations under stable conditions, and where consensus is possible. The model which we now present cannot thrive on consensus as it builds upon the dynamics of conflict, of separateness and on the acquisition of power for the exclusive use of the 'group', or organisation.

The hybrid model for action

Target AGGREGATE with POTENTIAL for ACTION	GROUP as the NUCLEUS for ACTION	ACTION as the STRATEGY for CHANGE	COMPLEX ACTION as the VEHICLE for CHANGE	CHANGE as the MEDIUM for ORGANISATION	Target the INDIVIDUAL for CHANGE
	ORGANISATION as the NUCLEUS for ACTION	COALITION as the VEHICLE for CHANGE	UNITY as the PLATFORM for POWER	POWER as the PLATFORM for CHANGE	

In this complex model we are presented with a choice of relationships. The nature of the target population is one factor and we shall deal with two variants of this in order to demonstrate how the model works and how the contrasting characteristics of the constituent groups determine the intervention method.

Seeking out the 'outsiders'   Our first example is concerned with those marginalised people who are forced into a form of segregation from the wider community. This may mean, in the purely physical sense, that they live an existence which is separate, such as the street kids of the *favellas* of Brazil, the shanties of Eastlea, Zimbabwe or Kings Cross in London. We mean those who reside in the subways and alleyways and in the drains of major cities of the developed world, the runaways, the mentally ill, the rejects or the self-excluded. In some cases they constitute a semi-criminal sub-class. Mere existence outside the formal social support systems of the society which defines their environment, places them in a state of resistance. This, alone, may result in them being perceived as deviant and threatening. Some may drop in or out of the 'host' community by choice, or when under compulsion by one social regulator or another. Sometimes these aggregates of humanity constitute a stable segment, sometimes the membership fluctuates widely. Seasons, social policies, whimsy, or whatever the cause of their detachment, they remain virtually untouched by strategies designed to include or assist them.

This group also includes those that live in the midst of the organised community, but who are effectively excluded by virtue of the stigmas and the narrow boundaries of freedom which their economic and social circumstances impose. These include many of the single parents who are forced to live in the shoddy estates in Britain, the legendary rural and urban literacy students of Freire's Brazil, the limbo status of many refugees (Donnison, 1991; Freire, 1974; Murray, 1990). They live from hand to mouth on minimal state handouts or occasional paid work. They declare little to the tax collector. They survive, occasionally on their wits, more often on their sense of humour. They are paralysed by the lack of their own force, and by the pressure of the rest of society. This apparent inertia does not constitute brain death, just the abandonment of potential.

The 'adjustment' of society to economic and social forces produces casualties. If these casualties are not responsive to the form in which any Aid is proffered, or if the Aid does not include the casualties as part of its target, the casualties remain casualties. In the developing economies of the South, Structural Adjustment Programmes have elicited a variety of state and NGO responses (Clark, 1992; Rondinelli, 1993; Stiefel & Wolfe, 1994). Many are forced to just concentrate on primary support, the basics for life, and no more. We must find an alternative, if only to demonstrate that community development has something to offer in every human situation.

Korten focuses on these developing economies. He outlines the extent to which the policy-makers of development have fallen foul of their own ideologies and past mistakes, and that they have put the future of whole generations, if not the whole civilisation, at risk. He identifies the 'over-consumers', the 'sustainers' and the 'marginals', three groups, only one of whom is secure within the new economic order of 'adjustment'. For the 'marginals', survival, itself, cannot be ensured (Korten, 1992). This situation is still being kept under some control in the Northern countries, through their extensive welfare systems and the deployment of ad hoc services to mop up the worst casualties.

The clash of these diametrically opposed ideologies: the 'Structural Adjustment' school and the people centred development faction, is not likely to be resolved in time to bring relief to the 'underclasses' of both the North or the South. For them, there is just one generation of pain. It is here that we must impose the rationale for community development.

208

Someone in the complex of socio-economic intervention must make their presence known and an attempt must be made to address the crises with which they are presented. This must be done on the terms of the victims of these policies, and not as a tidying up exercise for the perpetrators.

Target aggregate with potential for action

Target AGGREGATE with POTENTIAL for ACTION	GROUP as the NUCLEUS for ACTION	ACTION as the STRATEGY for CHANGE	COMPLEX ACTION as the VEHICLE for CHANGE	CHANGE as the MEDIUM for ORGANISATION	TARGET the INDIVIDUAL for CHANGE

We have identified the aggregate of people on which we wish to focus. We might identify them as a 'community', but we cannot do this until we have established that there are connections that can be identified which will make further development intervention valid. Their circumstances are those which render them vulnerable to control, exclusion and stigma. Their autonomy is limited to the times when they are not under direct supervision, or when they are not forced into dependency due to their deprivation. There is no reason why they should respond in any way to another, unsolicited intrusion from 'outsiders'. There is considerable risk for all concerned in this approach. But the worker must develop a relationship with individuals within this aggregate and must attempt to construct an extensive ethnography of the context within which contact and dialogue will be established.

We wish to emphasise that the model presented above does mark a break with the general ethos of the preceding chapters. Nevertheless, the qualities and patterns of engagement which have been discussed earlier are still applicable in this situation. The values, immediate goals and action framework may have shifted somewhat, but, for the worker, the development of skills and insight is a cumulative process, and not subject to compartmentalisation. It is not realistic to start out on an initiative of this nature with the intention of producing 'development' patterns of the order which we have suggested hitherto. The target for the worker is to 'pull on the skin' of the subject group/aggregate, to get to grips with the cultural codes, the parameters, the boundaries of space and behaviour, and to learn how these are expressed within the 'community'. The worker must be free to make this attempt, free from the constraints of time-bounded targets, outputs, outcome expectations and peer pressure. At the same time, the worker has standing and a personal investment in the trappings of the wider social context. This must not be abandoned or injured in this process.

We are not asking that the worker becomes completely submerged in this new culture, such as posing as an itinerant. Nevertheless, the approach must be aimed at becoming as well informed as possible, and as well connected to the individuals who make up this aggregate. For this, it must be based on direct experience, and upon close, personal contact, not on hearsay (thus the ethnography). The worker must be open to the acquisition of information and there must be a base for establishing contact which does not immediately build barriers of suspicion, reaction or aggression. All of the latter are bound to arise in some form or other, but steps must be taken to minimise them. A *'raison d'être'* for the intervention must be created which provides 'cover' and some credibility for the worker in the initial stages, as the worker has to make personal contact and personal relationships which will endure. This whole process is a test for the 'non-judgemental' approach of the social worker. Depending on the target population, the tolerance levels of the worker could be tested severely.

The purpose of this intervention is to establish what linkages exist between individuals *within* the target community. The next stage is to try to make these linkages the target for exercises which will strengthen them. Through this process, activities can be developed out of the perceived needs and priorities of those 'connected' in this way. In addition, from building on the existing skills and facilities available to the subjects of this exercise, attempts will be made to involve the group in the analysis of the forms of processes in which they are engaged. It has been suggested that a special 'Union' of workers may be required to create a defensive bloc with which to resist the pressures of isolation and social disapproval (Burghardt & Fabricant, 1987). Deploying these skills and widening the scope of these activities will be the primary strategy for the worker once the contact and initial inputs have been successful. The worker is being asked to achieve a relationship of trust which is based upon sharing knowledge and achieving social acceptance and integration into the 'community'. The perspective of the 'Unattached' needs to be inverted (Morse, 1965).

In this situation, it is the worker who becomes the unattached from the agency, and from the pressures of conformity with the expectations of professional peers and the wider society. The worker must be shown to be personally resourceful, and not reliant on established systems of service, which are likely to be objects of distrust to this target group. Taking up a position 'alongside' the marginalised people is taken literally (O'Gorman, 1990). What follows will be the growth of a form of dependence. In social work/development parlance, this is seen as dysfunctional to self-reliance and dubious professional practice (Oakley & Flores, 1994; Rahman, 1993b). We have argued that, as the role of the professional changes, so the relationship between the worker and the target community changes. We would argue that there is a role for dependence, and that it is in everybody's interest that it continue. Dependence changes its form, depending on the nature of the organisational formation that is taking place. There is no objective case for withdrawal. The rationale for it is usually based upon financial reasons, or a confused interpretation of the role of social work. Halmos' accusation that social work is compromised through the development of an alliance between the 'client' and the professional for political outcomes is contradicted by the assertions of the liberation theologians. In some cases (in all cases?), the worker must be seen to be *of, with and for* the client (Halmos, 1978; Kirk, 1989). In this example, the creation of mutual trust and inter-personal reliance, in the face of societal opposition, is vital. It is on the back of this relationship, that the way forward is to be designed (Campbell, 1993).

Group as the nucleus for action

Having established a one-to-one relationship with a number of people, and directed sufficient energy and skill to create and strengthen ties between these individuals, the next stage can be contemplated. This is a planning phase for what may become a vehicle for social change. The basics of group work are employed to build the foundations for social cohesion which goes beyond the shallow demands of mere sociability. The intention is to engage this mini-community in a process whereby they identify targets and processes through which they can transform their relations with each other and also with any of those intrusions of the 'outside' system that they might wish. It is the creation of a form of social organisation that is the first level objective of the worker. It maybe that the history of this group has already created the necessary bonds and social devices to enable them to recognise the nature and purpose of collective cohesion and mutual association. The quality of the information which has been assembled about the specific individuals in this situation will have informed the worker. The worker is in the middle of a process whereby the people are being 'objectified' by the worker's agenda, but the medium for expressing this is through the 'subjective' relationships which have been established.

This is a period of intensive exposure and face-to-face activity. The worker has to target those members of the 'community' that appear to be more active and amenable to participation. There is an element of frank discussion and coercion about it. Identifying the collective needs of the group to all its members, and the suggestion of a means towards solutions to some of them, may prove to be attractive, at least to some. The worker is in a position to suggest possible benefits which might follow. This group will be well aware of the negative aspects of their situation. Despite the likelihood that the worker's actions will appear to be more of the same, this 'group' of people must be encouraged and supported to seek positive and affirmative outcomes in settings which hitherto have proved negative. Selling the positives is the worker's priority. Providing direct support will reduce the risk of failure. Gradually, it will become apparent that there are gains to be made and the worker should exploit any strengths in personalities and situations to progress these initiatives. The initial objectives, in practical terms, can be very modest indeed: a party, a visit, a co-operative task. These activities can be developed into more complex objectives once success is achieved. As positive outcomes are realised, the worker begins to focus on the encouragement and development of person qualities and the creation of indigenous leadership for the group. The exploitation of any charisma and/or power characteristics of the personalities concerned should be utilised as a tactical expedient.

The primary objective of this phase is to establish the potential of networks and leadership within the group. In this situation, we are looking for the potential of movement, collective movement, in any direction that may demonstrate that there is advantage in strengthening ties, sharing opinions and aspirations, and for pooling energies. This is the first step in defensive and 'preventative' work, as much as it is development in the sense of moving forward. Conservation of the means for development is of vital importance. The worker will concentrate on getting people into contact with each other, on a casual and informal basis. They will be helped to establish mutual recognition and be 'assisted' to identify commonalties of circumstance, behaviour and needs. This is complemented by positive and reinforcing encouragement, and it is all done in the time and in the space of the people involved. If it is attempted in the setting of some service agency or other artificial surroundings, there will be a reaction. Either the people will generate another dependence syndrome, based upon the structural impact of the setting, or else they will see their activity as a thing apart, not as an organic part of their existence. Some groups will be more amenable and more able to respond. It might be said that the less able, the greater is the need for concentrated action. For some, the possibility of collective action is still some time away. They will be the immediate sufferers from personal, social and physical burdens that preclude any other activity, other than those needed for the barest survival. For them, the emergency services, and the more benign pressures of social control, provide the framework for existence. This form of dependence has to be broken down and replaced by one of mutuality.

Community development practice is, to some large extent, about backing winners. The worker seeks the 'positive' opening for movement and organisational potential. Those that do not 'take advantage' of the offer of change and betterment are often put aside until there is time and resources to spare to give the extra support and encouragement that they need. This task is often abandoned by default. The worker needs 'results' as much as the target population can benefit from 'empowerment'. Going back for the stragglers could be a costly and futile exercise. In this example, the target group have already demonstrated their 'failure', relative to the power manifested by those apparently secure in the mainstream. The group from the 'underclass' has nowhere to go, but if they can be given some purpose through witnessing their own success in small ways, then they may develop hope for greater achievement (Grosser, 1965). For those not able to set out at the start of this intervention, they can be given a positive role model to follow. The gains at first are going to appear to be small, but they will represent great effort, persistence and faith. For the worker, the distance back to the slower ones is not going to be far. The strengthening of the resolve and confidence of the initial target group might be used to collect the others and to carry them along until, and if, they pick up their own momentum.

Action as the strategy for change

The next step is to involve the group in a direct action to demonstrate that they can achieve some benefit from joint effort. There is no form or structure associated with this 'group', and so it up to the worker to contrive, through careful planning, an experience, in which as many play a part as can be induced. This activity can be of a very small and transitory nature. A celebration, a modest modification to the environment, a service for one person, or more, who cannot manage it alone. The worker will be in a very influential position. This extends over identifying the task, motivating and mobilising the group, allocating small roles and assisting those unfamiliar with the task to achieve their target (Grosser, 1976). The establishment of leadership from the group, and enlisting help throughout the process from as many as are willing and able, will be a directive, as well as a non-directive, task. The action has to succeed and, although it has been described as a one-off activity, the intention is to keep the movement alive. For this reason, success which can be quantified is an essential outcome.

Feedback, the dissection of the process, frame by frame, is the next task. It is necessary that the worker establish a mechanism for this new collective to share their experiences together, and that they be not to be allowed to disperse until that process has been accomplished. This represents the essence of directive intervention in the extreme. There is no need to disguise it for what it is. Development, for those in no position to resist, has a material, or structural impact. People in this marginalised and passive situation need to understand their reality. They can now be assisted to re-examine it for themselves. For that they need a trigger mechanism. To have taken part in some form of activity which was their own, and which they could claim ownership, will have the most relevance. The role of the worker as a full participant is acknowledged as one of many, thus reducing its importance (Freire, 1972). The achievement of the collective, including the worker, is built up as the example which may serve as a model for the future.

The existence of indigenous leadership, even if it is not representative, is important. It may be charismatic or coercive; or built on weak or transitory qualities. If it is not there, it may have to be invested, in order to get the 'group' through a critical phase. As the worker has not entered into this relationship with the intention of walking away once the first smell of success has been detected, the issue of the quality of leadership can be tackled at a later stage. The establishment of a group consciousness about the effect that collective action can make on the social and material environment, needs to be demonstrated over an extended time period. The reinforcement and encouragement of leadership is part and parcel of this process, in the first instance, and so it must be encouraged to flourish. For those without power, the establishment of a centre of power in their midst is a necessary building block for the future. The success in allowing indigenous leadership to emerge depends on the quality of the worker's relationship with that leadership. This is a crucial factor. The empowerment of the leadership is part of the process of empowering the larger group. Awareness of the nature of power and the relative powerlessness of the group in the face of the greater society is the aim of the worker. Once the pattern of collective activity has been established over a number of planned actions, the worker is in a position to confront the group with the implications of their success. The 'choice' which is

214

before them is whether or not to consolidate their achievements. At this level, any gains are positive indicators of achievement. The dangers of incorporation, of either the leadership or the group members, are still some way away in developmental terms (Arnstein, 1968; Cannan, 1975).

The worker's role is to support the leadership, to promote the group's direction and cohesion, and to attempt to propel the group into decisions which will continue the process of collective activity. The attempt is to assist this group, as individuals, and through group activity, *'to translate and actualise ....(their).... values into a socially desirable repertoire of behaviours'* (Devine & Wright, 1993). This confronts, and seeks to confound, the value system which presents the 'underclass' as feckless, and which wishes to impose a regime of 'tough love' upon them (Brager, 1963; Devine & Wright, 1993; Lister, 1990; Lopes, 1994; Murray, 1990, 1994). There are unconfirmed reports from the United States, that advocates of 'communitarianism', not satisfied with fencing off their own neighbourhoods into security bunkers, are bent upon *fencing in* the 'underclass' within the ghettos of deprivation. While access to the poorer areas of Britain is still possible, steps must be taken to discover a more society-sensitive solution. Special qualities will be required of the worker in this situation. Factors which may determine eligibility, such as sex, cultural background and race, will all have to be tested in the field, alongside the personal qualities of personality, training, skill and resilience. As will be seen in the next section, the selection and preparation of workers in this situation will have to be considered from a strategic, as well as a short-term perspective. The work which has been described is intensive and ties up a worker into a limited number of initiatives at any one time. There will be strong expectations that at least a medium-term commitment will be required - two to three years of sustained endurance under very difficult circumstances. After that, achievements cannot simply be abandoned. Agencies must consider this at all times. It will be necessary for a funding and planning agency to consider the implications of under-resourcing an undertaking such as this.

Complex action as the vehicle for change

The strategic dimension of this work is based upon the premise that, at the bottom of the social and economic order, groups engaged in self-help and self-advocacy will, in themselves, make little or no impact upon the wider community or society. It is also understood that many aggregates of individuals, for reasons of extreme deprivation, unconventional behaviour, stigma or for reasons of their own, may never be accepted as they are by those who consider their own social situation to be 'mainstream' or 'normal'. A worker may then be engaged with some groups which find that they are at the very margins of entry into these 'mainstream' communication and activity patterns. For them, any movement towards entry may appear to be the most desirable goal, but entry for others may not be. It may be for reasons of personal choice, culture or other characteristics (e.g. desire for separatist status) that they will continue to choose to be 'outsiders'. Development with both of these status groups will present the worker with a complex and sensitive set of strategic questions (Rahnema, 1993). Not least of these, is how to test the boundaries between groups and how to determine what options exist for choice and change. Is it possible to open up communication channels between them, and might some form of co-operation become possible? These are the essential questions for workers to have open and constantly before them as they move to engage an 'outsider' initiative.

From the beginning of this process, the target had been to change the perspective of individuals about their immediate social and survival needs. The next stage in development is to stimulate the formulation of goals which will result in change targets in the environment around them. This, in turn, will have knock-on effects on each of them. Recognition needs to be established that some success as been possible so far, but that the goals which were striven for were of only limited and marginal importance. The development of leverage on a greater set of social forces will need more than wishful thinking and short-term compliance with voluntary disciplines. The *'transformation'* of the relationship between these marginalised people and society rests on their ability to demonstrate a) a viable presence and b) the potential for influence. All this is dependent upon their own ability to come to terms with a fresh understanding of the society in which they survive. We now enter the arena of *'transformation for change'*, as it has evolved from the teachings of the Gandhians, Paulo Freire, feminists and, most recently, from Africa and Latin America. The mobilisation of the poor against seemingly insuperable odds of war, authoritarian regimes, famine, drought and AIDS, continues to make gains (Ankrah, E., 1992; Chinchilla, 1992; Clarke, 1993; Dominelli, 1990; Freire, 1972;1973;1985; Hope, et.al., 1984; Mosse, 1993; Narayan, 1967b).

Transformation for change marks the road towards liberation. Through the exploration of the issues dominating their own reality, people can break out of their dependence on the 'received wisdom' of others and begin to sort out things for themselves. This process depends on the transformation of the social (or religious) group into an agency for participatory education. The meetings, and their problem-posing approach to education and raising

216

consciousness, are part of a carefully structured process. The linkages with others are moulded, and solidarity is forged. Through this, the value of the group becomes recognised and internalised. Mutual dependence, linked with the spirit of co-operation and goal achievement cements the relevance of collective activity. From the formation of the group, the concept of either a communal or organisational formation can be developed. This model underpins the creation of 'Christian base communities' in Latin America, and elsewhere, where the lead is provided by the Roman Catholic Church (Boff, 1985; Burdick, 1992; Burkey, 1993; Dussel, 1992; Hope, et.al., 1984; Illich, 1973; Marins, et.al., 1989; Rowland, 1988; Stiefel & Wolfe, 1994). To some great extent, this is a spiritual movement, but it has as many secular adherents as it does religious. There is evidence of competition within the religious sector (Burdick, 1992), and some, who are obviously starting out along the parochial road, go to lengths to set out their secular stall as being of the greatest priority. Liberation, for the liberated theologians, belongs to all of creation, and not just to the chosen (Balleis, 1992; Berridge, 1993; Boff, 1985; Hope, 1984), although St. Paul might have an opinion on this (Acts 2. 42-46).

The professional task here is to develop a grasp of the nature of social relations into an understanding of power through action. The achievement of mutual recognition and social solidarity will change their group's perceptions of power over their own, immediate, circumstances. This will present them with choices:

♦ whether or not to widen their circle of contact, and their system of solidarity;
♦ whether or not to make proposals relating to their own needs, or those which concern other, more general, factors in their immediate environment;
♦ whether to seek changes in their circumstances through planned, and/or joint, effort?

There will be significant learning activities within this effort. They will discover the nature of compromise and negotiation, of the *quid pro quo*, of planning and of contracting one's own actions for the shared benefit of all. There will also be the exposure to some risk and ventures will be taken into the unknown. These may all be daunting, if not incomprehensible, to them. The nature of the professional task is to enable the meeting of those who believe that such action is at least worth considering.

In the first instance, meetings between representatives of the groups can be brought together informally. If there are other professional workers in the area, then they can prepare the ground amongst their own contacts. Their active co-operation may be desirable, or it may not be. Screening the qualities of other professionals and identifying their personal and professional agendas, will test their dependability. The emphasis is still on informal actions, taken in concert, which can demonstrate mutuality and the benefits of pooled resources. The first task of the professional is to facilitate the sharing of mutuality and then managing the development of future relations through the achievement of medium scale goals.

Change as the medium for organisation

Dudley presents the problem of moving through awareness, through analysis and into a change and action programme. He poses the dilemma which faces the researcher in search of the highest priorities of need in an area where culture and communications are only partly understood and the gulf between expectations is at its widest. This he calls *maximum serendipity* (Dudley, 1993). Conditions facing the 'captive' villager in a developing economy will vary considerably from those facing a victim of poverty and exclusion in the First World. Nevertheless, there is a basic lesson to be learned from their predicament. If the language of the church has to be modified for it to reach the estranged and oppressed masses, surely the language of development can be modified to include the capabilities and aspirations of the poor instead of oppressing them further (Beresford, 1993; Burdick, 1992; Dudley, 1993; Kelly & Sewell, 1988; Richardson, 1983) Even the language of the World Bank appears to have been affected (Salmen, 1987). In the depersonalised cities of the North, the idea of taking collective action may seem alien to many (Beresford, 1993; Beresford & Croft, 1993), particularly to those at the social extremities. But the professional task is to get them into motion on an organised basis.

There are two significant factors which need to be mastered: perceived need and leadership. The intention is to mould the aggregate of groups and supporters of the initial activities into some form of collective effort. This will confront the appropriate system which controls resources they need for change. They will have to prepare for this. Joint action, on issues serving their own, collective, needs may have to be accomplished before they can see that joint activity is beneficial to their own concept of self, and that collective action is capable of realising social goals.

Basic survival mechanisms can be put somewhat behind them if this model proves to be successful. This is an important threshold which has to be passed. The difficulty for the professional is in reading the multiplicity of needs that may have been presented. Choice, professional choice, will have to be made over the selection of the time, the direction and the method employed for tackling this next test of joint action and solidarity.

The lead has been given by the *Women in Development* approach, and Andersen spells out how best the most vulnerable can have their interests safeguarded through positive frameworks and thorough-going policies (Andersen, 1992). She identifies many historical failures of policy and of resolve in their implementation, but the pressure has to be maintained until favourable conditions are won over. The more marginalised the group, the more vulnerable the participants, the more the responsibility devolves upon the professional in the field to act responsibly and assertively, on their behalf, if necessary.

One of these sensitive areas is the assessment of need. We shall return to the issue of Rapid Needs Assessment in more detail later [this term appears in various guises and forms, containing the following words: 'Rapid', 'Participatory', 'Rural', 'Appraisal' and 'Procedures'], but under most circumstances, it is not going to be feasible to conduct anything like a representative survey of the needs this loose form of group. This is particularly true with a formation which is just beginning to function as such. Intuition and guesswork have been mentioned as the all-to-often refuge of a profession under pressure from the twin forces of ill-preparedness and unrealistic demands (Griffith, 1993; Pottier, 1993). But it may well have an important role to play here, until things can be stabilised. The question of ownership is the element which lies behind the professional initiative, but the circumstances will dictate to what extent ownership is transferred. It will become clearer in the next chapter, where the other half of this hybrid model is described, that professional ownership, on some terms, may be more compatible with outcomes which stretch the participants to their limits.

Power does not lie intrinsically with the people. It has to be established through some form of contest, even with the worker, to some extent. It is around this issue that the great divide between 'idealists' and 'pragmatists' takes place. Participation, in this model, is a process that is being driven by the energies and the 'strategic plan' of the professional. Exposure to, and understanding of, the predicament of the poor and the marginalised, must suffice as the best insight which may ever be available. This may not be good enough from a theoretical point of view, and the worker must strive for excellence at all times. Nevertheless, critical decisions have to be taken at every step along the way.

The group/organisation may be *deciding* that direct action is the best form of defence against continuing oppression. In this case, casting the most vulnerable against greater forces than their own, would be disastrous.

219

They cannot be expected to take on anything like full responsibility. They can hardly be capable of visualising the consequences, and they will not have any expertise in tactical, not to mention strategic, behaviour. One-off actions have to be experienced, and then evaluated within the wider social and historical framework before their importance becomes apparent.

The worker will take responsibility for the lead in planning, although any indigenous leadership would be harnessed and integrated to the fullest possible extent. In some instances, rehearsal may not be possible, but the worker must take every opportunity to prepare the group, and in particular any leadership figures, for what may be involved, and then to conduct an elaborate post-mortem after the task has been accomplished, whatever the outcome.

The secret in organising for change at this level of relative inexperience and vulnerability, is to choose targets which are well within the range of expectation and achievement of the participants. In this instance, the goal is the formation of a formally recognised organisation. Recognition by the participants is as important for them as it is for the outside world. If the group can be successful in a simple activity, and if they are able to have their identities strengthened though this process, then further actions can be planned and the sense of common purpose established.

Targeting the individual for change

Intervention with the most vulnerable and marginal people is to be purposeful and deliberate. There is no intention of *'validating'* their current lifestyles (Etzioni, 1995a p. 34), but of bringing in structured change - at first *to* them and, later, *with* them Making contact and the development of trust with individuals in extremely marginalised situations is a difficult and painstaking business. There can be no substitute for patience, time and dogged perseverance. Creating the right approach, and presenting as an approachable personality, is as acceptable a way as any other. Having something, material or tangible to offer will not necessarily create the appropriate atmosphere. Being there, in a manner which does not represent a forceful intrusion, and being amenable to share in the circumstances of the people is a statement of good faith. The intention of this exercise is to work alongside them. If necessary, to work with each person until they all establish the will and the skills to play a wider role within their own environment. Beyond that, the worker needs to build a bridge between the localised and personal activity and the wider context of formal society. The establishment of any form of obvious dependency at the outset will create the wrong perception of the way in which the relationship should develop. This may turn out to be unavoidable, however, and should be kept as an 'alive' issue for ongoing monitoring.

There will be a constant search for leadership potential. The worker will be on constant outlook for individuals with personal skills which can be exploited, or developed. The creation of contrived exercises can bring a person, who has little confidence or experience, to recognise that personal accomplishments are a form of leadership. The informality of the social situation can be projected into more formal settings. People can be assisted to understand that they have the necessary attributes with which to enter into closer tie with others and to undertake planned activity towards a commonly desired goal.

Work will be done intensively with individuals, as the necessary structures and networks may not yet be in place for focused work with a group. If group activity is possible from the beginning, then the task is at least one step closer to the formation of organisational structures and action planning. The selected leaders and the worker will become a closed group in the planning phase. The intention is to give exposure to the others (and the leaders) of the experience of risk, action and achievement. The deliberate and rational dissection of the history of the events and their outcome become the first, personal and subjective, evaluation of this form of activity. On this the future of the enterprise rests. If the outcome is positive, then more examples of self-help and co-operative action can be planned. In these, later, events, the role of indigenous leadership can be strengthened and developed as a focus for the worker's enhanced strategy.

This 'leg' of the template has described the professional route in transforming the perceptions of an unconnected aggregate of 'outsiders' into a group with the collective exposure to successful action. Small, successful, 'happenings' can then be used as a platform to consolidate groups into small, ongoing organisations, networks or patterns of collective activity. Intensive work with key individuals (leaders) can bring more pressure to bear and help to sustain 'organisation' boundaries. It is not going to be easy, as the previous experience of this aggregate of people has not been positive. Neither have they the qualities which are generally rewarded in our society. They are to be assisted through the endeavour of the worker and the acquisition of power for themselves through collective effort. Once this process has started, the professional task is to see that it feeds upon itself.

8 Social Action for Change - II: The Insiders

We have approached the problems to be encountered by the professional worker who intervenes from the position of a personal or institutional mandate. We have charted the strategy to be adopted when the group is powerless and where there is no clear view of how the predicament can be improved. The hybrid model will now be used to demonstrate how the professional role can be shaped by the 'client' constituency in a more purposeful manner. Here, the professional will be described in a mercenary capacity, as the employee of the community. Nevertheless, many of the considerations remain the same as in the earlier example, but there are fresh, and more taxing responsibilities to be taken on board. If the professional is to retain personal integrity, and remain 'in charge' of the process, while at the some time being at the mercy of the employer for salary and orders, a great deal of personal accomplishment will be required. Some of the value assumptions implicit in this statement will also be examined.

Outside North America, the vast majority of community development programmes and projects are funded directly by the state, or by local government, or by local or national NGO's in some sort of funding or policy relationship with government (Chanan, 1992; Chanan & Vos, 1990; Frazer, 1991; Lansley, et.al., 1989; Lees & Mayo, 1984; Rondinelli, 1993; UN Bureau, 1955; UN Secretary General, 1961; Wann, 1995). From the earliest writings on community development in the U.K., the implicit assumption has been that development is the benign instrument of the state. The established power system, alone, directs its direction and flow. It can exercise this prerogative at will, according to political expedient, and no proper alternative has yet been established to counter-balance this image (BAGUPA, 1995; Calouste Gulbenkian, 1968, 1973, Thomas, 1983, 1995).

In many respects, this is useful and necessary. The regeneration of large urban areas requires planning and co-ordination. Large forces are needed, and the management of co-operation across sectors of the economic and welfare complex is a task best suited to government - even if the lessons drawn from developing economies warn us to be careful with centralised solutions to local problems (Chambers, 1986; Chanan, 1990; Clark, 1991;

Hambleton & Huggett, 1988; Lansley, et.al., 1989; Oelschlaegel, 1991; Puddephatt, 1988; Tam, 1995; Toye, 1993). The real problem arises at the point of implementation, at the street level. The planners of general development initiatives would see community development as a natural complement to wider social and economic changes. Decentralisation, consultation, participation and human development programmes will all ease the impact and provide the mechanism for adapting to inevitable change (Booth, 1994; Edwards, 1994).

Writers who have disagreed with this paradigm were usually of the persuasion that social work/community development was itself part of the problem of oppression. On this basis, they advocated that it was the community which should develop its own activists. This was in line with Leninist and Gramscian thinking, where the domination of the capitalist state, and it agents, must be confronted and cast aside (Bolger, et.al., 1981; Corrigan, 1975; Corrigan & Leonard, 1978; Fleetwood & Lambert, 1982; Jacobs, 1975; Jones, 1983; Mayo, 1982; Wooley, 1970). In the London Borough of Notting Hill, in the 1960's, confrontation with the Council highlighted the limitations, and even the dangers of centralising power within the community (Baldock, 1979; O'Malley, 1970). Their chosen alternative to exposing the community to the dubious agenda of a state-funded worker (Cockburn, 1977), was to rely on local activists. Their activities could be regulated by the natural processes of identification with class goals and the force of local democratic processes. This presumption is challenged by Michels, who claims that oligarchy and anti-democratic consolidation will result. The rise of a new elite, a 'political class', which is creative and adaptive, is sure to occur (Michels, 1962). Other share this scepticism where the faith in an indigenous leadership is seen to be naive (Pruger & Specht, 1969). In one early and high profile example, the rise and fall of the Notting Hill Neighbourhood Council, due to the internal squabbling and factionalism was witnessed first hand. The alternative, independent residents' action produced *'a decade of struggle'* for some small gains in policy (Clark, 1975; O'Malley, 1970, 1977). It seemed to be all form, and no content.

The original model for British community action was taken up from the left- ideological starting point of working class community power. The magazine, *Community Action*, was dedicated to the premise that local activists (many of whom who were, in fact, dedicated, local, *middle class* professionals, with technical skills and contacts in influential places) would take the lead in organising protest, resistance to oppression and action. The 'local state' was the main target, despite the contradiction that these activists were, at the same time, trying to defend the structures of the Welfare State.

223

This was in a climate of economic decline and, latterly, radical economic restructuring (Cockburn, 1978; London/Edinburgh, 1979; Macintosh, 1987; Mayo, 1975, 1980). This movement had a long pedigree, and has been idealised somewhat. The involvement of organised labour in the lives of the community predates the British welfare state legislation. Between the World Wars, the Miners' Welfare Fund spawned a coalfields-wide network of 'Institutes' which contributed greatly to the social cohesion and general well-being of the community. This tradition survives in some places today, and it served as the foundation for the women's action in defence of their coalfields and miners' jobs at the time of the miners' strike of 1984-85 (Mayo, 1994; UN Secretary, 1961; Waddington, 1994).

In fact, the community action momentum was effectively hijacked by the government's *Community Development Project,* 1968-78 (CDP), and the transformation of the *Young Volunteer Force Foundation* (a community service and educational trust established in 1968 by government) into the *Community Development Foundation* (CDF), in 1989. The latter is funded as a parastatal agency, through the Home Office, in contractual relationships with local authorities and quangos. Today, it has all but abandoned its 'project' and direct development role, in favour of consultancy and think-tank activity (CDF, 1995; Loney, 1983; Thomas, 1995). The vulnerability posed by the connection with government finance, as demonstrated by the abrupt curtailment of the CDP in 1978, restricts the options open to local agency interventions. Militancy, or explicit confrontation with official policies, as envisaged in the community action mould, would not survive very long. An attempt at an independent approach by the Young Liberals, appears to have completely run out of steam (Hain, 1976).

Baldock tries to explain the reluctance of the British to carry through with their community activism. He suggests that it is their inability to learn that there has actually been no effective power shift over many generations of left-wing struggle, or liberal wishful-thinking. Organised resistance to the capitalist exploitation of labour has failed to create sufficient confidence. The net result has been reformist, incremental and gradual (Baldock, 1979). The trade union movement failed to cut through its own self-imposed 'class struggle at the point of production' ideology. Because of this, it never gave any public credibility or recognition to the connection between social reproduction at home, and economic reproduction at work. Because of this, it failed also to endorse a community development, or a community action, manifesto, or come up with any community programme of its own. This was despite the strident calls for structural change by the CDP projects, the fragmentation of the working class residential communities through 'comprehensive slum clearance programmes', the contraction of welfare services, and the emergence of permanent long-term unemployment for hundreds of thousands of their members. The rise of community action in the 1970's, appeared to suit the ideological outlook of Marxists, other socialists and libertarians alike, but it failed to produce a viable answer in organisational terms. Perhaps it was the pre-occupation with this form of 'ideology'. that contributed to its relative impotence (Sayer, 1986).

As such, it certainly obscured the potential of another model of community action which emanates from the United States. This is the *Community Organizing* model, which relies heavily on professional input, rather than spontaneous class action or political idealism. Community organising is a model developed by the American trade union and community activist, Saul Alinsky. Alinsky made a name for himself as a professional organiser of working class communities in the Chicago meat packing district, *Back of the Yards* (Slayton, 1986). In 1949, he published the fruits of this experience. This was a book that was to be both his manifesto and his almost forgotten testament, *Reveille for Radicals*. In this, he summoned the 'radical' who: 'actually believes what he says, ...to whom the common good is the greatest personal value,....who genuinely and completely believes in mankind, ...for the radical, the bell tolls unceasingly and everyman's struggle is his fight.' (Alinsky, 1969, p. 15). He was using the word 'radical' in the way Milton Friedman uses the word 'liberal'. Alinsky had witnessed in the Labour movement and in the residential districts of the poor, the deep divisions which marked out the ethnic, religious and economic communities in the American city. If the endemic social problems were ever to be overcome, if the structural causes of these inequalities were to be eradicated, and if the prejudices and social barriers were ever to be surmounted, then a new and radical form of social engineering was needed. Unity must be forged across the traditional boundaries and the best way in which to weld a community together was to unite, as if in warfare, in conflict against the opposition.

Alinsky had been deeply impressed by the strength of local branches of the trade unions, and the neighbourhood organisations in the communities with which he had worked. The quest, in developing his intervention technique, was how to galvanise those individual and separate strengths into one common cause. The mobilisation of these small factions, around issues of self-interest, seemed to be the only feasible answer to his dilemma (Alinsky, 1969). The unlikely answer was to set up a local representative assembly, the *Back of the Yards Neighbourhood Council*, in 1938. Any community organisation, boasting a minimum of ten members, was eligible to join. The inaugural meeting was overwhelmed with the response of 109 local organisations. The idea of the broad-based community organisation was born (Henderson & Salmon, 1995). The new *Council* immediately threw itself behind the cause of the meat packers, who were engaging in industrial action. In this way, Alinsky was able to remain consistent with his trade union loyalties. He had shrewdly calculated that the workers and the members of his 'council' were tightly inter-twined, through religion, family connections and neighbourhood organisation. It is a pity that this insight into the links between economic and social life failed to impress itself on the trade unions of Britain in the 1970's.

Alinsky decided to put a professional stamp on his new intervention technique. He secured financial backing and set himself up in independent practice: the *Industrial Areas Foundation* was born. This was an organisation which projected an uncompromising and business efficiency approach to what other purists might prefer to provide as a humanistic and altruistic service. Over the years, buoyed up by his own irrepressible energy, together with an abrasive and propagandist approach, Alinsky and the I.A.F. carved a formidable reputation for themselves. Successive high-profile confrontations, public condemnations as a communist, agitator, anti-Christian, Catholic militant, Jew, at least one gaol term, etc., and successes over formidable adversaries for the communities in which he worked, ensured his place in the annals of social work (Bailey, R. Jnr., 1974; Fish, 1973; Grosser, 1976; Henderson & Salmon, 1995; Swedner, 1982c). His methods have been described as coercive by those that see confrontation as counter-productive. These accusations are often made implicitly, by including descriptions of Alinsky's work in broader contexts, where threatening or potentially violent situations are being discussed (Brager, 1973; Spergel, 1969). He also stands accused of building a myth around his achievements with little empirical evidence to support his claims. The sin of committing virtually nothing to paper (except for the two 'texts'), and making no effort to provide an 'academic' discussion of his methodology and analysis, contributed to this schism. His wilful exploitation of street politics and conflict, and the uncompromising adherence to the 'put the money on the line' approach ensured that he remained controversial (Brager & Specht, 1973; Davies, 1988; Henderson & Salmon, 1995). Nevertheless, there have been those who advocate the import of his techniques into Britain, and there have been many imitators and variants, which is the sincerest form of flattery (Calouste Gulbenkian, 1973; Jameson, 1988; Pitt & Keane, 1984).

The IAF model is a hybrid. It is part-business in the mould of Tom Peters: redefine the problem, clear away all the clutter, target and act upon the objectives in the most decisive and effective manner, allocate clear responsibilities to the component parts of the organisation, etc. (Peters & Waterman, 1982). It is part-conservative 'old school' development in that it cleaves towards the establishment for its values, its dependence on middle class or aspirant leadership (Chambers, 1986; IAF, 1978). It is part of the new wave of empowerment and participation models, in its pragmatic and educational role (Alinsky, 1972; Chambers, 1992b, 1994; Fagan, 1979; IAF Network, 1988). Alinsky developed a number of key principles to underpin his approach:

- ◆ develop a broad based organisation drawn from community organisations representing the widest possible spread of self-interest;
- ◆ identify clear and 'winnable' targets for action;
- ◆ develop a multi-issue agenda for action;
- ◆ engage a professional organiser to manage the programme.

This is no short-life, protest campaign. It develops a strategy for social justice and the achievement of continuing change. Power is developed and used in direct political *actions* for the achievement of social and economic objectives. Tactics include the stripping away of the barriers between the 'private and personal' identity and characteristics of powerful people whom they wish to target, and the institutional role which these people perform at work. 'Targets' have self-interests, too! It is through exploiting these, as well as the dynamics of the political process, that they force compromise and negotiation. Every action is thoroughly researched in advance and evaluated afterwards. The management and conduct of every action is accountable directly to the participants, who are the members of the constituent member organisations. Action is designed to be enjoyable (Alinsky, 1957, 1969, 1972; IAF, 1978; IAF Network, 1988; Pitt & Keane, 1984).

The determining factor, is obtaining independent funding for the strategy. Without it, the exercise is doomed to curtailment or deflection. In the United States, and now in Britain (Davis, 1991), the Churches have provided the bulk of the up-front funding. This underpins the salary of the organiser and the base-line research into community priorities. Thereafter, the constituent organisations contribute their membership dues. The recognition by many religious institutions that plight of the poor is not improving, that centralised economic and administrative power and institutionalised discrimination is destroying the fabric of the urban areas, and the new stirring of grass-roots theology are all making their impact (Archbishop, 1985; BAGUPA, 1995; Leech, 1988; Pargeter, 1992; Church

227

in Wales, 1988a, b & c). Grave crises may require radical solutions. The conventional channels can offer little beyond welfare benefits, moral homilies and courses in practical self-defence for 'the active citizen' (Atkinson, 1994, 1995; Barr, 1991; Donnison, 1991; Etzioni, 1993; Field, 1989; Wann, 1994). Until the boundaries of tolerance of the establishment are tested by the more marginalised and impoverished sections of society, they will remain a disadvantaged, fragmented and malleable. There will be no real incentive for any change in the power relations in society. As more and more of them slip over the edge into the inert and humiliated 'underclass', the remainder can continue to be dependant on fate and the benefits of the 'trickle down effect'.), The Alinsky approach now has many variants in practice. These fit together to form a distinct strand of American social work methods - *Community Organization* (Rothman, 1979).

Aggregate with potential for action

In this model, we are not looking for the development of services or facilities for the community. The action model has been constructed because there already are defective services, and/or exploitative pressures upon this community from outside forces, which are arresting its natural, diverse development. The motivation of this approach is to redress imbalances, to confront violations of natural justice, to restore rights to people who are being denied them through improper means. It is the desire to change the passive, private citizen into an active, aware and public participant that lies behind this approach.

Target AGGREGATE with POTENTIAL for ACTION	ORGANISATION as the NUCLEUS for ACTION	COALITION as the VEHICLE for CHANGE	UNITY as the PLATFORM for POWER	POWER as the PLATFORM for CHANGE	TARGET the INDIVIDUAL for CHANGE

As these individuals are already participating in organisational activity (or will be if they are recruited through this process), then the human potential of the whole community is going to be greatly enhanced (Hope, et.al., 1984).

Coleman identified those areas of social tension and potential conflict which will motivate citizens into becoming participants in social protest activities (Coleman,   1957 cited in Brager, 1969, p. 268). These centre on the need to register objections, plus being a member of an organisation. Membership of an organisation empowers a person to act as a public entity, albeit in concert with others, for, perhaps, the first time in their lives. In our model, the selection of an initial aggregate of concerned people can be achieved through a number of approaches. In the Alinsky approach, the group must already be in existence and must be prepared to deliver a mechanism that can pay the larger part of the fee in advance. This is the sponsor organisation. Their future role will depend on whether or not they are 'of' the community, or concerned 'outsiders'. If they continue to play a role, themselves, in the development of the action programme, then they will have to agree to modify any authority which they may believe that they have over the scope and nature of the programme. This will include widening their relationship with the rest of the community and submitting to its will over any future role which they may have.

In other situations, the initial intervention may come from a community development agency itself. There is an important distinction that has to be made at this stage. The organiser is to be engaged (and possibly trained and retained) by the agency (such as IAF), but will be employed by the community where the action programme is to take place. If the organiser's employer is the primary funder and not the community in which the worker is to operate, then the autonomy of the worker is stronger than the power of the community. This means that the worker is in a better position to control the shape of the organisational development and the ensuing programme of action. The worker will be subject to all kinds of 'political' pressure. This could be brought to bear on a distant employer through indirect means, especially if large interests are involved (Brager, 1963; Grosser, 1976; Industrial Areas Foundation, 1978). The worker must be directly accountable to the people who depend on the outcomes of the action programme. This includes the power to hire and fire the organiser. This model is about the generation of conflict, possibly considerable conflict between the community formations and the wider society. We cannot allow the worker the luxury of facing two ways. If this happens, the community will be the loser. Even the mediation of a consultancy agency (which might 'own' the professional) cannot really be allowed to intrude on this special inter-dependent relationship. The stakes for the community formations will become too high, as we shall see.

We will approach this issue as if the 'ownership' of the initiative is in the hands of a small community organisation. The organiser is engaged and the potential of the whole community has to be assessed in order to determine the priority for action. It is likely that the original group may have some clear ideas about priorities. It is NOT in anyone's interest that planning and action takes place unless there has been a properly researched investigation into the community and its potential for action. At the present stage, the community is virtually anonymous. There is diversity of culture, of small and larger community organisations which span every activity from religion, social and interest activity, and even criminal networks. Whose interests are the most representative? If it is the 'self-interest' of the whole community that has to be the focus of collective action, then the self-interest of the community has to be aroused.

Organisation as a nucleus for action

The organiser must now assume that the community represents a totally unknown quantity. The organiser faces a clear field for development, but, of course, this is not strictly true. All communities have their special political and social histories and contain within themselves many conflicts, unresolved tensions and competing systems. However, the organiser will approach the situation as if seeing a clear slate. Potentials have to be revealed afresh, and a platform on which future action can be based must be identified. The community must be focused on the future, and not on the past. In this way, new formations and energies can be generated.

An IAF organiser, using a team introduced for this purpose, will conduct a survey of 2-5,000 face-to-face interviews with citizens and representatives of community organisations, and then analyse the results. Only then would a range of issues be selected for targeting. Some local organisations have their own, on-going programme of activity. Some may be involved in social action, other will have a low profile, a low public energy interest. It is in the interest of all, if this model is to work, that all these differing perspectives must be mobilised. Each small, local organisation is the nucleus for the formation of a broad-based organisation in the area. The survey will inform the organiser what the key issues are, where there is discontent and where individual or small-scale activity would prove powerless. Collective action, on the other hand could, and will be shown, to be decisive.

The first activity is to draw together those organisations which can form an easy and natural alliance for a joint venture. They can be identified from the information drawn from the survey. What the organiser is seeking is a quick and successful 'action' which will raise awareness in the community: that something is happening; that it was done by local people through action on their own and within their own range of resources; that they had reversed a power relationship and had brought changes to their quality of life and expectations about community and the future. They need to be invited to meet, and their approval will be obtained for a collective strategy. There can be nothing prescriptive, and it will take some time for them to discover that they are not signing on to a political lobby, or a pressure group. They are to be the action programme, themselves: the committee, the members, and any supporters that can be recruited.

The purpose in employing a professional organiser is to provide a direct, efficient, focused programme for the new coalition organisation. The scale of this operation may have been designed to be small, but its impact must create a momentum such that it over-rides their traditional separateness - those natural boundaries which small organisations erect around themselves, and which keep their interests separate from those of others around them.

The 'quality' of organisation to be found in each will be tested by the demands which the collective will make upon them as the programme develops. The intention of the organiser is to impose upon, and/or infuse into, these small local groups the spirit of community action. They must take the risk of seeking the goal of community achievement and victory over greater odds. They are to be awakened to their own self-interest and it can be best served through this broadly based process.

This first campaign is designed as the prototype of the larger 'actions' which will shape the rise to power and influence of the greater organisation which is planned. Above all, it needs to mobilise on an issue about which dissent can be shown, over which a protest can be rehearsed and within which an enemy can be identified. An enemy must be objectified and then defeated through an action campaign. This is the model that will be practised, again and again, on a widening field of activity and up an increasing scale of importance.

The methods are described in the following section, but the broad principles are: demonstrating success through action; clarifying issues of power, natural justice, and collective opinion; increasing people's demands through raising their confidence in their collective capability; guaranteeing satisfaction of local needs and demands. Pay-off for all participants is the *quid pro quo* of community action. It is a contractual relationship, reinforced through shared experience and beneficial achievements.

This is not an alliance. It is the creation of a new organisation which can, and will, assume responsibility for representation for the whole community in its dealings with power-related issues which have a bearing on community life (see Bailey, Jnr., 1974, and Fish, 1973, for comprehensive description of the process; also, IAF, 1978; Pitt & Keane, 1984). This entails achieving intra-communal consensus for the exploitation of conflict with external forces.

There is a time dimension to this development process. In the IAF model, the organiser is usually hired on a two-year contract. There are reasons for this that lie outside the concerns of the action plan itself (see conclusion of this chapter), but the main reasons are operational. Firstly, it is in the nature of organisations that there will be a need to change and restructure as time progresses (Child, 1984). If the programme is successful, there will be strategic changes. The organisation may change from being a protest organisation to becoming a co-ordinator of services. In some situations, it may become a supplier itself (Fish, 1973). There will be changes in personnel and in the priority and scale of its objectives. At the present stage in its development, the organiser has to combine the disparate parts of the community into a structure capable of short-term strategies and consolidation. This phase is make-or-break time for the community as a power base, its programme of protest activity, and for the organiser. Failure now would mean the wastage of the scarce resources, disillusion among the most committed participants and a loss of initiative. This might prove too great a setback to overcome in any future attempt to mobilise support. These objectives have to be realised within a reasonable time scale. at the end of a two-year period, it should be possible to evaluate the progress and restructure the strategy. The dependence on the organiser will have changed to more of a working partnership, than a developmental process. The main players on the community/employer side will be seasoned campaigners and they will be in charge of the operation, in all its aspects. The kind of person that they might need as their employee may have changed.

The strategy for the organiser is to build a broad based organisation out of these smaller ones through:

♦ mounting a public relations exercise emphasising the success of the first 'actions' calling for community solidarity to consolidate this;
♦ doing as much behind-the-scenes work as is necessary to draw in other community organisations on the back of the public relations campaign;
♦ holding a mass meeting of organisations, adopting a structure for representation on a central 'council', outlining a possible constitutional link-up between constituents, developing a bottom-up accountability mechanism and planning a direct action and protest approach;
♦ developing a recruitment capability within the new community formation, using the good offices of active, member organisations;

232

- polarising issues, identifying short and long-term goals for the community;
- defining priorities of self-interest/collective interest for localised action/s (small-scale, low intensity, soft target);
- the 'council' - plans, rehearses and implements a tactical 'action', drawing on collective support;
- mass meeting - evaluates the action for strengths and weaknesses, highlights the learning points;
- the 'council' - targets the next priority/tactic in programme/level of escalation;
- contracts each organisation for recruitment and delivery of resources (human and material) for the next action;
- repeats the cycle.

Success, learning from experience, building collective strength, understanding the processes and objectives of action, contributing and sharing in the process and its human as well as institutional rewards (excitement, fun, collective exuberance, contributing personal skills and energies, being valued in a dynamic process) - these are the indices of an effective participation activity. If the organiser can deliver these qualities, then the question of organisational solidarity is assured. The constitutional basis for action is important, for legal as well as questions of accountability and probity. But it is the people who make the organisation work.

Unity as a platform for power

This is not a party-political activity, and it aims to unite all factions against the forces which are depriving the community of the satisfaction of its needs. Local political party branches may well attempt to join, and exploit, the broad-based organisation. It is therefore imperative that the momentum and morale themselves act as a deterrent. It is possible for factions, or agents of outside forces, to attempt or engineer take-overs of the new coalition's constitutional structures. This is the way in which the organisation will lose momentum. If it appears to be sectarian, it will be deflected or lose general support. The internal structures must be sustained in a balanced form (Miller, 1987). This is the benefit of the 'mass meeting' approach. These take place on a regular basis, at least once a year. It is at these functions that the overall policy of the organisation is reviewed and the principal officers elected. Nobody knows the dynamics of the community better than the members of the community itself. Where an outsider-organiser can be misled through a relatively short period of

233

exposure, local politicians and factional supporters are well-known to many in the community - especially to their immediate rivals in their respective areas of influence.

The broad-based organisation contains many built-in checks and balances against factional take-over. It is a living federation of interest, and everyone is conscious of the need to keep their self-interests well to the fore. Balancing the short-term objectives (the localised, personal and intimate concerns of each small constituent member organisation) against the long-term, larger scale and weighty power plays of real social change issues, is the collective responsibility of the organiser and the central executive of the council. If the momentum is going the way of the long-term strategy, it must be sustained. Time, advantage, public opinion and political expediency must all be harnessed to the point where they can be their most use.

The smaller concerns, the concerns of the locality are, nevertheless, as vital to the goodwill and support as a big public victory may be. Success at street level must continue to be the bedrock of the consolidation process. The strategic thinking must constantly orchestrate the whole organisation towards the satisfying of these causes. Morale has to be maintained at every level, but especially at the street level. It has to be stressed that this is a 'bottom-up' organisation. The more an organisation becomes used to functioning effectively, its leadership begins to rest on its laurels, and adopt an entrenched position (Michels, 1962). The contract of the organiser will contain a specific duty to serve the interests of the constituents. This is one of the mechanisms which preserves the vitality of the organisation. As the existence of the broad-based organisation is predicated to self-interest, then self-interest must be honoured.

Boyte describes the continuing centrality of the local parish to what has become a powerful influence on the politics of San Antonio, Texas (Boyte, 1984). The (Mexican-American) citizens recognise how their own organisation brought relief from the seasonal flooding, once they had organised their own civic action organisation, COPS (Communities Organised for Public Service) and brought real pressure to bear on the (white) civic establishment. In Chicago, it is the same. Since the 1950's, successive civic groups, representing the migration patterns of big city America, have sustained The Woodlawn Organisation (TWO). This was the organisation which contested the urban redevelopment plans of the University of Chicago - and won, thanks to the organisational skill of Alinsky. But it did not stop with him, or the original residents' organisations. As in San Antonio, as it was with the United Farm Workers of California, as it was to a large extent in South Austin, Chicago, it was the exploitation of common interest that cemented the local organisations. In these cases, it was often the position of a local church or other institution, and the capacity to work across denominational lines, or other immediate interests that enabled social solidarity to triumph. In the largely Roman Catholic areas/groupings (San Antonio; the fruit pickers of Cesar Chavez, the Bronx Churches, the San Francisco Organizing Project), Their common religious connection made it easy for the organiser to discover and build upon a mutually recognised thread (Boyte, 1984, Fish, 1973; Jameson, 1988; Miller, 1987).

The responsibility for the organisation's leadership, and for the organiser, is to consolidate the power base, to develop an appropriate public image, and to underpin the organisation with sound financial base (donations, membership dues from constituents, fund raising). Winning the respect of the establishment through a trade-off of power-plays and compromise arrangements established the organisation as a formidable player in the political arena of the locality. It is in the interest of the organisation to be an ongoing and essential part of the local political brokerage pattern. No civic leader should be able to consider a policy for the organisation's area without first getting the organisation to consider the issue, drawing on their own expert opinion and getting their own compromise accepted. This is not the way in which the British political machines are used to working. But we live in a post-ideology age, and we have a lot to learn from San Antonio, Texas.

If the organisation has won its place in the loyalties of the local community, through solid success in campaigns for local issues and civic improvements, then the time will come when it appears that there is nothing left to be done. This is a time of extreme danger for the organisation. Inertia will kill off all the gains. In politics, those with the long-term strategy are those that carry the day in the end. The organisation cannot afford to stagnate, or even lose momentum, for even a short while. The 'opposition' are awaiting just such an opportunity to undo the gains, to manipulate the factions within the organisation that have been 'released' from their responsibilities, and wrest power away from the people again. The poor, and the survivors near the bottom of the economic and social hierarchy, lack influence and good connections. They do not command the compliance of layers of public officials, mindful of influence and social standing, who may be anxious to curry favour and protect their interests while they rest. Their new-found social buoyancy depends upon their maintaining an active role within a dynamic organisation. They will, in fact, have offended a few sensitivities on their way to political influence in the area. They will find, as they have found out in their actions, that they should not rely on favours. Power is won, and then it is defended. These groups in society need to remain active and alert. The only way in which to ensure that the community is alive and able to cope with the next crisis, is to keep it alert, working and looking for the next challenge. This is the time that it may be appropriate for the organisation to switch its activities from defence to service. Using the same 'self-interest' rule for determining priorities, the organisations should seek out the most beneficial mechanism, to serve the greatest number and across the widest area, and embark on a self-help strategy - or they may decide on another route.

Power as the platform for change

It must be borne in mind that a relatively new organisation must take the time to consolidate its position. At the same time, it will become obvious that power is a relative concept and, in the case of our organisation, the power that it commands is limited to the range of influence that its own efforts can generate. If it wants to extend its sphere of influence, then it will have to consider new strategies.

From San Francisco, to Portland, Oregon, and in Los Angeles in the West; across America through San Antonio, Texas; Lincoln, Nebraska; and Denver, Colorado; to the South Bronx and in Brooklyn on the East Coast, the people's organisations have progressed well beyond the neighbourhood and its local affairs. Not that they have forgotten their roots, it is just that, if you have a good organisation, why not use it for the maximum effect. The broad based organisation is an organisation forged through the voluntary recruitment of other, smaller organisations, to form a larger one. The same principle is employed to create a city-wide or a county-wide organisation. Community organisations, seeking to tackle the structural issues of their environment, recognise that they need to pool their power, their resources and their creativity. To do this and to bind the participants together in a purposeful endeavour, they need a new organisation. They may also need a new organiser.

The theory is that, given a number of power players, an alliance between them can equalise any imbalance in the political arena. In the case of broad based organisations, there are expectations that the institutional behaviour of those organisations will be in line with that of the smaller constituent bodies, of which it is but the titular head. In normal, traditional political alliances, the opportunism and horse-trading that goes on is out of keeping with the transparent and high profile activities which active, organisational members have now come to expect. Smoke-filled rooms and constitutional manipulation are not the stuff of participatory democracy. It may be that an alliance with the 'normal' political machinery may have to be made in order to effect change or to gain ascendancy in some critical situation. But this mechanism is not to be preferred. In one of the best publicised coups in Southern California, concerted action by three broad based organisations, under the auspices of the Industrial Areas Foundation, forced the State Industrial Welfare Commission to legislate a higher minimum age for one million, low wage workers (IAF Network, 1988). This was in the face of fierce opposition from the State Governor and the State Retailers Association. This Network was based on the ecumenical work and organisational development across 73 parishes. It represented the interests of over 200,000 citizens and, before the statutory Commission buckled in, it had won the active support of the Mayor of Los Angeles, Senator Robert Kennedy, the major trade unions and a broad collection of local business and trade associations. The Minimum Wage was raised 90 cents, to $4.25 an hour, ...'the highest in the Nation' (*Los Angeles Times*, December, 22, 1987). This organisation then went on to develop a fourth constituent member organisation, and continued with its work.

This development was not new to the State of California. In San Francisco, local organisations had been active for many years. An alliance was set up representing: '...*the denominations...(of) Roman Catholic, Jewish, Lutheran, Episcopal, Methodist, Community and Church of God in Christ. The labor unions include the San Francisco Labor Council, San Francisco Federation of Teachers, Building Service Employees Union, Hospital and Institutional Workers, Hotel and Restaurant Employees and Bartenders Union, International Ladies Garment Workers Union, International Longshoremen's & Warehousemen's Union, San Francisco Firefighters and Theater Unions SEIU.*' (*San Francisco Examiner*, December 12, 1982). This organisation was branded as ......' *"fascist" by Housing Commissioner, Preston Cook, who was not allowed to speak at a recent organisational meeting.*' .... and as.... '*a formidable force'*, by the Deputy Mayor of San Francisco (*San Francisco Chronicle*, May 16, 1983). Their main targets were the provision of affordable housing and cleaning up the City. These high level operations represented the fruits of long-term strategic thinking, and the benefit of involving the people, from the bottom up, and keeping them involved and empowered all the way through the many years of development.

The organiser plays a key role in this exercise. This is both a social planning exercise and a carefully choreographed 'action'. The organising council of this complex organisation has to be kept in touch with grass-roots feeling. It has to rely on their full participation and resource backing through what may be a long and exposed process. The troops have to be kept entertained. It has to be fun, as well as beneficial. Issues, such as the changing of the minimum wage, are bound to take on a level of abstraction, even if the hourly wage is a factor in most participants' lives. The sheer scale of the operation is beyond most people's comprehension. This is one of the reasons why the Church organisations make such an appropriate vehicle for sponsoring these activities. They hold well publicised weekly assemblies for their members. They have a leadership structure which combines high status figures with ordinary members of the laity. They run a lot of service-based activities which are good vehicles for communication and reinforcing community ties. They have a way of raising money, too. This also allows the professional organisers to concentrate their efforts on engineering the play at the top, where the conflict will break out. The social issues which are to be the focus, and the civic or commercial leaders who are to be targeted require detailed study and careful tactical treatment.

On his return from a visit to the United States, and the IAF circuit, the newly appointed Organising Secretary of the Church of England's Community Organising Foundation declared: 'The Church's role in Britain today as a key intermediary body in the political arena has never been more critical and, as such, Church people need an instrument or strategy which is firmly rooted in the "world as it is", in order to achieve the "world as it should be". This strategy needs to be firmly based in the communities.' He goes on, '*Community organising* has the potential to provide British Churches with the detailed and methodical strategy for social change which they presently lack. Simultaneously, it has the chance of introducing hope and fresh options for opposition and political leadership into our increasingly discredited and shabby democratic system.' (Jameson, 1988, pp. 2 & 6).

There had been some efforts by the Church of England, and the nation's churches collectively, to develop a strategy for intervention at community level across a more secular front, and on a developmental basis. The British Council of Churches established a community work agency in 1977: The Community Work Resource Unit. This was 'substantially funded by the Home Office' (Webster, 1989). The big break through came with the publication of *Faith in the City*, in 1985 (Archbishop, 1985). This gave a clear line for intervention at the base of the problem. The Church of England established its Urban Fund and set out to raise £18 million. To date, they are still a little short of this target, but they have already distributed £5 million, to over 200 projects (BAGUPA, 1995). The British Council of Churches' Community Work Alliance, established in 1991 and which has gone through difficult financial times, now seems to be emerging once again. Nevertheless, these initiatives are too little and too late to make a significant impact on the structural issues which confront the Urban Priority Areas which were analysed in *Faith in the City*. The financial embarrassment faced by the Church of England over disastrous property deals at the end of the U.K. property boom have obviously been a setback for large scale philanthropy. Nevertheless, the churches remain the largest independent institutions committed to social justice, and their lead is going to be crucial if these questions are to be addressed adequately.

There are, of course, differences of opinion within the ranks of the faithful about the best strategic place for their scarce resources. Alinsky's methods have been equated with those of the Mafia (Hasler, 1990), while the more evangelical wings of the faith would prefer the emphasis to be placed upon a community of prayer (Marchant, 1989). In Wales, the tendency has been for the church-funded projects to favour a non-confrontational strategy, based upon Freirean principles of individual growth, rather than Freirean confrontation for change (Davies & Evans, 1993). Harry Salmon writes about the concerns around the IAF methods: 'More has been said about the dangers than of the positive features of 'Community Organising', but that is because they need to be faced up to now if this new initiative is to provide community work with a sense of direction.' (Salmon, 1989, p. 6). These sentiments are certainly supported in this discourse.

Despite its hard-faced, business-like approach and its mercenary, cash-on-the- line attitude, community organising is community development in a very uplifting, as well as in a material sense. It seeks to perfect the capacity of the citizen to understand the processes of citizenship and to participate in them at every level. It seeks to inculcate the participant with the confidence to pay this role, and also with the sense of responsibility to play it to the full. Enlightened self-interest can only come with enlightenment. Participatory, first-hand experience is the best way of learning how the fruits of collective action pay off, and how the exercise of power can be shared across as many as enjoy the same enlightenment.

Targeting the individual for change

Community development begins and ends with the individual. In this model we have demonstrated that it is possible to transform the marginalised and cowed, semi-passive resident of a locality into a member of a vibrant and powerful institution. The individual, whether self-selected or drafted for leadership duties, or merely a fee-paying participant, is propelled through a set of personal and collective experiences which made a profound impact on a person's ability to function, both as a citizen, and as a member of the local community. The organiser has concentrated on one quality - self-interest, and has manipulated the social forces that enable the person to achieve satisfaction. This satisfaction may not be the one issue or need which first drew out the individual into taking part in the first place. The human capacity to reason, and to calculate the relative merits and benefits of compromise for the attainment of partial satisfaction, is fundamental to the model. The acquisition and exercise of power, in this collectivist arrangement, depends on hitting the best possible, attainable target. This experience teaches its own lessons, and the process is on its way.

In its own way, it is the development equivalent of holding the proverbial tiger by the tail. Many a good citizen has hankered after power, but done little to achieve it. Being faced with the reality of engineering political and social forces, and actually exercising real power, is a daunting experience. For those who never really believed that they ever could, or ever would be able to influence the forces around them, the effects can be electrifying. Once the facts sink in, there are sobering implications as well. The costs of relinquishing hard-earned gains soon become clear. The citizen discovers that it is difficult ever to let go of it again. The organiser's role is to assist the citizen, through the mechanisms of the organisation, to come to terms with this and to enjoy being in that situation. Expanding the horizons of the organisation's potential, and increasing the scope which the citizen sees for the whole enterprise is the impetus for the development process to go on.

There are costs for the organiser in all this. Despite being trained and supported by a retaining organisation such as IAF, the organiser is accountable to the organisation for wages and support. The organiser has to deliver the goods, ensure proper planning, arrange successful actions, achieve targets, and train effective leadership for the organisation. This is a tall order, and there are obvious risks to person, health and the fear of failure. There is the additional problem of burnout after prolonged exposure to the pressures of this form of activity. The organiser has to be carefully selected and requires support in the form of supervision and mentoring if the contractual obligations are going to be fulfilled. The community leaders are not going to be aware of these factors. After all, they have paid their money, and this is the expert, on a good salary. The kind of worker who is attracted to this form of activity has to be resilient in the extreme and must also revel in the entrepreneurial atmosphere which is engendered. This is not the kind of work for a 'fixer' or an opportunist. It takes calm, reflective and intelligent analysis and planning to construct a community strategy for social change. These traits have, at the same time, to be accompanied by those which thrill to the prospect of risk, tension and change. It is the entrepreneurial spirit. This is the kind of personality that is suppressed in British social work. Perhaps it is the non-statutory sector which can take the lead and demonstrate that there is a future for creativity and enterprise in British social welfare. They must some of their 'independent' moneys to do so. The present is the time to demonstrate that community development is an essential ingredient if social work is to have a future.

9 Evaluation

In this chapter, we shall attempt to explore the position of evaluation in the structure of a community development project. There is an urgency surrounding this subject as there are conflicting issues at stake. We shall show that the control and resourcing of this aspect of intervention is too strongly bounded by the values and expectations of those in positions of power - sponsors/donors and employers, and not under the control of the professionals with field accountability. This leaves them vulnerable, and it begs the question of the real position of the 'customers' or consumers in the equation. Midgley points to the mixed outcomes of economic and social progress over the recent decades. He highlights the 'distortion' of development that has taken place. This 'distortion' refers to the emergence of 'grinding poverty' for some sectors of the population, while other sections experience affluence and expectations of even higher standards of living. Communities (particularly the inner cities) are devastated in physical and social terms through low investment, and the rise in crime, unemployment and social deprivation (Midgley, 1995).

Elsewhere, Midgley demonstrates how globalisation has changed the focus for many workers and how international structures and forces shape the development environment for everyone (Midgley, 1997). We need urgently to address the question of why Midgley's pessimism about the outcomes of social development contrasts so markedly with the apparent optimism of certain practitioners in the UK. Barr, et.al., provide an uncompromising framework for the analysis of community development projects. They should be judged by their capacity to empower the community, from the individual upwards, to the creation of an influential centre of power. This community will now achieve progress and sustained impact on the environment, economy and engage in self-support and maintenance (Barr, et.al., 1996a, p.10).

One cannot dismiss these sentiments out of hand, but then we have a number of grave conflicts to assimilate somehow. Uphoff attempts to peer behind the scenes at the political realities surrounding development work. On the international stage, NGO's are apparently less restricted than agencies which are directly driven by bureaucrats or political systems, are beginning, nevertheless, to cluster around the honey-pots of power and influence. This is in line with the 'contract culture' described in chapter 2, in the UK situation. Uphoff discusses the tendency for even locally-based NGO's to have decreasing sensitivities to the needs and wishes of their beneficiaries (Uphoff, 1995 p. 21). He calls for a 'culture of evaluation' (p. 27) and less evaluation which becomes self-serving. Patton (1997 p. 22) suggests that, as many an evaluation study is never used, and its conclusions ignored, that any evaluation which is not predicated to action has little real significance. Both Uphoff and Patton include the role and aspirations of the professional worker in their scenario, whereas Barr, et.al., still hanker after the world as it should be. We shall attempt below to resolve some of these difficulties.

The immediate consequence of this analysis must be to ask where responsibility lies. What responsibility do professional workers have towards their client communities? They are the first hand witnesses to the effects that their employers' policies are having on hapless and dependent communities. Are workers ignorant or innocent of the effects that they have? If either is the case, then what methodology are they using to inform themselves of the consequences of their actions? If they have the means of detecting the effects of their interventions, are they using them? If they are neither ignorant nor innocent, and they have the means of detecting the effects of their programmes, then how are they using the material that they have at their disposal? Community development is a long-term, social change process. Career and programme structures may not allow individual workers to follow any specific development programme from the start to the finish. Nevertheless, many will move in and out along the way. The 'case notes' will be handed on. In addition, each of the aggregate of professions which supply the corps of development personnel, have their own, direct interest in assessing the efficacy of their methods. Each will promote the qualities which a particular specialism makes to the success of the whole. They train and accredit their graduates in keeping with the standards of their trade. If they want the credit, then they must be responsible for the outcomes. For this reason, evaluation is a two edged weapon in the hands of the professional. It is the means of measuring the effects, and an aid to plotting the way forward. It is also the tool to employ when questioning the whole basis of the exercise. This work is addressed primarily to social workers. Taking the line advocated by the exponents of citizen empowerment, the social worker must be proactive, using the models that *prevent* social breakdown and promote an ecological balance, rather than regulation, reaction and control (Chambers, 1992a; Friedmann, 1992; Hancock, 1993; Pratt & Boyden, 1985).

Evaluation is the only effective way in which the value of the intervention can be assessed, but measuring the outcomes will, of course, reflect more than just professional ability. It will highlight the disparities between the actual needs within the target community, and the political ideology and framework within which it is set (Rondinelli, 1993; Porter, et.al., 1991). How strongly has the professional chosen to deploy development resources in line with the priorities of the major funding agencies? Would deviation from these and the concentration on 'minority causes' find the more powerful interests involved withdraw their support? The experience of the British Community Development Project clearly illustrates this dilemma. Evaluation will, at least, aim to throw light on these issues. After that, it becomes a question of ethics, even morality. Some of the ethics have become a little tarnished as we have allowed ourselves to be led away from the centre field, and on to the periphery of social development (Midgley, 1995). Harry Specht was one of the first to point out that the costs for a profession of bucking the ideology of the system would be severe and have detrimental effects on professional status (Specht, 1973, p. 346).

One of the more contentious aspects surrounding the employment of social workers, is the premise that their labours produce a 'result'. There is the fabled social work strike of 1978/79, after which the comment, 'What strike? I did not miss them at all!', summed up the position of many clients. The clients' apparent resilience to their loss of support during this period, could be said to reflect the effectiveness of the workers' empowerment model. 'Radical non-intervention' (pre-planned absence, without leave or apology), just proved their point. By way of contrast, the workers of the Community Development Project, were deemed to be too much of a good thing by their employers, and so they were purged.

But if these events are considered rationally, these points demonstrate serious flaws in the respective intervention approaches of the two professional groups. In both cases, the workers failed to make an effective impact on crucial forces within their survival network. They failed to convince their sponsors, or their clients, that their services were essential and/or irreplaceable. Both groups lost their struggles, and, in the case of the CDP, they lost their jobs as well. It highlights the lack of suitable evidence that was available to them with which to confront the public, or the government, about the rectitude of their case. There was inadequate evaluative material available, and this represented poor foresight by the workers, and their supporters. They should have anticipated the possible outcomes, and developed a strategy for the presentation of evidence at all appropriate levels in their disputes. At the very least, each group should have made more impact on the system than they did.

Today workers are faced with a very different picture. There is a price

244

on everything and a complaints' procedure just waiting to be invoked for every risky or undefended action. In the past, professionals may have believed, arrogantly, that they did not need to justify their actions, or they may have feared that too close an inspection may have weakened their mystique. This time has passed. Professionals must embrace evaluation, and the accompanying appraisal and monitoring, purely to assert the strength of their methods and the effectiveness of their interventions. Being informed themselves must surely be a priority. It is one of the best defences against political or malicious attack. It is also an effective weapon against any form of unwelcome scrutiny. Information is also an essential property in the empowerment process, and in the business of justification for the continuation of employment contracts, or rationale for the development of intervention models.

In developed countries, social work should be about intervention, change and the development of best practice techniques. In reality, it is characterised by full schedules, resource scarcities and crisis conditions. As such, it often has to rely on the results of other agents, who undertake research and policy analysis to produce the validation for the work. Their results do not filter down to the work face until the crucial decisions have been made about the deployment of workers and the intervention priorities. If evaluation was considered to be a high priority in practice, then workers on the ground would be in possession of vital and contemporary information about the state of their performance. In some sectors and in some settings, this is already common practice. It is for this reason that we must draw on the information that is available, and design models for ourselves which would, in the first instance, allow for the empowerment of the worker. With empowered workers, empowerment of the client may follow. We will trace some of the sources and models of practice of evaluation, so that we can be the better judges of how to assemble the most relevant material, and how best to use it.

Scientific surveys and the measurement of quantity

In some countries, evaluation is now a firmly established practice. This is most evident in developing countries, where governments and donor funders seek justification in various quarters for their policies. There are emergent trends in this process which highlight the diversity of the agendas that are in contention. There are lines of international accountability, as well as local political sensitivity. As far as evaluation enquiry is concerned, these varying priorities reflect different evaluation preferences.

At one level, the price/effectiveness approach is the first choice. This model is most clearly presented in a recent 'guide for project managers'. The main concern here is to 'develop' a community through direct intervention. The emphasis is on providing an efficient and accountable programme for achieving centrally approved physical or service improvement, social change, or new formations (Cusworth & Franks, 1993). When evaluating this process, the core characteristics of a *conventional* approach would be: 'a desk study, document content analysis, quantitative survey, analysis of results and written report.' (Marsden, et.al., 1994, pp. 97-98; and Casley & Lury, 1987). Outcomes are measured against baseline data or the throughput of activity that results from the introduction of a new facility or social/economic formation. The development process is often visualised and planned around the concept of a 'project cycle'. This admits the evaluation procedures into the process on a pre-determined basis. Progress is tested against pre-set targets, including product quality control (Cusworth & Franks, 1993). The targets are often set at the most basic level, and the ease of measurement can be seen as a priority (Casley & Kumar, 1987).

One fact is plain. In this approach, the introduction of a significant physical change in the environment does not usually place much weight on the active involvement of the human component. The ensuing, and inevitable, modification of existing social processes around this development, is just allowed to take its course. The 'achievement' of the project's goals could be stated in terms of financial accounting, and little more. Evaluation reflects values which seek to measure the *quantity* of planned change, in isolation from other factors, which may not have been planned. This approach can often be employed, even where the population, itself, and not the environment, is the target of intervention and change techniques. The standard enquiry into the 'before and after' status of the community can '.....produce conclusions that were irrelevant, incomprehensible or too lengthy' (Pratt & Boyden, 1985, p. 99). It is evident that this form of evaluation is an instrument of scientific enquiry *into* the community, and the terms of reference are set *externally* from it. The timing of this kind of study is set by the external interests and the relevance of the outcomes to the local population will lose any immediacy which more rapid findings might have brought.

Realisation is beginning to dawn on the planners and operational workers of physical development (school-building projects, schools, and the like), that the exclusion of the people from start of the exercise can make their work more problematical, especially if the terms of reference are subsequently changed. For example, Dennis describes how the intrusion of new considerations or criteria distorts the model. The human and social ingredients of the development process are grudgingly recognised when contractors are forced to consider the effects that social issues may have on (for example) the long-term financial viability of the scheme. For example, service income may not have been a factor when the project began. If the 'beneficiaries' cannot actually afford to use the service once the project is completed, then the whole project may prove to be unjustifiable. What if the people do not actually want the new feature, and would not pay for it, even if they could? 'Sustainability' is closely linked to the social dimensions of development, and it has now 'emerged' as a factor (unwelcome?) on the development manager's list of project variables. Instead of taking the community for granted, they have to be included in the process of project planning and delivery. Evaluation is central to this process. It is suggested that foreign project managers are best served if they can be shielded from considerations like this - and from economic fluctuations which might affect their salaries (Dennis, 1993, pp. 220 - 221).

The quantity measurement approach reflects the 'hard' edge of development policies. It continues the tradition to separate out the *social* from the *physical* aspects of development. For a long time, it was not considered important that the social aspects of development were always predicated to, and dependent upon the implementation of physical development programmes. The realisation is now coming, that there are social costs in the traditional approach, and that there are social and developmental benefits in an alternative view. However, there is still considerable conflict over priorities between development economists and the advocates of social development Sen, 1988,; Toye, 1993). The disparity between these categories of goal objectives could not be more apparent than when the effects of development policies are assessed against purely theoretical models. It is here that the lack of concern for the human element in the broad development process becomes most evident (Chinnery-Hesse, *et al.*, 1989). If the people either cannot benefit (e.g. uneven implementation of programme), or are prevented from benefiting (e.g. putting administrative blocks on take-up of grants or welfare support), then the supposed 'benefits' may be nothing more than window-dressing for the consumption of other interests. If communities are to benefit, but if they should refuse to co-operate in the programme or prove to be inept, then planners and project strategists will have to determine how to integrate more variables into their model before they decide on their priorities. An alternative perspective is badly needed. This is the only way in which the new 'customer', or consumer, will be accommodated, and induced to participate.

There is one, long-running policy area where the 'alternative' dimension was not considered until the macro-level policies were firmly in place. The effects have been startling, and it is no wonder that the people were not asked in advance. The fruits of 'structural adjustment' have been the destruction of the life chances of perhaps a generation of citizens in some African countries (Ankrah, M., 1987; Balleis, 1994; Clark, 1992; Cornia, 1987; Gibbon, 1993; Korten, 1992; Robinson, 1992; Sparr, 1994a; Toye, 1993). At the same time as these macro-economic forces were having their draconian effects, especially on the rural poor, those working with the problems on the ground were acutely aware that they were only considering half of the 'problem' on which they were focused. Todaro stipulates that policies for economic development should *'be sensitive to the uniqueness and diversity of Third World societies.'* He continues, *'We must recognize that there are few, if any, 'universal' principles or 'laws' of economics ....'* (Todaro, 1989, p. 9). This approach was pre-empted by Cornia, et.al., in their UNICEF study. They go to great lengths to describe the alternative policies which could be implemented to soften the blow of necessary adjustments or to tackle the problems in a different way (Cornia, et.al., 1987). In addition, this should not be just a prescription for newly developing economies. Where structural adjustment is concerned, there are direct comparisons that can be made between countries with economies at different levels of development. These factors over-ride differences in culture and can offer penetrating insights into the nature of shared problems (Clarke, 1989). In 1976, the 'gnomes of Zurich' summoned Harold Wilson to Switzerland to discuss the British economy. They made him an offer which he could not refuse over the level of public spending, inflation and the featherbedding of obsolete business. Since that time, the British economy was subject to an escalating structural adjustment policy, and the consequences have been felt over a thirty-year period. After a reasonable assessment period (11 years), Toye reports that the effect of structural adjustment on developing countries has been an increase in exports, but that national investment and economic growth has not been influenced greatly. 'What comes out most clearly is that the outcome is quite disappointing compared with the advance claims and expectations raised.....' (Toye, 1993, p. 198; see also, Berridge, 1993).

Because of the potential for co-operation in getting to grips with the causes, and with possible solutions, to these difficulties, countries in both the North and the South can, and should, examine their experiences together. The difficulty is to break free of the restraints that the traditional economic development model holds over the 'conventional evaluation

248

methods'. Progress towards developing a mutually understood method of evaluating development programmes might be one positive step in this direction. One step could be to bring the point of evaluation down to the locality where the effects of the programme are experienced most vividly. At this level, there is a need to get behind the raw figures that may be used to illustrate progress in quantitative terms. It is the quality of the resultant experience, as felt by the immediate recipients, that is the judge of the model.

The questions that have to be asked afresh are: what is evaluation; for whom, or for what is it done; how is it done; where and by whom is it done? Oxfam have produced a Guide to evaluation which provides easy access and generous coverage of these questions (Rubin, 1995). The first distinction that needs to be made, is that, for evaluation to be effective, it should be a continuous process. It must be flexible enough to provide meaningful information to the major stakeholders in the development process, but also adaptable to change as the process unfolds. It is best explored through examining the project cycle, which has been portrayed in various guises. Basically it represents a circle of learning and action which admits monitoring, reflection and evaluation processes. The opportunity to learn from history, rather than make the mistake of repeating it, can be clearly demonstrated (Cusworth & Franks, 1993; Lattimer, 1994; Marsden et.al., 1994; Mikkelsen, 1995; Smale, et.al., 1988; Swedner, 1989d).

Appraisal, rapid appraisal and participatory methods

Responsibility for the introduction of this kind of programme, or project design, rests with the outside agencies, and their planners (Marsden, 1994a; Vargas, 1991). At the *formulation* stage of the programme, the social/cultural, financial, economic and geo-environmental context needs to be agreed in order that the feasibility of the scheme can be assessed. Formulation entails the recognition, in broad terms, of the need to establish an intervention or policy change. What are the changes that are envisaged? How do they fit into the broad policy field of the responsible agency, and with what priority? Various l models will be considered, and a decision made regarding the preferred focus for the application of resources, the management and accountability structure, and some general guidelines regarding the scale of the activity.

Following the formulation of the basic policy to take an initiative in this way, the first actual steps to launch the project should be accompanied by a thoroughly planned *appraisal* stage. It is from, and through, this appraisal process that indicators for measurement can be established. These indicators are the changes that can be shown to be the result of the intervention, and which can illustrate the quality of change that has taken place. In the past, this appraisal process was usually carried out at the centralised planning point, or, in many cases, not at all.

The operational workers were often faced with drawing up their own profile and analysis of the area's problems *after* they had begun their intervention (Carley, 1987). This virtually guaranteed a mismatch between the policy and the intervention goals. One of the issues commonly raised regarding the development of a baseline appraisal, is that the process is costly and time consuming. It can be compared to the 'conventional' evaluation survey. The methods tend to be established within the guidelines of the objective scientific model. The results take a long time to analyse, by which time they are obsolete (Chambers, 1993; Rondinelli, 1993).

In the following diagram, the evaluation process is spread across the centre of the circle, which represents the project planning cycle. The implementation decisions are represented along the bottom axis. The various stages of evaluation are described below, but the main feature is that the process is a continuous one.

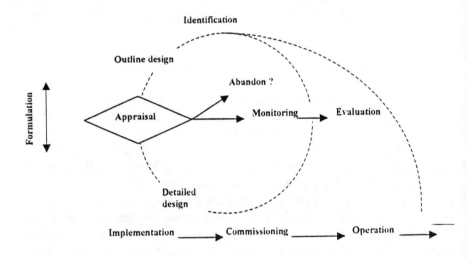

Figure 6: The project cycle
Source: Cusworth & Franks, 1993

The collection and analysis of information is followed by further planning and a modified implementation process. Accountability requirements, and

250

other public relations functions are met through the compilation of reports and the dissemination of information based upon this data. The 'loop', which links the operation process with the planning and design cycle, ensures that those responsible for policy are kept in touch with the operational conditions.

It is because of the interconnectedness of the processes of project *formulation* and the activities during the *appraisal* stage, that the 'good practice' framework for evaluation needs to be established. The appraisal process will also provide the operations and evaluation systems and their baseline information, from which measurement of progress can be made.

Armed with baseline information, the appraisal of a programme or project's feasibility can be made. The project framework can be fine-tuned to suit the objectives of the funding and regulatory agencies. Doubts about the 'fit' with the local culture and the local priorities have to be allayed. There will be many instances when there are likely to be conflicts of interests, depending on the model which the external agency brings with it, and the acceptability of this framework to some, or all of the recipient community. Over the years of operating the conventional 'top-down' model, the obvious distance between the planners and the supposed 'beneficiaries' of development gradually became apparent.

In the 1970's, the need for a re-think of tactics and methods gave rise to the technique known as Rapid Rural Appraisal (RRA). This is still a 'top-down' approach to data collection, but the nature of the data collected is qualitatively different from that retrieved in the 'traditional' survey (Chambers, 1980, 1992a, 1993; Edwards, 1994; Porter, 1983; Pratt & Boyden, 1985; World Health Organisation, 1988).

As its name describes, RRA is a method of gathering the most accessible information together, in the shortest possible time, in order to draw inferences on which new policies, or frameworks for projects, can be based. The information is drawn from a number of levels, and then this is analysed to produce a rough, but serviceable picture. 'Science' is sacrificed to serve the interests of necessity. The intention is to get policies to 'fit' current circumstances, and not to build in a relevance gap from the start. RRA goes as far as to consider possible outcomes of a planned programme, given the findings from the study and the options which these generate (Pottier, 1993).

Using RRA techniques, information is gathered to ensure the greatest possible spread across the range of sources available. Using this information, an 'information pyramid' is constructed, which constitutes the baseline of the appraisal process. The 'pyramid' is described by Arnett and

Rifkin (World Health Organisation, 1988). It comprises information (from the top, downwards) on:

♦ policy (from the level of decision making);
♦ services and formal institutions (records search, using professional network);
♦ the physical, socio-economic, broad over-view (from central statistics, professionals in the area, and other experts);
♦ community composition and attitudes (obtained in the field, by specially recruited local leaders and/or employees of operational agencies).

Information, which provides a framework for this appraisal, is gathered from studying policy documents and interviewing officials and others in authority. After than, public records, specialist data (doctors' and clinical statistics, local authority data, etc.), and any other available repositories are also consulted. The essential data-seeking activities on culture, local community structures and perceived needs, are field exercises. They are conducted either by the planning team, or by any available individuals (para-professionals, skilled persons, etc.) who can be released for training and deployment. In the case of a comprehensive study of Village Development Workers in Zimbabwe, the workers themselves were deployed, rotated geographically around the country so as not to survey their own regions (Min. of Community and Co-operative Development, 1989). It is important that as much of the information that is needed for the base of the pyramid is compiled from the information provided by the community itself. This comprises: insight into the culture and belief systems, local structures, leadership and attitudes towards change, directions of preferred change, and the like. There is a need to obtain as broad a representation as possible in the respondents to this study. Community leaders are often targeted, but where a social of demographic profile of the community exists, care should be taken to achieve full coverage.

On some occasions, and if there is no alternative, school children, community organisations, or other resources could be employed to gather the information (Tobayiwa, 1993). This shift away from using the specially prepared employee should not be considered to be a cheap option, and an opportunity to lower standards (Chambers, 1992a; Pottier, 1993). A rapid assault on a community is not the most subtle way in which to gather sensitive information. The interviewers have to be prepared carefully for their task and there is a high level of supervision required if they are not normally exposed to this form of activity. If corners are cut in the study, and the findings diluted, the results will not stand up once the process of implementation begins.

The idea is to compensate for the lack of a full, and scientifically constructed survey, with the ability rapidly to cross-reference information obtained from many sources. The RRA pyramid permits the community to be 'mapped' from within, as well as from external sources. If care is taken in setting up the study, some triangulation is possible. Professional opinion and insight from the community leadership can be cross-referenced with grass-roots' feelings. This form of intervention might appear to be best suited to areas of development where the sensitivities of the local community are not considered to be immediately relevant (e.g., a programme of health promotion), or not considered to be important as a matter of policy (e.g. by government).

Despite cynical and dismissive reactions, it still represents the best cost-effective trade-offs '...between quantity, accuracy, relevance and timeliness of information.'(Cornwall, et.al., 1994, p. 108). This statement reflects the boundary that divides the values that are presented by the *participatory* school of development, and those that adopt a centralist and managerial approach. This draws us back to the ideology of the beginnings of community development. Appraisal, in its most instrumental form, is not too far away from the colonial model described by Batten, and the United Nations (Batten, 1957; Colonial Office, 1943; UN Bureau, 1955). Subsequent, highly participative models of RRA bring us closer to the *process* approach of Murray Ross (Ross, 1955). We shall consider these below.

The 'project cycle' model of project planning and evaluation, provides sponsors with the information that they might need to terminate the process if, and when, criteria of success or failure manifest themselves. It puts into stark relief the fact that the power of the sponsor is the arbiter over the criteria for continuation or closure. It is at this point, that the staff of the agency find that they are to be subject of decisions which may have serious effects on the lives of the people with whom they have been working.

The workers know better than most what is at stake, what has been going well or badly, and what information has been selected for policy decisions to be made. Because those on the ground will have a relatively small role in the determination of decisions of this nature, but have the unenviable task of explaining the consequences of these actions to the 'beneficiaries', they are trapped in a problematic situation. It is full of contradictions which may never be resolved in the life of a project. This is one of the

253

issues which can be addressed by the employment of more inclusive forms of evaluation.

People centred development, monitoring and evaluation

Partly because of the lack of relevance of development projects to local conditions, or because of the widening gulf between centralised macro-development policies and their effects on the ground, operational workers have begun to develop a more *people-centred development* strategy. Workers were drawn into closer and closer co-operation with the local community in search of methods which might better ensure more sensitive and beneficial outcomes (Chambers, 1986; Dudley, 1993; Korten, 1992). These steps saw the development of a model which drew the consumers into the fabric of the evaluation process: Participatory Rural Appraisal (PRA), or Participatory Project Appraisal (PPA). The 'evaluation' is itself a process. The development professionals and citizens together become aware of, and reflect upon, the issues and methods of development and change as they happen, from the beginning and throughout the development process. This is a running appraisal process. Goals are agreed and outcomes are assessed collectively. Separate records and analysis may well be required by the funders, but these formal aspects of the 'project' are not of pressing concern of the participants in the exercise. Workers have to face both ways, and ensure that they are clear in their priorities. They must 'defend' the participatory process from the outside pressures at all costs, or the process itself will be distorted.

The challenge which participatory evaluation poses to the more formal approach dates its lineage back to the Institute of Development Studies workshop in 1979 (Chambers, 1980, 1986, 1992). Chambers draws attention to the fact that it has been the operational agencies (mainly NGO's) which are responsible for the extension of the action and planning principles, from those of RRA into those of PRA The academic community found that RRA, conceptually, could be harnessed within the bounds of 'scientific' research. The methods of RRA are described as being acquired through *didactic* methods, whereas PRA poses an *experiential* medium for the participants. Mikkelsen describes the essential differences between the 'modernization perspective' (rational, scientific) and the 'populist' (or participatory) methods. (Mikkelsen, 1995). Participants in the former (RRA) have to absorb the methods through a formal mechanism, and the PRA model is shaped by the participants in their search for a way through their development and social situations. Mikkelsen considers that both approaches were considered to be heresy when they first emerged (Mikkelsen, 1995, p. 99), and it can be readily imagined why centralised administrations and distant donor agencies want to know, in unambiguous terms, what their contributions have achieved. In some instances, the operational workers in PRA mode, were (and are) working towards a model for self-reliant, user project management (Burkey, 1993).

One advantage of both the RRA and PRA methods, as opposed to the 'traditional' survey, is the close attention to detail which can be maintained. Information can be made available within a short time-scale, and, if managed properly, on a regular basis. This form of detail is the kind which can be more readily developed the greater the degree of intensity and sensitisation of the participation process. Participants in the project, once aware of the methods of measurement, become conscious of their function in the allocation of resources, in providing feedback on their own inputs, and their capacity to comment on the overall benefit of the investment which they, and outsiders, may have made. Once the indicators of appraisal have been agreed, they become the basis for monitoring the progress of the whole project, or of specific components of it. The workers, conscious of the duality of their role in the evaluation process and their duty to represent the interests of the funders, as well as to support the participants, can abstract vital information from both levels. This greatly strengthens their hand in their influence over decision making. They understand the progress of development from the grass roots level and they can anticipate longer range processes from a more formal analysis of the data.

Monitoring is a mechanism of continuous observation and measurement of progress. It is designed to allow for programme adjustment, if necessary, during the development process, between the full-scale evaluation points in the timetable. It gives indications of trends in change and of direction. Through its use, steady and timely feedback is available to the participants on the effectiveness of the design of the original programme, and its appropriateness to the local situation. It can embrace both qualitative and quantitative aspects of change, but additional or separate means may have to be developed to ensure that each is given equal treatment, if this is desired. The project can only be expected to provide so much output in this direction, as its priorities will be towards other kinds of output (Beaudoux, et.al., 1992). This may entail the employment of separate systems of measurement and development work, which run in parallel to each other.

One aspect of the monitoring process is to keep the indicators of social development in focus. These are the factors which will serve as the measures of success of the programme when the evaluation process is drawn together. Marsden, et al, identify four major constellations of indicators: income, consumption, self-reliance and social mobility (Marsden, et.al., 1994, p. 109; see also Harding, 1991). Some processes are going to be more suitable to participative methods than may others. For example, these could arise where cultural resistance to change is anticipated, and where the presentation of actual evidence of these changes might result in the rejection of other aspects of the project's activity (i.e. evidence of the degree of financial independence of women after a co-operative development initiative). Considerable tact (or caution) is going to be required if sensitive information is to be made public. Expertise in development practice includes managing use of personal and institutional power, and the control of information is a major aspect of this responsibility. If, as in the past, the continued power of the elite (including the operational staff) is to be maintained through the control of information, then that must be agreed at the outset of the programme. It is not in the interests of the programme, or of the participants, that disputes over the ownership of information arise during the developmental period. Friedmann suggests that the fabric of society in a state of change, and under the strains of internal conflict over priorities and values, may have to change under the processes of development. The culture, itself, may have to shift into new belief systems or social formations if the changes, which may be seen to be beneficial, are to be accommodated (Friedmann, 1992). The instruments of development may precipitate this process, and the deliberate actions of the professional may have a decisive influence on them. Ethically, the actions of the professional should not impede or further distort the natural development of events, and yet....

In his discussion on evaluation, Rubin introduces the *consumers* of the development process into the equation at the very earliest opportunity. Rubin firmly embeds the role and value of the consumer as an essential ingredient of the process. Development theory is replaced by *development issues*, the culture of the development planner is *multi-disciplinary* and focused as much upon the *process* of development, as upon material change. The essential quality of the process, and the target for measurement, is *quality* itself. In participatory evaluation, the experts have the responsibility to assist the consumer to evaluate, through and during their direct experience of the development process, rather than to be passive recipients or reactive victims (Mikkelsen, 1995). The difference between the external, or 'objective', model and its participatory challenger, is that, in the latter, the development professional researches alongside the poor, rather than in isolation. The researcher shares the experience and the knowledge base, as perceived from the outside agency. The consumer, or citizen, shares the local knowledge, the personal and collective experience of the impact of the programme. Rubin insists that the evaluation process should not be used for decision-making (Rubin, 1995, p.28). There are grounds here for serious misunderstandings to arise. The participants are led to believe that, in the PRA process, they are putting into practice their priorities and preferences for development. But if they are going to be restricted if they 'go too far', there will be confusion. The operational workers must be in a position to define their boundaries to the participants, and explain the limits of their authority over resource allocation. If they lack the authority to go with the citizens along the road of choice and preferred goal attainment, then they should them know in advance. There will be great frustration if they do not. If this process of participatory evaluation and experiential development methods is taken to its logical conclusion, then the connections with the Latin American (Freirean) *conscientization* can readily be made. In this instance, the method is called *Participatory Action Research*. This entails using techniques such as:

♦ recovery of history - through collective memory, interviews and oral histories, relics;
♦ valuing local culture and traditions - arts, sports, rituals;
♦ production and diffusion of new knowledge - new communication methods, including literacy.
(Adapted from Cornwall, et.al., 1994 p. 110; Hope, et.al., 1984)

The 'evaluation' design becomes more a process of continuing appraisal. This is an appropriate decision making mechanism. The goals of the next 'project' can be set through the sharing of knowledge from each and every level in the equation. Thus armed, the different components can go forward together to discover the most practical and beneficial way to target their resources.

Anthropology and the conflict of values

The objectives of development are desirable changes in the material and social relations of the community. However, the existing relationships between the community and its total environment have a cultural significance which embody the community's historical developmental and value systems. Change of any kind will: a) disturb this relationship, and b) create a cultural reaction, which may retard the capacity of that community to benefit fully from the changes.

Development theory has centred largely on the imperatives of the economy or of governance. It has stemmed from a standpoint which originated in policy and the measurement of progress and the considerations of ethics and process objectives have been left to those at the level of implementation.

If participatory techniques are to be fully integrated into development, then planners and community development professionals will have to build a model for application in each community. This must build in from the start a mechanism which will be sensitive and responsive to the effects which tampering with local cultural mores will have. It may well be that some of the direct objectives of a development initiative is to produce a definite shift in the local culture (gender divisions, child labour practices, debt relationships, etc.). The tensions and conflicts which this will bring needs to be anticipated by planners and appropriate methods must be adopted by intervening professionals.

Behind this shift in thinking comes the impetus given to development concepts by anthropology. The challenge posed for anthropology is, whether its ethnographic approach can break out of the static academic framework, and contribute something to project planning and management? The value given to 'local knowledge' can only fully be understood and incorporated if its full cultural significance is recognised (Marsden, 1994a, 1994b). Pressures for change can, and will, be made from the outside. Three functions of development are identified: *action in the field, support in achieving the objectives of such action*, and *financial assistance required for the first two*. Each function represents a different perspective and a different focus for vested interests. Each interested party (agency/donor/government), representing one or more of these factors, will seek to ensure that any evaluation design will reflect the benefits of its own interests most favourably (Beaudoux, et.al., 1992). While these interests will be known to their owners in advance, they may not be declared fully until there is some form of crisis. If they are introduced arbitrarily, well into the development of a programme, and this distorts the direction or nature of the process, then there a sense of disillusionment can develop. This is more likely to manifest itself in the operational staff, as the consumers may have a more fatalistic appreciation of the local power structure.

The introduction of anthropological methods raises another issue of considerable importance. Detailed understanding of the local culture, places the operational staff in full knowledge of how that culture may conflict with some of the outputs which may be high on the programme's agenda. Confrontation with the local traditions, and the vested interests around those traditions, raise the question of how change is to be sought. Gender relations are a prominent issue. For example, policy priorities, and integral values, may dictate that the development process will not simply accept the cultural 'set'. For example, if programme design is structured to ensure that the allocation of resources, and opportunity, will empower women and change their current socio-economic and dependent status, changes may be forced upon the community. This means that, if the role and special place of women in their communities, is to be valued, developed, and not exploited on the same terms that classical, linear development theory would allow, then the contribution by women must be developed by women themselves in the first instance. It must not just be harnessed to accommodate arbitrary policies, and their narrow outcome requirements (Beaudoux, et.al., 1992; Chant, 1989; Moser, 1991; Townsend, 1993). As Moser states, '.....unless women speak, data will only reflect men's view of the world.' (Moser, 1993, p.97). Nobody can substitute for their voice in this process. The difficulty is, that there are also 'internal' constructs which act as impediments (see 'monitoring', above). In this example of gender relations, can an anthropological approach serve as a key to open up the planning process? Can it express the specific messages, which are sometimes contradictory, that each culture might express through its women? If this is possible, then the terms of reference of appraisal must be adjusted to include it.

The question still remains: which value system is best served through dispassionate enquiry? Does anthropology represent a contrived 'detachment' which may deliver a form of 'understanding', but will fail to provide a means of interpreting the desired changes of the development programme into the vernacular of the local culture. There is the question of implicit ideological bias, and no enquiry is value-free (Marsden & Oakley, 1991; Moser, 1993). The distinctions between different analytical approaches, such as those between sex, gender and/or women's political organisation identify different levels of priority. Institutionally, these standpoints are represented by *Women in Development* (WID), *Gender and Development* (GAD), and *Development Alternatives for a New Era* (DAWN). They identify different attitudes towards the autonomy of women, and present different degrees of challenge to vested interests in the indigenous community. At the one end of the spectrum, the development of women's social and economic role (WID) is designed to extend their *effective functioning* under the pressures of economic and social oppression. At the other end, there are expectations that they will *mobilise* against the system that confines them to a secondary status (Antrobus, 1991; Chinnery-Hesse, et al, 1989; Moser, 1991, 1993). Will appraisal, monitoring, participative structures for experiential development and evaluation tell us whether or not these formations are successful? Can they be more successful than the (dispassionate) interests of 'cost-benefit analysis'? How will they fare against the (far from dispassionate) voices of vested interest and tradition? And who is 'right' (developmentally) in the final analysis?

One of the important questions that has to be asked is, what level of critical awareness is to be encouraged during this process? If the interaction between the citizens and the staff of the operational agencies results in a questioning of the whole basis of the 'development' process in this instance, then there will be a potential for real conflict and dissent' (Lister, 1994). Pottier sets out the current 'buzzwords', which may yet find themselves consigned to the dustbin of history: *sustainability, the human factor, participatory research*, but which are currently defining the shape of accepted practice (Pottier, 1993). We have yet to discover whether or not the apparent 'openness' of Northern democracies in their attitude towards their aid programmes, is mirrored in their programmes for 'regeneration' or 'partnership' at home. Serious critique of the evaluation processes themselves may give us the answer.

Evaluation in context

Evaluation is an integral part of the development programme. It is one of the processes which should be planned ahead of the commencement of the *formulation* stage, and it is the one process that outlasts the termination of the initiative. Depending on the methods employed, evaluation can require the participation of people who are involved at all levels, and at every stage in the life of the scheme. Evaluation is that part of the methodology which attempts to counter the distorting forces of chance, opportunism, or petty politics on the fortunes of development. Structures, which are established to meet the needs of the evaluation model, provide boundaries which can be crossed only after deliberate decisions have been made, and which acknowledge the abandonment or redesign of the evaluation model itself. There are, of course, practical limitations to the resources allocated to evaluation. But community development, being the creature that is, may produce effects that take time to mature, or even take time to emerge. This means that the effects of a particular intervention may continue to be felt long after the formal structures have been dismantled.

The methods of evaluation, and their validity, are still evolving. This means that descriptions of preferred methods and the formulation of models are still in the experimental stage. Nevertheless, the absence of an evaluation mechanism must devalue the impact that any programme will make on posterity. This need not diminish the practical effects that the programme may have on its area of intervention. It just means that an opportunity to verify the connections between measured inputs against outcomes has been missed. Many programmes fall into this category, and they have contributed to the mystique of the process, and the attendant professionals.

Evaluation can serve many purposes. It is a mechanism for informing interested and disinterested parties and vested interests, and allows for comparisons to be made between activities of similar nature, or between measurable variables. It is a means of establishing opportunity costs, and of selecting choices of operational method. For operational staff, it is a management tool. It is a part of the project framework, and by complying with its disciplines, workers can fulfil their expectations that there will be some measurement which will signify various stages in the development process. Through the refinement of their evaluation methods, they can develop confidence in the value and success of their efforts, and in their own competence. At the 'end' of the programme, some overall estimate of the magnitude of change can be made with greater assurance. Evaluation offers a historical assessment to be made so that the costs and benefits can be put into perspective through reasoned analysis.

We have shown that the process of evaluation is not merely the domain of the professional. In addition to the needs and the demands of the sponsors of development, the immediacy of the involvement of the workers and their consumers ensures that measurement of outcomes will reflect heavily on the perceived worth of all participants. It will contribute to the picture of self-worth and of the esteem in which various parties to the process hold each other. Where the evidence of evaluation points towards lack of progress, failure or misapplication of resources, it becomes a lever for apportioning blame or relocating authority or control over the future of the endeavour. It is a potent agent and it has to be handled wisely.

Of critical importance, are the *terms of reference* of the evaluation model. These are constructed from the competing pressures of the varied interest groups involved in setting up the scheme. These terms of reference shape the boundaries of the study field. They include the scope for measurement; confining it within certain avenues of enquiry, limiting it to particular paths, or levels of investigation. It is not unknown for the resources for evaluation to be deliberately omitted from the budget during the planning process, or it may be that there are taboo areas, where no evaluation may penetrate - for example, incursions into political fiefs, or the market interests of sponsors. These may be zoned off limits from the start, or they may emerge as 'sensitive' areas, which cannot be probed to deeply. These constraints frustrate attempts to establish 'scientific' enquiry methods. There are already restraints built into the system. There are resource implications in the design of any scheme, and levels of experience and skill in building an evaluation process will vary across any team of workers. Well funded programmes will be able to afford continuous monitoring and regular evaluation points in the time scale. Poorer programmes will have to make do with what they can salvage from competing claims on scarce resources. All these will contribute to the limitations of the evaluation.

One of the objectives of evaluation is to test the potential of the model for future replication elsewhere, or for it to be repeated within the original area, but in a different arena. It follows that the instruments of measurement and the application processes are recorded, together with a record of the experience of implementing the evaluation process. Flaws must be identified and remedied, and records must be kept of the rationale for deciding when and why changes had to be made. It can be seen that, in order for this process to be effective, the resourcing of the evaluation process has to allow for the secondary level of outcome.

Evaluation serves as one medium for the education of the participants in the ways of development. This is one of the good reasons for involving all stakeholders in the evaluation. Focusing on the needs of measurement, focuses the participants on the development processes themselves. 'Social development encompasses a very broad concern for the development of people, for the improvement of people's lives and for giving some control over the forces, and some involvement in the decisions, which effect their lives. The aim of both the donor and operational agencies should be to help people to choose their own destiny and to handle their own development.' (Pratt & Boyden, 1985, p. 140).

The first level of recognition is to be aware that planning and the modelling of development patterns is not a magical or restricted business. Almost anyone can do it, if they are prepared to apply themselves, and if they are sufficiently motivated. It is a part of the community development process to promote this activity within the community. The application of rational analysis to the processes of social and economic development, breaks into the cycle of passivity, acceptance or tradition-for-its-own-sake. This development can be followed up with a secondary level of capacity-building. This is the translation of the principle of evaluation, itself, into the rationale of community activity. If the introduction of evaluation can bring about the adoption of further, sustainable evaluation on the part of the participants, then the model of evaluation can be said to be a success.

262

People are not going to waste their time with abstract hypotheses. They will be more likely to replicate a process which can be shown to have beneficial outcomes. The monitoring of development and change, beyond the life of a targeted intervention, becomes the prerogative of the community. Assessment of progress, especially where there are scarce resources, or where there are issues involved concerning survival, or viability for certain valued activities, is an indicator in its own right of the success of a development intervention. The training of participants in the ways of evaluation and the disciplines of measurement should be well established in the agenda of a programme's development plan.

As a major stakeholder in the programme, the professional worker has a strong interest in the outcomes of evaluation. It is essential that information be obtained in order that some measure of progress and standards of achievement can be ascertained. Motivation is bound up with the reinforcement of values and the relevance of skills. Without these indicators, the professional will have difficulty in maintaining direction and purpose in the activity. Without the sort of information which evaluation provides, the professional has no control over the process. Loss of control puts the professional into the wilderness as far as management and autonomy is concerned.

Project and evaluation context

We wish, now, to re-introduce the broad framework of the model which has been progressively adapted throughout this volume. In Figure 6, we introduced the 'project framework' concept and apply it to the various target dimensions of a social development project (Harding, 1991; Marsden, et.al., 1994). This framework introduces the agency of the 'project' as the focus for *inputs* and the planning of strategies. The *outcomes* become stepping stones towards the achievement of the overall *aims* of the development process. The broad aims of the project and development initiative are stated at the top of the diagram, and the layout below reflects the areas for monitoring and evaluation throughout the development process. The energies of the 'project' can be directed (upwards, in this diagram) towards goals in any sector. They can be projected in any number or combination of initiatives, and they can target outcomes of varying degrees of complexity. In the previous statements of the template management model, we have considered that the successive 'stages', from left to right, might represent movement across a template of development progress. In this rendition, although each stage does represent a form of increased complexity, it might also be considered alone, as a discrete phase

263

in developmental activity. Activity might continue at any level, and no change might be possible for some time.

It is at the level of the individual, and that of community-wide initiatives, that issues surrounding the extent and influence of local participation can be resolved. It is here that a judgement will be made concerning the measurement of external forces, and their degree of influence. Once the intervention target shifts across the figure to the right, through social planning and on to service infrastructure, the community's active participation will modify from individual participation to representational models.

In this final version of the template model, there is an expectation that, in addition to the intention of increasing the functioning ability of individuals and groups, the worker and the strategists of complex organisations will have objectives across a much wider perspective. For this reason, we have included within the 'framework' each dimension of the human condition, from individual status, to the environmental setting of the project.

It is expected that the impact of a social development project will have some impact on each of these dimensions. While it may be considered that there is a 'hierarchy of objectives' in terms of measurable social change (Casley & Kumar, 1987), the success of the support and development impetus that is given in each sector, makes its own contribution to the success of every other dimension of the model. Leadership experience given to individuals in small groups influences the political impact of their cause, and of those to which they lend their support. This process has its knock-on effect all the way up the scale, to the level of the environment.

An individual worker, or a planned project initiative, may be designated to intervene at a particular level in the community, and with a pre-determined focus. This may preclude much concern for other dimensions of community life, and it is a theoretical and policy level constraint on workers which will soon come under pressure. Even if they are able to contain their own activities within the prescribed area, workers will discover that external factors play a large role in determining their freedom of action and directions of development. Pressure will come from the established culture, from traditional ways of doing things, and from other priorities, which make a superior claim on the project participants' loyalties.

The successes of community development will result in articulate community organisations entering the public arena of planning processes and of political pressure groups. It is for these reasons, that project workers must take a pro-active interest in the whole of their social and material environment. When planning a specific evaluation design for their

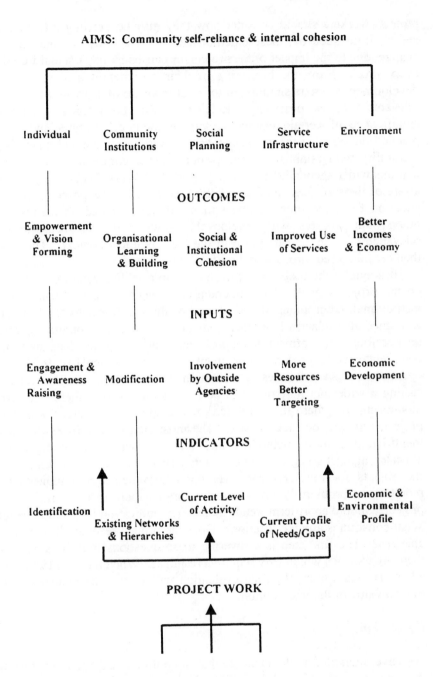

AIMS: Community self-reliance & internal cohesion

| Individual | Community Institutions | Social Planning | Service Infrastructure | Environment |

OUTCOMES

| Empowerment & Vision Forming | Organisational Learning & Building | Social & Institutional Cohesion | Improved Use of Services | Better Incomes & Economy |

INPUTS

| Engagement & Awareness Raising | Modification | Involvement by Outside Agencies | More Resources Better Targeting | Economic Development |

INDICATORS

| Identification | Existing Networks & Hierarchies | Current Level of Activity | Current Profile of Needs/Gaps | Economic & Environmental Profile |

PROJECT WORK

Figure 7: Project and evaluation context
Source - S. Clarke & C. Hawker (1991) unpublished

265

project, workers should consider how they may be exerting influence on, and be influenced by, these external factors. There will be indicators of change, due to the impact of the project, or caused by other social forces, at every level. From the beginning of their own deployment in the area, development workers should aim to become aware of as many of the more relevant ones as possible. 'Relevance' will be gauged against the significance of certain change factors to the local culture, and to the planned direction of the project's work. Staying in touch and maintaining credibility with established organisations in the community, will require that this wider agenda be given a high priority. Workers may only become aware of the significance of these after they have been exposed to the local situation for some time. Some will be of more immediate interest than others, but workers will develop their own scale for measuring the relevance of each, and its place in the local political context. These will then be monitored throughout the life of the scheme.

It is one of the problems of evaluation to establish what the effects are on the project's goals of the interaction between these different levels - institutional, environmental, etc. Some of these external forces may have an immediate impact, while others may not. Under some conditions, it may be possible for a project to address each and very level as part of a comprehensive approach. For many workers, particularly those with operational responsibilities, in addition to monitoring and evaluation, casting a wider net may prove to be impossible. Where there is external monitoring, or where there are dedicated evaluation resources within the project, this will be much easier. The most significant processes can be identified in a more methodical and analytical way. Weighting can be allocated against an agreed scale of importance and these can then become the objects for measurement. Having determined which indicators to monitor, the problem is how to use this information for the benefit of the project. Should short-term trends be taken as indication long-term change? What constitutes a panic reaction? Does the project react at all to external changes? The first step in answering these questions is to be aware that there are changes which may require a response. When the monitoring, and adjustments are over, the final evaluation will inform the planners of the overall value of the intervention.

Conclusion

We have attempted to demonstrate that the political realities at every level in community life demand that citizens develop, and then sustain, an active and determined interest in their social, economic and political environment.

266

The professional community development worker, who has provided so much of the analysis, motivational mix and technical know-how at every level, has to keep the pressure on to ensure that it all continues to happen. At the same time, the professional will need to stay in touch (in control, possibly) with the whole process, while the organisations that have been developed, mature. A vital and dynamic component of maturation will be the establishment of external relations within the wider political context.

As a consultant, the professional will remain 'ahead of the game' and will see the threats and possibilities before most others involved. Why should this be the case? Can a worker not just let go and let natural forces have their way? Has self-determination for the organisation simply been a hollow slogan which conceals a really sinister motive - professional imperialism (Midgley, 1981)? It is at the level of project evaluation that so many of the inherent tensions and conflicts are revealed. The 'globalisation' of issues and socio-economic forces may lead many to believe that 'small is beautiful' and that the rightful business of community development is at the work-face, rooted in the locality of community. The horizons of any particular project may tend to contract in response to internal pressures, not least, the sheer delight at getting on with the job.

Funding pressures, terms of reference for projects, political stratagems in high places will all have their influence on establishing the priorities for dealing with local issues. The 'parish-pump' approach serves the interest of workers with narrow horizons as well as vested interests elsewhere. Managing the stakeholders is, after all, an essential quality of the good servant (Young, 1996 p. 140).

We have shown how the forces of the 'market' have already penetrated deeply into the realms of personal welfare. Economic and financial considerations are now shaping the form and direction of local social investment. Professional workers are more than ever before the witting, or unwitting, agents for these forces. It is vital that they realise fully just what their position has become.

Profession-wide awareness, coupled with a sense of realism about what constitutes gains and successes for their citizen-clients, must become an urgent priority. The citizen-client has limited choice, and walking away is rarely an option. The citizen is stuck with the lottery of the personal integrity of the worker. This often is dependent on the degree of professional autonomy which can be rested away from the employer. All this involves awareness of the issues (Breitenbach, 1997), a preparedness to assume risk, and the relative strengths which the professional can derive from a personal constituency within a community and its organisations.

Bibliography

Abbott J. (1995), 'Community Participation and its relation to Community Development', *Community Development Journal*, Vol. 30, No.2, pp. 158-67.

Adams R. (1990), *Self-Help, Social Work and Empowerment,* Macmillan/BASW, London.

Alcock P, Christensen L. (1995), 'In and Against the State: community-based organisations in Britain and Denmark in the 1990s', *Community Development Journal,* Vol. 30, No.2, pp. 110-20.

Alinsky S.D. (1957), *From Citizen Apathy to Participation,* Industrial Areas Foundation, Chicago.

Alinsky S.D. (1969), *Reveille for Radicals,* Vintage Books, New York.

Alinsky S.D. (1972), *Rules for Radicals: A Programmatic Primer for Realistic Radicals,* Vintage Books, New York.

Allman P. (1988), Gramsci, 'Freire and Illich: Their Contributions to Education for Socialism', in Lovett, T. [ed], *Radical Approaches to Adult Education: A Reader,* Routledge, London, pp. 85-113.

Andersen C. (1992), 'Practical Guidelines', in Østergaard L. [ed], *Gender and Development: A Practical Guide,* Routledge, London, pp. 165-97.

Anderson P. & Davey K. (1995a), 'Communitarianism: Import Duties', *New Statesman and Society,* Vol. 8, No. 342, March 3, pp. 18-20.

Anderson P and Davey K. (1995b),Tough on Crime, *New Statesman and Society,* Vol. 8, No. 343, March 10, p. 21

Ankrah E.M. (1992), 'AIDS in Uganda: Initial Social Work Responses', *Journal of Social Development in Africa,* Vol. 7, No. 2, pp. 53-61.

Ankrah M.E. (1987), 'Radicalising Roles for Africa's Development: Some Evolving Practice Issues', *Journal of Social Development in Africa,* Vol. 2, No. 2, pp. 5-26.

Antrobus P. (1991), 'Women in Development', in Wallace T. and March C. [eds], *Changing Perceptions: Writings on Gender and Development,* Oxfam, Oxford. pp. 311-17.

Arce, A., Villarreal M., de Vries, P. (1994) 'The social construction of social development', in Booth, D. (ed.) *Rethinking social development: theory, research and practice,* Longman, Harlow, pp. 152-71.

Archbishop of Canterbury's Commission on Urban Priority Areas (1985), *Faith in the City: A Call for Action by the Church and Nation,* Church House Publishing, London.

Archbishop of Canterbury's Commission on Rural Areas (1990) *Faith in the Countryside,* Churchman Publishing, London.

Armstrong J. and Henderson P. [eds] (1992a), *The Contribution of Community Development*, Community Development Foundation, London, p. 8.

Armstrong J. and Henderson P. [eds] (1992b), *Putting the community into community care*, Community Development Foundation, London.

Armstrong R. (1971), 'Community Development and Community Organisation - Allies of Rivals?' *Community Development Journal*, Vol. 6, No .2, pp. 103-9.

Arnstein S. (1968), 'A Ladder of Citizen Participation', *Journal of the American Institute of Planners*, Vol. 35, No. 4, pp. 216-24.

Association of Community Workers (1983), *Community Work - which way forward?* Association of Community Workers, London.

Association of Metropolitan Authorities. (1989), 'Community Development: The Local Authority Role', in Perkins B. and Goody H. [eds], Association of Metropolitan Authorities, London.

Association of Metropolitan Authorities/Federation of Community Work Training Groups, (1990), *Learning for Action: Community Work and Participative Training*, A.M.A. London.

Atkinson D. (1995a) *The Common Sense of Community*, Demos, London.

Atkinson D. (1995b), 'Adding Participation to Representation', in Atkinson D. [ed], *Cities of Pride: Rebuilding Community, Refocusing Government*, Cassell, London, pp. 138-44.

Audit Commission. (1986), *Making a Reality of Community Care*, H.M.S.O. London.

Audit Commission. (1989), *Urban Regeneration and Economic Development: The Local Government Dimension*, H.M.S.O. London.

Audit Commission. (1992a), *Community Care: Managing the Cascade of Change*, H.M.S.O. London.

Audit Commission. (1992b), *The Community Revolution: Personal Social Services and Community Care*, H.M.S.O, London.

BAGUPA (Bishop's Action Group on Urban Priority Areas). (1995), *Staying in the City: Faith in the City ten years on*, Church House Publishing, London.

Bailey R. Jr.(1974), *Radicals in Urban Politics: The Alinsky Approach*, [2nd ed], University of Chicago Press, Chicago.

Bailey R. (1973) *The Squatters*, Penguin, London.

Bailey R. (1980) 'Social Workers: pawns, police or agitators', in Brake M. & Bailey, R. *Radical Social Work Practice*, Edward Arnold, London.

Baldock P. (1982), 'Community work and social services departments', in Craig G., Derricourt N., & Loney M. [eds], *Community Work and the State: towards a radical practice*, Routledge & Kegan Paul, London, pp. 24-35.

Baldock P. (1977), *Community Work and Social Work*, Routledge & Kegan Paul, London.

Baldock P. (1979), 'Community Action and the Achievement of Popular Power', in Chekki D.A. [ed], *Community Development: Theory and Method of Planned Change*, Vikas Publishing House, New Delhi. pp. 154-67.

Balleis S.J., P. (1992), *ESAP & Theology,* Social Series No. 1, Mambo Press/Silveira House, Gweru, Zimbabwe.

Balleis S.J., P. (1994), *A critical guide to ESAP,* Silveira House and Mambo Press, Gweru.

Barclay P.M. (1982), *Social Workers: their role and their task,* National Institute for Social Work/Bedford Square Press, London.

Barclay Sir P. (Chair). (1995), *Joseph Rowntree Foundation Inquiry into Income and Wealth,* Joseph Rowntree Foundation, York.

Barnardos South Wales/S.W.England Division. (1990), *Race Equality Strategy,* Barnardos, Cardiff.

Barr A. (1995), 'Empowering communities: beyond fashionable rhetoric? Some reflections on Scottish experience', *Community Development Journal,* Vol. 30, No.2, pp. 121-33.

Barr A. (1991), *Practising Community Development,* Community Development Foundation, London.

Barr A. (!976), *Professionalism and Community Work,* Association of Community Workers, Newcastle-upon-Tyne.

Barr A. (1977), *The Practice of Neighbourhood Community Work,* Dept. of Social Administration University of York, York.

Barr A., Hashagen, S. & Purcell, R. (1996a) *Monitoring and Evaluation of Community Development in Northern Ireland,* Voluntary Activity Unit, DHSS, Belfast.

Barr A., Hashagen, S. & Purcell, R. (1996b) *Measuring Community Development in Northern Ireland: a handbook for practitioners,* Voluntary Activity Unit, DHSS, Belfast.

Bassett P. (1995), 'In the 1990s, the union no longer makes us strong', *The Times.* September 13, p. 28, London.

Batson B. and Smith, J.(1995), *Organisational Development in the Community: Application, Tools and Discussion,* International Social Policy Research Unit, Leeds.

Batten T.R. (1957), *Communities and their Development,* Oxford University Press, London.

Batten T.R. (1962), *Training for Community Development: A critical study of method,* Oxford University Press, London.

Batten T.R., Batten M., in collaboration. (1965), *The Human Factor in Community Work,* Oxford University Press, London.

Batten T.R., Batten M., in collaboration. (1967), *The Non-Directive Approach in Group and Community Work,* Oxford University Press, London.

Bauzon K.E. (1992), *Development and Democratization in the Third World: Myths, Hopes and Realities,* Crane Russak, Washington D.C.

Beaudoux E., de Crombrugghe G., Douxchamps F., *et al.*(1992), *Supporting Action Development: from identification to evaluation,* COTA Macmillan, London.

Benington J. (1974), 'Strategies for change at the local level: some reflections', in Jones D. and Mayo M. [eds], *Community Work One,* Routledge & Kegan Paul, London, pp. 260-77.

Benington J. (1976), *Local Government becomes Big Business,* CDP Information & Intelligence Unit, London.

Benson J.K. (1980), 'The Inter-organizational Network as a Political Economy', in Etzioni A. and Lehman E.W. [eds], *A Sociological Reader on Complex Organisations,* [3rd ed], Holt, Reinhart & Winston, New York. pp. 349-68.

Beresford P. (1993), 'A Programme for Change: current issues in user involvement and empowerment', in Beresford P. and Harding T. [eds], *A Challenge to Change: Practical Experiences of Building User-led Services,* National Institute for Social Work, London, pp. 9-30.

Beresford P., Croft S. (1993), *Citizen Involvement,* Macmillan/BASW, London.

Berger P. L. (1974), *Pyramids of Sacrifice: Political ethics and social change,* Penguin, London.

Berkley N., Goodall G., Noon D., Collis C. (1995), 'Involving the Community in Plan Preparation', *Community Development Journal,* Vol. 30, No. 2, pp. 189-99.

Berridge S.J. A. (1993), *ESAP and Education for the Poor,* Social Series No. 5, Mambo Press/Silveira House, Gweru, Zimbabwe.

Biddle W.W. (1966), 'The 'Fuzziness' of definition of Community Development', *Community Development Journal,* Vol. 1, No. 2, pp. 5-12.

Biddle W.W. (1968), 'Deflating the Community Developer', *Community Development Journal,* Vol. 3, No.4, pp. 191-4.

Biddle W.W., Biddle L.J. (1965), *The Community Development Process: The Rediscovery of Local Initiative,* Holt, Rinehart and Winston, Inc. New York.

Biddle W.W., Biddle L.J. (1968), *Encouraging Community Development: A Training Guide for Local Workers,* Holt, Rinehart & Winston Inc. New York.

Binns I. (1973), 'What are we trying to achieve through Community Action?' *Community Action* Vol. 1, No. 6, pp. 12-3.

Blair A. (1995), 'The Party of the Family', *The Times,* March 30; also *The Financial Times* , March 18.

Blau P.M., Scott W.R. (1963), *Formal Organisations: A Comparative Approach,* Routledge & Kegan Paul, London.

Blaustein, A.L. & Fau, G. (1972) *The Star-Spangled Hassle: White Power and Black Capitalism,* Doubleday, New York.

Boff L. (1985), *Church, Charism and Power: Liberation Theology and the Institutional Church,* SCM Press, London.

Boff L. (1989), *Faith on the Edge: Religion and Marginalized Existence,* Harper Row, San Francisco.

Bolger S., Corrigan P., Docking J., *et al.*(1981), *Towards Socialist Welfare Work,* Macmillan, London.

Booker I. (1962), 'A Sicilian Experiment', *Community Development Bulletin,* Vol. XIII ,No .3, pp. 93-6.

Booth D. (1994) 'Rethinking social development: an overview', in Booth, D. (ed.), *Rethinking social development: theory, research and practice,* Longman, Harlow, pp. 3-41.

Borda O.F. (1992), 'Social Movements and Political Power in Latin America', in Escobar A. and Alvarez S.E. [eds], *The Making of Social Movements in Latin America: Identity, Strategy and Democracy,* Westview Press, Boulder, Colorado. pp. 303-16.

Boyte H.C. (1984), *Community is Possible,* Harper & Row, New York.

Bradshaw J. (1977), 'The Concept of Social Need', in Gilbert N. and Specht H. [eds], *Planning for Social Welfare,* Prentice-Hall, Englewood Cliffs, New Jersey. pp. 290-96.

Brager G. (1963), 'Organising the Unaffiliated in a Low-Income Area', *Social Work,* Vol. 8, No .2, pp. 34-40.

Brager G., Specht H. (1973), *Community Organizing,* Columbia University Press, New York.

Braidotti R., Charkiewicz E., Hausler S., *et al.* (1994), *Women, The Environment and Sustainable Development: Towards a Theoretical Synthesis,* Zed Books/INSTRAW, London.

Braye S., Preston-Shoot M. (1995), *Empowering Practice in Social Care,* Open University Press, Buckingham.

Breitenbach E. (1997) 'Participation in an Anti-Poverty Project', *Community Development Journal,* Vol. 32, No. 2, pp. 159-68.

Briscoe C. (1976), 'Community work in social service departments', *Social Work Today,* Vol. 1 7, No. 2,

Britton B. (1983), 'The Politics of the Possible', in Jordan B. and Parton N. [eds], *The Political Dimensions of Social Work,* Basil Blackwell, Oxford. pp. 130-45.

Brokensha D., Hodge P. (1969), *Community Development: an Interpretation,* Chandler, San Francisco.

Bryant B., Bryant R. (1982), *Change and Conflict: A study of Community Work in Glasgow,* Aberdeen University Press, Aberdeen.

Bryman A., Cramer D. (1990), *Quantitative data analysis for social scientists,* Routledge, London.

Bulmer M. (1986), *Neighbours: The Work of Philip Abrams,* Cambridge University Press, Cambridge.

Burdick J. (1992), 'Rethinking the Study of Social Movements: The Case of Christian Base Communities in Urban Brazil', in Escobar A. and Alvarez S.E. [eds], *The Making of Social Movements in Latin America: Identity, Strategy and Democracy,* Westview Press, Boulder, Colorado. pp. 171-84.

Burghardt S., Fabricant M. (1987), *Working Under the Safety Net: Policy and Practice with the New American Poor,* Sage, Newbury Park, Calif.

Burke E.M. (1975), 'Citizen Participation Strategies', in Kramer R.M. and Specht, H. [eds], *Readings in Community Organization Practice*, [2nd ed], Prentice-Hall, Englewood Cliffs, New Jersey. pp. 196-207.

Burkey S. (1993), *People First: A Guide to Self-Reliant, Participatory Rural Development*, Zed Books, London.

Burns D. (1991), 'Ladders of Participation', *Going Local* ,No.18, pp. 14-5.

Butcher H. (1993a), 'Why Community Policy? Some Explanations for Recent Trends', in Butcher H., Glen A., Henderson P. & Smith G. [eds], *Community and Public Policy*, Pluto Press in association with Community Development Foundation, London, pp. 55-75.

Butcher H. (1993b), 'Introduction: Some Examples and Definitions', in Butcher H., Glen A., Henderson P. & Smith G. [eds], *Community and Public Policy*, Pluto Press in conjunction with Community Development Foundation, London, pp. 3-21.

Butcher H., Collis P., Glen A., *et al.*(1980), *Community Groups in Action: Case Studies and Analysis*, Routledge & Kegan Paul, London.

Calderon F., Piscitelli A., Reyna J.L. (1992), 'Social Movements: Actors, Theories, Expectations', in Escobar A., Alvarez S.E. [eds], *The Making of Social Movements in Latin America*, Westview Press, Boulder, Colorado. pp. 19-36.

Callinicos A. (1990) 'Reactionary Post-Modernism?', in Boyne, R Rattansi, A. (eds.), *Post-Modernism and society*, Macmillan, London.

Calouste Gulbenkian Foundation. (1968), *Community Work and Social Change: a Report on Training*, Longman, London.

Calouste Gulbenkian Foundation.(1973), *Current Issues in Community Work*, Routledge Kegan Paul, London.

Campbell B. (1993), *Goliath: Britain's Dangerous Places*, Methuen, London.

Cannan C. (1975), 'Welfare Rights and Wrongs', in Bailey R. and Brake M. [eds], *Radical Social Work*, Edward Arnold, London, pp. 112.-28.

Carley J. (1991), 'The influence of Paulo Freire's ideas on theories of social change', in Jones J. and Tilson J. [eds], *Roots and Branches*, Open University/Health Education Authority, pp. 44-53.

Carley M. (1987), *Rational Techniques in Policy Analysis*, Gower, Aldershot.

Cary L.J. (1970a), 'The Role of the Citizen in the Community Development Process', in Cary L.J. [ed], *Community Development as a Process*, University of Missouri Press, Columbia. pp. 144-70.

Cary L.J. (1970b), 'Introduction', in Cary L.J. [ed], *Community Development as a Process*, University of Missouri Press, Columbia. pp. 1-6.

Cary L.J. (1979), 'The Present State of Community Development: Theory and Practice', in Chekki D.A. [ed], *Community Development: Theory and Method of Planned Change*, Vikas, New Delhi. pp. 32-45.

Carmichael S., Hamilton, C.V. (1967) *Black Power: the politics of liberation in America*, Vintage, New York.

Casley D.J., Lury D.A. (1987), *Data collection in Developing Countries,* [2nd ed], Clarendon Press, Oxford.

Casley D.J., Kumar K. (1987), *Project Monitoring and Evaluation in Agriculture,* John Hopkins University Press/World Bank/IFAG/FAO, Baltimore.

Casley D.J., Kumar K. (1988), *The Collection, Analysis and Use of Monitoring and Evaluation Data,* John Hopkins University Press/World Bank, Baltimore.

Castells M. (1977), *The Urban Question,* Edward Arnold, London.

Castells M. (1983), *The City and the Grassroots,* Edward Arnold, London.

CCETSW (1974), *The Teaching of Community Work,* CCETSW, London.

CCETSW (1979), *Council Policy for the Teaching of Community Work within the Personal Social Services,* CCETSW, London.

CCETSW (1981), *Paper 15.1: Guidelines for courses leading to the certificate of qualification in social work CQSW,* CCETSW, London.

CCETSW (1989), *Paper 30, Requirements and Regulations for the Diploma in Social Work, DipSW.* CCETSW, London.

CDF (1995), *Regeneration and the Community in Wales: Guidelines to the community involvement aspects of the Welsh Office's Strategic Development Scheme,* Community Development Foundation, London.

CDP Information and Intelligence Unit (1975), *The Poverty of the Improvement Programme,* C.D.P. Information and Intelligence Unit, London.

CDP Information and Intelligence Unit (1977), *Gilding the Ghetto The State and Poverty Experiments,* C.D.P. Information and Intelligence Unit, London.

Cernea M.M. (1991), 'Knowledge from Social Science for Development Policies and Projects', in Poulton R, & Harris M, *Putting People First: Sociological Variables in Rural Development,* [2nd ed], Oxford University Press, New York. pp. 1-41.

Chamberlayne P. (1973), 'Community Action in the U.S.A'. *Community Action,* Vol. 1, No. 10, pp. 32-3.

Chambers R. (1980), *Rapid Rural Appraisal: Rationale and Repertoire,* Institute of Development Studies, Brighton.

Chambers R. (1986), *Normal Professionalism, New Paradigms and Development,* Institute of Development Studies, Brighton.

Chambers R. (1992a), *Rural Appraisal: Rapid, Relaxed and Participatory,* Institute of Development Studies, Brighton.

Chambers R. (1992b), 'Spreading and Self-improving: a strategy for scaling-up', in Edwards M. and Hulme D. [eds], *Making a Difference: N.G.O's and development in a changing world,* Earthscan, London, pp. 40-8.

Chambers R. (1993), *Challenging the Professions: Frontiers for rural development,* Intermediate Technology, London.

Chambers R., Pacey A., Thrupp L.A. (1989), *Farmer First: farmer innovation and agricultural research,* Intermediate Technology Publications, London.

Chanan G. (1992), *Out of the Shadows: Local Community Action and the European Community,* European Foundation for the Improvement of Living and Working Conditions, Shankill, Co. Dublin.

Chanan G., Vos K. (1990), *Social Change and Local Action: Coping with Disadvantage in Urban Areas,* European Foundation for the Improvement of Living and Working Conditions, Shankill, Co. Dublin.

Chant S. (1989), 'Gender and Urban Planning', in Brydon L. & Chant S. [eds],*Women in the Third World: Gender Issues in Rural and Urban Areas,* Edward Elgar, Aldershot, pp. 213-39

Chechoway B. (1995), 'Six strategies of community change', *Community Development Journal,* Vol. 30, No.1, pp. 2-20.

Cheetham J., Hill M.J. (1973), 'Community Work: Social Realities and Ethical Dilemmas', *British Journal of Social Work,* Vol. 3, No.3,

Chekki D.A. (1979), 'A Prolegomena to Community Development and Planned Change', in Chekki D.A. [ed], *Community Development: Theory and Method of Planned Change,* Vikas, New Delhi, pp. 3-24.

Child J. (1984), *Organization: A Guide to Problems and Practice,* [2nd ed],. Paul Chapman, London.

Chinchilla N.S. (1992), 'Marxism, Feminism and the Struggle for Democracy in Latin America', in Escobar A. and Alvarez S.E. [eds], *The Making of Social Movements in Latin America,* Westview Press, Boulder, Colorado, pp. 37-51.

Chinnery-Hesse M., Agarwal B., Ariffin J., *et al.*(1989), *Engendering Adjustment for the 1990s,* Commonwealth Secretariat, London.

Church in Wales Board of Mission: Division for Social Responsibility (1988b), *Faith in Wales: Part 1: The Challenge to Faith* , Church in Wales, Penarth.

Church in Wales Board of Mission: Division for Social Responsibility.(1988a), *Faith in Wales: Part 2: An Atlas of Disadvantage,* Church in Wales, Penarth.

Church in Wales Board of Mission: Division for Social Responsibility.(1988c), *Faith in Wales: Part 3: An Atlas of Advantage,* Church in Wales, Penarth.

Church in Wales Board of Mission: Rural Commission. (1992) *The Church in the Welsh Countryside: a Programme for Action by The Church in Wales,* Church in Wales, Penarth.

Clark G. (1976), 'Neighbourhood Self-Management', in Hain, P. [ed], *Community Politics,* John Calder, London, pp. 97-115.

Clark J. (1991), *Democratizing Development: The Role of Voluntary Organisations,* Earthscan, London.

Clark J. (1992), 'Policy influence, lobbying and advocacy', in Edwards M. and Hulme D. [eds], *Making a Difference: N.G.O's and development in a changing world,* Earthscan, London, pp. 191-202.

Clarke, S. (1978) *Working on a Committee,* Community Projects Foundation, London.

Clarke S. (1998) 'Community Development and Health Professionals', in Symonds, A & Kelly, A. (eds.), *The Social Construction of Community Care,* Macmillan, London, pp 125-134.

Clarke S. (2000 forthcoming) 'How Little Things Change: a tale of two cities in community development', in Clarke, S, Byatt, A., Hoban, M., Powell, D. (eds), *A South Wales Reader in Community Development*, University of Wales Press, Cardiff.

Clarke S.J.G. (1989), 'Current Development Dilemmas in Wales: A Crisis for N.G.O's.', in Commonwealth Secretariat. [ed], *Strategic Issues in Development Management: Learning from Successful Experiences,* Commonwealth Secretariat, London, pp. 17-188.

Clarke S.J.G. (1993), 'Looking for an Appropriate Method for Engaging the Underclass', in Hall N. [ed], *Social Development and Urban Poverty,* School of Social Work, Harare, pp. 17-24.

Cockburn C. (1977), *The Local State: Management of Cities and their People,* Pluto Press, London.

Coke J. (1991), 'Training for Community Health Work', in Jones J., Tilson J. *et al.* [eds], *Roots and Branches,* Open University/Health Education Authority, Milton Keynes. pp. 196-200.

Colenutt B. (1979), 'Community action over local planning issues', in Craig G., Mayo M. & Sharman N. [eds], *Jobs and Community Action,* Routledge & Kegan Paul with ACW, London, pp. 243-52.

Colonial Office: Advisory Committee on Education in the Colonies. (1943), *Mass Education in African Society,* H.M.S.O. London, Colonial No.186.

Community Action (1972), Editorial. 'Stirrings in Golborne', *Community Action,* Vol. 1, No. 7, pp. 30-32.

Community Development Foundation (1995) *Regeneration and the Community: Guidelines to the community involvement aspect of the SRB Challenge Fund,* C.D.F., London.

Constantino-David K. (1992), 'The Philippine experience in scaling-up', in Edwards M. and Hulme D. [eds], *Making a Difference: N.G.O's and development in a changing world,* Earthscan, London, pp. 137-147.

Conyers D. (1982), *An Introduction to Social Planning in the Third World,* John Wiley & Sons, Chichester.

Coppin M. [ed], (1991), *The contribution of community work,* Kookynie Press/Assn. of Rural Social Welfare, Perth, Western Australia, p. 5.

Corina L., Collis P., and Crosby C. (1970), *Oldham CDP Final Report,* Dept. of Social Administration, University of York, York.

Corkey D., Craig G.(1978), 'CDP: Community Work or Class Politics?' in Curno P. [ed], *Political Issues and Community Work,* Routledge & Kegan Paul, London, pp. 36-66.

Cornia G.A. (1987), 'Social Policy Making: Restructuring, Targeting, Efficiency', in Cornia G.A., Jolly R., Stewart F. [eds], *Adjustment with a Human Face: Protecting the Vulnerable and Promoting Growth,* Oxford University Press, Oxford, pp. 165-182.

Cornia G.A., Jolly R., Stewart F. [eds],(1987) *Adjustment with a Human Face: Protecting the Vulnerable and Promoting Growth,* Oxford University Press, Oxford.

Cornwall A., Guijt I., Welbourn A. (1994), 'Acknowledging process: challenges for agricultural research and extension methodology', in Scoones I. and Thompson J. [eds], *Beyond Farmer First: Rural peoples knowledge, agricultural research and extension practice,* Intermediate Technology Publications, London, pp. 98-116.

Corrigan P. (1975), 'Community Work and Political Struggle: what are the possibilities of working with the contradictions?' in Leonard P. [ed], *The Sociology of Community Action - No 21,* Sociological Review, Keele, pp. 57-73.

Corrigan P., Leonard P. (1978), *Critical Texts in Social Work and the Welfare State,* Macmillan, London.

Coulshed V. (1990), *Management in Social Work,* Macmillan/B.A.S.W. London.

Cox D.J., Derricourt N.J.(1975), 'The de-professionalisation of community work', in Jones D. and Mayo M. [eds], *Community Work Two,* Routledge & Kegan Paul, London, pp. 75-89.

Cox F.M. (1974), 'Alternative Conceptions of Community: Implications for Community Organization Practice', in Cox F.M., Erlich J.L., Rothman J. & Tropman J.E. [eds], *Strategies for Community Organization: A Book of Readings,* [2nd ed]. F.E. Peacock, Itasca, Illinois, pp. 224-34.

Craig G, Mayo M. (1995), 'Editorial Introduction: Rediscovering Community Development: some prerequisites for working 'In and Against the State'', *Community Development Journal,* Vol. 30, No. 2, pp. 105-9.

Croft S., Beresford P.(1989), 'Decentralisation and the Personal Social Services', in Langan M. and Lee P. [eds], *Radical Social Work Today,* Unwin Hyman, London, pp. 97-119.

Cruikshank J. (1994), 'The Consequences of our Actions: A Value Issue in Community Development', *Community Development Journal,* Vol. 29 ,No.1, pp. 75-89.

Crummy H. (1992), *Let the People Sing: The Story of Craigmillar,* Helen Crummy, Newcraighall.

Cusworth J.W., Franks T.R.(1993), 'Development and Development Projects', in Cusworth J.W. and Franks T.R. [eds], *Managing Projects in Developing Countries,* Longman, Harlow, pp. 1-14.

Czerny S.J., M.F. (1992), 'Liberation Theology and Human Rights', in Bauzon K.E. [ed], *Development and Democratization: Myths, Hopes and Realities,* Crane Russak, Washington D.C. pp. 135-40.

Dahrendorf R. (1973), 'Market and Plan', in Etzioni A. and Etzioni-Halevy E. [eds], *Social Change: Sources, Patterns and Consequences,* [2nd ed]. Basic Books Inc. New York. pp. 500-504.

277

Daley J, M., Wong P. (1994), 'Community Development with Emerging Ethnic Communities', *Journal of Community Practice,* Vol. 1, No.1, pp. 9-24.

Daoutopoulos G, A. (1991), 'Community Development in Greece', *Community Development Journal,* Vol. 26, No.2, pp. 131-8.

Darville G., Smale G. [eds], (1990), *Partners in Empowerment: Networks of Innovation in Social Work,* National Institute for Social Work, London.

Dasgupta, S. (1962) *A Poet and a Plan: Tagore's experiments in rural reconstruction,* Calcutta, Thatcher & Spink.

Dasgupta S. (1967), 'The Professional Social Work Approach', in Dasgupta S. [ed], *Towards a philosophy of social work in India,* Gandhian Institute of Studies/Popular Book Services, New Delhi. pp. 9-16.

Dasgupta S. (1968), 'Social Work and Social Change: A Case Study in Indian Village Development', in Truitt, W., H. [ed], Extending Horizons Books, Boston, Mass.

Dasgupta S. (1979), 'Three Models of Community Development', in Chekki D.A. [ed], *Community Development: Theory and Method of Planned Change,* Vikas, New Delhi. pp. 60-75.

Davies I.(1988), 'The IAF Training Programme and Philosophy of Organising', *Christian Action Journal,* pp. 12-5.

Davies I., Evans A. (1993), *Partners in Action: A Partnership in Community Development between the Church in Wales and the Children's Society,* Church in Wales Publications, Penarth, Wales.

Davies M. (1985), *The essential social worker: a guide to positive practice,* Community Care/Wildwood House, Aldershot.

Davis A. (1991), *What was Faith in the City really about?* Christian Urban Resources Unit, University of Bradford, Bradford.

De Graaf M. (1986), 'Catching Fish or Liberating Man: Social Development in Zimbabwe', *Journal of Social Development in Africa,* Vol.. 1, No.1, pp. 7-26.

Dennis C. (1993), Current Issues in Development Management, in Cusworth J.W. and Franks T.R. [eds], *Managing Projects in Developing Countries,* Longman, Harlow, pp. 217-29.

Depts. of Health, S.S., Wales. (1989), *Caring for People: Community care in the next decade and beyond,* H.M.S.O., London. Cm 849.

Devine J.A., Wright J.D. (1993), *The Greatest of Evils: Urban Poverty and the American Underclass,* Aldyne de Gruyter, New York.

Diani M., Eyerman R.(1992), 'The Study of Collective Action: Introductory Remarks', in Diani M. and Eyerman R. [eds], *Studying Collective Action,* SAGE, London, pp. 1-21.

Dixon J. (1990), 'Will Politically Inspired Community Work be evident in the 1990s", *Community Development Journal,* Vol. 25, No. 2, pp. 91-101.

Dixon J. (1995), 'Community Stories and Indicators for Evaluating Community Development', *Community Development Journal,* Vol. 30, No.4, pp. 327-36.

Dixon R. (1993), *The Management Task,* Butterworth Heinemann/Institute of Management, Oxford.

Dobson R. (1995), 'Judicial reviews may boost court challenges', *Community Care,* No. 23, March 29.

Dolci D. (1959), *To Feed the Hungry: Enquiry in Palermo,* MacGibbon & Kee, London.

Dominelli L. (1990), *Women and Community Action,* Venture Press, London.

Dominelli L. (1994), 'Women, Community Work and the State in the 1990s', in Jacobs S. and Popple K. [eds], *Community Work in the 1990s,* Spokesman, Nottingham. pp. 51-66.

Dominelli L. (1995), 'Women in the Community: feminist principles and organising in community work', *Community Development Journal,* Vol. 30, No.2, pp. 133-43.

Donnison D. (1991), *A Radical Agenda: After the New Right and the Old Left,* Rivers Oram Press, London.

Donnison D. (1994), *Act Local: Social Justice from the Bottom Up,* Commission on Social Justice, London.

Drucker P.F. (1968), *The Practice of Management,* Pan Books, London.

Drucker P.F. (1990), *Managing the Non-Profit Organization: Practices and Principles,* Butterworth Heinemann, Oxford.

du Sautoy P. (1956), 'Training for Community Development', *Community Development,* Vol. VIII, No.1, pp. 2-4.

du Sautoy P. (1962), *The Organization of a Community Development Programme,* Oxford University Press, London.

du Sautoy P. (1966), 'Community Development in Britain', *Community Development Journal,* Vol. 1, No.1, pp. 54-6.

Dudley E. (1993), *The Critical Villager: Beyond Participation,* Routledge, London.

Dunham A. (1958), *Community Welfare Organization: Principles and Practice,* Thomas Y. Crowell, New York.

Dussel E. (1992), 'Theology and Economy: The Theological Paradigm of Communicative Action and the Paradigm of Community Life as a Theology of Liberation', in Bauzon K.E. [ed], *Development and Democratization in the Third World: Myths, Hopes and Realities,* Crane Russak, Washington D.C., pp. 119-134.

East Dyfed Health Authority et.al. (1992) *Project Llanelli Gwendraeth Valley: consultations with service users in Pontyberem, Kidwelly & Tumble,* East Dyfed Health Authority, Carmarthen.

Edwards M. (1994), 'Rethinking Social Development: the search for 'relevance', in Booth D. [ed], *Rethinking social development: theory, research & practice,* Longman, Harlow, pp. 279-97.

Ellis J. (1989) *Breaking New Ground: Community Development with Asian Communities,* Bedford Square Press, London.

Else R. (1980), 'Community Work in a New Town', in Henderson P., Jones D., & Thomas D.N. [eds], *The Boundaries of Change in Community Work,* George Allen & Unwin, London, pp. 130-38.

Environment Dept. of (1988), in Warburton D., Wilcox D. *et al.* [eds], *Creating Development Trusts: Case Studies of Good Practice in Urban Regeneration,* H.M.S.O. London.

Escobar A., Alvarez S.E (1992), *The Making of Social Movements in Latin America,* Westview Press, Boulder, Colorado.

Esteva G. (1993), Development, in Sachs W. [ed], *The Development Dictionary: A Guide to Knowledge and Power,* Witwatersrand University Press, Johannesburg. pp. 6-25.

Etzioni A. (1964a), *Modern Organizations,* Prentice-Hall, Englewood Cliffs, New Jersey.

Etzioni A. (1964b), 'Towards a theory of societal guidance', in Etzioni-Halevy E. and Etzioni A. [eds], *Social Change: Sources Patterns and Consequences,* Basic Books Inc. New York. pp. 145-160.

Etzioni A. (1968), *The Active Society: A Theory of Societal and Political Processes,* Collier-Macmillan, London.

Etzioni A. (1969), 'Preface', in Etzioni A. [ed], *The Semi-Professions and their Organization: Teachers, Nurses, Social Workers,* Free Press, New York. pp. v-xvii.

Etzioni A. (1970), *Demonstration Democracy,* Gordon & Breach, New York.

Etzioni A. (1993), *The Spirit of Community: The Re-invention of American Society,* Touchstone, New York.

Etzioni A. (1995a), 'Responsibility', in Atkinson D. [ed], *Cities of Pride: Rebuilding Community, Refocusing Government,* Cassell, London, pp. 33-6.

Etzioni A. (1995b), 'Nation in need of community values', The Times. February 20, p. 9, London.

Evans C., Hughes M. (1993), *Tall oaks from little acorns. - the Wiltshire experience of using users in the training of professionals in care management,* Wiltshire Users' Network & Wiltshire Social Services Department, Calne.

Fagan H. (1979), *Empowerment: Skills for Parish Social Action,* Paulist Press, New York.

Fainstein N., Fainstein S.S.(1993), 'Participation in New York and London', in Fisher R. and Kling J. [eds], *Mobilizing the Community: Local Politics in the Era of the Global City,* Sage/Urban Affairs Annual Review, Newbury Park, Calif., pp. 52-74.

Farrow D. (1993), 'Community Work Principles and Rural Housing, in Wiltshire', in Henderson P. and Francis D. [eds], *Rural Action: A Collection of Community Work Case Studies,* Pluto Press, London, pp. 127-36.

Federation of Community Work Training Groups. (1992), *Setting up a Community Work Skills Course,* Federation of Community Work Training Groups, Sheffield.

Felvus J. (1994), *Consumer participation on the Public Sector: Applying theory and practice to Health Commissioning in Gwent,* [MSc thesis], University of Wales Cardiff,

Feuerstein M. (1986), *Partners in Evaluation: Evaluating Development and Community Programmes with Participants,* Macmillan, London.

Field F. (1989), *Losing Out: The Emergence of Britain's Underclass,* Blackwell, Oxford.

Fish J.H. (1973), *Black Power, White Control: The Struggle of the Woodlawn Organization in Chicago,* Princeton University press, Princeton, N.J.

Fisher R. (1993), 'Grass-Roots Organizing Worldwide: Common Ground, Historical Roots, and the Tension Between Democracy and the State', in Fisher R. and Kling J. [eds], *Mobilizing the Community: Local Politics in the Era of the Global City,* Sage/Urban Affairs Annual Review, Newbury Park, Calif., pp. 3-27.

Fisher R., Kling J. (1993), *Mobilizing the Community: Local Politics in the era of the Global City,* Sage, Newbury Park, Calif.

Fleetwood M., Lambert J.(1982), 'Bringing Socialism Home: Theory and action for a radical community action', in Craig G., Derricourt N. & Loney M. [eds], *Community Work and the State: towards a radical practice,* Routledge & Kegan Paul, London, pp. 48-59.

Foster G.M. (1957), 'Guidelines to Community Development Programmes', *Community Development Bulletin,* Vol. VIII, No. 2, pp. 32-8.

Fraggos C. (1968), 'A Settlement's role in C.D: a decade of experience', *Community Development Journal,* Vol. 3, No .4, pp. 201-10.

Francis D., Henderson P., Thomas D.N., (1984), *A Survey of the Community Workers in the Untied Kingdom,* National Institute of Social Work, London.

Frazer H. (1981), 'Community Work in the 80's', in Frazer H. [ed], *Community Work in a Divided Society,* Farset Co-operative Press, Belfast. pp. 20-32.

Frazer H. (1991), 'Integrated Approaches to Development', in van Rees W. [ed], *A Survey of Contemporary Community Development in Europe,* Dr. Gradus Hendriks-stichting, The Hague. pp. 67-76.

Freeman J. (1965),*The Tyranny of Structurelessness,* Anarchist Workers Association, Kingston.

Freire P. (1972a), *Cultural Action for Freedom,* Penguin, London.

Freire P. (1972b), *Pedagogy of the Oppressed,* Penguin, London.

Freire P. (1976), *Education: The Practice of Freedom,* Writers and Readers Publishing Co-operative, London.

Freire P. (1985), *The Politics of Education: Culture, Power and Liberation,* Macmillan, London.

Friedmann J. (1992), *Empowerment: The Politics of Alternative Development*, Blackwell, Cambridge, MA.

Gallagher A. (1977), 'Women and Community Work', in Mayo M. [ed], *Women in the Community*, Routledge & Kegan Paul, London, pp. 121-41.

Gallardo W.G., Encena II, V.C., Bayona N.C. (1995), 'Rapid Rural Appraisal and Participatory Research in the Philippines', *Community Development Journal*, Vol. 30, No.3, pp. 265-75.

Gibbon P. (1993), *Social Change and Economic Reform in Africa*, Nordiska Afrikainstitutet, Uppsala.

Gilbert N., Specht H. (1974), *Dimensions of Social Welfare Policy*, Prentice Hall, Englewood Cliffs N.J.

Gilbert N., Specht H.(1975), 'Socio-Political Correlates of Community Action: Political Integration and Political Influence', in Leonard P. [ed], *The Sociology of Community Action*, Sociological Review, University of Keele, Keele. pp. 93-112.

Gilbert N., Specht H.(1977), 'The Incomplete Profession', in Specht H. and Vickery A. [eds], *Integrating Social Work Methods*, George Allen & Unwin, London, pp. 219-32.

Gilbert N., Specht H., Terrell P. (1993), *Dimensions of Social Welfare Policy*, [3rd ed]. Prentice-Hall, Engelwood Cliffs, New Jersey.

Ginsburg N. (1979), *Class, Capital and Social Policy*, Macmillan, London.

Glampson A., Scott T., Thomas D.N. (1975), *A Guide to the Assessment of Community Needs and Resources*, National Institute of Social Work Training, London.

Glastonbury B. (1971), *Homelessness near a Thousand Homes: A Study of Homeless Families in South Wales and the West of England*, George Allen & Unwin, London.

Glen A. (1993), 'Methods and Themes in Community Practice', in Butcher H., Glen A., Henderson P. & Smith G. [eds], *Community and Public Policy*, Pluto Press in association with Community Development Foundation, London, pp. 2.-40.

Glugoski G., Reisch M., Rivera F.G. (1994), 'A Wholistic Ethno-Cultural Paradigm: A New Model for Community Organisation Teaching and Practice', *Journal of Community Practice*, Vol. 1, No.1, pp. 81-98.

Goetschius G.W. (1969), *Working with Community Groups*, Routledge & Kegan Paul, London.

Goldstein, H. (1973) *Social Work Practice: a unitary approach*, University of South Carolina Press, Colombia, S.C.

Goode W.J. (1969), 'The Theoretical Limits of Professionalization', in Etzioni A. [ed], *The Semi-Professionals and their Organization*, The Free Press, New York. pp. 266-313.

Grace M., Romeril B. (1994), 'The Youth Homeless Taskforce in Melton', *Community Development Journal*, Vol. 29, No. 3, pp. 257-67.

Gramsci A. (1971), [trans. Hoare Q. and Nowell Smith G.]. *Antonio Gramsci: Selections from the Prison Notebooks,* Lawrence & Wishart, London.

Greve J., Page D., Greve S. (1971), *Homelessness in London,* Scottish Academic Press, Edinburgh.

Griffith G. (1993), 'Project Appraisals: The Need for Methodological Guidelines', in Pottier J. [ed], *Practising Development: Social Science Perspectives,* Routledge, pp. 138-52.

Griffiths H. (1974), 'Carrying on in the middle of violent conflict: some observations of the experience in Northern Ireland', in Jones D. and Mayo M. [eds], *Community Work One,* Routledge & Kegan Paul, London, pp. 5-21.

Griffiths S.R. (1988), *Community Care: Agenda for Action,* H.M.S.O., London.

Grosser C.F. (1965), 'Community Development Programs Serving the Urban Poor', *Social Work,* Vol. 10, No. 3, pp. 15-21.

Grosser C.F. (1976), *New Directions in Community Organization: From Enabling to Advocacy,* [2nd ed]. Praeger, New York.

Gutierrez G. (1988), *A Theology of Liberation: History, Politics and Salvation,* SCM Press, London.

Hadley R., McGrath M. (1984), *When Social Services are Local: the Normanton experience,* George Allen and Unwin, London.

Hain P. (1976), 'The Future of Community Politics', in Hain P. [ed], *Community Politics,* John Calder, London, pp. 9-34.

Halmos P. (1978), *The Personal and the Political: Social Work and Political Action,* Hutchinson, London.

Hambleton R., Hoggett P.(1988), 'Beyond Bureaucratic Paternalism', in Hoggett P. and Hambleton R. [eds], *Decentralisation of Democracy: Localising Public Services,* School for Advanced Urban Studies, Bristol. pp. 9-28.

Hancock T. (1993), 'The Healthy City from concept to application: implications for research', in Davies J.K. and Kelly M.P. [eds], *Healthy Cities: Research and Practice,* Routledge, London, pp. 14-24.

Handy C. (1988), *Understanding Voluntary Organizations,* Penguin, London.

Handy C. (1990), *Inside Organizations:21 Ideas for Managers,* B.B.C. Books, London.

Hanmer J. (1991), 'The Influence of Women on Community Development and Health', in Jones J. and Tilson J. [eds], *Roots and Branches,* Open University, Milton Keynes. pp. 37-43.

Harding P. (1991), 'Qualitative Indicators and the Project Framework', *Community Development Journal,* Vol. 26, No.4, pp. 294-305.

Harloe M., Horrocks M.(1974), 'Responsibility without Power: the case of social development', in Jones D. and Mayo M. [eds], *Community Work One,* Routledge & Kegan Paul, London.

Hasler J. (1990), 'Community Organising - an Offer You Might Refuse', in Ballard P. [ed], *Issues in Church Related Community Work,* Collegiate Faculty of Theology, University of Wales Cardiff, Cardiff. pp. 99-102.

Hattersley R. (1987), *Choose Freedom: The Future of Democratic Socialism,* Penguin, London.

Hawtin M., Hughes G., Percy-Smith J. (1994), *Community Profiling: auditing social needs,* Open University Press, Buckingham.

Hay R.W. (1989), 'Food, Aid and Relief-Development Strategies', *Journal of Social Development in Africa,* Vol. 4, No.2, pp. 7-26.

Heginbotham C. (1990), *Return to the Community: The Voluntary Ethic and Community Care,* Bedford Square Press, London.

Henderson J. (1976), 'The U.N. approach to Social Development', *Community Development Journal,* Vol. 6, No.3, pp. 148-55.

Henderson P., Salmon H. (1995), *Community Organising: The U.K. Context,* Community Development Foundation/Churches Community Work Alliance, London.

Henderson P., Thomas D. N. (1987), *Skills in Neighbourhood Work,* [2nd ed]. Allen & Unwin, London.

Hettne B. (1995), *Development Theory and the Three Worlds,* Longman, Harlow.

Higgins J., Deakin N., Edwards J., *et al.* (1983), *Government and Urban Policy: Inside the Policy Making Process,* Basil Blackwell, Oxford.

Hill C.W., Jones G.R. (1992), *Strategic Management Theory: an integrated approach,* [2nd ed]. Houghton Mifflin Company, Boston, Mass.

Hills J. (1995), *Joseph Rowntree Foundation Inquiry into Income and Wealth,* Joseph Rowntree Foundation, York.

Hodge P. (1964), 'Community Organisation and the Bristol Social Project', *Community Development Bulletin,* Vol. XV, No.4/5, pp. 164-6.

Hodge P. (1970), 'The Future of Community Development', in Robson W.A. and Crick B. [eds], *The Future of the Social Services,* Penguin/The Political Quarterly, London, pp. 66-80.

Hogg C. (1994), *Involving the Community: Guidelines for Health Service Managers,* National Consumer Council, London.

Hogg C. (1994), *Beyond the patients' charter: working with users,* Health Rights, London.

Hope A., Timmel S., with Hodze C. (1984), *Training for Transformation: A Handbook for Community Workers,* Mambo Press, Gweru, Zimbabwe.

Howarth, C., Kenway, P., Palmer, G. & Street, C. (1998) *Monitoring Poverty and Social Exclusion: Labour's Inheritance,* New Policy Institute/Joseph Rowntree Foundation, London.

Hugman R. (1991), *Power and the Caring Professions,* Macmillan, London.

Hutson S., Liddiard M.(1993), 'Agencies and Young People: runaways and young homeless in Wales', in Pottier J. [ed], *Practising Development: Social Science Perspectives,* Routledge, London, pp. 34-49.

Illich I. (1973), *Deschooling Society,* Penguin Books, London.

Industrial Areas Foundation. (1978), *Organizing for Family and Congregation,* Industrial Areas Foundation, New York.

Industrial Areas Foundation Network of Southern California. (1988), *A Win for the Working Poor: The Moral Minimum Wage Campaign: UNO:SCOC:EVO*, Industrial Areas Foundation, Ponoma, Calif.

Jacobs S. (1994), 'Community Work in a Changing World', in Jacobs S. and Popple K. [eds], *Community Work in the 1990s*, Spokesman, Nottingham. pp. 156-74.

Jameson, N. (1988a), *Organising for a Change*, Citizen Organising Foundation, Birmingham.

Jameson N. (1988b), 'Organising for Change', *Christian Action Journal*, pp. 4-5.

Jankowicz A.D. (1995), *Business Research Projects*, [2nd ed]. Chapman & Hall, London.

Jenkins D.E., Patey E.H. (1990) *Involvement in Community: A Christian Contribution*, Williams Temple Foundation, Manchester.

Jenkins S. (1995) 'Milk and water communities', *The Times*. March 25, p.16, London.

Johnson P.(1995), 'Blair talks the language of Thatcher', *The Times*. March 24, p.16, London.

Jones C. (1983), *State Social Work and the Working Class*, Macmillan, London.

Jones J. [ed], (1991), *Roots and Branches*, Open University, Buckingham,

Jones J., Macdonald J. (1993), C.D.J. 'Editorial Introduction', *Community Development Journal*, 28, No.3, pp. 199-205.

Jones T. (1993), *Britain's Ethnic Minorities*, Policy Studies Institute, London.

Jordan B., Parton N.(1983), 'Introduction', in Jordan B. and Parton N. [eds], *The Political Dimensions of Social Work*, Basil Blackwell, Oxford. pp. 1-24.

Kaplan R. D. (1994), 'The Coming Anarchy', *Atlantic Monthly*, February, pp. 44-76.

Kee A. (1990), *Marx and the Failure of Liberation Theology*, SCM Press, London.

Kelly A. (1991) 'The Contribution of Community Work' in Coppin, M. (ed) *Community Work: Solutions or Illusions*, Kookynie Press, Perth, Western Australia.

Kelly A., Sewell S. (1988), *With Head, Heart and Hand: Dimensions of Community Building*, [3rd ed]. Boolarong, Brisbane.

Khindulka K. (1975), 'Community Development: Potentials and Limitations', in Kramer R.M. and Specht H. [eds], *Readings in Community Organization Practice*, [2nd ed]. Prentice-Hall Inc. Englewood Cliffs, New Jersey. pp. 175-83.

Kirk A. (1989), 'A Different Task: Liberation Theology and Local Theologies', in Harvey A. [ed], *Theology in the City: A Theological Response to 'Faith in the City'*. SPCK, London, pp. 15-31.

Kirkpatrick D. J. (1974), 'How Close is American to British community development?' - some impressions, *Community Development Journal*, Vol. 9, No. 2, pp. 108-16.

Knight B. (1993), *Voluntary Action*, Home Office, London. p. i.

Korten D.C. (1992), 'People-Centered Development: Alternative for a World Crisis', in Bauzon K.E. [ed], *Development and Democratization in the Third World: Myths, Hopes, and Realities*, Crane Russak, Washington D.C. pp. 53-79.

Kuenstler P. (1960), *Community Organisation in Great Britain*, Faber, London.

Lambert J. (1978), 'Political Values and Community Work Practice', in Curno P. [ed], *Political Issues and Community Work*, Routledge & Kegan Paul, London, pp. 3-16

Langan M. (1993a) 'New Dimensions in Social Work', in Clarke, S. *A Crisis in Care? Challenges for Social Work*, Sage/Open University, London.

Langan M. (1993b), 'Who cares? Women in the Mixed Economy of Care', in Langan M. and Day L. [eds], *Women, Oppression & Social Work: issues in Anti-Discriminatory Practice*, Routledge, London, pp. 67-91.

Lansley S., Goss S., Wolmer C. (1989), *Councils in Conflict: The Rise and Fall of the Municipal Left*, Macmillan, London.

Lattimer M. (1994), *The Campaigning Handbook*, Directory of Social Change, London.

Lawless P. (1989), *Britain's Inner Cities*, [2nd ed]. Paul Chapman, London.

Leaper R.A.B. (1968), *Community Work*, National Council of Social Service, London.

Leech K. (1988), *Struggle in Babylon: Racism in the Cities and the Churches of Britain*, Sheldon Press, London.

Lees R., Mayo M. (1984), *Community Action for Change*, Routledge & Kegan Paul, London.

Lehman E.W. (1980), 'A Paradigm for the Analysis of Inter-organizational Relations', in Etzioni A. and Lehman E.W. [eds], *A Sociological Reader on Complex Organizations*, [3rd ed]. Holt, Reinhart & Winston, New York.

Leonard P. (1975a), 'Introduction: The Sociology of Community Action', in Leonard P. [ed], *The Sociology of Community Action - No. 21*, Sociological Review, University of Keele, Keele. pp. 5-20.

Leonard P.(1975b), 'Towards a Paradigm for Radical Practice', in Bailey R. and Brake M. (ed). *Radical Social Work*, Edward Arnold, London, pp. 46-61.

Leonard P. (1979), 'Restructuring the Welfare State', *Marxism Today*, pp. 7-13.

Lister I. (1994), Concsientization and political literacy: a British encounter with Paulo Freire, in McLaren P.L. and Lankshear C. [eds], *Politics of Liberation: Paths from Freire*, Routledge, London, pp. 62-73.

Lister R. (1990), *The Exclusive Society: Citizenship and the Poor*, Child Poverty Action Group, London.

Littlejohn E.R., Hodge P. (1965), *Community Organisation: Work in Progress*, National Council of Social Service, London.

Litwak E., Hylton L.F.(1980), 'Inter-organizational Analysis: A Hypothesis in Co-ordinating Agencies', in Etzioni A. and Lehman E.W. [eds], *A Sociological*

Reader on Complex Organisations, [3rd ed]. Holt, Reinhart & Winston, New York. pp. 269-83.

Local Government Information Unit. (1995), *The 1995 Housing white paper - Our future homes: opportunity, choice, responsibility,* Local Government Information Unit, London.

London Edinburgh Weekend Return Group. (1979), *In and Against the State,* Pluto Press, London.

Loney M. (1983), *Community against Government: The British Community Development Project 1968-78,* Heinemann, London.

Long N., Villareal M.(1994), 'The Interweaving of Power and Knowledge in Development Interfaces', in Scoones I. and Thompson J. [eds], *Beyond Farmer First: Rural People's Knowledge, Agricultural Research and Extension Practice,* Intermediate Technology, London, pp. 41-51.

Lopes C. (1994), *Enough is Enough! For an alternative diagnosis of the African crisis,* Nordiska Afrikainstitutet, Uppsala.

Lotz J. (1979), 'Learning Community Development: A Canadian Perspective', in Chekki D.A. [ed], *Community Development: Theory and Method of Planned Change,* Vikas, New Delhi. pp. 189-97.

Lovibond S. (1990), 'Feminism and Postmodernism', in Boyne R. and Rattans A. [eds], *Postmodernism and Society,* Macmillan, London. pp. 154-86.

Macdonald J.J. (1992), *Primary Health Care: Medicine in its Place,* Earthscan, London.

MacGarry S.J.,B. (1993) *Growth? Without Equity?* Silveira House and Mambo Press, Gweru.

Machiavelli N., (trans. George Bull). (1975), *The Prince,* [2nd ed]. Penguin Books, London.

MacInnes J. (1987), *Thatcherism at Work,* Open University Press, Buckingham.

MacIntosh M., Wainwright, H. (1987) *A Taste of Power: the politics of local economies,* Verso, London.

Manderson L., Aaby P. (1992), 'Can rapid anthropological procedures be applied to tropical diseases?' *Health Policy and Planning,* Vol. 7.,No.1, pp. 46-55.

Marchand M.H., Parpart J.L. (1995), *Feminism, Postmodernism, Development,* Routledge, London.

Marchant C. (1989), 'Evangelicals and Community Work', *Christian Action Journal,* pp. 12-3.

Marcuse H. (1968), *Repressive Tolerance,* [Unpublished].

Marins J., Trevisan T.M., Chanona C. (1989), *The Church from the Roots: Basic Ecclesial Communities,* CAFOD, London.

Marris P. (1974), 'Experimenting in social reform', in Jones D. and Mayo M. [eds], *Community Work One,* Routledge & Kegan Paul, London, pp. 245-59.

Marris P. (1982), *Community Planning and Conceptions of Change,* Routledge & Kegan Paul, London.

Marris P., Rein M. (1967), *Dilemmas of Social Reform: Poverty and Community Action in the United States,* Routledge & Kegan Paul, London.

Marsden D. (1994a), 'Indigenous management and the management of indigenous knowledge', in Wright S. [ed], *Anthropology of Organizations,* Routledge, London, pp. 41-55.

Marsden D. (1994b), 'Indigenous Management and the Management of Indigenous Knowledge', in Wright S. [ed], *Beyond Farmer First: Rural Peoples' Knowledge, Agricultural Research and Extension Practice,* Intermediate Technology, London, pp. 52-6.

Marsden D., Oakley P. (1991), 'Future Issues and Perspectives in the Evaluation of Social Development', *Community Development Journal,* 26, No.4, pp. 315-28.

Marsden D., Oakley P., Pratt B. (1994), *Measuring the Process: Guidelines for Evaluating Social Development,* INTRAC, Oxford.

Marston S.A., Towers G. (1993), 'Private Places and the Politics of Spaces: Spatioeconomic Restructuring and Community Organizing', in Tucson and El Paso., in Fisher R. and Kling J. [eds], *Mobilizing the Community: Local Politics in the Era of the Global City,* Sage/Urban Affairs Urban Review, Newbury Park, Calif. pp. 75-102.

Mason D. (1995), *Race & Ethnicity in Modern Britain,* Oxford University Press, Oxford.

Mayo M. (1972), 'Some fundamental problems of Community Work on Housing Estates in Britain', *Community Development Journal,* Vol. 7, No.1, pp. 55-9.

Mayo M. (1975), 'Community Development: A Radical Alternative?' in Bailey R. and Brake M. [eds], *Radical Social Work,* Edward Arnold, London, pp. 129-43.

Mayo M. (1979), 'Radical Politics and Political Action', in Loney M. and Allen M. [eds], *The Crisis of the Inner City,* Macmillan, London, pp. 131-48.

Mayo M. (1980), 'Beyond CDP: reaction and community action', in Brake M. and Bailey R. [eds], *Radical Social Work and Practice,* Edward Arnold, London, pp. 182-96.

Mayo M. (1982), 'The European Poverty Programme: why re-invent the broken wheel?', in Craig G., Derricourt N. & Loney M., *Community Work and the State: Towards a Radical Practice,* Routledge and Kegan Paul, London.

Mayo M. (1994), *Communities and Caring,* Macmillan, London.

Mayo M. (1982), 'Community Action Programmes in the early eighties - what future?' *Critical Social Policy,* Vol.. 1, No.3, pp. 5-18.

McAndrew B. (1993), *Changing Organisations,* Longman, Harlow.

McLaren P.L., Lankshear C.(1994), *Politics of Liberation: Paths from Freire,* Routledge, London.

McMurray A. (1993), *Community Health Care Nursing: Primary Health Care in Practice,* [2nd ed]. Churchill Livingstone, Melbourne.

Meyer C.H. (1970), *Social Work Practice,* Free Press, New York.

Michels R. (1962), *Political Parties: A Sociological Study of the Oligarchical Tendencies of Modern Democracy,* The Free Press, New York.

Midgley J. (1981), *Professional Imperialism: Social Work in the Third World,* Heinemann, London.

Midgley J. (1986a), 'Community Participation, the state and social policy', in Midgley J., Hall A., Hardiman M. & Narine D. [eds], *Community Participation, Social Development and the State,* Methuen, London, pp. 145-60.

Midgley J. (1986b), 'Community participation: history, concepts and controversies', in Midgley J., Hall A., Hardiman M., & Narine D. [eds], *Community Participation, Social Development and the State,* Methuen, London, pp. 13-44.

Midgley J. (1987), 'Popular Participation, Statism and Development", *Journal of Social Development in Africa,* Vol. 2, No.1, pp. 5-16.

Midgley J. (1992), Review Article', *Journal of Social Development in Africa,* Vol. 7, No.2, pp. 63-72.

Midgley J. (1995), *Social Development: The Developmental Perspective in Social Welfare,* Sage, London.

Midgley J. (1997) *Social Welfare in a Global Context,* Sage, Thousand Oaks, Calif.

Mikkelsen B. (1995), *Methods for Development Work and Research: A Guide for Practitioners,* Sage, New Delhi.

Miles M.B., Huberman A.M. (1994), *Qualitative Data Analysis: An Expanded Sourcebook,* Sage, Thousand Oaks, Calif.

Miller M. (1987), 'Organizing: a map for explorers', *Christianity and Crisis,* Vol. 47, No.1, pp. 3-9.

Miller S.M., Rein M.(1975), 'Community Participation: Past and Future', in Jones D. and Mayo M. [eds], *Community Work Two,* Routledge & Kegan Paul, London, pp. 3-24.

Ministry of Community and Co-operation (1991) *The Evaluation of the Effectiveness of the Village Community Worker Training Programme,* Min. of Community & Co-operation/SIDA, Harare.

Mizrahi T., Rosenthal B., (1992), 'Managing Dynamic Tensions in Social Change Coalitions', in Mizrahi T. and Morrison J.D. [eds], *Community Organization and Social Administration: Advances, Trends and Emerging Principles,* Howarth Press, New York. pp. 11-40.

Mobray M. (1995), 'The medicinal properties of localism: a historical perspective', in Thorpe R. and Petruchenia J. [eds], *Community Work or Social Change? An Australian Perspective,* Routledge & Kegan Paul, London, pp. 41-58.

Morris R. (1970), 'The Role of the Agent in the Community Development Process', in Cary L.J. [ed], *Community Development as a Process,* University of Missouri Press, Columbia. pp. 171-94.

Morris R., Binstock R.H.(1980), 'Organizational Resistance to Planning Goals', in Resnick H. and Patti R.J. [eds], *Change from Within: Humanizing Social Welfare Organizations*, Temple University Press, Philadelphia. pp. 132-47.

Morse M. (1965), *The Unattached*, Penguin, London.

Moser C. 1993) *Gender, Planning and Development: Theory, Practice & Training*, Routledge, London.

Moser C. (1992) *From residual welfare to compensatory measures: the changing agenda of social; policy in developing countries*, Silver Jubilee Papers 6, Institute of Development Studies, Univ. of Sussex, Brighton.

Moser C.O.N. (1991), 'Gender Planning in the Third World: meeting practical and strategic gender needs', in Wallace T. and March C. [eds], *Changing Perceptions: Writings on Gender and Development*, Oxfam, Oxford. pp. 149-57.

Mosse J.C. (1993), *Half the World, Half a Chance: An Introduction to Gender and Development*, Oxfam, Oxford.

Mouzelis N. (1994), 'The state in late development: historical and comparative perspectives', in Booth D. [ed], *Rethinking social development: theory, research and practice*, Longman, Harlow, pp. 126-151.

Mullins L.J. (1989), *Management and Organisational Behaviour*, [2nd ed]. Pitman, London.

Mulwa F.W. (1988), 'Participation of the Grassroots in Rural Development: 'The Case of the Development Education Programme of the Catholic Diocese of Machakos, Kenya", *Journal of Social Development in Africa*, Vol. 3, No.2, pp. 49-65.

Murray C. (1990), *The Emerging British Underclass*, IEA Health & Welfare Unit, London.

Murray C. (1994), *Underclass: The Crisis Deepens*, IEA Health & Welfare Unit/Sunday Times, London.

Muzaale P.J. (1987), 'Rural Poverty, Social Development and their Implications for Fieldwork', *Journal of Social Development in Africa*, Vol. 2, No.1, pp. 75-85.

Narayan J. (1967a), 'The Concept of Loka-Sakti', in Dasgupta, S. [ed], *Towards a philosophy of social work in India*, Gandhian Institute of Studies/Popular Book Services, New Delhi. pp. 106-11.

Narayan J. (1967b), 'Revolutionary Social Work', in Dasgupta, S. [ed], *Towards a philosophy of social work in India*, Gandhian Institute of Studies/Popular Book Services, New Delhi. pp. 88-93.

Nevin B., Shiner P.(1995), *The Single Regeneration Budget: Urban Funding and the Future for Distressed Communities*, CLES, Manchester.

Nevin B, Shiner P. (1995), 'Community Regeneration and Empowerment: A new approach to partnership', *Local Economy*, Vol. 9, No 4, pp. 308-22.

290

Nicholson T. (1994), 'Institution building: examining the fit between bureaucracies and indigenous systems', Wright S. [ed], *Anthropology of Organisations,* Routledge, London, pp. 68-86.

Nkukila A.I. (1987), 'The Role of Popular Participation in Programmes of Social Development', *Journal of Social Development in Africa,* Vol. 2, No.1, pp. 17-28.

Ntebe A. (1994), 'Effective Intervention Roles of South African Social Workers an Appropriate, Relevant and Progressive Social Welfare Model', *Journal of Social Development in Africa,* Vol. 9, No.1, pp. 41-50.

O'Gorman F. (1990), 'Some Reflections on Community Development Experiences in Brazil', *Community Development Journal ,*Vol . 25, No.4, pp. 384-90.

O'Malley J. (1970), 'Community Action in Notting Hill', in Lapping A. [ed], *Community Action,* Fabian Society, London, pp. 28-36.

O'Malley J. (1977), *The Politics of Community Action,* Spokesman, Nottingham.

Oakley P. (1986), 'Evaluating Social Development: 'How Much' or 'How Good'?' *Journal of Social Development in Africa,* No.2, pp. 89-99.

Oakley P., Flores O. (1994), 'Community Development in Latin America: The current state of play - Editorial Introduction', *Community Development Journal,* Vol. 29,No.4, pp. 295-7.

Oakley, P., Marsden, D. (1984) *Approaches to Participation in Rural Development,* International Labour Organisation, Geneva.

Oakley P. *et al.* (1991), *Projects with People: The practice of participation in rural development,* International Labour Organisation, Geneva.

Oelschlägel D. (1991), 'Between possibility and restriction, Community work as a professional strategy in the social field' in van Rees W. [ed], *A Survey of contemporary Community Development in Europe,* Dr Gradus Hendriks-stichting, The Hague. pp. 25-34.

Ohri A. (1982), *Accreditation - the Next Step,* 36 Association of Community Workers, Sheffield.

Ohri A., Manning D., & Curno P. [eds], (1982) *Community Work and Racism,* Routledge and Kegan Paul, London.

Orme J., Glastonbury B. (1993), *Care Management: Tasks and Workloads,* Macmillan, London.

Osei-Hwedie K. (1990), 'Social Work and the Question of Social Development in Africa', *Journal of Social Development in Africa,* Vol. 5, No. 2, pp. 87-99.

Pargeter R.P. (Chair). *From Charity to Empowerment: The Church's Mission alongside the Poor and Marginalised People,* Committee for Community Relations, Catholic Bishops' Conference for England and Wales, London.

Parpart J.L. (1995), 'Deconstructing the Development 'Expert': Gender, development and the 'vulnerable' groups', in Marchand M.H. and Parpart J.L. [eds], *Feminism, Postmodernism, Development,* Routledge, London, pp. 221-43.

Parry G. (1972), 'The Idea of Political Participation', Parry G. [ed], *Participation in Politics,* Manchester University Press, Manchester. pp. 3-38.

Patti R.J. (1980), 'Organizational Resistance to Change: The view from below', in Resnick H. and Patti R.J. [eds], *Change from Within: Humanizing Social Welfare Organizations,* Temple University Press, Philadelphia. pp. 114-31.

Patton M.Q. (1997) *Utilization-Focused Evaluation: the new century text,* 3rd Edn., Sage, Thousand Oaks, Calif.

Payne M. (1986), *Social Care in the Community,* Macmillan/BASW, London.

Peirce, N.R., Steinbach, C.F. (1987), *Corrective Capitalism: the rise of America's community development corporations,* Ford Foundation, New York.

Perlman, J.E. (1976) 'Grassrooting the System', *Social Policy,* Vol. 7, No. 2., pp 4-20.

Peters T.J., Waterman Jnr. R.H. (1982), *In Search of Excellence,* Harper Row, New York.

Phillips L. (1987), 'Docklands for the People', Mackintosh M. and Wainwright H. [eds], *A Taste of Power: The Politics of Local Economics,* Verso, London, pp. 298-325.

Pincus A., Minahan A. (1973), *Social Work Practice: Model and Method,* F.E. Peacock, Itasca, Illinois.

Pinker R.A. (1982), 'An Alternative View', in Barclay P.M. *Social Workers: Their Role and their Tasks,* Bedford Square Press/N.C.V.O. London, pp. 226-62.

Pitt J., Keane M. (1984), *Community Organising? You've never really tried it!: the Challenge to Britain from the USA,* J. & P. Consultancy, Birmingham.

Pityana N.B. (1989), 'Towards a Black Theology for Britain', in Harvey A. [ed], *Theology in the City: A theological response to 'Faith in the City',* SPCK, London, pp. 98-113.

Plowden Lady E. (1966), *Children and their Primary Schools (The Plowden Report),* H.M.S.O. London.

Popay J., Dhooge Y.(1989), 'Unemployment, cod's head soup and radical social work', in Langan M. and Lee P. [eds], *Radical Social Work Today,* Unwin Hyman, London, pp. 140-64.

Popple K. (1994), 'Towards a Progressive Community Work Praxis', in Jacobs S. and Popple K. [eds], *Community Work in the 1990s,* Spokesman, Nottingham. pp. 24-36.

Popple K. (1995), *Analysing Community Work: Its Theory and Practice,* Open University Press, Buckingham.

Popplestone G. (1971), 'The ideology of professional community workers', *British Journal of Social Work,* Vol. 1, No.1, pp. 85-104.

Porter D., Allen B., Thompson G. (1991), *Development in Practice: Paved with Good Intentions,* Routledge, London.

Porter M. (1994), 'Second-hand ethnography: some problems in analysing a feminist project, in Bryman A. and Burgess R.G. [eds], *Analysing Qualitative Data,* Routledge, London, pp. 67-88.

Pottier J. (1993), 'The Role of Ethnography in Project Appraisal', in Pottier J. [ed], *Practising Development: Social Science Perspectives,* Routledge, London, pp. 13-33.

Pratt B., Boyden J.(1985), *The Field Director's Handbook: An Oxfam Manual for Development Workers,* Oxfam, Oxford.

Pruger R, Specht H. (1969), 'Assessing Theoretical Models of Community Organization Practice: Alinsky as a Case in Point', *Social Service Review,* Vol. 43, No.2, pp. 123.

Puddephatt A. (1988), 'Local State and Local Community: The Hackney Experience', in Hoggett P. and Hambleton R. [eds], *Decentralising Democracy: Localising Public Services,* School for Advanced Urban Studies, Bristol. pp. 187-93.

Radford J. (1970), *From King Hill to the squatting association,* in Lapping A. (ed). Fabian Tract 400, Fabian Society, London.

Rahman M.A. (1990a) 'Qualitative Dimensions of Social Development Evaluation', in Marsden, D & Oakley, P., *Evaluating Social Development Projects*, OXFAM, Oxford

Rahman M.A. (1990b), 'The Case of the Third World: People's Self-Development', *Community Development Journal,* Vol. 25, No. 4, pp. 307-15.

Rahman M.A. (1993), *People's Self-Development Perspectives on Participatory Action Research,* Zed Books, London.

Rahnema M. (1993), 'Participation', in Sachs W. [ed], *The Development Dictionary: A Guide to Knowledge and Power,* University of the Witwatersrand Press, Johannesburg. pp. 116-31.

Rathgeber E.M. (1995), 'Gender and Development in Action', in Marchand M.H. and Parpart J.L. [eds], *Feminism, Postmodernism, Development,* Routledge, London, pp. 204-20.

Rein M. (1977), 'Social Planning: The Search for Legitimacy', in Gilbert N. and Specht H. [eds], *Planning for Social Welfare: Issues, Models and Tasks,* Prentice-Hall, Englewood Cliffs, New Jersey. pp. 50-70.

Resnick H., Patti R.J.(1980), 'An Overview of Organizational Change', in Resnick H. and Patti R.J. [eds], *Change from Within: Humanizing Social Welfare Organizations,* Temple University Press, Philadelphia. pp. 3-22.

Rex J. & Moore, R. (1967) *Race, Community & Conflict,* Oxford University Press, London.

Richardson A. (1983), *Participation,* Routledge & Kegan Paul, London.

Robinson M. (1992), 'NGO's and rural poverty alleviation: implications for scaling-up', in Edwards M. and Hulme D. [eds], *Making a Difference: NGO's and development in a changing world,* Earthscan, London, pp. 28-39.

293

Robinson M. (1995), 'Towards a New Paradigm of Community Development', *Community Development Journal,* Vol. 30, No .1, pp. 21-30.

Robson B. (1988), *Those Inner Cities: Reconciling the Social and Economic Aims of Urban Policy,* Clarendon Press, Oxford.

Roche C. (1992), 'It's not size that matters: ACORD's experience in Africa', in Edwards M. and Hulme D. [eds], *Making a Difference: NGO's and development in a changing world,* Earthscan, London, pp. 180-90.

Rondinelli D., A. (1993), *Development Projects as Policy Experiments: an adaptive approach to development administration,* [2nd ed]. Routledge, London.

Rose H. (1975), 'Bread and Justice: The National Welfare Rights Organization', in Leonard P. [ed], *The Sociology of Community Action,* Sociological Review, University of Keele, Keele. pp. 113-42.

Rose H., Hanmer J.(1975), 'Community participation and social change', in Jones D. and Mayo M. [eds], *Community Work Two,* Routledge & Kegan Paul, London, pp. 25-45.

Ross M.G. (1955), *Community Organization: Theory and Principles,* Harper & Brothers, New York.

Ross M.G. (1958), *Case Histories in Community Organization,* Harper & Brothers, New York.

Rothman J. (1974), *Planning and Organizing for Social Change: Action principles from social action research,* Columbia University Press, New York.

Rothman J. (1979), 'Three Models of Community Organization Practice, Their Mixing and Phasing', in Cox F.M., Erlich J.L., Rothman J. & Tropman J.E. [eds], *Strategies of Community Organization: A Book of Readings,* [3rd ed]. F.E. Peacock, Itasca, Illinois, pp. 25-44.

Rothman J., Erlich J.L., Teresa J.G.(1979), 'Fostering Participation', in Cox F.M., Erlich J.L., Rothman J. & Tropman J.E. [eds], *Strategies of Community Participation,* [3rd ed]. F.E. Peacock, Itasca, Illinois, pp. 385-90.

Rowland C. (1988), *Radical Christianity: A Reading of Recovery,* Polity Press, Oxford.

Rubin F. (1995), *A Basic Guide to Evaluation for Development Workers,* Oxfam, Oxford.

Runnicles D. (1970), 'The social worker and community action', in Lapping A. [ed], *Community Action,* Fabian Society, London, pp. 19-22.

Sacks J. (1995), *Faith in the Future,* Darton, Longman & Todd, London.

Sackville, A.W. (1977), *The Social Work Task,* B.A.S.W. Birmingham.

Salmen L.F. (1987), *Listen to the People: -Observer Evaluation of Development Projects,* World Bank/Oxford University Press, Oxford.

Salmon H. (1978), 'Ideology and Practice', in Curno P. [ed], *Political Issues and Community Work,* Routledge & Kegan Paul, London, pp. 67-84.

Salmon H. (1989), 'Community Work in a Cold Climate', *Christian Action Journal,* pp. 5-7.

Salole G. (1991), 'Participatory Development: The Taxation of the Beneficiary', *Journal of Social Development in Africa,* Vol.. 6, No. 2, pp. 5-18.

Sanders I.T. (1970), 'The Concept of Community Development', in Cary L.J. [ed], *Community Development as a Process,* University of Missouri Press, Columbia. pp. 9-31.

Sayer J. (1986), 'Ideology: The Bridge between Theory and Practice', *Community Development Journal,* Vol. 21, No.4, 294-303.

Schenck C.J, Louw H. (1995), 'A People-centred Perspective on People-centred Community Development', *Journal of Social Development in Africa,* Vol. 10, No.2, pp. 81-91.

Schler D.J. (1970), 'The Community Development Process', in Cary L.J. [ed], *Community Development as a Process,* University of Missouri Press, Columbia. pp. 113-140.

Schorr A., L. (1992), *The Personal Social Services: an outside view,* Joseph Rowntree Foundation, York.

Schuurman F.J. (1993a), 'Modernity, Post-Modernity and the New Social Movements', in Schuurman F.J. [ed], *Beyond the Impasse: New Directions in Development Theory,* Zed Books, London, pp. 187-206.

Schuurman F.J.(1993b), *Beyond the Impasse: New Directions in Development Theory,* Zed Books, London.

Scoones I., Thompson J. (1994), 'Introduction - Beyond Farmer First', in Scoones I. and Thompson J. [eds], *Beyond Farmer First: Rural People's Knowledge, Agricultural Research & Extension Practice,* Intermediate Technology Publications, London, pp. 1-14.

Scott J. (1994), *Poverty & Wealth: Citizenship, Deprivation and Privilege,* Longman, London.

Seabrook J. (1993), *Victims of Development: Resistance and Alternatives,* Verso, London.

Seale, B. (1970) *Seize the Time,* Vintage, New York.

Secretary of State for Wales (1998) *Better Health Better Wales,* London, Stationery Office.

Seebohm S.F., *et al.* (1968), *Report of the Committee on Local Authority and Allied Personal Social Services,* H.M.S.O. London. Cmnd. 3703.

Seers D. (1995), 'What are we trying to measure?' in Ayres R. [ed], *Development Studies: An Introduction through Selected Readings,* Greenwich University Press, Dartford, Kent. pp. 3-20.

Segal B. (1980), 'Planning and Power in Hospital Social Service', in Resnick H. and Patti R.J. [eds], *Change from Within: Humanizing Social Welfare Organizations,* Temple University Press, Philadelphia. pp. 275-86.

Sen G., Grown C. (1988), *Development, Crises and Alternative Visions: Third World Women's Perspectives,* Earthscan, London.

Shragge E. (1979), 'Neighbourhood Organizing: Methodology and Ideology', in Chekki D.A. [ed], *Community Development: Theory and Method of Planned Change,* Vikas Publishing House, New Delhi. pp. 168-88.

Silberman C.E. (1964), *Crisis in Black and White,* Random House, New York.

Slayton, R.A. (1986) *Back of the Yards: the making of local democracy,* University of Chicago Press. Chicago.

Skeffington A.M. (1969), *People and Planning,* H.M.S.O. London.

Smale G., Tuson G., Cooper M., *et al.*(1988), *Community Social Work: A Paradigm for Change,* National Institute for Social Work, London.

Smale G., Bennett W. [eds], (1989), *Pictures of Practice Volume 1: Community Social Work in Scotland,* National Institute for Social Work, London.

Smith C.S., Anderson B. (1972), 'Political Participation through Community Action', in Parry G. [ed], *Participation in Politics,* Manchester University Press, Manchester. pp. 303-18.

Smith J., Bishop .J, Salmon H., Spence D., Symons B., and Twelvetrees A. (1978), *Towards a Definition of Community Work,* Association of Community Workers, London.

Smith L. (1981), 'A model for the development of public participation in local authority decision making', in Smith L. and Jones D. [eds], *Deprivation, Participation and Community Action,* Routledge & Kegan Paul, London, pp. 1-36.

Smith L. (1995),*Community Development and the Children Act: The Prevention Option,* [Applied Social Studies],University of Wales Swansea.

Smithies J. (1991), 'Management Theory and Community Development Theory: Making the Connections', in Jones J. and Tilson J. [eds], *Roots and Branches,* Open University/Health Education Authority, Milton Keynes. pp. 242-57.

Smithies J., Adams L.(1993), 'Walking the Tightrope: Issues in Evaluation and Community Participation for Health for All', in Davies J.K. and Kelly M.P. [eds], *Healthy Cities: Research and Practice,* Routledge, London, pp. 55-70.

Sparr P. (1994a), 'What is Structural Adjustment?' in Sparr P. [ed], *Mortgaging Women's Lives: Feminist Critiques of Structural Adjustment,* Zed Books, London, pp. 1-12.

Sparr P. (1994b), 'Banking on Women: Where do we go from here?' in Sparr P. [ed], *Mortgaging Women's Lives: Feminist Critiques of Structural Adjustment,* Zed Books, London, pp. 183-207.

Specht H. (1975a) 'Disruptive Tactics', in Kramer, R. M. & Specht, H. (eds), *Readings in Community Organization Practice,* Prentice-Hall Inc, Englewood Cliffs, N.J.

Specht H. (1975b), 'The Dilemmas of Community Work in the United Kingdom: A comment', Reprinted in Henderson P. and Thomas D.N. (1981), *Readings in Community Work,* George Allen & Unwin, London, pp. 21-5.

Specht H. (1976), *The Community Development Project: National and Local Strategies for Improving the Delivery of Services,* National Institute for Social Work, London.

Specht H. (1977), 'Issues and Problems in Utilizing a Unitary Method', in Specht H. and Vickery A. [eds], *Integrating Social Work Methods,* National Institute for Social Work, London, pp. 248-55.

Spergel I.A. (1969), *Community Problem Solving: The Delinquency Example,* University of Chicago Press, Chicago.

Standing Conference for Community Development. 'New Challenges in Community Development', SCCD News. 1995; Vol. 12, pp. 1. Sheffield.

Stevenson O. & Parsloe, P. (1993) *Community Care and Empowerment,* Joseph Rowntree Foundation, York.

Stewart J., Spencer K., and Webster B. (1974) *Local Government Approaches to Urban Deprivation,* Home Office, London.

Stewart M. (1993), *Integrated Social Support in Nursing,* Sage, Newbury Park, Calif.

Stiefel M., Wolfe M. (1994), *A Voice for the Excluded: Popular Participation in development: Utopia or necessity?* Zed Books in association with UNRISD, London.

Stiles J., Dean C. (1978), *The Training Debate,* Association of Community Workers, London.

Stokes P. (1994), *Recreating the Civil Society,* Community Resource & Information Service Trust, Birmingham.

Sullivan, M. (1992) *The Politics of Social Policy,* Harvester Wheatsheaf, Hemel Hempstead.

Swedner H. (1982a), 'Risks and Shortcomings in Action Research and Community Work', in Swedner H. [ed], *Human Welfare and Action Research in Urban Settings,* Delegation for Social Research, Swedish Council for Building Research, Stockholm, pp. 191-206.

Swedner H. (1982b), 'The Role of Sociologists in Community Planning', in Swedner H. [ed], *Human Welfare and Action Research in Urban Settings,* Delegation for Social Research, Swedish Council for Building Research, Stockholm,. pp. 59-71.

Swedner H. (1982c), 'A White Island in a Black Sea', in Swedner H. [ed], *Human Welfare and Action Research in Urban Settings,* Delegation for Social Research/Swedish Council for Building Research, Stockholm, pp. 7-41.

Swedner H. (1982d), 'An attempt to present a Theoretical Framework for Social Work as an Academic Discipline', Swedner H. [ed], *Human Welfare and Action Research in Urban Settings,* Delegation for Social Research, Swedish Council for Building Research, Stockholm, pp. 241-52.

Taoiseach of Ireland (2000) *Programme for Participation and Funding,* Dublin, Government Publications Office.

Taoiseach of Ireland (2000) *Programme for Prosperity and Fairness*, Dublin, Government Publications Office.

Tam H. (1995), 'Enabling Structures', in Atkinson D. [ed], *Cities of Pride: Rebuilding Community, Re-focusing Government*, Cassell, London, pp. 129-37.

Thake S. [Edited by Smyth K.](1995), *Community Regeneration: A Challenge for Local Government*, Centre for Local Economic Strategies, London.

Thomas D.N. (1976), *Organising for Social Change*, George Allen & Unwin, London.

Thomas D.N. (1983), *The Making of Community Work*, George Allen & Unwin, London.

Thomas D.N. (1995), *Community Development at Work*, Community Development Foundation, London.

Thomason G.F. (1969), *The Professional Approach to Community Work*, Sands and Co. London.

Thorpe R. (1985), 'Community Work and Ideology: An Australian Perspective', in Thorpe R. and Petruchenia J. [eds], *Community Work and Social Change: an Australian Perspective*, Routledge & Kegan Paul, London, pp. 11-27.

Times [Editor]. (1995), *The Will and the Hope*, The Times, March 6, p. 19 London.

Tobayiwa C. (1993), 'The Effectiveness of Using School Children in Sample and Data Collection', *Journal of Social Development in Africa*, Vol. 8, No. 1, pp. 73-87.

Todaro M., P. (1989), *Economic Development in the Third World*, [4th ed], Longman, London.

Topping P., Smith G. (1977), *Government Against Poverty? Liverpool Community Development Project, 1970-75*, Social Evaluation Unit, Oxford.

Toren N. (1969), 'Semi-Professionalism and Social Work: A theoretical perspective', in Etzioni A. [ed], *The Semi-Professionals and their Organization*, Free Press, New York. pp. 141-95.

Townsend J. (1993), 'Gender Studies: Whose Agenda?' in Schuurman F.J. [ed], *Beyond the Impasse: New Directions in Development Theory*, Zed Books, London. pp. 169-86.

Townsend P., Abel-Smith B. (1965), *The Poor and the Poorest*, Bell, London.

Toye J. (1993), *Dilemmas of Development: Reflections on the Counter-Revolution in Development Economics*, Basil Blackwell, Oxford.

Tracey M. (1982), 'Influencing the Town Hall', in Henderson P., Wright A. & Wyncoll K. [eds], *Struggles and Successes on council Estate: Tenant Action and Community Work*, Association of Community Workers in the U.K. London, pp. 39-59.

Tropman J.E. (1972), 'A Comparison Analysis of Community Organization Agencies: The Case of the Welfare Council', in Spergel I. A. [ed], *Community Organization Studies of Constraint*, Sage, Beverly Hills, Calif., pp. 93-122.

Turton P., Orr J. (1993), *Learning to Care in the Community* [2nd ed], Edward Arnold, London.

Twelvetrees A. (1990), *Community Work*, [2nd ed]. Macmillan/BASW, London.

UKCC [U.K. Central Council for Nursing, Midwifery & Health Visiting] (1998) *Standards for Specialist Education and Practice*, London

Ukpong E.A. (1990), 'A Quest for Self-Glory or Self-Reliance: Upgrading the Benefits of Community Development Programmes', *Journal of Social Development in Africa*, Vol. 5, No.2, pp. 73-85.

UN Bureau of Social Affairs. (1955), *Social Progress through Community Development*, United Nations, New York.

UN Secretary General. (1961), *Community Development in Urban Areas* United Nations Dept. of Economic and Social Affairs, New York. ST/SOA/43.

UNESCO. (1963), 'Qualifications and Training for Community Development: Extracts from the Report of the Standing Committee of the Economic commission for Africa on S.W & C.D.' *Community Development Bulletin*, Vol. XIV, No. 4, pp. 131-33.

Uphoff N. (1991), 'A Field Methodology for Participatory Self-Evaluation', *Community Development Journal*, Vol. 26, No. 4, pp. 271-85.

Uphoff N. (1995) 'Why NGO'S re not a Third Sector: a sectoral analysis with some thoughts on accountability, sustainability and evaluation', in Edwards, M. and Hulme, D., *NGO's: Performance and Accountability: Beyond the Magic Bullet*, Earthscan, London.

Vargas LV. (1991), 'Reflections on Methodology of Evaluation', *Comm- unity Development Journal*, Vol. 26, No.4, pp. 266-70.

Vlassoff C., Tanner M. (1992), 'The Relevance of Rapid Assessment to Health Research and Interventions', *Health Policy and Planning*, Vol. 7, No.1, pp. 1-9.

Waddington P. (1979), 'Looking ahead - community work into the 1980's', *Community Development Journal*, Vol. 14, No.1, pp. 224-34.

Waddington P. (1994), 'The Values Base of Community Work', in Jacobs S. and Popple K. [eds], *Community Work in the 1990s*, Spokesman, Nottingham. pp. 3-12.

Wade A.D. (1963), 'Social Work and Political Action', *Social Work*, Vol. 8, No. 3, pp. 3-10.

Wann M. (1995), *Building Social Capital: self-help in a twenty-first century welfare state*, Institute for Public Policy Research,

Warren R.L. (1970), 'The Context of Community Development', in Cary L.J. [ed], *Community Development as a Process*, University of Missouri Press, Columbia. pp. 32-52.

Waste R.J. (1986), *Community Power: Directions for further research*, Sage, Beverley Hills, Calif.

Webster A. (1989), A National Church-Based Resource? *Christian Action Journal*, pp. 27-8.

Weil M. (1994), 'Editors Introduction to the Journal', *Journal of Community Organization*, Vol. 1, No.1, pp. xxi-xxxiii.

Wenger G.C. (1994), *Understanding Support Networks and Community Care: Network Assessment for Elderly People,* Avebury, Aldershot.

West Wales Health Commission (1993), *Local Strategy for Health 1993 - 2002,*Dyfed, East Dyfed & Pembrokeshire Health Authority, Carmarthen.

White H. (1994), 'Black Empowerment: Gaining strength and setting agendas', in Jacobs S. and Popple K. [eds], *Community Work in the 1990s,* Spokesman, Nottingham. pp. 94-103.

Whitfield D. (1972), 'Editorial Statement', *Community Action,* Vol. 1, No.1, p. 2.

Wiener R. (1980), *The Rape and Plunder of the Shankill,* [2nd ed]. Farset Co-operative Press, Belfast.

Williams F. (1995), 'An Overview of Community Care', in Henderson P. and Armstrong J. [eds], *Community Development and Community Care,* Community Development Foundation, London, pp. 3-5.

Willmott P., Young M. (1960), *Family and Class in a London Suburb,* Routledge & Kegan Paul, London.

Wilson E. (1977), 'Women in the Community', in Mayo M. [ed], *Women in the Community,* Routledge & Kegan Paul, London, pp. 1-11.

Wilson, E. (1980) *Only Half Way to Paradise: Women in Post-War Britain,* Tavistock, London.

Wilson E. (1990), 'These New Components of the Spectacle: Fashion and Postmodernism', in Boyne R. and Rattansi A. [eds], *Postmodernism and Society,* Macmillan, London, pp. 209-36.

Wilson T., Younghusband E. (1976), *Teaching Community Work: A European Exploration,* International Association of Schools of Social Work, New York.

Wistow G., Knapp M., Hardy B., *et al.*(1994), *Social Care in a Mixed Economy,* Open University, Buckingham.

Wood M. (1994), 'Should Tenants take over? Radical Community Work, Tenants', in Jacobs S. and Popple K. [eds], *Community Work in the 1990s,* Spokesman, Nottingham. pp. 144-55.

Wooley T. (1970), *The politics of Community Action,* Author, Motherwell, Lanarkshire.

Wooton B. (1959), *Social Science and Social Pathology,* Allen & Unwin, London.

World Health Organisation.(1986), *Ottawa Charter for Health Promotion,* WHO, Ottawa.

World Health Organisation. (1988), (Annett H. & Rifkin S. - University of Liverpool). *Improving Urban Health: Guidelines for rapid appraisal to assess community health needs: A focus on health improvements for low-income urban areas,* WHO & Swedish International Development Agency/SAREC, Geneva.

Wyburd G. (1963), 'A Question of Approach', *Community Development Bulletin,* Vol. XIV, No. 4, pp. 124-30.

Young M., Willmott P. (1962), *Family and Kinship in East London,* [Revised ed]. Pelican, London.

Young T.L. (1996) *How to be a better project manager*, Kogan Page/Industrial Society, London.

Younghusband, E.L. (1959) *Report of the Working Party on Social Workers in Local Authority Health and Welfare Services*, H.M.S.O., London.

Younghusband E.L. (1962), *Communities and Change: implications for social welfare*, National Council of Social Service, London.

Younghusband E.L. (1978), 'Training for community work', in Younghusband E. [ed], *Social Work in Britain, 1950 - 1975. a Follow-up Study*, Allen & Unwin, London.

Youth Service Development Council (1969), *Youth and Community Work in the Seventies*, H.M.S.O. London.

Zald M.N. (1975), 'Organizations as Polities: An Analysis of Community Organization Agencies', in Kramer R.M. and Specht H. [eds], *Readings in Commmunity Orgainization Practice*, [2nd ed]. Prentice-Hall Inc. Englewood Cliffs, New Jersey. pp. 87.-96.

Zutshi M. (1991), 'Community Development from within a Statutory setting - a contradiction of terms?' in Jones J. and Tilson J. [eds], *Roots and Branches*, Open University, Milton Keynes. pp. 93-100.

Zwanniken, W.A.C. (1968), 'Community Development in the Netherlands', *Community Development Journal*, Vol. 3, No. 3, pp. 93-100.

Zweig F.M., Morris R.(1975), 'The Social Planning Design Guide', in Kramer R.M. and Specht H. [eds], *Readings in Community Organization Practice*, [2nd ed]. Prentice-Hall Inc. Englewood Cliffs N.J. pp. 246-288.

Index

304

306

women, 25, 65, 207, 209, 211, 224, 230,
  262, 265, 266
Women in Development, 224, 266
Wood, M., 66
Wooley, T., 2, 64, 77, 203, 229
Wooton, B., 2
World Bank, 20, 200, 224
World Health Organisation, 6, 77, 257,
  258

Younghusband, E.L., 2, 201
Youth Service Development Council, 2

Zald, M.N., 122
Zutshi, M., 114
Zweig, F.M., 165